CREATIVITY IN LANGUAGE AND LITERATURE

The State of the Art

Creativity in Language and Literature

The State of the Art

Edited by

Joan Swann, Rob Pope
and Ronald Carter

palgrave
macmillan

First published 2011 by
PALGRAVE MACMILLAN

Palgrave Macmillan in the UK is an imprint of Macmillan Publishers Limited, registered in England, company number 785998, of Houndmills, Basingstoke, Hampshire RG21 6XS.

Palgrave Macmillan in the US is a division of St Martin's Press LLC, 175 Fifth Avenue, New York, NY 10010.

Palgrave Macmillan is the global academic imprint of the above companies and has companies and representatives throughout the world.

Palgrave® and Macmillan® are registered trademarks in the United States, the United Kingdom, Europe and other countries.

ISBN 978–0–230–57559–2 hardback
ISBN 978–0–230–57560–8 paperback

This book is printed on paper suitable for recycling and made from fully managed and sustained forest sources. Logging, pulping and manufacturing processes are expected to conform to the environmental regulations of the country of origin.

A catalogue record for this book is available from the British Library.

A catalog record for this book is available from the Library of Congress.

10 9 8 7 6 5 4 3 2 1
20 19 18 17 16 15 14 13 12 11

Printed and bound in Great Britain by
MPG Books Group, Bodmin and King's Lynn

Contents

List of Figures and Frames

Figures

Frames

Acknowledgements

The original motivation for this collection was a series of seminars on 'Transitions and Transformations: Exploring Creativity in Everyday and Literary Language', held at the Open University in 2007 and funded by the Arts and Humanities Research Council (AHRC). We are grateful to the AHRC for their support for this project. Thanks also to the seminar participants and other colleagues (writers, researchers, performers, educationists, film-makers and others with a professional interest in language and creativity) whose ideas and enthusiasm have, over the past few years, acted as a stimulus for the collection.

We would also like to express our thanks to our two anonymous reviewers for their valuable, critical comments on a first draft of the volume. We are grateful to Jess Mason from the University of Nottingham for assistance with the index to the book, and to Carol Johns-MacKenzie from the Open University for help with formatting and the administration of the project.

The authors and publishers wish to thank the following for permission to use copyright material: 6 Wing/C Kwan and Warner/Chappell Music, for song lyric extracts from '456 Wing', 'ABC Jun', 'Quan Cheng Jin Qing' and 'Xue Hai Wu Ya' on pp.59–65; Patience Agbabi and Canongate Books Limited, for 'Word' from Agbabi: *Transformatrix* on pp.36–8, and 'My light is spent' from Agbabi: *Bloodshot Monochrome* on pp.182–3; Caroline Ashley, for the poem 'Prophecy' on p.235; Christine Koutelieri, for the poem 'Captivity' on p.235; Cralan Kelder, for the poem 'The Common Finch' from *Bordercrossing Berlin*, on p.233; Faber and Faber and Louis MacNeice, for poetry extracts from 'Babel', 'Conversation', 'Plain Speaking' and 'The Mixer', from MacNeice: *Collected Poems* on pp.40–50; G.D. Jayalakshmi and Jayamac Productions, for the film still from *Arranged Marriage* on p.201; Hong Kong Observatory of HKSAR, for the chart 'Uranium-3 Radioactive Decay Series' on p.119; Libby Houston, for the poem 'Desolution' on p.234; Michelene Wandor and Arc Publications, for poetry extracts from *The Music of the Prophets* on pp.172–80; Oxford University Press India and Rukmini Bhaya Nair, for extracts from 'When the sky falls: creativity in poetry', in *Poetry in a Time of Terror: Essays in the Postcolonial Preternatural*, on pp.265–6; Oxford University Press, for the figure 'Dimensions of analysis', adapted from Maybin and

Swann: 'Everyday creativity in language: textuality, contextuality and critique', *Applied Linguistics* 28 (4): 497–517, on p.17; Mario Petrucci for the poems 'The Room' and 'Chain of Decay' from *Heavy Water* on pp.118 and 120; Phil Grabsky, for film stills from 'Heavy Water' on p.123; Stanley Pelter, for the poem 'Fish out of Water' on p.234; The Open University, for extracts from G.D. Jayalakshmi's interview with S. Upendran and R. Amritavalli from *The Art of English* on pp.103–5; and for extracts from an audio interview and video stills from Haggarty: *Storytelling* from *Children's Literature* on pp.186–8; Wimba UK/Blackboard UK and Blackboard USA, for the screenshot on p.152. Every effort has been made to trace all the copyright holders, but if any have been inadvertently overlooked the authors and publishers will be pleased to make the necessary arrangements at the first opportunity.

Notes on Contributors

Patience Agbabi is a Creative Writing Fellow at Oxford Brookes University, a Canterbury Laureate and a freelance poet. She is interested in the relationship between poetic form and performance, especially dramatic monologue, and recently received a Grants for the Arts award to write *Roving Mic*, a modern interpretation of the *Canterbury Tales* as a poetry slam. Her publications include *Transformatrix* (Canongate, 2000) and *Bloodshot Monochrome* (Canongate, 2008).

Daniel Allington is Lecturer in English Language Studies and Applied Linguistics at the Open University. He works between discourse analysis, the sociology of culture, and book history, combining an interest in the macrosocial processes that structure particular cultural products and producers as 'artistic', 'literary', 'creative', etc. with an interest in microsocial practices of interpretation and evaluation. His publications have appeared in journals including *Language and Literature, Poetics Today, Social Semiotics* and the *Journal of Literary Semantics*.

R. Amritavalli is Professor of Linguistics at the English and Foreign Languages University, Hyderabad. She has also worked to teach English using print, audio and video media. Her publications include *Language as Dynamic Text* (Allied Publishers, 1999), *English in Deprived Circumstances: Maximising Learner Autonomy* (Cambridge University Press, 2007) and the chapter on India (co-authored with K. A. Jayaseelan) in *Language and National Identity in Asia* (Oxford University Press, 2007).

Richard Danson Brown is Senior Lecturer in English at the Open University. His research interests include Renaissance and modern poetry; he is also a poet and translator. His publications include *The New Poet: Novelty & Tradition in Spenser's* Complaints (Liverpool University Press, 1999) and *Louis MacNeice & the Poetry of the 1930s* (Northcote House Publishers, 2009).

Lynne Cameron is Professor of Applied Linguistics at the Open University and ESRC Global Uncertainties Research Fellow. She is currently researching the discourse dynamics of empathy and the role of metaphor. Recent publications include *Metaphor and Reconciliation* (Routledge, 2010) and *Metaphor Analysis* (co-edited with R. Maslen, Equinox, 2010).

Ronald Carter is Professor of Modern English Language at Nottingham University. Recent books include: *Language and Creativity: The Art of Common Talk* (Routledge, 2004) and the *Cambridge Grammar of English: A Comprehensive Guide to Spoken and Written Grammar and Usage* (with Michael McCarthy) (Cambridge University Press, 2006). He has recently been chair of the British Association for Applied Linguistics and is interested in the literary and linguistic inflections of creative practice.

Guy Cook is Professor of Language and Education at the Open University. He has published widely on discourse analysis, applied linguistics, literature teaching and English-language teaching. He is currently particularly interested in creative language use in PR, marketing and public controversies. His books include *Language Play Language Learning* (Oxford University Press, 2000), *The Discourse of Advertising* (Routledge, 2001), *Applied Linguistics* (Oxford University Press, 2003), *Genetically Modified Language* (Routledge, 2004) and *Translation in Language Teaching* (Oxford University Press, 2010).

Jon Cook is Director of Creative and Performing Arts and Emeritus Professor at the University of East Anglia, where he has supervised PhDs in creative and critical writing since the programme began. He has also taught literary theory and philosophy, with an emphasis on Romanticism and ideology, in universities in Europe, India and the United States. His recent books include *Poetry in Theory: An Anthology 1900–2000* (Blackwell, 2004) and *Hazlitt in Love* (Short, 2007).

Ruth Finnegan is Emeritus Professor in the Faculty of Social Sciences at the Open University and is a Fellow of the British Academy. She works on the anthropology/sociology of artistic activity, communication and performance. Recent publications include *Communicating: The Multiple Modes of Human Interconnection* (Routledge, 2002), *The Oral and Beyond: Doing Things with Words in Africa* (University of Chicago Press, 2007), 'Creativity: but Where Do You Look?' in 'Community and Creativity', a special issue of *Oral History* (2009), and *Why Do We Quote? The Culture and History of Quotation* (OpenBook Publishers, 2011).

Angela Goddard is a Professor of English Language and a Higher Education Academy National Teaching Fellow. She is Head of Languages and Linguistics at York St John University, UK. A co-editor of the Routledge *Intertext* series, her research interests centre on the social values accorded to different types of communication and different groups of communicators.

Ben Haggarty has been pioneering the UK storytelling revival since 1981. Working in education and for the public, he has a repertoire of 350 traditional tales and myths. As the Crick Crack Club's artistic director he promotes adult storytelling events. He is Honorary Professor of Storytelling at the Arts University of Berlin (UDK). His graphic novel, *MeZolith*, created in collaboration with artist Adam Brockbank, examines stories and storytelling in Stone Age Britain.

Graeme Harper is Professor of Creative Writing at Bangor University and Inaugural Chair of the Higher Education Committee at the UK's National Association of Writers in Education. He is editor of *New Writing: The International Journal for the Practice and Theory of Creative Writing* and his recent publications include *On Creative Writing* (Multilingual Matters, 2010), *The Creative Writing Guidebook* (Continuum, 2008) and, as Brooke Biaz, *Camera Phone* (Parlor, 2010) and *Moon Dance* (Parlor, 2008).

G. D. Jayalakshmi is a British Asian film-maker and also Programme Leader for the BA degree in Film and TV, University of Hertfordshire. She worked as a producer/director with the BBC for 11 years before setting up her own production company. She is currently working on a feature project, *The Potter's Daughter*, for which she made *Arranged Marriage* as a pilot. It won her several awards – Best Black and Asian Film at Kino International (2003), Platinum Award at Worldfest Houston (2003) and Runner-up TAPS British Writer of the Year (2003).

Angel Lin is Associate Professor in the Faculty of Education, University of Hong Kong. She is interested in sociolinguistics, language play and identity, youth popular culture and new literacies, and language policy and planning studies. Her publications include *Problematizing Identity: Everyday Struggles in Language, Culture and Education* (Routledge, 2008) and *Bilingual Education: Southeast Asian Perspectives* (Hong Kong University Press, 2009).

Janet Maybin is Senior Lecturer in Language and Communication at the Open University. Originally trained as a social anthropologist, she has written extensively for Open University courses and also researches and writes on children and adults' informal language and literacy practices, focussing currently on voice and creativity. Recent publications include *Children's Voices: Talk, Knowledge and Identity* (Palgrave Macmillan, 2006) and *The Art of English: Everyday Creativity* (edited with J. Swann) (Palgrave Macmillan, 2006).

Rukmini Bhaya Nair is Professor of Linguistics and English at the Indian Institute of Technology, Delhi. After receiving her PhD from Cambridge University, Nair has taught at universities ranging from Singapore to Stanford. Awarded an honorary doctorate by the University of Antwerp in 2006 for her contributions to the fields of linguistics, narratology and literary theory, Nair's academic books include *Poetry in a Time of Terror* (Oxford University Press,

2009), *Narrative Gravity: Conversation, Cognition, Culture* (Oxford University Press, 2003) and *Lying on the Postcolonial Couch* (Minnesota University Press/ Oxford University Press, 2002). She is also widely regarded as one of India's leading poets, *The Ayodhya Cantos* (Viking Penguin, 1999) and *Yellow Hibiscus* (Penguin, 2004) numbering amongst her volumes of poetry.

Kate Pahl is Senior Lecturer in Education at the Department of Educational Studies, University of Sheffield. She is the co-director of the Centre for the Study of New Literacies at Sheffield. She is interested in looking at the intersections between material cultural studies and the uses of literacy in homes and communities. Her publications include *Artifactual Literacies: Every Object Tells a Story* (Teachers College Press, 2010) with Jennifer Roswell, and *Literacy and Education: The New Literacy Studies in the Classroom* (Sage, 2005) also with Jennifer Roswell.

Mario Petrucci is a poet, physicist, educator and broadcaster who has won many awards and held residencies at the Imperial War Museum and BBC Radio 3. A practitioner of site-specific poetry, he creates educational resources linking science with literary and textual studies, particularly on the science–poetry interface. His poetry collections include *i tulips* (Enitharmon Press, 2010), *Flowers of Sulphur* (Enitharmon Press, 2007) and *Heavy Water: A Poem for Chernobyl* (Enitharmon Press, 2004).

Rob Pope is Professor of English at Oxford Brookes University and a UK National Teaching Fellow. He is interested in the relations between creative and critical activity, and particularly in forms of rewriting (parody, adaptation, translation, intervention) as ways of combining the two. His publications include *Textual Intervention: Creative and Critical Strategies for Literary Studies* (Routledge, 1995) and *Creativity: Theory, History, Practice* (Routledge, 2005).

Fiona Sampson has published 17 books, most recently *Rough Music* (Carcanet, 2010) *Poetry Writing* (Hale, 2009) and *A Century of Poetry Review* (PBS Special Commendation, 2009), with ten in translation. She has been awarded the Newdigate Prize, been short-listed for the Forward single-poem and the T. S. Eliot prize, received a Cholmondeley Award and is a Fellow of the Royal Society of Literature. Forthcoming are the Newcastle/Bloodaxe Poetry Lectures and the Faber Poet-to-poet *Shelley*.

Elena Semino is Professor of Linguistics and Verbal art at Lancaster University. She is interested in stylistics, corpus linguistics and metaphor research. Her books include: *Cognitive Stylistics: Language and Cognition in Text Analysis* (John Benjamins, 2002) (with Jonathan Culpeper), *Corpus Stylistics: Speech, Writing and Thought Presentation in a Corpus of English Writing* (Routledge, 2004 (with Mick Short) and *Metaphor in Discourse* (Cambridge University Press, 2008).

Jane Spiro is Principal Lecturer in Applied Linguistics at Oxford Brookes University and a UK National Teaching Fellow. She is interested in the creativity of both learners and teachers in language education, and in the links between appreciative reading and creative writing. Her publications include two books with Oxford University Press, *Creative Poetry Writing* (2004) and *Storybuilding* (2007), a novel published in 2002, and poetry and stories, including a poem displayed on Oxford buses.

Peter Stockwell is Professor of Literary Linguistics in the School of English at the University of Nottingham, UK. His books include *Texture: A Cognitive Aesthetics of Reading* (Edinburgh University Press, 2009), *Cognitive Poetics* (Routledge, 2002), *Language in Theory* (with Mark Robson) (Routledge, 2005) and several textbooks, reference works and edited collections in stylistics, sociolinguistics and English language studies.

Joan Swann is Senior Lecturer and Director of the Centre for Language and Communication at the Open University. Her main research is in interactional sociolinguistics, and she therefore brings a socially oriented approach to the study of creativity and verbal artfulness. Books include *The Routledge Companion to English Language Studies* (co-edited with Janet Maybin) (Routledge, 2010), *The Art of English: Everyday Creativity* (co-edited with Janet Maybin) (Palgrave, 2006) and *A Dictionary of Sociolinguistics* (with Ana Deumert, Theresa Lillis and Rajend Mesthrie) (Edinburgh University Press, 2004).

S. Upendran is Professor in the Department of Materials Development at the English and Foreign Languages University, Hyderabad. He has scripted and produced several educational radio and television programmes, and specializes in the area of using authentic materials in language teaching. He has been writing 'Know Your English', a weekly column in the *Hindu*, one of India's national newspapers, for the past 17 years.

Michelene Wandor is a poet, playwright, fiction writer and musician. She is also a Royal Literary Fund Fellow and teaches on the Creative Writing Distance Learning MA at Lancaster University. *Musica Transalpina* (Arc, 2006) was a Poetry Book Society Recommendation. *The Author is not Dead, Merely Somewhere Else: Creative Writing Reconceived* (Palgrave, 2008) is the first UK history and critique of the discipline. *The Art of Writing Drama* (Methuen, 2008) draws on her award-winning career as a dramatist.

Prologue

What's (not) in a title

Creativity	Language	Literature
all abstract	all singular	all nouns

with capitals for good measure.

big block things   monumental like marble   so solid seeming
yet slippery-as-they-come   and not a little   wobbly

So let's take each term in turn
and not just polish but
pulverise   chip   crack   break   shatter grind   mix   bind   fix
slide   glide   swipe   clean   shine   sheen   and
See what happens!

'CREATIVITY' is the new kid on the block.
Not yet 150 years old! (first recorded in English in 1875).
Human, secular and more or less anyone's from the first.
Born of the sciences, social and otherwise.
Not religious.
Not particularly artistic.
Incipiently (some say insidiously) inclusive. But hey...

Culture is common
Creativity ordinary
E-v-e-r-y-d-a-y, some say

Certainly not to be confused – though it often is –
with older brother, father, great grandfather ...
'CREATION'
Also abstract, singular, noun
Yet far more august, awesome
(some say awfully stuffy)
half a millennium earlier.
Creation as in
God the Creator. As in
what artists do. As in

what you probably can't.
But what if Creativity were Creativities?
Would that really make a difference?
Say – a creativity for painters
of houses and a creativity for painters
of pictures. A creativity for makers
of music and a creativity for those who make a racket.
A creativity for her. A creativity for him.
       (But not them)
A creativity for you. A creativity for me.
Even a co-creativity for all of us together.
       (But not them!)
For what's the point of a creativity for each
and creativities for all
if no-one is not?

'LANGUAGE' is the second of the big block things
till you come to break it down and build it up
differently, amongst other things with itself.
As the $L=A=N=G=U=A=G=E$ poets might have said:
                Q. *What did the language say when it met-a-language?*
                A. *Search me!*
So yes, again, afresh
we can pluralise the singular, particularise the abstract.
For if Language is the notional totality of all verbal systems, actual and
potential, spoken, written and otherwise, in air, on paper, on screen, in
mind...
then strictly it doesn't exist.
Except of course as a word
The Word, Langue, Logos, Слово
in some specific language
material, medium, context, culture
of which there are many. And various.
And always already creative. Because...
                Speech   acts
                Word   worlds
                Dia   logues
                Building relationships, they say.

Now to that last big block thing
'LITERATURE'!
Whatever can we do with that?!

Here we go, in very short, in English:
Long ago, from Latin via French,
Literatur was the classier, courtly counterpart
to older, Anglo-Saxon 'writ' and 'writing'
(though the latter had grit and legal and holy writ behind it).
Then Literature was recognised as 'writing of value', 'oeuvres worth
    keeping'
often fictional and faintly secular, but also historical and philosophical.
(Among the devout there has always been doubt
about treating the Bible – that holy book of scripture – as literature.)
For a time, in some circles, the big L got narrowed to *belles lettres*.
In some circles it still is. But then opened up again to mean
what it always could: the *literature on the subject*
any subject – legal, advertising, technical, scientific, whatever.
Still, being *literary* can seem a luxury
When being *literate* is such a necessity.
But let's face it, when it comes down to it,
LIT is ...

       'what oft was thought but ne'er so well expressed' (Pope)
                         'news that *stays* news' (Pound)
         'truth told slant' (after Dickinson)
     'whatever gets taught' (before Eagleton).

So that's the end of *lit.*
and *lang.* and *creat.*
ivity
Or just the beginnings
if one wants to make a big cultural-historical, social-political, practical-
    theoretical
thing of it.
Which some do.
Us for example
and maybe you.

ROB POPE

Introduction: Creativity, Language, Literature

ROB POPE AND JOAN SWANN

In recent years there has been an explosion of interest in creativity, or artistry, in everyday language, and in potential continuities between such everyday creativity and literary language. Linguists have discussed the poetic nature of 'common talk', creativity in language play amongst children and adults, and the appropriation of literary-like patterns in genres such as advertising and Internet discourse. Ethnographically oriented research has added the study of creative language practices and their location within particular cultural contexts. Meanwhile, there has been a massive growth in Creative Writing as an educational practice and academic subject, often in or around English.

Literary language itself has come under scrutiny from those who would challenge or defend its singularity; and boundaries around the literary – and indeed around language – are pushed and prodded by those with an interest in transformation and change: in generic hybridity and creative play across modes, media and technologies. Writers have also engaged in theorizing creativity across language, literature and culture. In addition to its theoretical and research interest, such work has implications for the English curriculum at both school and HE level and may challenge traditional distinctions, e.g. between 'language' and 'literature'. This is a forum for the meeting of linguistic science, critical understanding and creative practice: the 'state' as well as the 'art' of all three may change as a result.

Interest in language creativity spans several academic areas, including English (English language and literature, creative writing) as well as linguistics (applied linguistics, stylistics and sociolinguistics), language studies, communication studies, cultural studies and media studies, anthropology and education. We hope this book will be a resource for teachers, students and researchers in these and related areas. We also hope it will support interchanges with creative practitioners within and outside the academy.

'Creativity' Words: A Continuing Conversation

From 'Creation' to 'Creativity': Ancient and Modern

To many people's surprise, the first use of the abstract noun 'creativity' recorded in the *Oxford English Dictionary* (2nd edn, 1989) is as recent as 1875. (It was not even included in the first edition of 1928.) From the first, 'creativity' tended to refer to a general human trait or capacity rather than a primarily divine or specifically artistic one. In his *Keywords: A Vocabulary of Culture and Society*, Raymond Williams (1983: 82–5) sums up the momentousness of this change thus: '*Creativity*, a general name for the faculty, followed in the early 20th century. This is clearly an important and significant history, and in its emphasis on human capacity has become steadily more important'. The divine or artistic senses were associated with the older term 'creation'. 'Creatio(u)n' had been around in English since at least the thirteenth century and was identified initially with 'God the Creato(u)r' and, by extension, from the late eighteenth century onwards, with more or less divinely inspired or naturally gifted 'creative artists'. Taken together, the 'create' words span an array of senses that may be schematically plotted thus:

Divine (archaic)	Special artistic (early modern)	Common human (later modern)
God the Creator	Creative artist	Creativity of humanity

What complicates and often confuses matters is the fact that *all* these senses are simultaneously available nowadays whenever a 'create' term is used. For – depending on context, assumptions and aims – it can be coloured by older senses that are more specifically artistic or sublimely divine, even while a broad gesture is apparently being made to embrace humanity at large.

Current claims for, and constructions of, creativity, predominantly in terms of the 'new', 'novel' and 'innovative', have to be seen in the context of a deeper historical perspective and a broader cultural understanding. Such claims may themselves be symptomatic of values associated with modernity in general and with Western modernity in particular. The standard definitions of creativity in the 'expert literature' produced by psychologists and educationists stress it as being 'new and valuable', 'novel and original', 'innovative and adaptive', etc. (These are all taken from Sternberg's influential *Handbook of Creativity* (1999): chs 1, 5, 7, 12 and 22.) Only Lubart (ch. 17) sounds a sustained note of caution about the modern Western assumptions that such definitions express. In their place he argues for a cross-cultural and historical perspective that (re)values ancient and traditional notions of making as craft and design and, indeed, shifts the emphasis to notions of creative being and becoming – not just getting and doing. Justin O'Connor issues a similar warning, with a sharper political-economic edge, at the close of his review of the research literature on *The Cultural and Creative Industries* (2007: 53–4): 'But maybe creativity is the problem... The creativity mobilised in the new spirit of capitalism is one based on a particular modernist artistic tradition of rule-breaking innovation, of the shock of the new'. So, with a view to an alternative politics as well as aesthetics, he adds pointedly, though also guardedly (ibid.: 54):

> In particular we might look to the ecological challenge to accumulation, which sees constant innovation as a form of waste... while also cautioning against a kind of New-age eclecticism which may itself go indiscriminately searching through past, marginal, indigenous and experimental cultures alike for the next big hit.

In short, the presumed 'newness' of creativity may itself be an obstacle. And so may any merely reactionary attempt simply to turn the clock back nostalgically or look longingly at the supposed simplicity or purity of other, non-Western cultures. All these terms – modern and ancient, Western and Eastern or (non-Western) – carry with them the appeals and perils of binaries in general. What may initially serve as valuable contrasts to provoke thought can quickly turn into unthinking reflexes.

Old Terms for New? Inspiration, Imagination, Originality, Genius, Invention

We must also bear in mind many other terms that are freely and apparently naturally associated with the 'creativity' debate. These all regularly and routinely crop up in policy statements as well as informal conversation, and yet each has its own distinctive associations and complex, often contentious and contradictory, history. Chief amongst these are *inspiration, imagination, invention, originality* and *genius*. Each of these words has expressed and will continue to express meanings and values that vary radically depending on the current rate of change – and cultural rate of exchange – in which it is implicated. Though all may get pressed together to serve some apparently homogenized agenda, each brings its own cultural baggage that needs unpacking and scrutinizing separately. A very brief review of each term in turn will confirm the possibilities as well as the problems opened up by a fully historical and critical sense of what they have meant – and may yet mean differently (see Pope 2005: 52–89 for an extensive overview and further references).

Inspiration may still be infused with its root sense of 'breathing-in' (from Latin *in-spirare*): this is the sense that Patience Agbabi celebrates in her performance piece 'Word' and expressly draws attention to in her commentary on it, 'Give Me (Deep Intake of Breath) Inspiration' (Chapter 2). In general, however, inspiration now tends to mean energy or stimulation, even just influence, of many kinds; though the sense of the divine *afflatus* (breath) may still be invoked on occasion (see Clark 1997).

Imagination has always had the capacity to refer or appeal to 'images' that are far more than merely visual and to 'imagery' that is by no means tied to poetry alone. Imaginative capacities have themselves at various points been extensively characterized as everything from 'gardens' and 'houses' to 'mirrors' and 'books', and 'lamps' and 'labyrinths' – even to 'infinite libraries' and 'halls of mirrors' (see Kearney 1998).

Originality is a particularly tricky and apparently contrary concept. Up to the late eighteenth century it had the primary sense of 'ancient, traditional, from the beginning' (a sense that is still with us in the phrase 'original inhabitants' and the archaic notion of 'aborigines', 'from the beginning', 'primitives'); this was itself the ancient or classical sense. However, from the late eighteenth century onwards 'original' increasingly tended towards the opposite and now-dominant sense of 'novel', 'innovative', 'never-been-done-before' (in the modern sense of 'an original idea', 'strikingly original'); this is the modern or romantic sense. Interestingly, the distinction between the two can be activated by something as slight yet significant as a change of article: '*the* original painting' refers us back to the initial version (not a copy) and invokes the earlier sense; '*an* original painting' refers us to a kind of painting that has not been done before and assumes the later sense. It is therefore important to weigh whether the originality one has in mind looks back, forwards or, indeed, attempts to do both at once (see Chapter 3 by Richard Danson Brown, Chapter 20 by Rob Pope and Chapter 23 by Daniel Allington; see also Attridge 2004: 35–40).

Genius is another term with a remarkably wide array of historical senses, many of which survive into contemporary usage. Initially, from Roman times and before, it was associated with 'genius of place' (*genius loci*) and could be identified with whole 'peoples' or 'tribes', too (Latin *(in)gens*); whence references to the German/English/Chinese 'genius for'). In the late eighteenth century it commonly meant the characteristic trait of anyone, their primary but not necessarily exceptional distinguishing feature: 'Every man has his genius', observes Dr Johnson in 1780. Though even then it was beginning to acquire its currently dominant sense of 'an exceptional talent' and tending to be used with the indefinite article to designate an individual, 'a genius'. Typically, and problematically, such individuals were explicitly – and often still are implicitly – gendered as masculine and the term applied more or less exclusively to prominent men: Albert Einstein, Stephen Hawking, Bill Gates and, in retrospect, Leonardo da Vinci, Wolfgang Amadeus Mozart and William Shakespeare. In *A Room of One's Own*, Virginia Woolf (1992 [1929]: 63) remarks ruefully that 'genius of a sort must have existed among women, as it must have existed among the working class'; but the fact that the term was hardly ever applied to them massively obscured this fact. Meanwhile, it remains possible to identify 'genius' with time rather than person or place. In Germany it was common to refer to the high Romantic period of *Sturm und Drang* as *Genieperiod*; and a BBC radio series on great scientific inventions and inventors was called 'Moments of Genius' (BBC Radio 4, 2010). Clearly, as with the supposed 'Eureka moment' of discovery, the act of genius may be as much bound up *in the event* with the 'when' as the 'who' and the 'where' (see Chapter 24 by Guy Cook; see also Preminger and Brogan 1993: 455–6; Howe 1999).

Invention, meanwhile, we may note, went through a similar kind of volte-face to that undergone by 'original', only at a slightly earlier historical moment. In the sixteenth-century sense it still retained its root etymological sense of 'finding out' (from Latin *invenire*, *inventum*, to find out, found); hence rhetorical *invention*, referring to the finding and gathering of materials, and 'inventory', an itemized list of contents. But thereafter, particularly under pressure from the seventeenth-century scientific revolution, it tended increasingly to acquire its now-dominant, primarily technological sense of 'making up' (e.g. the invention of the steam engine, Davy lamp, telephone, computer, etc.). As such, the term has a shifting and dynamic relation with the concept of 'discovery' (itself complex), which can refer to the scientific discovery of oxygen but also to the 'discovery' of, say, North America or Australia – which happened many times and is invariably framed from a Western European point of view (see Howe 1999: 176–87).

In all these ways, the continuing history and teeming conversation that characterizes the 'creativity' words is at once clamorously confusing and fabulously rich. Such terms and concepts as those featured above – and many more picked up and turned over in the pages that follow – may appear to be natural and necessary fellow-travellers with 'creativity'. But in reality many are much older and each has its own vexed and complex – if not plain contrary – story to tell. Mixing all these up with the potential meanings as well as actual applications of such a relative newcomer on the scene as creativity (the term first appeared in the late nineteenth century, remember) makes for a heady mix indeed. What's more, these are living verbal histories in which we each have our say, ongoing cultural conversations to which we all contribute. The latest word is always ours: the first or last word, never. That is perhaps the most crucial – critical and creative – lesson we can learn from a contemporary history of the 'creativity' words.

Culture is Un/common, Creativity is Extra/ordinary

These are the axes on which many debates on creativity revolve – sometimes just going round in circles, occasionally getting somewhere else. They are partly interchangeable, too, so we also find talk of creativity being more or less common or uncommon and culture being more or less ordinary or extraordinary; and of both of them being in various ways 'everyday' or 'exceptional'. At any rate, there is a dynamic in play which, if it is not to be self-defeating or simply seize up, has to be conceived as moving in some direction or switching dimension. In short, there must be a purposeful sense of historical process if not exactly progress.

'Culture Is Ordinary' is the title of an influential essay first published by Raymond Williams in 1958, later elaborated around the proposition that 'creativity is as ordinary as culture' in the first chapter of his *The Long Revolution* (1961). To this he added the important qualification that 'there are no ordinary activities, if by "ordinary" we mean the absence of creative interpretation. We create our human world as we have thought of art as being created' (ibid.: 27). In the area of youth culture in particular, Paul Willis and others in *Common Culture: Symbolic Work at Play in the Everyday Cultures of the Young* (1990) offered a strongly evidence-based as well as political argument for 'a vibrant symbolic life and symbolic creativity in everyday life, everyday activity and expression', especially 'the multitude of ways in which young people humanize, decorate and invest with meaning their common and immediate life spaces and social practices – personal styles and choice of clothes, selective and active use of music' (ibid.: 1–2). Variations on this championing of the creativity of common culture can be found throughout contemporary Cultural and Media Studies; indeed, they are part of the foundational rationale of these comparatively recent subjects (see Jones 2009: 52–7).

All these issues can be framed conversely, however, with the emphasis upon culture as *un*common and creativity as *extra*ordinary. From this perspective, the array of opinion and insight is if anything even more varied. At one extreme lies the reactionary rhetoric of Roger Scruton (2001), lamenting the passing of an elite culture of creative artists and proposing a restitution of narrowly idealist, resolutely non-materialist aesthetics. In another direction, virtually another dimension, we have Derek Attridge's subtle arguments for *The Singularity of Literature* (2004), with its fresh inflections of 'invention' (combining its ancient sense of 'finding out' with a modern sense of 'making up'), partly derived from the 'deconstruction' of Derrida (1992) and driving towards 'reconstructions' ('stagings', 'performances', 'displays') that are uniquely tuned to each intelligence and sensibility that has learnt to respond (also see Chapter 26 by Jon Cook).

Meanwhile, there are many insightful and openly idiosyncratic positions somewhere in the middle(s). On one side there is George Steiner's *Grammars of Creation* (2001) with his pointed and poignant acknowledgement that 'creation in its classic sense and connotations' – inflected in terms of the 'divine' and 'artistic' senses identified above – 'turns out to have been a magnificently fruitful invention' (32). On another side is Peter Abbs's sustained and openly combative argument in *Against the Flow: Education, the Arts and Postmodern Culture* (2003). Abbs is expressly *for* an arts and crafts approach based on a 'living inheritance of examples and procedures transmitted by the culture' and a 'symbolic vocabulary' of 'metaphors, models, ideas, images, narratives, facts' that can stimulate and sustain a 'flowering of consciousness'. He is vigorously *against* both 'an individualistic expressive arts paradigm' (wrongly seen as 'progressive', he says) and a 'consumer democracy' where a combination of naked market forces and veiled public accountability conspire to make it 'impossible for profound levels of creativity to be released' (ibid.: 2, 17, 59; also see Jones 2009: 48–50). Abbs's position is complex and vexed, partial and sometimes idiosyncratic. In fact that might be said of all the arguments reviewed above, whether nominally *for* or *against* 'common' and 'everyday' or 'extraordinary' and 'singular' creativity and/or culture. Readers must therefore decide for themselves where – or whether – they wish to place the oblique in that last phrase or any of those preceding. Invoking 'extra/ordinary' creativity and 'un/common culture' is an apparently even-handed option, of course. But so is fence-sitting. Learning to juggle and removing the fence are also options. We explore the initial utility and eventual futility of binary thinking at many points in the book. Ronald Carter expressly returns to this issue in the Epilogue. For the moment, we shall move directly to multiples and pluralities.

Multiple Creativities for Each and All?

Creativity may be grasped as not one thing, but many. The plural form may be superficial or significant, depending on how it is handled and what it is taken to mean. Howard Gardner's work (1998) helps set the scene with the trajectory of his work moving from multiple intelligences to plural creativities. Both of these have implications for plural learning styles: spatial, kinetic and tactile, for example, as well as verbal, aural/oral, visual and, latterly, what has been dubbed 'emotional intelligence'. Anna Craft's 'little c' and 'big C' creativities (Craft et al. 2001) offers another take on this, the former equated with fresh learning of any kind and the latter with achievements, discoveries and inventions that are recognized as generally significant by the authorities in some field (after Csikszentmihalyi 1996). This in turn may be compared with

Margaret Boden's (2004) distinction between 'P-creativity' (Person-centred, psychological) and 'H-creativity' (Historical, world-changing) – respectively, "'Tis new to thee' and "'Tis new to everyone', so to speak. Boden's argument, like her labelling, is less overtly hierarchical and more discriminating than Craft's in the kind of relative valuation implied. (The latter qualifies and elaborates her position in Craft 2011.) Meanwhile, in a broader perspective, we need to recognize all the 'Multi-'s: Multimodality, Multimedia and Multiculturalism. These also open up the possibility of creativity in and through many senses, perceptions, modes, media, periods and cultures (see Kress and Van Leeuwen 2001; also Marsh 2010). We pick up some of these multi-s shortly, when situating language in relation to communication at large and learning in particular. They are treated at length in Part 2, and expressly reinvoked in Chapter 27 by Ruth Finnegan.

Creative Learning, Industries, Partnerships

'Creativity' and 'creative' have become buzz words, rallying calls and weasel words in many areas of commercial enterprise and public policy from the late twentieth into the early twenty-first centuries. This has been especially marked in the UK in education ('creative learning'), employment ('creative enterprise') and culture ('creative industries'). Indeed, so ubiquitous and pervasive – some would say invasive – has the rhetoric of creativity become in the modern corporate state that for better and worse it offers (or threatens) to blur the boundaries between education and employment altogether, with projects and programmes such as 'Creative Partnerships', for example. A brief review of the characteristic rhetorics and discourses of 'creativity' in and around contemporary UK education policy will help set the scene (see Banaji et al. 2006; O'Connor 2007). This extends from the setting up of the Department of Culture, Media and Sport in 1997 to the latest reports on 'innovation' in education, business and industry.[1] 'Innovation', rather like 'invention' earlier, is often used instead of or alongside the 'create' terms; it gives them a technical edge, projecting a kind of 'creativity with attitude'.

The richness, complexity and contentiousness of approaches and arguments in this area may be gauged by a representative sampling of the main topics, by chapter heading, treated in just a couple of the reviews of the recent research literature:

> Creative genius; Democratic and political creativity; Creativity as economic imperative; Play and creativity; Creativity and cognition; The Creative Affordances of Technology.
>
> (Banaji et al., *The Rhetorics of Creativity*, 2006)

Cultural conservatism; Mass culture and progressive education, 1945–65; Cultural Studies in the new order: Common Culture, 1980s; Creativity and economic change, 1990s; Cultural and Creative Industries, to the present.

(Jones, *Culture and Creative Learning*, 2009)

Reading through these reports and reviews, what comes through time and again is a fundamental tension between two models of creativity. These may be characterized as:

- creativity for personal growth and cultural awareness;
- creativity for the knowledge economy and employment.

These two models may be seen as complementary or in conflict: certainly they tend to compete and sometimes they may cooperate (in a more or less corporate kind of way). For graphic convenience, the overall situation may be further modelled as follows, with two-way flow-arrows connecting all the items, around and across, and 'creativity' as the term at issue in the centre:

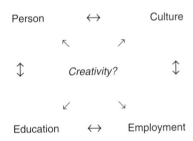

Figure 1.1 **A dynamic model of creativity in the public sphere**

Creativity in Relation to Reading and Rewriting

Much of the work reviewed above has emphasized production, whether in terms of creative processes of production or the outcome of such processes in creative texts or other artefacts. However, accounts of reading, or the reception of literary and other texts, also differ in the extent to which this is seen as a creative activity. And different conceptions of reading have implications for how we conceive of writing. For instance if all reading is in some sense a form of rewriting (recasting what one reads in one's own mind), and if much writing is a form of rereading (recasting the resources of the language and texts as found into what one makes of them), at what point can a really fresh reading or writing be said to appear? This also has a bearing on what may be meant by creativity. For if human creation is not from nothing (*ex nihilo*, on divine lines) but from something or someone else (*ex aliis*, say, a broadly materialist view), is it all really just a matter of re-creation? (See Pope 1995, 2005 and Chapter 20 in this book; see also Knights and Thurgar-Dawson 2006.)

These are questions that bulk large and have been very variously addressed in many areas of theory and analysis. Debate ranges (sometime rages) from 'Reception Aesthetics' (associated chiefly with Iser 1978 and Jauss 1982) with its roots in Western European phenomenology to 'Reader Response Criticism' (Bloom 1973, Bleich 1978, Fish 1980) with its roots in Anglo-American prag-matism and individualism (see Holub 1984; Bennett 1995). Such debates tend to draw on earlier twentieth-century Eastern European traditions of formal and functional analysis (Mukarovsky 1970 [1936], Jakobson 1960) and, in the early twenty-first century, are increasingly informed by insights from physiology and psychology and artificial intelligence as well as linguistics and critical theory, and currently assume the form of Cognitive Poetics and Text World Theory (see Chapter 16 by Peter Stockwell; see also Oatley 2003). Famously – some would say infamously – there has been much heat and some light generated by responses to Barthes's essay 'The Death of the Author', especially its provocative last line: 'the birth of the reader must be at the cost of the death of the author' (Barthes 1977; and compare Wandor 2008 and her Chapter 12 in this book).

Nowadays there is a rich array of approaches that may be broadly character-ized as forms of 'reading-as-rewriting', each with its own more or less distinct project of what may be called 're-vision as re-valuing'. Marxist, new historicist, feminist, gay, psychoanalytic and post-colonial approaches all have their criti-cal agendas and regimes of reading, often partly overlapping – reading for class, gender, sexuality, trauma, ethnicity, and powers and pleasures of many kinds. Meanwhile, openly post-structural and deconstructive 'readings' may issue in kinds of (re)writing and (re-)presentation that exploit devices of lay-out and graphology and strategies of textual organization (crossings-out, collage, paral-lel and hybrid text, alternative annotations) usually associated with experimen-tal poetry, drama and fiction and the more literary kinds of philosophy (for examples, see Chapter 13 by Patience Agbabi and Chapter 20 by Rob Pope; see also Sheppard 2008). Alongside these traditions, research on the history of reading, and the empirical study of contemporary reading practices (how people actually read and discuss their responses to literary texts, as opposed to more idealized conceptions of reading) offer insights into reading and reception as literary activities that are very different from those familiar in the literature and language classes of formal education (see Chapter 17 by Joan Swann).

Linguistic Approaches to Creativity in Language

Set against these broader debates about creativity, contemporary empirical research has highlighted the prevalence of linguistic creativity even in the most routine utterances. The swell of evidence has led several researchers to identify continuities between such 'everyday' creativity and literary language. This research tradition forms a major stimulus for the present volume, and is the starting point for many of the chapters that follow.

Three Approaches to Linguistic Creativity

'The central fact to which any significant linguistic theory must address itself is this: a mature speaker can produce a new sentence of his language on the appropriate occasion, and other speakers can understand it immediately, though it is equally new to them ... the class of sentences with which we can operate fluently and without difficulty or hesitation is so vast that for all practical purposes ... we may regard it as infinite.'

(Chomsky 1964: 7)

'[Creativity] is the everyday process of semiotic work as making meaning.'

(Kress 2003: 40)

'Creativity is a pervasive feature of spoken language exchanges as well as a key component in interpersonal communication, and ... it is a property actively possessed by all speakers and listeners; it is not simply the domain of a few creatively gifted individuals.'

(Carter 2004: 6)

The idea of 'creativity' is important in several areas of linguistics. In his theory of transformational generative grammar, for instance, Noam Chomsky referred to 'the "creative" aspect of language' (1964: 8) to denote its productivity: the fact that it enables speakers and listeners to produce and understand entirely novel sentences that they have not encountered before. In this sense, 'creativity' refers to an essential property of the language system rather than to language use that is creative in a literary or poetic sense, although the ability to produce novel sentences allows for the possibility of literary creativity.[2] This distinction between, in Guy Cook's terms, creativity *of* and *with* the system is addressed briefly in Chapter 24 of this volume.

In a rather different intellectual vein, socially oriented research on language in use (e.g. in the areas of applied linguistics and sociolinguistics) has come to see this as a relatively creative process in which language users constantly refashion linguistic and other communicative resources rather than reproducing static rules of language use. While emanating from a different discipline, such research is consistent with the work of Williams and others, cited earlier, that foregrounded the commonness of 'culture' and 'creativity'.

Gunther Kress and Theo Van Leeuwen (e.g. 2001), for instance, have developed the concept of 'design' to account for the integration of different modes in the production and interpretation of texts. Design necessarily involves transformation, however slight, and in this sense the 'semiotic work' of meaning-making is always creative. Similarly, within the study of language variation and diversity, a significant body of research has focused on speakers' appropriation of language varieties to style themselves and others – a shifting, creative performance of particular personae (Coupland 2007; Eckert 2000; Pennycook 2007; Rampton 2005). Practice-based approaches to the study of literacy have also emphasized the creative role of participants as active, strategic agents, using literacy practices to represent or create histories, social relationships and social identities (Bloome et al. 2005). Within these and similar traditions of enquiry researchers do not see the communicative strategies adopted by individuals as entirely unfettered, but there is an emphasis on language users' creativity within and in relation to social, contextual and medium-specific constraints (Maybin and Swann 2007).

It is against the backdrop of this general trend that research has begun to document the pervasiveness of creative language that may be considered, in various ways, literary-like. The extracts below provide examples, including features such as wordplay, repetition, metaphor and imagery often associated with poetry and other literary texts. Extract 1 comes from a study by Ronald Carter of a substantial (5-million-word) corpus of spoken interaction: this is an example of word play – a near pun based on the similarity in form between *reason* and *raisin*. Carter notes that initially he was not looking for evidence of creativity, but found this was surprisingly common in his data. In Extract 2, two speakers echo and re-echo one another's words, giving their interaction a poetic texture (similar forms of interactional repetition recur throughout Carter's data). Extract 3 comes from research on language play by Guy Cook, who focuses on word play of various sorts and on the playful construction of imaginary or fictional worlds evident in children's rhymes and riddles; adult forms such as Valentine messages; adverts; and more serious genres such as oratory, poetry and song. In Extract 4, from research by Janet Holmes on workplace humour, creativity turns not on wordplay or other manipulation of linguistic form but on the discursive play evident in conversational joking – in this case Sam comments humorously on the length of a meeting and the chair, Jill, maintains the humorous tone in her response. The final extract comes from research on narrative by Michael Toolan: here, a speaker selects words and phrases (*amazingly scary*, *unbelievable screech*, a *massive... stone wall*) to create powerful images of the events in her story and intensify the feeling of danger.

Some Examples of Language Creativity

Extract 1   *Members of a family are preparing food for a party:*

C	Foreign body in here. What is it?
B	It's raisins and [inaudible]
C	Er oh it's rice with raisins is it?
D	No no no. It's not supposed to be [*laughter*] erm
C	There must be a raisin for it being in there.
	[*laughter*]

(Adapted from Carter 2004: 93)

Extract 2   *Three children are engaged in small-group discussion in a class-room. They have been asked to consider a moral dilemma – what should happen to a boy who stole chocolates for his mother, who was sick. Two of the children are speaking in this extract:*

Emily	Right em
Gemma	I think he should be punished and grounded
Emily	[I think he should be punished and grounded
Gemma	[I think he should be grounded
Emily	For em like a couple of weeks mmh
Gemma	I think he should be (.) at least a month because like imagine if like you stole
Emily	The police would find out
Gemma	The police would [find out
Emily	[And then your mum would be really
Gemma	And your mum would be really angry
Emily	Your mum would be really angry
Gemma	She'd be like panicking and
Emily	Everything
Gemma	She'd probably get even more ill
Emily	Exactly
Gemma	Imagine how she'd feel (.) OK

(Unpublished data[3])

Note: (.) = brief pause; square brackets = beginning of overlapping speech.

Extract 3   *Beginning of a rhyme for young children:*
Diddle diddle dumpling my son John/Went to bed with his trousers on

(Cited Cook, 2000: 24)

Extract 4 *A Board meeting in a small IT company is almost finished and the main agenda items have been covered. The participants are now discussing only minor points. Jill is the chair of the meeting:*

Sam: ke- keep going until there's only one person standing
Jill: [*laughs*] oh you've been to our board meetings before
             [*laughs*]

(Holmes, 2007: 525)

Extract 5 *Part of a story told by a student about a near accident in a car:*
...so we were like [laughing intonation] coming over this hill not too fast but fast enough for it to be amazingly scary erm and he pressed the brakes again and we started to skid and I'll never forget the unbelievable screech as as we started to move towards the right of the road and there was a massive sort of erm err stone wall that we were heading towards and I've [laughing intonation] never been so scared in my life...

(Toolan 2006: 59)

A great deal of research, such as the studies reported above, involves creativity in spoken interaction (see also Norrick 2001; Tannen 2007). Studies have also, however, looked at creativity in written texts and practices (from diaries and letters, graffiti, signs and leaflets, and various electronic texts, to canonical literature – see examples in Goodman and O'Halloran 2006; Maybin and Swann 2006).

This body of work is not inconsistent with the more general, theoretical re-viewing of all language use as creative and indeed some researchers would align themselves with this view. In many cases, however, research with a specific focus on literary-like creativity sees this, while prevalent, as distinctive – as a type of language use that stands out and, however fleetingly, draws attention to itself. In Extract 2 above, the creative patterning is more covert – while it is evident in a transcript it is unlikely to be noticed by speakers. In other extracts, however, linguistic or discursive patterns are more marked and, where we have evidence of this, they are responded to by others – by laughter in Extracts 1 and 4. Such usage corresponds to one of the functions of language identified by Roman Jakobson, which he termed the *poetic function*: an occasion in which there is a 'focus on the message for its own sake' (1960: 356). Jakobson is referring here to the highlighting of the linguistic form of a message (word play, rhyming, etc.). While this is a dominant function of poetry, taking precedence over other functions such as conveying information, it is also evident in non-literary texts, although in this latter case other functions may be dominant.

Alongside the identification of creative forms in discourse, there has also, importantly, been a focus on the socially embedded nature of language creativity, and on its interactional, interpersonal and affective meanings within specific contexts of use. Such language is often seen as inclusive in various ways. Carter (2004) argues that creative episodes, in his data, are associated with informal, friendly relations and in this context they function to align viewpoints and create convergence. Tannen (2007), similarly, argues that language that she sees as 'poetic' creates involvement in the conversational topic and between speakers. On the other hand, Cook (2000) notes that while play may serve to include others it may also exclude, e.g. in humorous taunts or put-downs.[4] The examples cited above all provide evidence of inclusion and the creation of involvement, but in Extract 2 the closeness of the two children speaking together may also exclude a third member of the group who does not speak on this occasion (elsewhere in the discussion there is more overt friction between Emily and Gemma, and Dan, the third member of their group). Extract 4 demonstrates the fairly complex negotiation of relationships in the workplace, in which a teasing comment has the potential to subvert authority, but in this case the humour in both Sam's remark and Jill's response also takes the edge off the criticism.

Maybin and Swann (2007) develop a more overtly contextualized approach to language creativity, drawing on linguistic anthropological notions of *performance* (Bauman 1986; Bauman and Briggs 1990; Hymes 1975), and a dialogical model of language associated with the Russian literary theorist Mikhail Bakhtin.

Performance in this sense may be defined as:

> a mode of communication, a way of speaking, the essence of which resides in the assumption of responsibility to an audience for a display of communicative skill, highlighting the way in which communication is carried out, above and beyond its referential content. (Bauman 1986: 3)

This idea is closely associated with Jakobson's poetic function. Performance calls attention to the act of expression itself and to the performer. For Bauman it is: 'the enactment of the poetic function, the essence of spoken artistry' (ibid.).

Bakhtin (e.g. 1984 [1929], 1981 [1935], 1986 [1953]) sees language not as a unified whole, but as highly differentiated:

- Language itself is *heteroglossic* – it includes different social languages, associated with particular social groups and contexts of use (e.g. the language used by different professional groups, by older people or younger people). There are often tensions and struggles between such social languages.

- At the level of particular utterances, too, language is *polyphonic* or multi-voiced: any utterance reproduces the *voices* of other speakers and contexts of use. Words, phrases, discourses carry with them the 'taste' of these prior speakers and contexts. This is most obvious where speakers are actually quoted, i.e. in direct speech; but it permeates language use more generally (e.g. reference to someone being grounded in Extract 2 will derive its associations from previous contexts of use).
- Language use is *dialogic*, both in the sense that it addresses a particular person/people and a particular context, and in drawing on other voices (in this latter sense any utterance is a response to previous utterances, contexts or people).
- The associated term *intertextuality* is often used (from Julia Kristeva 1986) to refer to 'chains of communication' – the idea that all utterances or texts are made up of words and meanings from other utterances/texts.

This view of language would see utterances as always having an evaluative dimension (i.e. reflecting a speaker's evaluative stance or viewpoint). Bauman and Briggs (1990) argue further that, because they call attention to themselves, performances have an enhanced potential for evaluation and critique. An example here would be the workplace extract (Extract 4) where Sam's comment serves as a humorous critique of his boss.

Such ideas have been highly influential in contemporary language study and have implications here for the study of language creativity. In terms of the 'creativity words' discussed above, creativity would be seen not as something completely novel or original, but as a process of transformation, where words and phrases, or communicative practices, are taken up and recontextualized – i.e. bringing associations from prior contexts, but also refashioned, and imbued with particular meaning in the current context of use. Such ideas about creativity underpin several chapters in this volume (Chapters 4, 9, 10, 11, 17, 18, 20).

To summarize these rather complex arguments:

- creativity has been identified as a common feature of language use;
- some researchers see all language use as creative; others restrict the term to particular types of language (e.g. metaphor, word play, the use of powerful imagery);
- in this latter case, attention is drawn to the form of language; this process has been termed the poetic function of language, but it is not restricted to poetry;
- some researchers focus, not just on creative forms of language, but on language creativity as a contextualized practice – so that its meaning is dependent on particular contexts of use;

- in this case, creativity may be seen as a matter of performance (however fleeting this is), designed for a particular audience in a particular context;
- drawing on ideas from Bakhtin, language creativity is also seen as a process of transformation, where words and expressions draw on meanings from prior contexts, but are also reinvested with meaning in the current context of use;
- like any form of language use, language creativity reflects the values and standpoints of speakers and listeners; some researchers argue that, because creative episodes stand out, this increases their potential as a means of critique (of other people, standpoints, etc.).

On the basis of these ideas, Maybin and Swann set out a schematic representation of different ways of analysing language that may contribute to the study of language creativity (see Figure 1.2).

Some Implications for the Relationship between Everyday and Literary Creativity

Anthropological conceptions of performance, building on Jakobson's poetic function, apply to literature (literary performances) but also more broadly

Dimension of analysis	Analytical focus	Examples
Textual	Linguistic forms and structures, at word/sentence level and above; may also include formal multimodal analysis.	Word play; narrative structure; voice quality used to enhance the point of an ironic or playful comment; placement of emoticons in electronic chat.
Contextualized	How language is used by participants in specific interactions, and/or how it shapes, responds to, and is shaped by particular sociocultural and sociohistorical contexts (the balance varies in different analyses).	Joint construction of a narrative, or word play, and how this is responded to by others; the cultural understandings necessary to make sense of a joke; economic, social and technological conditions associated with contemporary electronic creativity.
Critical	Creativity as necessarily evaluative, with the potential for more developed critique of social relations/positions and associated values.	Conversational narrative that indexes a speaker's moral stance; joking that subverts or critiques authority; the potential of poetic language to call attention to a critical stance.

Figure 1.2   Dimensions of analysis

Source: Adapted from Maybin and Swann (2007: 513).

to language creativity wherever this occurs. They serve as a way of bringing together a microperformance in conversational word play and a fully developed literary work. They also allow researchers to explore commonalities and differences between everyday and literary creativity.

While for convenience we have referred so far to relationships between the 'everyday' and the 'literary', clearly neither of these is a unitary, undifferentiated category. The idea of 'multiple creativities', discussed earlier, would suggest here that instances of creative language use relate to each other in complex and contextually specific ways, varying across texts, genres and contexts to a range of aesthetic, affective and interpersonal effects.

In addition to broadening conceptions of creativity and challenging the distinctiveness of literary language, the ideas discussed above pose challenges to conventional conceptions of the nature and functions of language itself. Carter for instance suggests that 'creative language may be a default condition, a norm of use from which ordinary, routine "non-creative" exchanges constitute an abnormal departure' (2004: 214). And Cook, similarly, states that 'it might be that, both ontogenetically and phylogenetically, the first function of language is the creation of imaginative worlds: whether lies, games, fictions or fantasies' (2000: 47).

How this book is organized

The ideas sketched out above form a historical and disciplinary backdrop for the present volume, and are variously elaborated and extended, played with, challenged or contested in the contributions from different authors. We have tried to bring together and to mix up contributors with a range of disciplinary, aesthetic, ideological and practical perspectives on creativity, language and literature. These include scholars, teachers and researchers in English Language and Literature, Literary Studies, Linguistics, and Education; and creative practitioners in Writing (novelist, poet, dramatist, storyteller, literary editor) and Film (director), all of whom have been or are currently also involved in teaching Creative Writing, Performance, Drama or Film Studies.

The contributions themselves are different in nature: many are conventionally academic, concerned with analysis, argument or debate. Practitioners bring a more personal and reflexive perspective to their own engagement with creative practices. But we also include a wider range of formats: an interview discussing bilingual joking; a poem with a commentary by the author; extracts from an interview with a storyteller and an illustration of his performance; a brief extract from a lecture on creativity in poetry; a poetic 'A–Z of textual re-creation'.

The volume therefore forms a kind of vortex – in a more contemporary scientific idiom, it acts as a 'strange attractor' – to draw together a wide but not disparate range of people, activities and institutions, and ways of presenting ideas about creativity, language and literature. The contributors and editors have done this because they believe it is not only an exciting and energizing thing to do but also a desirable and perhaps even necessary one. In short, to be upbeat and open about it, we reckon this is one of the shapes of things to come. But even if this eventually proves not to be the case, being more modest and unassuming, it is hoped that the idea and design of the book will have modelled at least one of the shapes that things might become.

Part I extends the earlier discussion on the relationship between the 'everyday' and the 'literary', focusing on multiple creativities and the potential instability of boundaries between these. Authors take contrasting positions on the relative distinctiveness of, and relationships between, a range of diverse creativities – drawing on insights from linguistics/language studies, literary scholarship and cultural studies, and poetry/performance art. The theme of literary value/aesthetics surfaces across chapters.

Part II further elaborates these ideas in the consideration of creativities across different modes, media and technologies, and the potential offered by multimodal, and often ethnographically grounded, understandings of creative practices. Analysis and commentary foreground processes of transformation and (re)contextualization in writing and performance, face-to-face and electronic discourse, material texts and film.

Part III turns to processes of reception, response and 'creative interpretation'. The role of the audience, imagined and actual, has already been highlighted in relation to performance and film, and 'production'/'reception' necessarily blur in interpersonal interaction. The focus here is on imagined responses to film from different audiences, literary reading, editing and judging, and the dynamic of rereading and rewriting. There is reflection throughout on the nature of critical response and on conceptions of aesthetic judgement and literary value.

Part IV concludes the volume by pointing to some persistent questions and ongoing debates – on the historical construction of creativity, around contested notions of 'genius', and about the problematics of teaching 'creative writing'. Further perspectives on creativity in language and literature are supplied through philosophy, aesthetics, performance and multimodal communication. An epilogue to the volume offers 'postscripts and prospects' for studies in creativity, language and literature at large.

NOTES

1. For example and in particular: *All our Futures* (National Advisory Committee on Creative and Cultural Education, 1999); *Creativity: Find it, Promote it* (Qualifications and Curriculum Authority, 2003); *Nurturing Creativity in Young People: A Report to Government to Inform Future Policy* (Roberts, 2006); *Creating Growth: How the UK Can Develop World-class Creative Businesses* (NESTA, 2006); *Education for Innovation* (NESTA, 2007); *Innovation Nation* (DIUS, HMSO, 2008).
2. See Chomsky's discussion of what he termed 'true creativity' as manifested in the arts and sciences (Chomsky 1966).
3. These data come from a project directed by Neil Mercer, called Thinking Together in Primary Classrooms, and analysed by Joan Swann in previous research. We are grateful to Neil Mercer and the Thinking Together team for permission to cite data from their project.
4. Some practices are more ambiguous. For instance competitive play – sounding, verbal duelling, etc. – may involve ritual insults which combine competition with inclusion/involvement.

REFERENCES

Abbs, P. (2003) *Against the Flow: The Arts, Postmodern Culture and Education*. London: Routledge/Falmer.

Attridge, D. (2004) *The Singularity of Literature*. London and New York: Routledge.

Bakhtin, M. (1981 [1935]) 'Discourse in the novel' in Holquist, M. (ed.) *The Dialogic Imagination: Four Essays by M.M.Bakhtin*, trans. C. Emerson and M. Holquist. Austin, TX: University of Texas Press.

Bakhtin, M. (1984 [1929]) *Problems of Dostoevsky's Poetics*, ed. and trans. by C. Emerson. Manchester: Manchester University Press.

Bakhtin, M. (1986 [1953]) 'The problem of speech genres', in Emerson, C. and Holquist, M. (eds) *Speech Genres and Other Late Essays*, trans. V.W. McGee. Austin, TX: University of Texas Press.

Banaji, S., Burn, A. and Buckingham, D. (2006) *Rhetorics of Creativity*. London: Arts Council and Creative Partnerships.

Barthes, R. (1977) *Image–Music–Text*, ed. and trans. S. Heath. London: Fontana.

Bauman, R. (1986) *Story, Performance and Event*. Cambridge: Cambridge University Press.

Bauman, R. and Briggs, C. (1990) 'Poetics and performance as critical perspectives on language and social life'. *Annual Review of Anthropology* 19: 59–88.

Bennett, A. (1995) *Reader Response: A Reader*. London: Longman.

Bleich, D. (1978) *Subjective Criticism*. Baltimore: Johns Hopkins University.

Bloom, H. ([1973] 1997) *The Anxiety of Influence*. 2nd edn. Oxford: Oxford University Press.

Bloome, D., Carter, S.P., Christian, B.M., Otto, S. and Shuart-Faris, N (2005) *Discourse Analysis and the Study of Classroom Language and Literacy Events: A Microethnographic Perspective*. London: Lawrence Erlbaum Associates.

Boden, M. (2004) *The Creative Mind: Myths and Mechanisms*, 2nd edn. London: Routledge.

Carter, R. (2004) *Language and Creativity: The Art of Common Talk*. London/New York: Routledge.

Chomsky, N. (1964) *Current Issues in Linguistic Theory*. The Hague: Mouton.

Chomsky, N. (1966) *Cartesian Linguistics*. New York: Harper and Row.

Clark, T. (1997) *The Theory of Inspiration*. Manchester: Manchester University Press.

Cook, G. (2000) *Language Play, Language Learning*. Oxford: Oxford University Press.

Coupland, N. (2007) *Style: Language Variation and Identity*. Cambridge and New York: Cambridge University Press.

Craft, A., Jeffery, B. and Leibling, M. (eds) (2001) *Creativity in Education*. London: Continuum.

Craft, A. (2011) *Creativity and Education Futures*. Stoke-on-Trent: Trentham.

Csikszentmihalyi, M. (1996) *Creativity: Flow and the Psychology of Discovery and Invention*. New York: HarperCollins.

Derrida, J. (1992) *Acts of Literature*, ed. D. Attridge. London and New York: Routledge.

Eckert, P. (2000) *Linguistic Variation as Social Practice*. Oxford: Blackwell Publishers.

Fish, S. (1980) *Is There a Text in This Class? The Authority of Interpretive Communities*. Cambridge, Ma: Harvard University Press.

Gardner, H. (1998) *Extraordinary Minds*. London and New York: HarperCollins.

Goodman, S. and K.A. O'Halloran (eds) (2006) *The Art of English: Literary Creativity*. Basingstoke: Palgrave Macmillan.

Holmes, J. (2007) 'Making humour work: creativity on the job', in Swann, J. and Maybin, J. (eds) *Language Creativity in Everyday Contexts*. Special Issue of *Applied Linguistics* 28(4): 518–37.

Holub, R. (1984) *Reception Theory: A Critical Introduction*. London: Methuen.

Howe, M. (1999) *Genius Explained*. Cambridge: Cambridge University Press.

Hymes, D. (1975) 'Breakthrough into performance', in Ben-Amos, D. and Goldstein, K.S. (eds) *Folklore: Performance and Communication*. The Hague: Mouton.

Iser, W. (1978) *The Act of Reading: A Theory of Aesthetic Response*. Baltimore: Johns Hopkins University Press.

Jakobson, J. (1960) 'Closing statement: linguistics and poetics' in Sebeok, T.A. (ed.) *Style in Language*. Cambridge, MA: M.I.T. Press.

Jauss, H.R. (1982) *Toward an Aesthetic of Reception Theory*. Minneapolis: University of Minneapolis Press.

Jones, K. (2009) *Culture and Creative Learning: A Literature Review*. London: Arts Council and Creative Partnerships.

Kearney, R. (1998) *Poetics of Imagining: Modern to Postmodern*, 2nd edn. Edinburgh: Edinburgh University Press.

Knights, B. and Thurgar-Dawson, C. (2006) *Active Reading*. London and New York: Continuum.

Kress, G. (2003) *Literacy in the New Media Age*. London: Routledge.

Kress, G. and Van Leeuwen, T. (2001) *Multimodal Discourse: The Modes and Media of Contemporary Communication*. London: Arnold.

Kristeva, J. (1986) 'Word, dialogue, and the novel', in T. Moi (ed.) *The Kristeva Reader*. New York: Columbia University Press.

Marsh, J. (2010) *Childhood, Culture and Creativity: A Literature Review*. Sheffield: Creativity, Culture and Education.

Maybin, J. and Swann, J. (eds) (2006) *The Art of English: Everyday Creativity*. Basingstoke: Palgrave Macmillan.

Maybin, J. and Swann, J. (2007) 'Everyday creativity in language: textuality, contextuality and critique' in Swann, J. and Maybin, J. (eds) *Language Creativity in Everyday Contexts*. Special Issue of *Applied Linguistics* 28(4): 497–517.

Mukarovsky, J. (1970 [1936]) *Aesthetic Function, Norm and Value as Social Facts*, trans. Mark E. Suino. Ann Arbor, MI: University of Michigan.

Norrick, N.R. (2001) 'Poetics and conversation'. *Connotations* 10(2–3): 43–267.

Oatley, K. (2003) 'Writingandreading: the future of cognitive poetics' in Gavins, J. and Steen, G. (eds) *Cognitive Poetics in Practice*. London and New York: Routledge.

O'Connor, J. (2007) *The Cultural and Creative Industries: A Literature Review*. London: Arts Council and Creative Partnerships.

Pennycook, A. (2007) *Global Englishes and Transcultural Flows*. Abingdon, UK: Routledge.

Pope, R. (1995) *Textual Intervention: Critical and Creative Strategies for Literary Studies*. London: Routledge.

Pope, R. (2005) *Creativity: Theory, History, Practice*. London and New York: Routledge.

Preminger, A. and Brogan T. (eds) (1993) *The New Princeton Encyclopedia of Poetry and Poetics*. Princeton, NJ: Princeton University Press.

Rampton, B. (2005) *Crossing: Language and Ethnicity among Adolescents*. 2nd edn. Manchester: St Jerome Press.

Scruton, R. (2001) 'What is creativity?' Lecture at Hay-on-Wye Book Festival, 30 May 2001, previewed in *The Sunday Times, Review*, 20 May 2001.

Sheppard, R. (2008) 'Poetics as conjecture and provocation'. *New Writing: The International Journal for the Theory and Practice of Creative Writing* 5(1): 3–26.

Steiner, G. (2001) *Grammars of Creation*. London: Faber and Faber.

Sternberg, R. (ed.) (1999) *A Handbook of Creativity*. Cambridge: Cambridge University Press.

Tannen, D. (2007) *Talking Voices: Repetition, Dialogue and Imagery in Conversational Discourse*, 2nd edn. Cambridge: Cambridge University Press.

Toolan, M. (2006) 'Telling stories' in Maybin, J. and Swann, J. (eds) op. cit.

Wandor, M. (2008) *The Author Is not Dead merely Living somewhere Else: Creative Writing Reconceived*. London: Palgrave.

Williams, R. (1961) *The Long Revolution*. Harmondsworth: Penguin.

Williams, R. (1983) *Keywords: A Vocabulary of Culture and Society*, 2nd edn. London: Fontana.

Willis, P. with Jones, S., Canaan, J. and Hurd, G. (1990) *Common Culture: Symbolic Work at Play in the Everyday Cultures of the Young*. Milton Keynes: Open University Press.

Woolf, V. (1992 [1929]) *A Room of One's Own*, ed. M. Shiach. Oxford: Oxford University Press.

PART I

CREATIVITIES: TEXTS IN CONTEXT, GENRES IN PRACTICE

Introduction to Part I

The contributors to this part take as their starting point the fluidity of various sorts of boundaries – for instance, between everyday language and literature, between genres, and between languages. Whether explicitly or by implication, this affects how we conceive of traditional hierarchies between genres, and how we evaluate different forms of creativity.

A great deal of research on linguistic creativity has involved language that, in some way or other, can be considered poetic, and poetic language – across different genres – is a major theme in this part.

In **Chapter 2** Patience Agbabi discusses her poem *Word* and more generally her approach to writing and performing poetry. Agbabi tries to bridge the gap between 'page' and 'stage'. Performance, she writes, 'elevates' the word from page to stage, and her choice of term here deliberately subverts a conventional literary hierarchy.

Word is poetic in a formal/linguistic sense (in its manipulation and play with poetic form); in its play with generic conventions and border crossing (mixing 'the iambic pentameter into a rap without disguising its "I am(b)s" but multilayering its meaning: "I am/bicultural ..." '); and with respect to features developed in performance (the significance of a pause/deep intake of breath). A major focus of the chapter however is on poetic processes: in writing, forgetting everything else and getting 'into the groove'; in performance, working oneself up into the 'performance zone', where words can fly. In all these ways – textual, compositional, performance – poetry occupies a distinctive creative space, as poets strive to put 'the best words in the best order'.

Agbabi's account here of creativity across the modes of speech and writing, and of her interaction with an audience in performance, prefigure the later discussions in Parts II and III.

In **Chapter 3**, Richard Danson Brown discusses poetry and commentary by the twentieth-century poet Louis MacNeice. Brown's analysis and close reading provide a counterpoint to applied linguists' arguments about the literariness of everyday language. MacNeice and some of his contemporaries are engaged in a converse process – the literary appropriation of the everyday. MacNeice writes that 'the poet is a specialist in something which everyone practices', but for Brown this is a gesture towards 'an *ideal* of conversation' (our italics): the practice of poetry remains distinct with the poet drawing on talk as raw material, artfully 'fusing disparate poetic idioms and linguistic registers'.

When literary or literary-like language is used in conversation, it may have a poetic function (of drawing attention to itself) but it also needs to serve a range of interactional and interpersonal functions and the importance of these may equal or surpass the poetic. When 'everyday' phrases, even clichés and nursery-rhyme-like refrains, occur in poetry, they carry with them the resonances of other contexts of use, but they are also reframed as 'literary' and their primary function becomes poetic.

Angel Lin (**Chapter 4**) takes us from canonical poetry to hip hop, a global art form that has interested many researchers because of its appropriation and reinvention by performers in different local contexts. Lin discusses the work of Fama, a Hong Kong group who hybridize Western hip hop with local styles and practices, creating a new style that distinguishes Fama from their predecessors and chimes with the popular mood of the day.

Lin's analysis highlights the formal properties of Fama's rapping style – in particular their blending of the resources of three languages, Cantonese, English and sometimes Putonghua, and the possibilities this affords for creative linguistic play and innovation across the structures of these languages. Lin's interest is also in how these bilingual practices invoke a particular local identity – suave, urban, fun-making – common to Fama and their student audience.

In **Chapters 5 and 6**, Lynne Cameron and Elena Semino discuss metaphor, an archetypally poetic form. Both Cameron's and Semino's work, however, draws on cognitive metaphor theory, which sees metaphor as an inherent property of the human mind. The argument here is that we habitually understand the world metaphorically – we see one thing in terms of another. Literary metaphor is able to build on and extend such routine metaphorical thinking. This is reflected in studies of metaphor in discourse, such as Cameron's and Semino's work, which would see metaphorical language use as habitual, and not restricted to particularly striking or noticeable metaphors.

Cameron's thinking, in **Chapter 5**, is framed partly by her experience as an artist as well as a metaphor analyst. Following the literary theorist Bakhtin, she outlines a broad distinction between 'prosaic' and 'poetic' creativity, the former exemplified by metaphor in reconciliation talk and the latter by metaphor in poetry. For Cameron, ideas about 'clines' of literariness mask what is distinctive about poetic creativity: the work involved in 'constructing order and shape', building something that is then complete and becomes independent of its creator. Prosaic creativity, by contrast, is spontaneous and remains rooted in the context of its production. The ubiquity of creativity is also at issue – creativity that is 'everywhere' must be qualitatively different from creativity that is not constant – 'occasional bright moments in the long labour with material and ideas'.

Characteristics such as spontaneity and completion/independence relate also to differences between mode and medium – freestyle rap is more spontaneous than written poetry, for instance. Creativity across modes/media is addressed in Part II.

Semino, in **Chapter 6**, draws distinctions along different lines. She distinguishes 'creative' and 'conventional' metaphorical uses, but these do not map neatly onto Cameron's 'poetic' and 'prosaic'. Creativity in metaphor is, here, a matter of degree, having to do with the novelty of metaphorical associations in individual words as well as broader metaphorical patterns in discourse. Metaphors that are (relatively) creative occur across a range of everyday genres as well as in poetry. Semino analyses creative metaphor in texts that represent three genres – a novel, a doctor–patient interview and a scientific paper. She points out that metaphor is used in different ways in these three contexts, although in each case it is appropriate and may be seen as successful.

Both Cameron and Semino address issues of value. Cameron seeks to 'revalue the prosaic while retaining respect for the skills and expertise involved in crafting the poetic'. Semino makes a broader appeal to context specificity, arguing that the value or success of metaphor 'can only properly be discussed in relation to the text and genre in which it occurs'.

Chapter 7, the final contribution, takes us into a different creative genre: bilingual joking, explored in an interview between G. D. Jayalakshmi, S. Upendran and R. Amritavalli. Upendran and Amritavalli discuss several examples from their collection of Indian bilingual jokes, illustrating playfulness across languages and cultures. Their focus is partly on the formal complexity of bilingual punning and playing (as in Chapter 4 speakers are blending the resources of different languages). Word play is also seen as a culturally contextualised activity, serving to 'create community' and both integrate and explore tensions in bilingual identities.

Several themes emerge across these chapters:

- Creativity (creativities) are seen as **multiple** and **differentiated**: even in this small selection of papers, researchers analyse different forms of creativity, evident in different texts, genres and practices. Creativity may be seen as ubiquitous and routine (Cameron's 'prosaic' creativity), though for the most part it involves language that stands out in some way, consistent with the 'poetic function' of language.

- Contributors draw different types of **relationships and distinctions between creativities** – within poetry, between page and stage; more broadly between prosaic and poetic. Distinctions may be seen as matters of degree (creative and conventional metaphor) or as more differentiated (different types of creative metaphor). Literary creativity may be seen as an extension: as a polished, worked up version of the everyday. Creating or challenging distinctions may itself be a poetic act (the poetic use of everyday language).

- Authors focus on creativity at the level of **text** (and on formal properties such as metaphor, word play, rhythm, language choice) – e.g. Brown, Cameron, Semino, Lin, Upendran and Amritavalli. Textual analysis may draw on different analytical traditions and languages of description – Brown's close reading of poetry; Cameron's and Semino's linguistic analysis of metaphor drawing on insights from cognitive metaphor theory. There is also a focus on creativity as **process**, e.g. in composition and performance, including design for an audience – provoking the imagination, eliciting audience responses (Agbabi).

- Creativities are seen as **contextualized practices**: though this may be expressed in different ways, all chapters see language creativity (production and interpretation) as locally, culturally and historically situated – e.g. metaphor use as specific to different contexts of use, MacNeice's writing alongside that of other early twentieth-century British poets, the cultural and historical meanings of bilingual joking. The related idea that creativity is, in various ways, **dialogical** (both locally co-constructed and responsive to prior texts and practices) is implicit here – e.g. in the co-construction of creative episodes in reconciliation talk; in Fama's hip hop, seen in the context of earlier styles. These points are developed further in Part II.

- Language creativities are (therefore) intimately bound up with various sets of interactional and interpersonal processes: e.g. the construction of **relationships** through metaphor; the creation and juggling of **identities** in hip hop and bilingual word play.

All the above have implications for judgements of **literary value**: the differentiated, contextualized and locally functional nature of language creativity suggests that its understanding and appreciation must also be contextualised, and that we need a plural and dynamic conception of aesthetics. Cameron seeks to value the poetic *and* the prosaic; Agbabi to subvert hierarchies between writing and performance; Semino insists that metaphor needs to be judged in relation to the task at hand. These ideas disrupt conceptions of Literature as being particularly highly valued as a cultural practice or seen as a descriptive benchmark for linguistic creativity. They are further elaborated, played with and contested in the parts that follow.

2

Give Me (Deep Intake of Breath) Inspiration

Patience Agbabi

Give me a word, any word and I'll give you an instant rap fat with complex rhymes and cross-cultural refs over a rough 4/4 beat. Except I'm not a real rapper bestowed with that particular creative superpower, the ability to freestyle. So give me a word, any word and a day free of admin and chores and maybe I'll come up with something decent that rhymes, with the odd cultural reference over an irregular beat. Doesn't have quite the same ring does it?

When I wrote *Word*, 'Word!' was the in-word in black British culture, Brixton via the Bronx. It was the late 1990s. At a poetry performance if you said something deep, an audience member would say 'Word!', i.e. 'I agree, you're speaking truth, sista.' Maybe it harked back to the biblical connotation of *the* word, the gospel truth. (People still refer to *Word* as *The Word*, which I rather like.) I could imagine people shouting 'Word!' at the preacher; and poets, let's face it, are supposed to have insights, divine or otherwise. They put the best words in the best order. They cast a spell. For a spell to be effective it has to be said aloud. By naming my poem 'Word' I was celebrating the *spoken* word, from scripture to preacher, from page to stage.

Around that time I created a neologism, 'wordshop', because I hated working at weekends and that was the only way I could trick myself into teaching. The word 'word' was magic. It had the power to transform drudgery into fun. My wordshops focused on elevating the word from the page to the stage. I use the word 'elevate' deliberately to subvert the literary hierarchy that says the condensed stuff replete with classical literary allusion is superior to the musical stuff replete with popular cultural allusion. Performance poets are rubbished and ridiculed by certain 'page' poets because they celebrate the power of the spoken over the written word. But for the word to be performed aloud it has to *fly* off the page. Except in the case of the superhero(ine) freestylers who write nothing down.

At this stage I should introduce my rap mentor, Carl St Hill. I speak in the present tense although he died in 2004. I met him ten years earlier on our Rap Poetry Tour though I'd seen him perform with his band, Free Speech, for years, at gigs where 'the line between rap and poetry was as thin as the paper it was written on' (this quote was used for the front of our tour flier). Hanging out with Carl was being totally immersed in hip hop culture. He wore the clothes, he walked the walk, he talked the talk. Rap was the soundtrack to his life and he made me awesome tapes then spent days explaining the cross-cultural references of various tracks. I can't remember any of it now, he should have written it down, but that wasn't his style. Man, could he freestyle! Give him a word, any word and he'd fly with it, he'd play off its sound, sense, and chuck in a dozen references from anything from contemporary rap to the Bible. On that tour, he swallowed some chewing gum halfway through a song and managed to freestyle his way out of it. The audience went wild. If you can freestyle you don't need drugs and neither does your audience. And though Carl explained that if you do it enough it's not really spontaneous because you develop the ability to mix excerpts from previous freestyles whilst conjuring the fresh line, I still maintain if you can freestyle well you're a genius. Carl was aka Mo' Skills, i.e. rap genius.

Being totally immersed in hip hop culture from time to time as well as Carl's friendship post-Rap Poetry Tour inspired me to take more risks with my own rap (and non-rap) poetry. It gave me the confidence to find my own voice. It gave me the permission I needed. Let's face it, rappers are mostly black, male, inner-city, working-class youth. I was black, female, just discovered I was living in zone 3 rather than zone 2, of a complicated cross-cultural class background then went to Oxford, late 20-something. I was much more rebellious post-university – I had more to rebel against – but my street cred was past tense. I was feisty though, which helped, and my gender gave me the freedom to rap on my own terms, rather than try to copy the men.

As the only woman on the tour, I felt I had to 'represent', i.e. show, my skills. Though I couldn't freestyle, it was the first time I'd done gigs which privileged rap *poetry* and that felt fresh. I'd been mistakenly labelled a rapper on publicity fliers for years but this tour exactly represented the continuum between poetry and rap, page and stage, and that would not only inspire *Word*, my poetical manifesto, but all my subsequent poetry. My oral-aural writing process — enjoying the act of enunciation, the delicious texture of the words in my mouth as well as the auditory thrill when I utter them – is replicated on the stage. There is something very special about the private act of writing, getting into 'the zone' I discuss later. Performing in public is also magical because the auditory thrill is shared, and in the case of *Word*, a musical poem with a refrain, there's a chance the audience will get some of that oral thrill by joining in.

My early 1990s pieces were old skool rap like the most famous one of all, *The Message*, i.e. over a 4/4 beat with the rhyme coming at the end of the line. By the mid-1990s I started playing around with line lengths, using a lot more internal rhyme and upping the wordplay. I also became more confident on stage, i.e. I'd encourage audience participation. I strongly believed, and still do, that a magical performance is as much about the audience as the performer. At a performance poetry night, the audience always applaud between poems. They used to call out *during* poems too, to encourage the poet. Call and response. A symbiosis of energy. A social event.

> Give me a word
> any word
> let it roll across your tongue
> like a dolly mixture.
> Open your lips
> say it loud
> let each syllable vibrate
> like a transistor.
> Say it again again again again again
> till it's a tongue twister ...

Word is a challenge to the audience. *They* have to be creative. *They* have to come up with something that will inspire not only themselves, but me, the performer. If it were a word*shop* or a school performance, they really would be expected to say something out loud. But as it's a performance, I let them off. The challenge is stated but the audience is then invited to sit back, relax, whilst I take them on a journey down memory lane to reacquaint themselves with the parts of speech. For some people, this is the opposite of relaxation because they found it difficult as a child and still find it hard to get their heads round the technical terms. They freeze. Thankfully, most people chuckle and go with the flow.

I perform *Word* at the beginning of a set to warm people up. It's accessible, musical, witty. It also helps warm me up! Quite literally, it gets my voice going and mentally it prepares me for the rest of the set. Around the late 1990s, when I was performing with polyvocal poetry pop group Atomic Lip, I became much more disciplined about warming up before a gig. By that I mean doing singing and acting vocal exercises ranging from tongue twisters to breathing in for three then seeing how long you could hold a note before going blue. I used to swim whole lengths underwater and I'm a slow swimmer so I have pretty good lungs. I discovered that warming up made a huge difference to my physical presence on stage. I felt more confident, centred and powerful. I could expand my vocal range, in volume and tone. I was in the performance zone. I was, to quote a member of Atomic Lip, 'on fire!'. And in that state, I found myself freestyling. OK I improvized a syllable, a breath. But it was quite significant.

Give Me (Deep Intake of Breath) Inspiration

Because *Word* was not just inspired by wordplay, the page–stage continuum, listening to other performers or even the act of performing itself, it was inspired by that magical moment when you swallow the metaphorical chewing gum and fly. For that split second, the full meaning of 'inspiration' took over and I came off script. Ever since, I've been unable to perform that line without the meaningful pause, the deep intake of breath. If you listen to the online recording at www.57productions.com there's no pause because there was no tangible audience. But for live performance, it's now part of the script. You had to have been there the first time it happened. That's the magic of *live* performance. It's of the moment. There's a sense that anything might happen. Words can fly.

Performing *Word* or any rap for that matter is a deeply pleasurable experience. You do indeed feel as if you're flying. It makes you high. Not as high as if you could freestyle, but let's face it, those words are a long long way from the printed page, and although I never deliberately change the order, the spell is effective. When you perform word you're omniscient and omnipotent. You're god. And god with a small 'g' feels pretty good. Who needs cocaine when your whole body is buzzing with that kind of confidence. And that kind of confidence is embedded in the *writing*, the original creation of the spell.

Now Write It Down ...

How did I write *Word*? I wrote it out loud. I heard it in my head and wrote it down. The first soundbites I scrawled on pieces of paper but once I got going I typed straight onto the computer. That's how I generally write. I used to enjoy the feel of the 10p biro between my fingers but then I got lazy. I composed *Word* in triplets, i.e. I kept coming up with these rhetorical ideas in the style: I came, I saw, I conquered. This was a departure from the old skool rhyming couplet:

> I got more skills than I got melanin
> I'm fired by adrenaline
> If you wanna know what rhyme it is
> It's feminine.

This was the first soundbite I came up with and a pretty accurate assessment of where I was at when writing the piece. Rap is all about posturing, about 'bigging yourself up', and as I'm a short woman with a small build I felt it necessary to big myself up and then some. When I was writing *Word*, my consciousness was on fire. Once you get into the groove you don't feel as if you're writing but that something else has taken over. The words are writing themselves, you are merely the conduit. It's word association cubed. Hours can pass without you knowing. You forget to eat, drink or check your emails. OK, I wasn't online in 1998 or whenever *Word* passed through my fingers onto the keyboard. But I'm talking about 'the zone' all writers get into when it's flowing. I achieve a similar feeling when I'm swimming in such a rhythm I forget I'm swimming, or that I have a body and a mind. I go into auto. It's quite wonderful. Of course, there's a bit more going on in your head when you're writing but it doesn't *feel* like it. Writing should appear effortless, say the manuals. But some of my best writing *is* effortless, the effortlessness you achieve after hours, weeks, maybe months of tapping away on a hot keyboard.

It's the closest I've ever got to freestyling. I still find multilayered titles very stimulating and in this case *Word* was the ignition. I wrote it in one sitting and barely changed it afterwards. It felt right on my tongue. There's one line, 'then you'll lose your fear of flying', which doesn't make sense as I never establish that the audience has a fear of flying in the first place. My literary mentor, Kwame Dawes, pointed this out at manuscript stage. Under normal circumstances I would have inserted a few more lines to create the balance, but by then I arrogantly thought, 'I can get away with this because it's raw,' (my first book was called R.A.W.) and more about the tongue than the typescript. If I were writing it now there'd be a whole stanza on how you need to let go of your inhibitions to fly with spoken word, both as audience member and performer. But I wouldn't be writing it now and that's the whole point. The poem is very much of its time and where I was at and who I hung out with.

My writing reflects my passions and in a poem like *Word* I was able to indulge these quite blatantly. The great thing about rap is it's 'in yer face'. It can be multilayered but the primary message is spelt out. I call *Word* my poetical manifesto because whilst it celebrates the word off the page, the rap impetus, it also celebrates the written word, the iambic pentameter, and name drops one of my favourite poems of all time:

> I am I am I am I am I am
> Bicultural and sometimes clinical,
> My mother fed me rhymes through the umbilical
> I was born waxing lyrical.
> I was raised on Watch with Mother

The Rime of the Ancient Mariner
And Fight the Power.

My creativity has always been fired by several canons. There's a fantastic crea-tive writing exercise called 'Be a Replicant', where you write down 100 favour-ite books, poems, stories, films, records, etc. then check the list for recurring themes to find your creative obsessions. It's a great way to brainstorm ideas. I hadn't come across the exercise when I wrote *Word* but Coleridge and Chuck D were inevitably to feature on my list. I don't know whether I'd invite them to my ideal dinner party though.

Word is about spreading the word, word of mouth being the best form of advertising. I wasn't saying to the audience, you've got to go to these perform-ance poetry clubs more; but hearing spoken word at these clubs or by these groups has inspired me to create this piece. A classic example of poetry being about itself. The name dropping was fun for those in the know but not off-putting for those who weren't. It was all part of the verbal trickery. Ultimately, the creation of *Word* was about word*play*:

> Give me a word
> Give me a big word
> Let me manifest
> Express in excess
> The M I X
> Of my voice box.

Wordplay is all about repetition, playing one word against another, and in this type of poem you can get away with tons. The form demands it. Typical rap is replete with full rhymes and assonance. I deliberately used consonance and alliteration as well. But what I did more than anything else was repeat lines and words. There's the refrain, 'Give me a word', that punctuates the message. Then there's: 'again again again again again' and 'I am I am I am I am I am'. The irregularity of the rhythm meant I could slip into iambic pen-tameter not only for dramatic emphasis but to *marry* page to stage. There's a maverick rap poet, MC Jabber, who managed to perform the line 'To be or not to be, that is the question' in a 4/4 beat. I wanted to do something else, mix the iambic pentameter into a rap without disguising its 'I am(b)s' but multilayering its meaning: 'I am/bicultural ...' (also an oblique reference to another contemporary poem by Remi Abbas of Urban Poets Society, *Ironic Iambic*). When I use the word 'bicultural' I'm not just talking about being black British, I'm talking about blurring the boundaries between the printed and the performed:

Give me a stage and I'll cut form on it
Give me a page and I'll perform on it.

Word has a strange relationship to the page. It is both of and not of the page. It is most well-known *off* the page. Yet it started its life on the page. I definitely wanted to include it in my second collection, *Transformatrix*, but Kwame said it didn't fit with the rest of the poems, which sat more firmly on the page than this hyperactive rap poem. He went on to say the only way it would work would be as a kind of prologue. Which is why the first poem of *Transformatrix* is now and forever will be entitled 'Prologue'. Like many of the characters in the book, *Word* has a protean existence. As a prologue, it becomes more static. It *must* come first. Whereas in performance, although I chose to open with it, I could perform it at any stage throughout the set.

I could also perform the poem as an entire set, twice, on National Poetry Day 2000 with 3,001 schoolchildren. That's 3,001 schoolchildren reciting *Word* simultaneously in various assemblies in southern England. We set what I call a 'Word Record' but it didn't make the Guinness Book of Records. You have to *break* a record to do that. We had to perform it twice because it was only three and a half minutes long and there was some rule that the reading had to be a minimum of five minutes. Many of the children were from primary school. A tiny dot of a girl came up to me to tell me she'd learnt it off by heart. I was very moved. It was a very strange National Poetry Day, performing a poem I'd performed hundreds of times with little variation but this time in the South Bank Centre as a group performance with a couple of hundred London schoolchildren and the knowledge that 2,800 others were simultaneously doing the same thing. Twice. When you perform with a large group you lose the hyperactive dynamic. It's like assemblies when the headteacher says good morning and the whole school says 'Good morning Mister Blah Blah.' When we speak en masse we speak in slow motion. Also, you have more time to ponder each word, and with a rhythmic piece, you're in danger of forgetting your lines. You're no longer flying, you're wandering, not lonely as a cloud, but accompanied by a crowd. It's surreal.

After the peculiar exercise was over I wandered across the river to the Poetry Cafe in the hope of hearing one of my sonnets on Radio 4. I missed the broadcast but it was a lovely feeling, that today, my words had reached many people, both orally and aurally, rap and sonnet. There's an epilogue to all of this. The opening of *Word* was subsequently printed on a wall at the South Bank Centre. The vinyl letters no longer exist but their imprint remains. Spoken word is written in stone.

Word

Patience Agbabi

Give me a word
any word
let it roll across your tongue
like a dolly mixture.
Open your lips
say it loud
let each syllable vibrate
like a transistor.
Say it again again again again again
till it's a tongue twister
till its meaning is in tatters
till its meaning equals sound
now write it down,
letter by letter
loop the loops
till you form a structure.
Do it again again again again again
till it's a word picture.
Does this inspire?
Is your consciousness on fire?
Then let me take you higher.

Give me a noun
give me a verb
and I'm in motion
cos I'm on a mission
to deliver information
so let me take you to the fifth dimension.
No fee, it's free,
you only gotta pay attention.
So sit back, relax,
let me take you back
to when you learnt to walk, talk,
learnt coordination
and communication,
mama
dada.
If you rub two words together you get friction
cut them in half, you get a fraction.

If you join two words you get multiplication.
My school of mathematics
equals verbal acrobatics
so let's make conversation.

Give me a preposition
Give me an interjection
Give me inspiration.
In the beginning was creation
I'm not scared of revelations
cos I've done my calculations.
I've got the high hopes
on the tightrope,
I just keep talking.
I got more skills than I got melanin
I'm fired by adrenaline
if you wanna know what rhyme it is
it's feminine.
Cos I'm Eve on an Apple Mac
this is a rap attack
so rich in onomatopoeia
I'll take you higher than the ozone layer.
So give me Word for Windows
give me 'W' times three
cos I'm on a mission
to deliver information
that is gravity defying
and I'll keep on trying
till you lost your fear of flying.

Give me a pronoun
give me a verb
and I'm living in syntax.
You only need two words to form a sentence.
I am I am I am I am I am
Bicultural and sometimes clinical,
my mother fed me rhymes through the umbilical,
I was born waxing lyrical.
I was raised on Watch with Mother
the Rime of the Ancient Mariner
and Fight the Power.
Now I have the perfect tutor

in my postmodern suitor,
I'm in love with my computer.
But let me shut down
before I touch down.

Give me a word
give me a big word
let me manifest
express in excess
the M I X
of my voice box.
Now I've eaten the apple
I'm more subtle than a snake is
I wanna do poetic things in poetic places.
Give me poetry unplugged
so I can counter silence
give me my poetic licence

and I'll give you metaphors that top eclipses
I'll give megabytes and megamixes.

Give me a stage and I'll cut form on it
give me a page and I'll perform on it.

Give me a word
any word.

(From Agbabi, P. (2000) *Transformatrix*.
Edinburgh: Canongate: 9.)

3

'Can't We Ever, My Love, Speak in the Same Language?': Everyday Language and Creative Tension in the Poetry of Louis MacNeice

RICHARD DANSON BROWN

'Everyday language' is arguably always in tension with written poetry as a textual practice, a sophisticated use of language which relies on visual as well as aural cues. Or as Elizabeth Bowen (1998: 10–11) puts it (through the mouthpiece of the desiccated novelist, St Quentin Miller, in *The Death of the Heart*): 'To write is always to rave a little ... Style is the thing that's always a bit phony, and at the same time you cannot write without style'.[1] Twentieth-century poetry in English, however, repeatedly gestures towards an ideal of conversational style; the work of Louis MacNeice (1907–63) is particularly intriguing in the ways in which it faces up to the tensions between everyday language and the demands of poetry. MacNeice would have agreed with Bowen – a fellow Irish writer whose career was also focused on London – that to write is to rave, yet the style which emerges from his poetry attempts to accommodate the 'phoniness' of literature with the radical potential of everyday language.

My title comes from the poem 'Babel' which MacNeice wrote in December 1942 in London.[2] He had returned two years earlier from a lecturing job and a failed love affair in the USA. *The Strings are False*, his unfinished autobiography which was also drafted at about this time, clarifies his dilemma. As a left-leaning writer who had come to prominence during the 1930s, MacNeice was initially unsure of what role he should play in the Second World War, even though, like his contemporaries W. H. Auden, Stephen Spender and C. Day Lewis, this was a conflict which they had long anticipated.[3] MacNeice's position was further complicated by his ambivalent feelings of national allegiance – what Terence Brown (1975: 10) calls his 'spiritual hyphenation' between the Ireland where he was born and the England where he was educated. To return to Europe was to commit oneself – with marked caveats – to the Allied cause and to the struggle against fascism:

> I had decided...that any choice now was a choice of evils and that it was clear which was the lesser. But it is hard to risk your life for a Lesser Evil on the off-chance of some entirely problematical betterment for most likely a mere minority in a dubious and dirty future. (MacNeice 1965a: 21)

'Babel' expresses similar misgivings in the context of an interrogation of communal aspirations to 'togetherness' through the biblical myth of the origins of different languages. If *The Strings Are False* looks fretfully towards 'a dubious and dirty future', 'Babel' goes back to the Book of Genesis to find a prophetic analogy for the cosmopolitan, fractured London of the 1940s:

> There was a tower that went before a fall.
> Can't we ever, my love, speak in the same language?
> Its nerves grew worse and worse as it grew tall.
> Have we no aims in common?...
>
> Can't we ever, my love, speak in the same language?
> We cut each other's throats out of our great self-pity –
> Have we no aims in common?
>
> (CP: 227–8.)

This is typically MacNeicean in its artful appropriation of everyday idioms and its focus on the tensions between collective hopes and pragmatic realities. It's also a provocative starting point for this essay because it shows MacNeice's radical, demotic poetics in action while simultaneously exploring his misgivings about that theory. The poem works through sophisticated counterpoint, in which the refrain lines 'Can't we ever, my love, speak in the same language?' and 'Have we no aims in common?' juxtapose the language of lovers with a blander, more public idiom. At the same time, the strongly endstopped rhyming lines recall popular forms such as the ballad stanza and the nursery rhyme: 'There was a tower that went before a fall. ... Its nerves grew worse and worse as it grew tall'.[4] The first line's variation of the proverbial 'pride comes before a fall' exemplifies MacNeice's sensitivity to everyday language, as a dormant metaphor is revived to provide an economic means of retelling the biblical story.[5] The poem taps into spoken idioms and literary traditions with strong oral roots. Nevertheless, in keeping with the biblical story, its attitude towards the possibility of mutual comprehension is pessimistic. By fusing disparate poetic idioms and linguistic registers, MacNeice holds out the possibility that in a London which has become 'a foreign city', 'we' as 'Exiles all' may 'speak in the same language'. Yet the shortfall in communication is aurally emphasized by ruptures in the formal pattern: the refrains are of unequal metrical length and fail to rhyme with one another; communicative idioms fail to cohere – there is no shared language nor any 'aims in common'. That the poem establishes no symmetry between these questions intimates that everydayness – even everyday creativity – may not alleviate social tensions.[6] Rather than offering a blueprint for a better world, 'Babel' challenges its cast of 'Patriots, dreamers, die-hards, theoreticians' to face up to the alternatives to solidarity: cutting each other's throats or going 'to the wall'.

Speaking the same language is for MacNeice – himself an accomplished linguist – an ideal which is never fully realized socially, politically or erotically.[7] He generates some of his best poetry from this tension, and in this essay I read linguistically conscious poems of the late 1930s and early 1940s to explore the ways in which his consciousness of the ambiguities of everyday language informs his work. In turn, MacNeice's demotic poetics resonates with the debates about everyday language and creativity raised by other contributors to this volume. While on the one hand MacNeice anticipates the radical dimension of this work with his ongoing sense of the value of the everyday, conversely his commitment to the demotic is exemplary of the risks of relying on 'ordinary' language as poems reveal the unpredictable psychological and aesthetic effects of common usage. The penultimate question in 'Babel', 'shall we go, still quarrelling over words, to the wall?', articulates MacNeice's sense of the values at stake in such work while his poetry continues to challenge conservative and idealistic impulses alike.

As Peter McDonald, the editor of the new edition of MacNeice's *Collected Poems* has recently argued, 'there are now several generations of readers ... for whom he is one of the essential poets of the twentieth century' (CP: xxxi). MacNeice's widespread influence is connected with his poetic accommodation of everyday language. As Philip Larkin put it in the aftermath of his premature death in 1963, 'his poetry was the poetry of our everyday life'.[8] In a very real sense, MacNeice's achievement, his seemingly easy accommodation of the conversational with the rhetorical, his *via media* between the poles of traditional form and experimentalism, as well as his pervasive concern with 'our everyday life', makes his work an essential primer in the contemporary poetic idiom.

MacNeice was a part of a generation for whom poetic theory came easily. As Robin Skelton quipped of the thirties generation, 'it almost seems as if the main task of many poets was to make an assertion about the poet's function, rather than to perform that function' (Skelton 1964: 30). Despite the attitudinizing of much 1930s criticism, MacNeice was comfortable with poetic theory and remains a poet for whom, as Edna Longley has argued, 'literary criticism [was] never a wholly separable category', and who 'explains himself better than most poets' (Longley 1998: 56, 1988: xiii). Yet he was no doctrinaire theorist, and the virtue (as well as on occasions the vice) of his criticism is his ability to explain complex ideas in readily comprehensible terms. As the 1930s wore on, comprehensibility was increasingly prized as poets like Auden, Spender and MacNeice reacted against the more high-brow, elitist poetics of writers like T. S. Eliot and Ezra Pound partly in response to the rapidly shifting political situation during the decade. In particular, Eliot's contention that modern poetry should become more 'difficult' in order to capture adequately the shifting outlines of the modern world was contestable both politically and aesthetically.[9] The reaction of Auden and MacNeice against Eliot is symptomatic of the broader shift in literary politics between the 1920s and 1930s, as a younger generation of radical writers rejected the perceived conservatism of their immediate forebears.

In the anthologies *The Poet's Tongue* (1935) and *The Oxford Book of Light Verse* (1938) Auden conceptualized poetry as 'memorable speech' (Auden and Garnett 1935: v), and redefined the capacious and hitherto irredeemably bourgeois category of light verse by placing canonical *vers de société* beside popular ballads. By printing black American ballads like 'Stagolee' and 'Frankie and Johnny' adjacent to the literary verse of writers like C. S. Calverley and Lewis Carroll, Auden problematized both conventional tastes and notions of the literary (Auden 1938: 440–56). Anthologies are important because of their reach and their capacity to shape public taste: *The Poet's Tongue* was directed towards schoolchildren, while *The Oxford Book* uses the prestigious Oxford brand to undermine traditional conceptions of what poetry 'ought' to be. As a contemporary review suggested with mock indignation:

> Light verse should be what most people mean by light verse...Mr. Auden, by political conviction and natural antipathy, dislikes precisely that society which has produced, in the usual connotation of the phrase, light verse. He prefers popular verse.[10]

In this context, it is worth noting that enthusiasm for popular poetry goes alongside scepticism about the Romantic model of the poet as a uniquely inspired individual. As Spender put it in a poem which paradoxically anticipates the 'world state' in strikingly Romantic terms, 'No more are they haunted by the individual grief/Nor the crocodile tears of European genius'.[11] Similarly, Auden's anthologies react against both the elitism of modernism and the vestigial romance of Shelley's model of the poet as an unacknowledged legislator (Shelley 1977 [1821]: 508). For Auden, 'poetry which is at the same time light and adult can only be written in a society which is both integrated and free' – or: in a better society, the poet becomes an *acknowledged legislator* (Auden 1938: xx).

MacNeice made the connection between a demotic poetics and everyday language more directly, though with a less polemical edge. His critical study *Modern Poetry* (1938) stresses the interrelations between poetry and speech:

> The poet is a specialist in something which everyone practises...every one...puts together words poetically every day of his life...
>
> Every one practises love-talk, and the poet distils from this something which through its shape and balance will more than compensate for the lack of the spoken word, the tones of the voice. (MacNeice 1938: 31, 178)

As these examples demonstrate, there's a canny pragmatism in MacNeice's model, which does not deny the difference between poetry and conversation. Poetic form – the 'shape and balance' the poet gives to 'talk' – distinguishes it from its raw, conversational sources. Since Wordsworth's *Lyrical Ballads*, the claim that poetry should mirror 'the language really spoken by men' has become a critical truism: almost all poetry aspires – or genuflects towards – speech as the more authentic medium.[12] MacNeice, however, was doing more than recapitulate Wordsworth. MacNeice's model of the poet as specialist is at odds with the Romantic idea of the poet-seer. And in place of Wordsworth's distinction between nature and artifice, MacNeice stresses that language is creatively manipulated by all language users – there is no such thing, in this view, as 'natural' language, a language which does not bear the hallmarks of artifice.[13]

MacNeice's thinking partly derives from Christopher Caudwell's Marxist literary history *Illusion and Reality* (1937). Despite his general disdain of Marxist critics, MacNeice quoted from Caudwell's formulations of the social role of the bourgeois poet throughout his career:[14]

> poetry in some form is as eternal to society as man's struggle with Nature, a struggle of which association in economic production is the outcome. In poetry itself this takes the form of man entering into emotional communion with his fellow men by retiring into himself. Hence when the bourgeois poet supposes that he expresses his individuality and flies from reality by entering a world of art in his inmost soul, he is in fact merely passing from the social world of rational reality to the social world of emotional commonness. (Caudwell 1937: 141)

The 'social world of emotional commonness' would stand as a good epigraph to MacNeice's best work: the individual speaking voice is not a rarefied seer so much as someone with a gift for poetic 'shape and balance' who uses his or her experiences to enter into 'emotional communion' with a diverse readership. His commitment to everyday language is part of a broader poetic project which embraces the everyday as a legitimate subject for poetry. This is a leitmotif of his work, from 1930s poems like 'Hidden Ice', which observes 'There are few songs for domesticity/For routine work, money-making or scholarship', through to later poems like *Autumn Sequel* (1953) which focuses extensively on MacNeice's own office job as a BBC producer, to convey a lively sense of the interplay between routine and holiday: 'Everydayness is good; particular dayness/Is better, a holiday thrives on single days' (CP: 89, 397). Indeed, *Autumn Sequel* exemplifies MacNeice's commitment to radio in its humorous version of his recruitment to the BBC during the Second World War by E. A. Harding. Harrap, the Harding persona, argues that although the job will entail writing propaganda, 'after all/Homer liked words aloud' (CP: 88), working for the BBC would enable MacNeice to write in a context which – for all its technological novelty and propagandist contingency – overlapped with his training and literary predelictions.

Though after the 1930s Auden, Spender and Day Lewis all in various ways were to modify their literary politics, MacNeice remained constant both to his non-partisan politics and to the broad contours of the communicative poetics outlined in *Modern Poetry*.[15] This means that his poetry is particularly amenable to being read in relation to more recent developments in cultural and linguistic theory. To cite two influential examples: both Michel de Certeau's *The Practice of Everyday Life* and Ronald Carter's *Language and Creativity: The Art of Common Talk* are congruent with aspects of MacNeice's thinking. Though de Certeau's ambitious work resists easy summary, his attack on 'The Scriptural Economy' of modernity emphasizes the ways in which the totalizing social and cultural systems of writing are haunted by the impossible desire to recapture the vanished authenticity of the ordinary speaking voice: 'we can distinguish between writing's effort to master the "voice" that it cannot be but without which it nevertheless cannot exist... and the illegible returns of voices cutting across statements and moving like strangers through the house of language, like imagination' (de Certeau 1988: 159). To MacNeice's question, 'Can't we ever, my love, speak in the same language?', de Certeau replies, 'No, but we are always dependent on and haunted by real, fragmentary voices even as we parasitically repress them through writing'. De Certeau's dedication of the book 'To the ordinary man' is also relevant: the invocation of the 'absent figure' of a modern Everyman mirrors MacNeice's concentration on everydayness and his versions of the Everyman story in poetry and drama.[16]

The work of Ronald Carter and other applied linguists tends to be more optimistic and empirical in its exploration of 'common talk'. Carter recalls

MacNeice and Caudwell in his attack on elitist conceptions of the literary: 'literary language is not an exclusive, once and for all phenomenon, to be located only in certain types of text' (Carter 2004: 64 and *passim*). Based on evidence from large recorded corpora of ordinary conversations, Carter reveals literary techniques of repetition, metaphor and alliteration (amongst others) in a wide range of ordinary conversational exchanges. In this sense, his work exemplifies MacNeice's contention that 'the poet is a specialist in something everyone practises'; more precisely, for Carter, we are all, when we talk, poets of the contingent, conversational moment.

Though Carter and de Certeau share a broadly progressive political agenda, they differ in the ways in which they regard 'everyday language'. In de Certeau's view, the everyday is constantly being eroded by the scriptural – indeed, everyday life is precisely what is absent from his intricate pages: what is practised in the book is not the everyday so much as a range of interdisciplinary approaches to the problem of how to locate and specify that elusive life. In contrast, Carter argues that linguistic corpora give measurable evidence of 'common talk' which compels a rethinking of the conventional parameters of the everyday and the literary. This distinction between what could be characterized as pessimistic and optimistic views of language can give a framework for reading MacNeice's 'language' poems. As we have seen with 'Babel', these texts typically move in opposing directions – on the one hand, genuine communication in everyday language is canvassed as a possibility which might lead to collective solidarity. In this light, 'ordinariness' continued to have a subversive potential and utopian resonance for MacNeice. On the other hand, language itself, whether spoken or written, is often felt as a constricting and deadening medium through which the isolated individual is repressed. In one of his most famous poems, 'Prayer Before Birth', an unborn child anticipates the linguistic systems of socialization: 'forgive me/For the sins that in me the world shall commit, my words/when they speak me, my thoughts when they think me' (CP: 213). In this almost anarchist formulation, the individual is scripted by a hostile world: words, like sins and thoughts, are imposed on, and constitutive of, a dislocated, involuntary identity.

'Prayer Before Birth' is the first poem in MacNeice's wartime volume *Springboard* (1944), and its pessimism about the role of language in socialization is prominent in his poetry at this time. What might be called the anarchistic scepticism of this work helps to clarify another difference between MacNeice and later theorists. Carter's democratic view of conversational creativity entails an attempt to recode what are usually called clichés as 'formulaic language', which speakers can revive and remodel in conversation (Carter 2004: 129). MacNeice's view of such formulae is significantly more complicated. In *Homage to Clichés*, a poem of the mid-1930s, he embroiders a three-page text from formulaic language, while intimating that 'This whole delightful world of cliché and refrain' may entail the erosion of individual identity: 'watch the approved response/This is the preferred mode' (CP: 66–8). The poem is part linguistic fantasia and part nightmare, in which truistic phrases and metaphors slip under pressure of repetition from the familiar to the unsettling. The refrain lines, which irregularly punctuate the poem, 'This is on me' and 'What will you have, my dear? The same again?', morph from snatches of bar room badinage to threats by proxy. In this text, ordinary language may well be creatively manipulated, but it is not a neutral communicative idiom. Nevertheless, MacNeice's attitude to commonplace language remained ambivalent. In the 1956 radio play *Carpe Diem*, the protagonist Quintus defends his favourite poet Horace from the accusation of being a purveyor of commonplaces by arguing 'What is a commonplace? Being born, making love – growing old – what could be more commonplace activities, yet the human race still goes in for them'.[17] As Quintus defends Horace's political inconsistency, so it could be argued that MacNeice's response to commonplace and cliché was at times deliberately vague; nevertheless, his sense of the deadening potential of truistic language remains strikingly at odds with Carter's more positive view.

In the remainder of this essay, I will explore MacNeice's thinking about the ambiguity of everyday language through three poems of the early 1940s: 'Conversation', 'Plain Speaking' and 'The Mixer'. Rereading these important yet often overlooked poems in turn helps to interrogate what we mean by everyday language and creativity. In reading these poems, I am interested in the ways in which MacNeice appropriates ordinary language technically and thematically. 'Conversation' and 'Plain Speaking' are poems about language which manipulate conversational and poetic idioms in new ways, witnessed in the choice of rhyme, metaphor or metrical pattern. In contrast, 'The Mixer' is a social poem which threatens to be sidetracked from its subject by its closing linguistic simile.

'Conversation' and 'Plain Speaking' were written in America in March 1940 and were first collected in the American only *Poems 1925–1940* (1940), then in *Plant and Phantom* (1941). They are effectively extensions of debates from the 1930s about the language of poetry. 'Conversation' centres on the relationship between the isolated individual and language as a social construction. Building from the opening observation 'Ordinary people are peculiar too', it uses the image of 'the vagrant in their eyes' to symbolize that peculiarity (CP: 169). The final stanza is exemplary of the tense balance the poem establishes between a peculiar ordinariness and intransigent social obligations:

> Vagrancy however is forbidden; ordinary men
> Soon come back to normal, look you straight
> In the eyes as if to say 'It will not happen again',

> Put up a barrage of common sense to baulk
> Intimacy but by mistake interpolate
> Swear-words like roses in their talk.

The impersonal injunction against 'Vagrancy', supported by 'a barrage of common sense', is short-circuited by the conversational interpolations of 'Swear-words like roses'. Ordinary people, in other words, fight to repress subversive 'Intimacy', yet conversational 'mistakes' – or perhaps Freudian slips – betray consciously unacknowledged possibilities. As the first stanza puts it, the vagrant 'sneaks away while they are talking with you/Into some black wood behind the skull,/Following un-, or other, realities'. In this context, it's worth noting the way in which the clichéd gesture of subservience – 'It will not happen again' – is corrected and undermined by the 'Swear-words'. MacNeicean 'common talk' is then a covert action against impersonal authority which may be concealed even from the speaker.

The tension between the social and the individual is also shown by the poem's seemingly informal idiom. In reality, MacNeice plays intricate games with line length, metre and rhyme to give the impression of conversation. Like much of his poetry, 'Conversation' avoids regularity: very few lines are conventional iambic pentameter; instead, they vary from having six, five or four major stresses; there is no predetermined metrical pattern. Consider the end of the second stanza (stressed syllables are emboldened):

> He may **pick up** among the **pine need**les and **burrs**
> The **lost purse**, the **dropped stitch**.

It would be difficult, and largely unrewarding, to characterize such a rhythm according to conventional scansion; rather, stresses are distributed according to the speech accent.[18] To an extent, such accent will depend on the ear of the individual reader; it is possible to read the start of the first line with an alternative stress pattern: 'He **may** pick **up**'. The effects of such intricate accentual patterns are manifold. By using, as throughout the poem, heavy enjambment, MacNeice partially disguises the interlocking rhyme scheme (ABACBC), enhancing the impression of speech. And by recurring to something like the classical spondee,[19] in which two stressed syllables are placed beside one another ('**pick up**', '**pine need**-', '**lost purse**', '**dropped stitch**', all anticipating '**Swear-words**' in the last stanza), the verse is perceptibly slowed down giving the chance for the objects mentioned to be fleetingly materialized in the reader's mind. The slurred rhymes – 'burrs' makes a half-rhyme with the earlier 'yours' as well as a full internal rhyme with 'purse' – re-emphasize the poetic features of 'ordinary' language. Moreover, the conversational disguising of these organizing patterns underlines the poem's point that the subversive language act is encoded, or interpolated, within conventional registers.

In contrast, 'Plain Speaking' is from the outset a more exhibitionist text, which draws the reader's attention to its use of rhetoric:

> In the beginning and in the end the only decent
> Definition is tautology: man is man,
> Woman woman, and tree tree, and world world,
> Slippery, self-contained; catch as catch can.
>
> (CP: 206)

Although again the idiom is conversational – note the overflowing enjambment 'the only decent/Definition' – the focus on tautology and the list of tautological terms alerts the reader to a tension between text and title. Because of the bossy impatience of the opening line and a half, the poem invites the reader to assess the validity of the proposition. Is tautology the best definition of man, woman, tree and world? At any event, the risk is that tautology puts the poet out of business as a maker of analogies: 'man is man/Woman woman, and tree tree' is certainly arresting, but it's also a poetic cul-de-sac: a one-note riff which will only bear limited repetition.

Intriguingly, in *Poems 1925–1940*, the poem was called 'The Undeniable Fact', an undeniably less provocative title aesthetically or in relation to my argument (MacNeice 1940: 318–19). The first title coercively backs the assertion of the first stanza (which means that it is an undeniable fact that tautology is the only decent definition), whereas 'Plain Speaking' raises the question of whether to speak tautologically is to speak plainly (see also Marsack 1982: 88–9). MacNeice would have been aware that in exploring tautology, he was reviving a trope most clearly associated with the Shakespeare of the Sonnets:

> O, know, sweet love, I always write of you,
> And you and love are still my argument;
> So all my best is dressing old words new,
> Spending again what is already spent[20]

Shakespeare's contention is that by keeping 'invention in a noted weed', and by refusing to 'glance aside/To new-found methods and to compounds strange', he maintains faith in his lover. Poetic stasis is equated with amatory fidelity. It is, at best, a paradoxical claim inasmuch as tautology, while avoiding 'compounds strange', becomes an inorganic form of language far removed from 'plain speaking' as MacNeice's poem demonstrates. The speaking is only plain because it insists on absolute reciprocity between terms; in such terms no metaphor or comparison is exact enough – as the Soviet poet Osip

Mandelstam put it, 'Do not compare: the living is beyond comparison'.[21] Yet such linguistic absolutism almost inevitably subverts its own claims, as it ignores the metaphorical aspect Carter uncovers in 'common talk'. As Shakespeare demonstrates, tautological writing cannot avoid analogy – 'dressing old words new' and keeping 'invention in a noted weed' vividly suggest that writing poetry is analogous to choosing a wardrobe, an image which subtly points away from any idea of linguistic purity or nudity.

Thus in the central stanzas of 'Plain Speaking', tautology segues into metaphorical thinking: with 'their entities unfurled...a tree becomes/A talking tower, and a woman becomes world'. Conventional poetic order is temporarily restored, as the poem begins to see the tautological terms of the first stanza not as separate entities but as properties which can illuminate one another. Yet the close of 'Plain Speaking' recurs to something like Shakespeare's model of tautology as MacNeice faces the failure of metaphorical thinking:

> ...man from false communion dwindles back
> Into a mere man under a mere sky.
>
> But dream was dream and love was love and what
> Happened happened – even if the judge said
> It should have been otherwise – and glitter glitters
> And I am I although the dead are dead.

The register of these lines is significantly different from the assertiveness of the first stanza; we only have to compare 'man is man/Woman woman, and tree tree' with 'dream was dream and love was love and what/Happened happened' to appreciate that the poem is now speaking about a failed relationship. By introducing repeated past tenses, MacNeice transforms his tautologies from assertions to bitter retrospects. The 'false communion' of metaphorical thinking leaves the man diminished – 'a mere man under a mere sky' – who can only reiterate in tautological (and therefore elliptical) terms the value of what he has lost: 'what/Happened happened...and glitter glitters/And I am I'. This 'false communion', moreover, recalls Caudwell's model of poetry as 'emotional communion' (Caudwell 1937: 141): in place of the covert social relationships Caudwell envisages being fostered through the written practice of poetry, 'Plain Speaking' intimates that the communion between lovers is fragile linguistically and emotionally.

It should be clear from this discussion that 'Conversation' and 'Plain Speaking' approach the relationship between speech and writing in different ways. While both poems take their impetus from linguistic ambiguity, they incarnate divergent models of 'memorable speech'. 'Conversation' is a text where the peculiarity of individual discourse subverts commonsensical authority. It thus chimes with the work of de Certeau in postulating a poetics of conversational interpolation – what de Certeau would call 'ruses' – which problematizes the totalizing aspirations of external authority, or indeed 'The Scriptural Economy'.[22] In contrast, the title 'Plain Speaking' is a pun which misleads the reader into thinking that the poem is concerned with 'common talk'. In this case, 'plain speaking' is more properly the deliberate unadorned-ness of tautology, a paradoxical form of rhetorical display which queries the conventional rhetoric of poetic praise. Again, the poem rehearses the possibility of genuine communication – at one level, tautology promises to erase ambiguity in a 'self-contained' discourse – only to stress by the end that this possibility has not been realized. Language, like the things it refers to, is ultimately more 'Slippery' than 'self-contained'.

'The Mixer' is more externally focused, at least for its first two stanzas. Like many of the poems in *Springboard*, it attempts to convey the texture of upper-middle-class social life in wartime London through a compact character sketch. The protagonist is reminiscent of a character from Elizabeth Bowen's *The Death of the Heart*: like Major Brutt he is an ex-military man at a perennial loose end: 'he roams/Far and narrow, mimicking the style/Of other peoples' leisure'; 'He is only happy in reflected light/And only real in the range of laughter' (CP: 226).[23] However, the mixer's clubbable blandness is only achieved at a cost: 'Behind his eyes are shadows of a night/In Flanders but his mind long since refused/To let that time intrude on what came after'. He suppresses memories of the First World War in order to function socially; like Major Brutt, he is acutely aware of what is socially acceptable for a man like him.

These lines suggest a measure of dispassionate sympathy, yet the poem's final stanza uses an elaborate simile which reproaches the mixer's timidity through a key linguistic image:

> So in this second war which is fearful too,
> He cannot away with silence but has grown
> Almost a cipher, like a Latin word
> That many languages have made their own
> Till it is worn and blunt and easy to construe
> And often spoken but no longer heard.

The comparison of the protagonist to a commonplace piece of Latinate vocabulary works in a number of ways. Most prominently, the simile is disparaging: because he must offer an opinion about 'this second war which is fearful too', the mixer becomes like an unremarkable word which is 'often spoken but no longer heard'. He is part of the inane, conformist babble which forms the soundtrack in Babel. Moreover, the reduction of man into 'a cipher' again indicates the capacity of language to reinforce social control and to script individual responses.[24]

Yet there is a sense in which the elaborate terms of the simile exceed its ostensible referent. This is a very literary comparison, through which the Latin word almost becomes an actor in the poem. The simile's careful elaboration in the last four lines mimics the 'wearing' of the word by 'many languages'; in comparison with the violent enjambments and accent-driven rhythms of 'Conversation', 'The Mixer' resolves into more endstopped lines in which the iambic beat predominates. The formal qualities of the simile intimate the residual flexibility of the Latin word: a term which is 'worn and blunt and easy to construe' could be sharpened in the way that Carter sees formulaic language being revived by practice. Indeed, MacNeice's earlier chiselling of the cliché 'to wander far and wide' in 'he roams/Far and narrow' exemplifies the possibility which circulates throughout the poem. Though 'The Mixer' seems to repudiate everyday language, the way in which the simile dominates the poem bears witness to the residual force of that language.

From these texts of the early 1940s, it should be clear that MacNeice's view of everyday language was at once subtle and 'slippery'. A poem like 'Conversation' anticipates the thinking of applied linguists and cultural theorists in that it perceives a radical creativity in the ordinary which is not necessarily controlled by the forces of convention. Nonetheless, MacNeice's wariness of Romanticism and utopian aspirations is visible in the vigilance surrounding the applications of language in poems like 'Prayer Before Birth' and 'The Mixer'. From these texts, ordinary language emerges as at best a bland medium, which it is dangerous to ignore, through which the mechanizing processes of socialization can be constructed. For MacNeice, there was no such thing as 'plain speaking' in the conventional sense; his poetry is rather continuously alert to the ambivalences of ordinary language. The impulse towards tautology in 'Plain Speaking' illustrates the complexity of his thinking: while, on the one hand, tautological formulations are attractive precisely because they don't slip, on the other – as the poem is all too aware – it is in the nature of language and of relationships for words to be dynamic and shifting in their application. As a specialist in something which everyone practises, MacNeice continuously reminds his readers that language, like Nature, is 'Not to be trusted' and 'Deaf at the best' (CP: 202).

NOTES

1. For Bowen's friendship with MacNeice, see Stallworthy (1995: 292, 389).
2. All quotations from MacNeice's poetry come from *Collected Poems*, ed. Peter McDonald (London: Faber and Faber, 2007), afterwards cited in text as CP.

3. See Stallworthy (1995: chs 14–16) for the biographical context, and Brown (2009: 20–32) for MacNeice in relation to Auden, Spender and Day Lewis.

4. For MacNeice and nursery rhyme, see Brown (2009: 13–14, 117–18).

5. On the revival of dormant metaphor, see Carter (2004: 148). The biblical phrase derives from Proverbs 16.18: 'Pride goeth before destruction, and an haughty spirit before a fall', in *The Bible: Authorized King James Version*, ed. Robert Carroll and Stephen Prickett (Oxford: Oxford University Press, 1997): 736.

6. For further reflections on the form of 'Babel', see Brown (2009: 97).

7. MacNeice read Classics at Oxford, translated poems and plays from Ancient Greek, Latin and French among others; see Stallworthy (1995) for details.

8. Larkin (2001: 18). Larkin's piece was originally published in the *New Statesman* on 6 September 1963, three days after MacNeice's death.

9. Eliot (1921: 289). On a personal and professional level as publisher at Faber, Eliot was supportive of MacNeice, Auden and Spender; see Stallworthy (1995: 162–4 and *passim*); for further commentary on the reaction against Eliot, see Brown (2008: 35–8).

10. Unsigned review, 'Light Verse or Popular Verse?: Mr Auden's Anthology', *Times Literary Supplement*, 5 November 1938, p. 712.

11. Spender(2004: 18–19). For Spender's unpurged Romanticism, see for example MacNeice (1965a: 113–14) and Brown (2002).

12. Wordsworth (1984 [1802]: 602). The gendering of the formulations is noteworthy: like Wordsworth, MacNeice assumes in *Modern Poetry* that his readers and his model poet will be male (198); see also Brown (2009: 10–11).

13. See also Caudwell (1937: 107), on Wordsworth's theory: 'With this goes a theory that "natural", i.e. *conversational* language is better, and therefore more poetic than "artificial", i.e. *literary* language. He does not see that both are equally artificial – i.e. directed towards a social end – and equally natural, i.e. products of Man's struggle with Nature. They merely represent different spheres and stages of that struggle and are not good or bad in themselves, but in relation to this struggle. Under the spell of this theory some of Wordsworth's worst poetry is written.'

14. See Heuser (1987: 122, 145, 168, 205, 212), MacNeice (1965b: 27–8) and McDonald (1991: 114–15, 155–6).

15. For MacNeice's politics, see Heuser (1990: 72); for Auden's fluctuating position, see Smith (2004: 11–12); on Spender's retreat from Communism, see Sutherland (2004: 206 ff.); for Day Lewis, see Stanford (2007: 195–6).

16. De Certeau (1988: v, 1–2). For MacNeice's versions of Everyman, see among others MacNeice (1993) and Brown (2009: ch. 1).

17. Louis MacNeice, *Carpe Diem* (1956). Unpublished radio script held at the BBC Written Archives at Caversham, p. 14; on MacNeice and truistic language, see also Brown (2006: 362–8).

18. See MacNeice (1938: ch. VII) for his observations about the possibilities of 'less regular verse' (118).

19. I mean an *accentual* spondee, rather than the quantitative spondee of Greek and Latin poetry of two long syllables. Robert Pinsky uses the term 'spondaic' to highlight the difference between classical languages and English; see Pinsky (1998: 65). For the broader history of attempts to make English metrics mirror classical models, see Attridge (1974).

20. Shakespeare (1986: Sonnet 76, p. 114). See also Kerrigan's shrewd commentary on the sonnet in his Introduction: 'Yet the result is a poem which, for all its charm (and integrity), lacks the compelling excitement of a metaphoric sonnet such as 60, "Like

as the waves make toward the pebbled shore". In so far as Shakespeare exceeds the Erasmian *copia*, shunning "variation" for the sake of tautologous recurrence, his verse palls' (p. 29).

21. Mandelstam (1975: 139). This is one of the poem's from Mandelstam's Voronezh notebooks, dated 18 January 1937, and published posthumously.
22. de Certeau (1988: xv and *passim*): 'these procedures and ruses compose the network of an antidiscipline which is the subject of this book'.
23. Bowen (1998 [1938]); for Major Brutt's appreciation of his social position, see in particular pp. 285–98. Unsurprisingly, Brutt is an inveterate user of cliché – because unemployed, and embarrassed about his status, he repeatedly refers to having 'two or three irons in the fire' (p. 48 and *passim*). See also Longley (1988: 93).
24. See also McDonald (1991: 123) for the connection between 'The Mixer' and 'Babel': 'Language is seen here as one of the barriers between the self and the other transcended only in the gesture of articulation and communication which is the poem itself'.

REFERENCES

Attridge, Derek (1974) *Well-Weighed Syllables: Elizabethan Verse in Classical Metres.* Cambridge: Cambridge University Press; pbk 1979.

Auden, W.H. (ed.) (1938) *The Oxford Book of Light Verse.* Oxford: Oxford University Press.

Auden, W.H. and Garnett, John (eds) (1935) *The Poet's Tongue.* London: G. Bell and Sons.

Bowen, Elizabeth (1998 [1938]) *The Death of the Heart.* London: Vintage.

Brown, Richard Danson (2002) 'Your Thoughts Make Shape Like Snow: Louis MacNeice on Stephen Spender'. *Twentieth-Century Literature* 48(3): 292–323.

Brown, Richard Danson (2006) 'MacNeice in Fairy Land' in J.B. Lethbridge (ed.) *Edmund Spenser: New and Renewed Directions.* Madison: Fairleigh Dickinson University Press.

Brown, Richard Danson (2009) *Louis MacNeice and the Poetry of the 1930s.* Tavistock: Northcote House.

Brown, Terence (1975) *Louis MacNeice: Sceptical Vision.* Dublin: Gill and Macmillan.

Carter, Ronald (2004) *Language and Creativity: The Art of Common Talk.* London: Routledge.

Caudwell, Christopher (1937) *Illusion and Reality: A Study of the Sources of Poetry.* Reprinted: London: Lawrence and Wishart, 1977.

de Certeau, Michel (1988) *The Practice of Everyday Life*, trans. Steven Rendall. Berkeley: University of California Press.

Eliot, T.S. (1921) 'The Metaphysical Poets' in *Selected Essays.* London: Faber and Faber; 2nd edn 1932; 3rd edn 1951.

Heuser, Alan (ed.) (1987) *Selected Literary Criticism of Louis MacNeice.* Oxford: Clarendon.

Heuser, Alan (ed.) (1990) *Selected Prose of Louis MacNeice.* Oxford: Clarendon.

Larkin, Philip (2001) *Further Requirements: Interviews, Broadcasts, Statements and Book Reviews 1952–1985*, ed. Anthony Thwaite. London: Faber and Faber.

Longley, Edna (1988) *Louis MacNeice: A Critical Study*. London: Faber and Faber; reprint 1996.

Longley, Edna (1998) 'Something Wrong Somewhere?: MacNeice as Critic' in Kathleen Devine and Alan J. Peacock (eds) *Louis MacNeice and his Influence*. Gerrards Cross: Colin Smythe.

MacNeice, Louis (1938) *Modern Poetry: A Personal Essay*. Oxford: Oxford University Press.

MacNeice, Louis (1940) *Poems 1925–1940*. New York: Random House.

MacNeice, Louis (1965a) *The Strings are False: An Unfinished Autobiography*, ed. E.R. Dodds. London: Faber and Faber.

MacNeice, Louis (1965b) *Varieties of Parable*. Cambridge: Cambridge University Press.

MacNeice, Louis (1993) *One for the Grave* in Alan Heuser and Peter McDonald (eds) *Selected Plays of Louis MacNeice*. Oxford: Clarendon.

MacNeice, Louis (2007) *Collected Poems*, ed. Peter McDonald. London: Faber and Faber.

Mandelstam, Osip (1975) *Selected Poems*, trans. David McDuff. New York: Farrar, Strauss and Giroux.

Marsack, Robyn (1982) *The Cave of Making: the Poetry of Louis MacNeice*. Oxford: Clarendon; pbk 1985.

McDonald, Peter (1991) *Louis MacNeice: the Poet in his Contexts*. Oxford: Clarendon.

Pinsky, Robert (1998) *The Sounds of Poetry: A Brief Guide*. New York: Farrar, Strauss and Giroux.

Shakespeare, William *The Sonnets and a Lover's Complaint*, ed. John Kerrigan. Harmondsworth: Viking.

Shelley, Percy Bysshe (1977 [1821]) *A Defence of Poetry*, in Donald H. Reiman and Sharon B. Powers (eds) *Shelley's Poetry and Prose*. New York: Norton.

Skelton, Robin (ed.) (1964) *Poetry of the Thirties*. London: Penguin; reprint 2000.

Smith, Stan (2004) 'Introduction' in S. Smith (ed.) *The Cambridge Companion to W. H. Auden*. Cambridge: Cambridge University Press.

Spender, Stephen (2004) *New Collected Poems*, ed. Michael Brett. London: Faber and Faber.

Stallworthy, John (1995) *Louis MacNeice*. London: Faber and Faber.

Stanford, Peter (2007) *C. Day-Lewis: A Life*. London: Continuum.

Sutherland, John (2004) *Stephen Spender: The Authorized Biography*. London: Viking.

Wordsworth, William (1984 [1802]) 'Preface to *Lyrical Ballads*' in Stephen Gill (ed.) *William Wordsworth*. Oxford: Oxford University Press; pbk 1986.

4

The Bilingual Verbal Art of Fama: Linguistic Hybridity and Creativity of a Hong Kong Hip-Hop Group[1]

ANGEL LIN

The Hong Kong Music Scene and Hong Kong Identity

The music scene in Hong Kong has centred around Cantopop (Cantonese pop songs) since the mid-1970s. With easy-listening melody and lyrics about the common working-class people's plight, Sam Hui's music and lyrical style marked the genesis of this popular music form in Hong Kong (Erni 2007). Cantopop has served as 'a strategic cultural form to delineate a local identity, vis-à-vis the old British colonial and mainland Chinese identities' (McIntyre et al. 2002: 217). Even after the return of Hong Kong to China in 1997 and the rising importance of Mandarin Chinese in the official domains and Putonghua (PTH)[2] in the service domains of Hong Kong (Luke 2003), Cantonese remains an important local Hong Kong identity marker and lingua franca among the majority of Hong Kong people (ibid.).

However, Cantopop since the 1990s has become increasingly about idol-making, churning out songs about love affairs mainly, losing much of the thematic versatility of Cantopop's early days (e.g. working-class life, friendship and family relationships, life philosophy, etc.) (Chu 2007). Hip-hop music, with its translocal defiant symbols and attitude, thus became an attractive alternative to the tired Cantopop melodies and themes in the mainstream music scene in the mid-1990s in Hong Kong.

LMF Enters the Hong Kong Music Scene:
Capitalizing on the Grassroot Cantonese Youth Identity

It was from this climate that LMF (LazyMuthaFuckaz) emerged in the mid-1990s, attracting urban youth with their indignant, socially relevant lyrics. Though they are generally seen as a hip-hop group, LMF's music style was actually a fusion of rock, hip-hop and pop-rap genres. Researching on the historical development of LMF, I interviewed Davy Chan, a former LMF member who composed and produced most of the music and songs for the group in the studio – 'a.room'. Davy mentioned that in the last-known line-up of LMF, only two members (MC Yan and DJ Tommy) had a hip-hop music background. However, the audience's image of LMF has always been largely one-sidedly that of a hip-hop group, chiefly because of the profiles of the vocalists of the group, especially that of MC Yan, who always identifies himself as a hip-hop artist (Lin 2008).

LMF was, however, disbanded in 2003. According to Davy, it was largely due to the loss of advertising sponsors with increasingly negative coverage of the group in the media.

From LMF's Rock-Rap to Fama's Pop-Rap:
Creating a 'Suave Schoolboy Bilingual Identity'

Since the disbanding of LMF, the hip-hop scene in Hong Kong has never been as animated as in the LMF days. However, Fama, a two-emcee group, was formed in 2000. In 2002 the two emcees came under the tutorage of DJ Tommy and were signed under his music production company. Fama has striven to keep local hip-hop music alive in Hong Kong. Although they remained marginal in the mainstream music scene in the early and mid-2000s, they are popular among college and high school students and are by far the only local hip-hop group that has enjoyed some degree of commercial success since LMF. In the late 2000s, they have gained increasing commercial success, not exactly for their music, but more for their talk-show skills; and they performed mainly as TV fun-show hosts in 2008–09.

This distinctive style of Fama seems to have been chosen early on. From day one, Fama had its own style which they seemed to want to distinguish clearly from the LMF style. Fama (phonologically standing in for the word 'farmer') as a name is also very unconventional for a hip-hop group, as Fama seems 'country' or 'folk' in its connotations rather than rock or hip hop. In contrast, LMF rocked the local music and media scene by being the first local popular band to put Cantonese 'chou-hau' (vulgar speech) into their lyrics (and their name, LMF) in publicly released albums and live performances (Ma 2002). LMF's lyrics were largely vernacular Cantonese. As Chan (2009) pointed out, Cantopop lyrics are traditionally characterized by the use of Mandarin Chinese spoken and sung in Cantonese. That is, the syntactic and lexical styles of Cantopop lyrics are those of 'high' Cantonese (Luke 1998), while the phonology is that of Cantonese.

So, the lyrical style of LMF is quite revolutionary in the Hong Kong mainstream music scene. It breaks away from the traditional lyrical style of Cantopop which uses a high variety of Cantonese or written Mandarin Chinese sung in Cantonese (Chan 2009). LMF lyrics consistently draw on a low variety of Cantonese (i.e. everyday vernacular Cantonese) and, when English (a potentially high variety in Hong Kong – see discussion by Chan 2009) was used, it was mainly English slang; for instance: 'Do you know what the fuck I'm saying?! Hahm-gaa-ling!' ('Hahm-gaa-ling' is a Cantonese 'chou-hau' expression literally meaning: 'To hell with your whole family!'). The combination of English vulgar words ('fuck') with Cantonese vulgar words ('Hahm-gaa-ling') is consistent with LMF's angry, grassroot lyrical style.

LMF's sociolinguistic positioning can thus be said to be mostly that of the Hong Kong Cantonese working-class youth – the speaking style projects a powerful, defiant, angry, Cantonese, working-class, masculine image, with lots of 'rage' – called 'fo' (which literally means 'fire') in Cantonese.

In this sense, LMF can be seen as a rock and pop-rap renewal of earlier socioeconomic concerns, as articulated by Sam Hui, an artist who enjoyed broad popularity among the working class (as well as among some middle-class audiences). Fama have, however, endeavoured to distinguish themselves from the expletive-laden polemics of their predecessors. Li (2006), in her unpublished MPhil study of hip-hop music in Hong Kong, pointed out that Fama seemed to want to rectify Hong Kong people's misconceptions about that music. In a song by Fama called 'F.A.M.A. Praise', the group rapped explicitly in their lyrics about these misconceptions:

三百萬個唔正常唔聽廣東說唱 <Three million people are abnormal and they don't listen to 'Chinese Narrative Singing'> (referring to Canto-rap in the text)
佢哋以為hip hop 就係粗口 <They think that hip hop is profane language>
點知聽到農夫幾首先至發覺 <However, there is a new discovery after listening to Fama's music>
等一等 咦 有啲野諗 <Wait, there's something to think about>
等 幾千萬個押韻從我口 <Wait, hundreds and thousands of rhymes coming from my mouth>

(Lyrics and translations from Li 2006: 51)

Fama never uses Cantonese 'chou-hau' in their lyrics. While LMF's lyrics were chiefly Cantonese (except for some English vulgar words), Fama are effectively bilingual, and their facility with both languages attests to their cosmopolitanism, especially when English is identified as a language of cosmopolitan citizens (Guilherme 2007). Indeed, one thinks of gentrified college students rather than working-class men when listening to Fama CDs (Lin 2007).

Although Fama's two emcees address popular misconceptions about hip hop, they do have an attitude of their own. For instance, they readily identify themselves as hip-hop artists who are more into fun-making than idol-making. In their lyrics they say they are more like 'siu-jeuhng' ('fun-making masters') than 'auh-jeuhng' ('idols'). In Hong Kong, if an artist has good looks he or she can go for the idol-singer route, and if the artist does not have good looks he or she can go for the fun-making, witty, humorous, talk show master route. They also jeer at those 'wannabe hip hop' artists who know little about hip-hop music but fit themselves out in hip-hop garb. In one of their songs they also critique the self-seeking, rude, pushy public manners of many Hong Kong people (e.g. they seldom greet strangers; they fight to get seats in public transport, etc.). Fama thus represents a new stance and a new identity as developed in Hong Kong's local hip-hop music scene after LMF. In contrast to LMF, they seem to enjoy having fun and making jokes along with putting forward social and media critique, while all the time stressing their genuine friendship with their music fans, and addressing the loneliness of many adolescents (called 'yan-bai ching-nihn' – 'hidden youth' – a term coined in the mass media in Hong Kong during the late 1990s and 2000s to refer to teenagers who stay at home all the time, interacting on the Internet rather than in face-to-face social situations). In short, they present themselves as genuine, caring friends of youths in Hong Kong, especially those struggling in schools and not knowing how to express themselves. In this sense, they can be seen as a Pop-Rap version of Cantopop groups such as I Love You Boyz, targeting a similar college/high school youth market. Despite Fama's explicit identification of their music as hip hop, their musical and lyrical styles are very much influenced by Cantopop, and can be said to be a Pop-Rap variation of mainstream Cantopop music genres and a reaction to LMF's grassroot Cantonese youth identity. In the next section we shall look in detail at how Fama capitalizes on a hybrid identity to appeal to a different market segment of the Hong Kong music audiences.

Fama: Crafting out a Hybridized Cantonese–English Identity through Bilingual Lyrics

Fama's two emcees draw on both Cantonese and English in their lyrics as well as the 'art names' that they have crafted for themselves. MC Six-wing (or '6-wing' or 'Six-wing') is the art name of Luhk Wihng-Kuehn. In Hong Kong, many young students have pet names or nicknames which are formed by playing on the bilingual features of their names. Six-wing represents an example of such a common cultural practice among schoolboys and young people in Hong Kong. The Cantonese word 'Luhk' (the family name of MC 6-wing) sounds the same as the word for number 'six' in Cantonese, and so MC 6/Six-wing has formed his English art name by this process. In his rap lyrics, he proudly raps his name in this bilingual way (English translations are given in pointed brackets < > after the Cantonese characters; the original English lyrics are highlighted in bold text):

Example 1

俾支筆我寫歌詞 <Give me a pen to write lyrics>
我寫左幾萬字 <I've written several thousand words>
俾支咪我 <Give me a mike to> **Rap**　我好寫意! <I'm very happy!>
我叫做 <I'm called> **S-I-X-W-I-N-G, S-I-X-W-I-N-G, Sing!**

(From the song: '456-Wing')

One has to listen to the way he raps his name to notice the Anglicized word-play that MC 6-wing has mobilized to craft out his English name in a fun, innovative, bilingual way. When he raps the English letters for his name in the song, '456-Wing' (which is basically a song about himself), he raps it in a characteristically Cantonese intonation. Here I have marked out the tones in which he raps the English letters of his name:

$$S^6\text{-}I^6\text{-}X^1\text{-}W^1\text{-}I^2\text{-}N^6\text{-}G^1$$

Cantonese has six commonly used contrastive tones (marked 1–6) and each syllable must be marked with a tone as tones are morphemically differentiating (Cantonese morphemes are mostly monosyllabic, and the same syllable spoken in different tones constitutes different morphemes). By rapping the spelling of his 'English' name (Six-wing) in a Cantonese tonal way, Six-wing has crafted out his bilingual identity in an innovative manner: in its segmental features, it is an English name, but in its suprasegmental features (tones and intonation), it sounds like a Cantonese name. Such clever Cantonese–English linguistic hybridity seems to be a feature of most of Fama's lyrics in their 2006 album, *Music Tycoons* (*Yam-ngohk Daaih-hang*).

MC C-gwan (Si-gwan)[3] has a similarly interesting alias. C-gwan's real name is Chehng Si-gwan. Since the Cantonese word 'Si' sounds like the English letter 'C', and 'gwan' is a polite term of address (like the English terms 'Mr' or 'Ms'), C-gwan has been used commonly in Hong Kong to mean 'Mr or Ms C', along with 'A-gwan' ('Mr or Ms A') or 'B-gwan' ('Mr or Ms B'), for referring to someone anonymously in a polite way. There is some self-deprecatory irony in this, implying that he is just a 'Mr C', some anonymous nobody in this world. And when he raps it in his song, 'ABC-gwan' (which is basically a song about himself), he has blended English into Cantonese almost seamlessly:

Example 2

OK 各位觀眾 <Okay, everyone of the audience>

我想問**ABC** 之後係個咩字呀？<I want to ask: after A-B-C, what is the next letter?>

(君!) <gwan!>

冇錯　咁我地大家一齊講一次「**ABC君EFG**」

<That's right, let's say it again together: 'A-B-C-gwan-E-F-G'>

Come on

人人開開心心　個個興興奮奮 <Everybody very happy, everybody very lively>

跟我講下英文　**ABC**君 <follow me to speak some English: A-B-C-gwan>

In Example (2) above, we can see that MC C-gwan blends English words and letters into his Cantonese lyrics which evolves around wordplay on his bilingual name: 'C-gwan'. And instead of calling upon his audience to rap A-B-C-D-E-F-G, he inserts his own name seamlessly into the alphabet song. The result is a clever conceit that many students in Hong Kong can readily recognize and enjoy.

As documented in the research literature (Chan 2009), code-mixing and code-switching enhance the poetic resources available to the lyricist and facilitate rhyming in the verses. Fama have frequently mixed English letters, words or phrases into their Cantonese 'matrix' to enhance both internal and sentence-final rhymes. For instance, in the following example, the English word 'seat' is used to rhyme with the final Cantonese word '鐵' ('tit') in the previous line (the rhyming words are italicized and the phonetic transcription of Cantonese words is given in the Yale System in round brackets ( ):

Example 3

你揸保時*捷 (jit)*　我司機揸地*鐵 (tit)* <You drive a Porsche; my driver drives an underground train>

你坐兩個人　我有二百個***seat*** <You carry two people; I have 200 seats!>

(From the song, 'The Whole City Rejoices')

In the next example, to enhance the rhyming resources in their lyrics, the emcees also draw on PTH. PTH is not a language spoken by most Hong Kong people as their native tongue (Cantonese being the lingua franca of the city), but it has become an important political language in Hong Kong since 1997. The rhyming bisyllabic words are italicized and their phonetic transcription is given in round brackets ( ):

Example 4

別人笑我訓*街邊* (*gaai-bin*)　我比他人更*開心*、(*kai xin*) {*spoken in PTH*}
<Other people laugh at my sleeping on the street; I'm actually more happy than many people!>

We can notice that 'gaai-bin' (Cantonese word meaning 'street-side') rhymes with the PTH-pronounced word 'Kai xin' (meaning 'happy'). When this line is rapped, the word meaning 'happy' is pronounced in PTH to make it rhyme with 'gaai-bin'. If the word is pronounced in Cantonese, the rhyme collapses – the Cantonese equivalent of 'kai xin' is 'hoi sam'.

We can see that by doing this verbal play with three languages, the rhyming resources are enhanced. And this is possible only because Fama's audience is a trilingual one. This audience is composed of local students and young adults who have been educated in English, PTH and Cantonese. As such, Fama invoke an ideal audience in the process of penning their lyrics – a suave, urban, hybrid crowd of multilingual youths. In an interview with Phat Chan, a former LMF vocalist, Phat made a similar observation to me about Fama's audience, as the Fama emcees are relatively well-educated themselves (e.g. Six-wing is a graduate of the Hong Kong Academy of Performing Arts, majoring in theatrical performance).

Sometimes English words are inserted into an otherwise Cantonese 'matrix' to serve discourse marking functions, thereby reasserting an English-speaking cosmopolitan identity. For instance, in the following example the insertion of the English words not only serves rhyming purposes (all the words rhyme: Go, no, oh, so, no), but also marks out the transitions of the different units in the stanza. They also call attention to themselves: i.e. the sudden switch to the English word in the otherwise Cantonese lyrics helps to draw the audience's attention to what is to follow; they help to demarcate and highlight boundaries of idea units (the English words serving as discourse markers are highlighted in bold).

Example 5

GO! 大大步走上前大大步
<big, big steps, making my own big steps>
走 屬於你自己既路, 唔好著人地對鞋, 走人地條路

NO! 我諗我搵到
<I think I've found it>
大大步走上前大大步 我冇博大霧 featuring?
< big, big steps, making my own big steps, I haven't tried to gain by featuring (in big stars' songs)>
話我博大路 我淨係知道有狗仔隊跟我
<they say I'm trying to gain by going mainstream, but I only know that no paparazzi follow me>
冇 o 靚妹仔跟我 仲憎我話我
<no young girls follow me, and they also hate me>
OH! 有人話我似阿rain.
<someone says I look like 'Rain'[4]>
SO!又話我似祖名
<someone says I look like 'Jo-mihng'[5]>
NO! 你話我似兩個巨星 我唔敢認
<you say I look like these two big stars, I dare not agree>
我淨係希望有一日你會話佢地兩個都幾似陸**WING**
<I only hope that one day you will say both of them quite look like Luhk-wing>
呢首歌我淨係要你識得 我Six Wing 我冇得逼你覺得我得
<with this song, I only hope you will get to know me Six-wing, I won't force you to think I'm great>,
但萬一你覺得我得 Throw Your Hands Up!
<but if you do find me great, throw your hands up!>
(From the song, '456-Wing')

In Example (5) above, we can see that the English words starting each sentence were all said in an exclamation tone. They seem to be parallel interjection particles, which serve the function of expressing the emcee's strong feelings, upon hearing what others say about him, in a parallel, repeated, semantic and emotional pattern somewhat like this:

Go! (Showing strong determination of the emcee to express his agency by finding and going his own way, and not by copying or following others. The emcee then urges the audience to go their own way too.)
No! (To reinforce his strong feeling when he urges the audience not to follow others.)
Oh! (To express his strong feeling of unhappiness and surprise at this: others say that he looks like 'Rain'.)
So! (To express his strong feeling about being repeatedly said to look like other big stars.)
No! (To express his determination to reject these comparisons and his desire to be recognized on his own.)

By using these English interjection particles in a systematic way (e.g. sentence-initial positions followed by a few lines providing the context of these emotions), the lines form a neat semantic and sound pattern. There are other interesting instances of code-switching in which the two emcees comfortably switch between English and Cantonese to joke about school life. For instance, in the example from a 2007 song from Fama titled '學海無涯' (literally 'No Shore to the Sea of Learning'), the two emcees crafted out a whole stanza of lyrics in English (Hong Kong-style English) amidst other mainly Cantonese-based stanzas:

Example (6)

Excerpts from the Song '學海無涯' ('No Shore to the Sea of Learning')	English translation of lyrics
A班俾人話係精英班	Class A is called the Elite Class
B班又俾人話係精靈班	Class B is called the Smarty Class
士多啤梨啤梨蘋果橙	Strawberries, pears, apples and oranges
ABCDE班點樣揀	How to choose between Classes A, B, C, D and E?
FAMA college beautiful life	FAMA college beautiful life
We have Six-wing and C-Kwan be your guide	We have Six-wing and C-Kwan be your guide
We need to 努力做人	We need to be a better person
HKCEE三十分	HKCEE 30 marks!
C班俾人話係傻仔班	Class C is called the Dummy Class
D班又俾人話係籮底橙	Class D is called the Bottom Class
士多啤梨啤梨蘋果橙	Strawberries, pears, apples and oranges
ABCDE班點樣揀	How to choose between Class A, B, C, D and E?
Biology makes me cry	Biology makes me cry
Chemistry makes me cry	Chemistry makes me cry
中西史都 make me cry	History and Chinese History make me cry
農夫D歌 makes me smile	Fama's songs make me smile

Notes: HKCEE is the shortened form for the Hong Kong Certificate of Education Examination, which is the most important examination facing all secondary school students (like the GCSE examination in Britain). Getting 30 marks in HKCEE means getting very good grades in the examination (A = 5 marks).

The above excerpts are taken from Fama's song about secondary school life in Hong Kong. Those who have gone through or are going through secondary schooling in Hong Kong will find the references in the lyrics very familiar, and they can evoke immediate emotional responses. The Fama emcees are particularly talented in crafting out bilingual lyrics to depict school life in Hong Kong, which is characterized by frequent Cantonese–English code-mixing and code-switching as many schools teach some subjects in English and some subjects in Cantonese. (The reader can visit the following link to listen to the song and see the music video, in which typical secondary school campus scenes are shown: www.youtube.com/watch?v=6dcZLW1or38.)

For instance, the code-mixed term, 'A-班' ('A-baan' means 'Class A'), is a common name for classes in Hong Kong schools. Typically, students are streamed into Class A, B, C, D or E according to their academic standards, with Class A usually being the top class and Class E the bottom class. Such an extremely competitive and elitist system has often done a lot of psychological damage to many Hong Kong students. The Fama emcees, capitalizing on this school reality, have crafted out lyrics that depict this harsh fact of school life but without making it more gloomy. They have simply added their humorous twist and light-hearted comments by using the metaphor of different kinds of fruits to remove the hierarchy of (or just to laugh away) this elitist streaming practice. By juxtaposing the two lines 'Strawberries, pears, apples and oranges' and 'How to choose between Class A, B, C, D and E?', the rappers successfully demystify the 'class' hierarchy and humorously make them all look colourful and desirable (merely as different kinds of fruits), turning the tables and giving students the choice and agency to choose their own class, if only discursively, lyrically, vicariously and not realistically. But this seems to be what popular culture does: they give you vicarious pleasure of what does not exist in reality. This process, and the somewhat fantastical reinscribing and reinventing of an otherwise grim school fact, in a fun, light-hearted way, represents exactly what so many Hong Kong students need to escape from or to laugh away their unhappiness. Instead of launching a serious critique of the cruel streaming practice of schools, Fama's approach still achieves the purpose of empathizing with students' feelings, even if not giving them long-lasting empowerment.

Another way in which Fama have shown themselves to be masters in creating bilingual lyrics that just push the buttons of many school fans' hearts is shown in the following code-mixed stanzas about Fama's role as a guide for students and giving them happiness and a beautiful life, and urging them to work hard to become a better person, despite their unhappiness in learning difficult school subjects such as biology, history or chemistry (which 'make them cry'):

FAMA college beautiful life
We have Six-wing and C-Kwan be your guide
We need to 努力做人
HKCEE 三十分
...

Biology makes me cry
Chemistry makes me cry
中西史都 make me cry
農夫D歌 makes me smile

...

The Fama emcees do not seem to have any psychological hang-ups about using English for the local Hong Kong audience and they seem to project the image of their audience as similar to themselves: as (formerly) young students in Hong Kong having the bilingual resources to decode, recognize and enjoy their 'bilingualness' and bilingual (and sometimes trilingual) rhymes and creative word puns.

Fama has thus marked out their lyrical style as totally different from their hip-hop forerunners, LMF. Davy Chan, an experienced music maker and producer in the Hong Kong music scene, as well as a former member of LMF, commented in an interview that Fama's fun lyrical style is more suitable for the current social atmosphere (in the mid- and late 2000s) than the social atmosphere of LMF in the late 1990s, when the economic situation in Hong Kong was poor and people in general harbored great resentment towards the government and the ruling elite. So, LMF had lots of rage (e.g. as expressed in the use of Cantonese vulgar words; see analysis in Lin 2008) in their lyrics and the public at that time seemed to resonate well with them. Things seem to have changed, and the fun, happy, humorous style of Fama seems to suit the current social atmosphere better. Phat Chan, another main vocalist and rapper of LMF, expressed similar sentiments about Fama. Phat expressed his own personal liking of Fama's lyrical style when in an interview he said: 'there are not so many things in society to always admonish about! Why not have fun?!'

In light of the above analysis, it can be said that Fama has demonstrated a great deal of local creativity in freely drawing on both Cantonese and English (and sometimes PTH) linguistic resources to break away from the stereotypical 'angry' hip-hop image of LMF and to hybridize creatively Western hip-hop rapping with local bilingual Cantonese-based fun-making language, into which they freely mix English words styles (see also Pennycook 2007 for a discussion of global Englishes through local hybrid hip-hop styles). This is part of many Hong Kong students' everyday conversational practice. This increasing linguistic creativity from the bottom up (i.e. emerging from popular culture and from students' everyday conversations) also seems to coincide with the development of increasing acceptance or attractiveness of globalized, cosmopolitan, multicultural, hybridized identities among Hong Kong young people.

NOTES

1. This chapter is a significantly revised and enriched version of an earlier paper by the same author, collected in Tam (2009).
2. Mandarin Chinese is the standard language of China. Its spoken form is called Putonghua (PTH). Mandarin Chinese texts can, however, be spoken with Cantonese pronunciations. In Hong Kong, for instance, the news broadcasters read aloud their news texts in spoken Cantonese while the texts are usually written in Mandarin Chinese. This is a formal or high variety of Cantonese.
3. C-Kwan is the name used in the public media. Here I also use C-gwan to be consistent with the Yale transcription system for transcribing Cantonese.
4. A Korean pop star.
5. Another pop star in Hong Kong: Jacky Chan's son.

REFERENCES

Chan, B.H.S. (2009) 'English in Hong Kong Cantopop: language choice, code-switching and genre'. *World Englishes* 28(1): 107–29.

Chu, S.Y.W. (2007) 'Before and after the fall: mapping Hong Kong Cantopop in the global era'. Paper presented at the International Conference on Inter-Asia Culture: Desire, Dialogue and Democracy, 4–5 May 2007, City University of Hong Kong.

Erni, J.N. (2007) 'Gender and everyday evasions: moving with Cantopop'. *Inter-Asia Cultural Studies* 8(1): 86–105.

Guilherme, M. (2007) 'English as a global language and education for cosmopolitan citizenship'. *Language and Intercultural Communication* 7(1): 72–90.

Li, W.C. (2006) 'The emergence and development of Hong Kong hip-hop and rap music since the 1980s'. Unpublished MPhil thesis, Department of Music, Chinese University of Hong Kong.

Lin, A.M.Y. (2007) 'Crafting out a bilingual identity with bilingual hip-hop lyrics in Hong Kong.' Paper presented at the International Symposium of Bilingualism, 30 May–2 June, University of Hamburg, Germany.

Lin, A.M.Y. (2008) ' "Respect for da Chopstick Hip Hop": The politics, poetics, and pedagogy of Cantonese verbal art in Hong Kong' in H.S. Alim, A.M. Ibrahim and A. Pennycook (eds) *Global Linguistic Flows: Hip Hop Cultures, Identities, and the Politics of Language*. Mahwah, NJ: Lawrence Erlbaum: 159–77.

Luke, K.K. (1998) 'Why two languages might be better than one: motivations of language mixing in Hong Kong' in C. Pennington (ed.) *Language Use in Hong Kong at Century's End*. Hong Kong: Hong Kong University Press: 145–60.

Luke, K.K. (2003) 'Language change in Hong Kong: diglossia and bilingualism'. Paper presented at the Conference of the Linguistic Society of China, 11–23 November, Macau. [Original in Chinese.]

Ma, E.K.W. (2002) 'Emotional energies and subcultural politics in post-97 Hong Kong'. *Inter-Asia Cultural Studies* 3(2): 187–90.

McIntyre, B.T., Cheng, C.W.S. and Zhang, W. (2002) 'Cantopop: the voice of Hong Kong'. *Journal of Asian Pacific Communication* 12(2): 217–43.

Pennycook, A. (2007) *Global Englishes and Intercultural Flows*. New York: Routledge.

Tam, Kwok-kan (ed.) (2009) *Englishization in Asia: Language and Cultural Issues*. Hong Kong: Open University of Hong Kong Press.

5

Metaphor in Prosaic and Poetic Creativity

LYNNE CAMERON

Metaphor makes connections across difference. In this chapter, I explore creativity as a metaphor researcher and as an artist. In my research, I engage in analysis; in practising art, I engage in creative synthesis. These opposing processes are used to probe the nature of linguistic creativity, to understand more about the practice of creativity in metaphor use, and to question the existence of a creativity cline proposed by Carter (2004).

The question of whether there is such a thing as non-creative art reinforces the usefulness of Bakhtin's distinction between the poetic and prosaic in language. The prosaic, ordinary and everyday use of language is creative but in a different way from the poetic, which is a project involving the crafting of language. The prosaic is unfinalizable, dialogic and shared; the poetic is completed, non-dialogic and distanced. I argue that making a distinction between poetic creativity and prosaic creativity allows us to support a revaluing of the prosaic while retaining respect for the skills and expertise involved in crafting the poetic.

I will elaborate the distinction between prosaic metaphor creativity and poetic metaphor creativity. Data from empirical studies of reconciliation conversations exemplify prosaic creativity, as speakers develop their own and other's metaphors in discourse activity. Analysis reveals something about the affordances of metaphor that are exploited in poetic creativity.

The last part of the chapter returns to the poetic as crafted synthesis and explores the mind–body–world interactions of poetic creativity through statements by the poets Seamus Heaney and Mark Doty. Their reflections on poetic metaphor creativity suggest that the power of poetic metaphor can be initiated by serendipitous visual images, and then generated by labour that responds to contingency and to the constraints of form. Metaphor can hold together a final piece of work through its symbolism and rich affordances for remindings and connections.

The Experience of Creativity in Art

I have been learning to draw and paint over the last 12 years, and have no hesitation in identifying creativity in the act of making art. Creativity happens when it does and will not be controlled. It emerges in the moment from multiple actions of different types. Drawing a line or shape incorporates knowledge about technique and materials. Physical actions interact with images: from books, postcards, or sketchbook drawings. Action, knowledge and visual input interact physically with the medium and paper or canvas. The medium exerts constraints on what can be done while offering various opportunities or affordances. Over the years of practice and lessons, the degree to which I can exploit constraints and affordances has changed.

Affect and emotion are involved alongside technical expertise. In my experience, affect comes to play a role when intense involvement in some part of the drawing or painting opens up a mental space for whatever is concerning me emotionally to make itself felt. Emotions seem to spread through my hands to the page, influencing what happens, and back from the developing image to the emotions as snatches of meaning or import. Activity moves back and forth between mind, body, image and medium.

Out of these various actions and interactions, in response to constraints and affordances, sometimes and to varying degrees of delight, what I would call 'creativity' occurs and something interesting appears on the paper. Moments of creativity are always contingent, at times to the extent of being a 'happy accident', as when frustration with what I see makes me rub out an entire section, producing a new and unpredicted mark that suggests the next move. The process of creativity here is one of synthesis, surprise and emergence that come about as a result of intense activity and attention.

In my experience of making art, creativity is a special rather than everyday occurrence. Furthermore, the creativity I experience in my art does *not* come from using the same tools that are used in my everyday life, as suggested by proponents of a creativity continuum (e.g. Carter 2004, 2007; Lakoff and Turner 1989; Maybin and Swann 2007). To take a simple example: in my everyday life I use an HB pencil, but for drawing this would be a most unlikely choice of tool – I would start with a 2B pencil and then move on to others of different hardness depending on the effect I want to create; I would hold the pencil differently in my fingers; I would think about degrees of pressure, the angle of the pressure, the length and orientation of strokes – none of which I ever need to think about when using a pencil to write a shopping list. In emphasizing the continuity of creativity between the everyday and the artistic or poetic, we risk losing a clear sense of how they differ and of the scale of that difference.

Creativity and Metaphor

I will now reconsider metaphor creativity on the basis of empirical studies of metaphor in discourse activity (e.g. Cameron 2003, 2007, 2010; Charteris-Black 2004; Deignan 2005; Musolff 2004; Semino 2008; Steen 2008). The discourse perspective focuses on metaphor as ordinary and everyday, inspired and informed by cognitive metaphor theory (initiated by Lakoff and Johnson 1980). Cognitive metaphor theory reversed an earlier focus on strong or vivid metaphors carefully crafted within drama, poetry and rhetoric, and instead directed attention to the ubiquity and frequency of metaphor in conventionalized ways of using language. A 'conceptual metaphor' is held to be a structure of thought that does not just connect two disparate ideas but provides cognitive architecture to link the two together in a way that enables understanding. People are held to use and understand a phrase like *building bridges* in reference to reconciliation after conflict by drawing on conceptual metaphors like LIFE IS A JOURNEY[1] and PERSONAL/POLITICAL DIFFERENCES ARE PHYSICAL DISTANCES. The metaphors combine to produce the idea that reconciling differences over time is like a journey across a divide or gap, and reconciliation is like building a bridge to cross that gap. The cognitive turn in metaphor theory downplayed not only the aesthetics of metaphor, but also the role of language and the multiple interacting factors that contribute to the linguistic form of metaphorical utterances. My discourse perspective redresses this lack of attention to language use while retaining the importance of the 'prosaic'.

Bakhtin's key idea of the 'prosaic', contrastive with 'poetic' (1981 [1935], 1986 [1953]), and developed by Morson and Emerson (1990), is that creativity springs from the disorder and mess of ordinary and everyday uses of language in the social world. Unordered prosaic creativity is held to be different in nature from artistic or poetic creativity, which requires work of a particular type and involves a different kind of complexity. Poetry or literary writing requires work to be done, constructing order and shape, making finished and complete what began as open and unfinalizable (Morson 1998). When writing a poem, everything is made to fit into the overall shape or pattern; there is no room in the finished version for the contingent or unordered. In a prosaic view of creativity, contingency is always active; there is always something that will not fit, and always the possibility of choice. That choice may be constrained but there is always more than one way forward. For Bakhtin, the small choices that we make all the time, our actions in each of the 'moments of multiple possibility' (Morson 1998: 678), are the site not only of creativity but of ethics, since each choice could make a difference to the future.

Prosaic Metaphor Creativity in Reconciliation Talk

Extracts from an empirical study illustrate the contingent and dynamic nature of prosaic creativity in the flow of talk. Data comes from conversations in which two people, separated by conflict and violence, try to understand each other. Jo Berry is the daughter of the British politician Sir Anthony Berry, who was a victim of a bomb placed in a Brighton hotel in 1984 by the Irish Republican Army (IRA). The bomb was planted by Patrick Magee, who was arrested, imprisoned for life and released under the peace agreement negotiated by the British government in 1999. Jo Berry and Pat Magee first met in 2000, at Jo's request, and have continued to meet since. Our work[2] analyses face-to-face conversations, a radio interview and an event presentation, capturing their developing interaction over a period of ten years. More details of the metaphor analysis and findings can be found in Cameron (2007, 2010).

The data samples used here to discuss prosaic metaphor creativity (from the conversations following Jo and Pat's second meeting in 2001, and their fourth meeting in 2002) centre around the topic of Pat Magee's responsibility for the death of Jo's father and the continuing impact of this death through to the next generation, Jo's daughters. Three systematic metaphors[3] (Cameron 2007, 2010) are used in relation to this topic:

- ACCOUNTING metaphors: actions in life as entries in an account book;[4]
- CONFRONTING metaphors: responsibility for the bomb and its consequences as something large encountered through MOVEMENT from one place to another;
- CARRYING metaphors: negative feelings and memories as something difficult to be carried.

Episode 1[5]

911	Pat	...(4.0) <X I'm even certain X> --
912		...(1.0) I am very conscious that sometime,
913		I'm going to have to,
914		...(1.0) talk with your daughter.
915	Jo	... hmh
916	Pat	and answer her questions.
917		...(1.0) and er,
918		...(1.0) I have to be as truthful as possible.
919		and er,
920		... I can't --
921		...(1.0) er,

922		...(1.0) <u>finesse</u> ... that reality.
923	Jo	... hmh
924	Pat	that --
925		you know,
926		the <u>bottom line</u>.
927		...(1.0) er --
928		...(1.0) the <u>struggle</u> was necessary.
929	Jo	hmh
930	Pat	.. you know,
931		it's a --
932		it's a --
933		... it's --
934		it's such a <u>painful</u> <u>thing</u> to <u>carry</u>.
935		.. you know,
936	Jo	hmh
937	Pat	.. when --
938		er,
939		... I'm <u>confronted</u>,
940		you know with the --
941		er,
942		... somebody who <u>suffered</u>,
943		.. as a consequence.

Pat here contemplates explaining his motivation to Jo's daughter, using the metaphor of *the bottom line* (line 926) to express his conviction that armed conflict in Ireland was politically necessary.[6] Technically, the phrase *the bottom line* is not the 'metaphor' but only part of it; this part, called the 'vehicle' term, is the incongruous or new idea that is brought into the discourse and connected to the idea being talked about (or metaphor topic). The vehicle comes from the domain of ACCOUNTING, where *the bottom line* refers to the final sum of income after subtracting all expenses. There is nowhere to go from this point; the sums are finished. The topic of this metaphor (i.e. what the vehicle refers to in the context of the talk) is Pat's belief that violence was necessary: POLITICALLY MOTIVATED ACTIONS AND CONSEQUENCES. After the metaphor, Pat continues to comment on how it feels to believe this, first with a CARRYING metaphor (934), *such a painful thing to carry*, and then with the *confronted* metaphor (939). The phrase *I'm confronted with* is taken to be used metaphorically because it is followed in 940 by a truncated noun phrase *the...*, which would suggest a non-animate noun such as 'suffering'. In line 942, he rephrases the argument of *confronted with* to *somebody*, which makes the confrontation literal rather than metaphorical. The metaphor dynamics reflect a process of 'literalization', a contingent move from metaphorical to literal use.

We can also note the apparent 'mixing' of linguistic metaphors, in which *the bottom line* becomes *a painful thing to carry*. Mixing is quite frequent in spontaneous conversation but never appears to cause problems in understanding. The consistent topic domain of POLITICALLY MOTIVATED ACTIONS AND CONSEQUENCES acts as a source of stability to help participants to make sense across the shifting vehicles.

Episode 2

The next extract is discussed elsewhere (Cameron 2007, 2010) for Pat's appropriation of the *healing* metaphor (1145). Here I examine the CONFRONT-ING metaphors. In line 1132, the consequence of Pat's politically motivated actions is *to be confronted with your pain*. The metaphor changes *pain* from an abstract notion into something physical that Pat cannot avoid noticing since it is in front of him. The JOURNEY aspect of *confront* is enhanced by the development to *something I have to go through* (1153), which again suggests difficulty for Pat from the size or nature of the obstacle. This is a critical point in the conversation, and in the reconciliation process, as Pat leaves the certainty of his political motivation (*the bottom line*) and allows himself to understand the grief that Jo and her family suffered.

1123	Pat	you know,
1124		...(1.0) I mean,
1125		.. that is a consequence.
1126		...(1.0) that's a co- --
1127		you know,
1128		and --
1129		er,
1130	Jo	.. hmh
1131	Pat	... be --
1132		be <u>confronted</u>,
1133		.. with your <u>pain</u>.
1134		... that's a consequence that --
1135		er,
1136		...(3.0) you know,
1137		I suppose I deserve.
1138		...(2.0) you know,
1139		...(1.0) and --
1140		er,
1141		...(2.0) seems very --
1142		how do you <u>put it</u>,

1143		er,
1144		...(2.0) maybe that's <u>part of</u> <u>healing</u> too,
1145		.. my <u>healing</u>.
1146	Jo	your <u>healing</u>.
1147		.. yeah.
1148	Pat	yeah.
1149		...(1.0) you know,
1150		er,
1151		...(2.0) it's --
1152		er,
1153		<u>something</u> I have <u>to go through</u>.
1154	Jo	... hmh
1155	Pat	... if I'm going to sort of --
1156		er,
1157		...(1.0) <X nearly / really X> retain my humanity.
1158	Jo	...(1.0) hmh
1159	Pat	because as I said,
1160		...(1.0) <u>at a certain stage</u> of my life,
1161		I <u>made</u> --
1162		...(1.0) you know,
1163		er,
1164		<u>tremendous</u> --
1165		and again,
1166		...(1.0) <u>enormous</u> decisions.
1167		...(1.0) that had consequences for other people.
1168	Jo	... hmh
1169	Pat	.. and there is --
1170		...(1.0) it's probably it's <u>part of</u> that.
1171		...(1.0) you know the <u>healing</u>.
1172	Jo	.. hmh
1173	Pat	because it's always <u>a price to pay</u> for it.
1174		... in terms of my humanity.

At the end of the episode, Pat mentions the topic of his *humanity*, i.e. the side of himself that imagines other people's feelings (1157, 1174). He uses a new metaphor *a price to pay for it* (1173) that links back to the vehicle domain of ACCOUNTING; no longer concerned with the finalized *bottom line* but with entries in the accounts. In this example of prosaic metaphor creativity, a vehicle that carries allusions to an earlier metaphor is used with a different topic.

Episode 3

The *bottom line* metaphor is used again, to refer, not to political beliefs, but to the personal consequences for Jo. This extract is fascinating for the rapidly changing agents in lines 1422–6, as Pat first accepts direct responsibility and then seems to shift it back to the organization, rather than himself as individual.

1419		and that's --
1420		<u>bottom line</u> is,
1421		that is true.
1422		.. I am the person who caused your <u>pain</u>.
1423		.. even though it was a --
1424		... it was the Irish Republican Army,
1425		it was the Republican <u>movement</u>,
1426		it was the Republican <u>struggle</u>.
1427	Jo	.. hmh
1428	Pat	that caused your <u>pain</u>.
1429		but I can't <u>walk away from</u> the fact that it was --
1430		...(1.0) I was directly,
1431	Jo	hmh
1432	Pat	[responsible] too for that.
1433	Jo	.. hmh

The contingent creativity in the use of the *bottom line* metaphor is twofold: first, it is used in the same form with a different topic (1420); secondly, the vehicle term is reformulated (1429) as *I can't walk away from the fact*. This phrase keeps the sense of a state of affairs that cannot be changed, but moves from the domain ACCOUNTING to MOVEMENT. Since he *can't walk away* from it, the *fact* of his responsibility is always close by him, echoing the sense of CONFRONTING.

Episode 4

In this extract from the conversation after Jo and Pat's fourth meeting, *price* metaphors occur twice (885, 892) in talk about the consequences of violence.

878	Pat	...(1.0) you can <u>stand over</u> your actions,
879		<u>on</u> an intellectual <u>level</u>.
880		.. justify the past.

881	... past actions.
882	...(2.0) but when you <u>start</u> <u>losing sight of</u> the --
883	.. t- the --
884	the fact that you're also harming a human being.
885	...(1.0) you <u>lose sight of</u> that,
886	or ignore it,
887	or you <u>find</u> it easier to ignore it.
888	... that's .. always had a <u>price</u>.
889	...(1.0) and some <u>way</u>,
890	well <u>down the line</u>.
891	...(1.0) you know,
892	you're going to <u>come</u> <u>face-to-face</u> with that <u>price</u>.

In 890, *down the line* is a MOVEMENT metaphor where distance in physical space refers to a period of time passing. In the last line, Pat asserts that, in his hypothetical world, *you're going to come face-to-face with that price*. To make sense of this superficially impossible idea, participants may use a metaphor scenario (Musolff 2004) in which *price*, which has so far been a metaphor for the consequences of violence, now becomes the obstacle that confronts Pat and is unavoidably visible. This example of prosaic creativity can only be understood through the dynamics of the talk that produced it; it is dialogic, contingent on previous talk and relies on shared meanings constructed between the participants.

Prosaic Metaphor Creativity: Summary

Examination of spontaneous talk around a small group of metaphors has illustrated aspects of prosaic metaphor creativity:

- metaphor shifting as vehicle terms are reused with new topics, and as vehicle terms change;
- movement between literal and metaphorical uses of the same terms;
- symbolization of the literal;
- reuse of the metaphors of another speaker;
- metaphor scenarios that construct coherence across apparently disparate metaphors.

Creativity of a more dramatic sort – the introduction of a novel and striking metaphor to shift perspectives on a topic – happens only very rarely.

A continuity view of metaphor creativity would stress the connection between metaphor in spontaneous interaction with processes of poetic metaphor creativity. However, if the bulleted points above equate to the everyday uses of an HB pencil, then poetic use of metaphor may be as different from this as the skilled use of pencils to create delicate or powerful drawings differs from writing a shopping list. In the next section, two contemporary poets describing metaphor in their work help to further explore the difference.[7]

Poetic Metaphor Creativity: 'Our Metaphors Go on Ahead of Us'

The Irish poet Seamus Heaney reflects on his creative processes in a series of written 'interviews' with a fellow poet (O'Driscoll 2008). Heaney quotes the words of W. B. Yeats to describe the completeness of a poem, the finalized order that Bakhtin contrasts with the prosaic and contingent:

> Even when the poet seems most himself [sic], he is never the bundle of accident and incoherence that sits down to breakfast; he has been reborn as an idea, something intended, complete. (Yeats 1961: 509)

Heaney comments on this:

> It's another way of accounting for the fact that, if a poem is any good, you can repeat it to yourself as if it were written by someone else. The completeness frees you from it and it from you. (O'Driscoll 2008: 197)

The completed poem (or painting) emerges from contingent activity over minutes, hours, days or months, and stabilizes in its 'complete' or 'finished' form, with further contingent action by the poet disallowed.[8]

Images that become analogy and metaphor can prompt the initiation of writing a poem. One of Heaney's poetry collections is entitled *Wintering Out* and he is asked if this is intended as a metaphor, 'to suggest the wintering out of cattle as well as the "winter of our discontent"?'. His response describes the visual image that produced analogical connections:

> It came ... from memories of cattle in winter fields. Beasts standing under a hedge, plastered in wet, looking up at you with big patient eyes, just taking what came until something else came along. Times were bleak, the political climate was deteriorating. The year the book was published was the year of Bloody Sunday and Bloody Friday.[9] (ibid.: 121)

The analogy connects the bleak winter weather with the bleak political times; the patience and strength of the cattle to survive the weather is connected to the patience and strength that the people of Ireland needed to survive the political violence. The linguistic metaphor of *wintering out* comes to hold all those ideas and emotions, condensed, in an act of poetic metaphor creativity, into the two-word phrase. Because of the work done by the poet, this metaphor is much richer than the metaphors used in spontaneous talk, in that it prompts multiple connections between the vehicle domain of the patient cattle and the topic domain of Ireland during the 'troubles'. The richness of the metaphor springs from the detail available in the vehicle domain and the rich scenario that can be activated behind the words.

Another contemporary poet, Mark Doty, has written about metaphor in the process of composing a poem, *A Display of Mackerel*, in a piece entitled 'Souls on Ice' (www.poets.org/viewmedia.php/prmMID/15847).[10] The poem was sparked by the strong visual image of shining rows of fish in a supermarket. The features of the fish that he noticed in the display become possible points of connection to human concerns, through the 'tool' of metaphor:

> Our metaphors go on ahead of us, they know before we do ... I can't choose what's going to serve as a compelling image for me. But I've learned to trust that part of my imagination that gropes forward, feeling its way toward what it needs; to watch for the signs of fascination, the sense of compelled attention ... Sometimes it seems to me as if metaphor were the advance guard of the mind; something in us reaches out, into the landscape in front of us, looking for the right vessel, the right vehicle, for whatever will serve.

The composing process begins with the vehicle domain of the fish – very different from the topic-controlled metaphors of spontaneous talk – as the poet explores words and phrases to describe the image: 'if I am lucky, the image which I've been intrigued by will become a metaphor, will yield depth and meaning, will lead me to insight'.

The exploratory description moves into metaphor and taps into the affective state of the poet: 'it's clear to me that these descriptive terms aren't merely there to chronicle the physical reality of the object. Like all descriptions, they reflect the psychic state of the observer'.

Eventually, a topic – 'interchangeability' – emerges for the mackerel as vehicle, and from this point on the two parts of metaphor, topic and vehicle, interact in the poem's development. The idea of the absence of individuality develops into 'the realm of theology' and then into the possibility of 'losing oneself' in the mass. Doty writes about the process of shaping the language, adjusting the lines, making connections between his emotions and what he'd written – the surprise of finding that the poem was already addressing another topic without him being aware of it, that of the loss of his partner to AIDS. The topics gradually get richer and more interconnected through the work that the poet does with the metaphor, through the interactions with the developed vehicle: 'I could not have considered these ideas "nakedly", without the vehicle of mackerel to help me think about human identity'.

Doty has described something of the messy, contingent processes of writing a poem, out of which comes the finished work, 17 stanzas each of three short lines: 'a poem is always a *made* version of experience' (his italics).

Conclusions

I have explored in this chapter some differences between poetic and prosaic metaphor creativity, and questioned the idea that the distinction between them is 'continuity'.

One difference in metaphor creativities that has emerged from contrasting poets with conversation participants is the relative priority of topic and vehicle. For the poets, the metaphor vehicle often strikes first and is then connected to a topic, with rich connections formulated. For the conversation participant, the topic domain is prior, in time and in relevance. Various vehicle terms appear in the conversation to express ideas and emotions about the topic; richness of domain development is replaced with multiple metaphors, sometimes connected through scenarios, but made sense of through their connection to the topic.

In both painting and poetry, the process of composition is long, slow and arduous (even though often exciting and enjoyable), bringing to bear years of learning and practice[11] that transform skills and knowledge. Both poetic processes aim at a completed piece of work that 'leaves' the artist and begins a life of its own out in the world. The prosaic process is spontaneous and in the moment, with little time for crafting language, and with no finished product as a desired outcome.

The prosaic uses of metaphor we have seen have been largely driven by contingency, and contingency is also a driving force in the composing of poems and the painting of pictures. However, once the poetic work is completed and finalized, contingency ceases to be relevant for the producer, although it will be back in play once the work is seen by others. Producing a finalized piece of art or poetry dispenses with contingency.

In poetic mode, creativity is not felt to happen constantly. Expert poets and artists experience creativity as occasional bright moments in the long labour with materials and ideas. When we find creativity 'everywhere' in prosaic uses of language, what we label 'creativity' must be something qualitatively different. Whether this difference between poetic and prosaic metaphor creativity is best explained as a discontinuity remains a puzzle.[12] Perhaps the question itself changes depending on the type of language and metaphor we think about. When we examine spontaneous conversation, we can find the elements or traces of devices and strategies that are used poetically. But when we start from the processes of experts, we may 'want to retain the distinction between everyday creativity and the special skill of creating telling, poetic, metaphorical images and forms that have the power to move us emotionally' (Cameron 2003: 266).

NOTES

1. Small capitals are conventionally used for conceptual metaphors.
2. Studies were funded by the Arts and Humanities Research Board (now Council) and the Economic and Social Research Council. Dr Juup Stelma was research assistant on the first project. The author thanks Jo Berry and Pat Magee for permission to use their conversations.
3. Small capitals plus italics are used to indicate systematic groups of metaphors, in which connected vehicle terms are applied to the same topic at the discourse event level. Cognitive metaphor theory would see them as derivative of more general conceptual metaphors but my discourse dynamics approach does not (see Cameron et al. 2009).
4. I am tempted to suggest a Catholic cultural influence on Pat here through the idea of purgatory and that sins must be paid for in some way. In the radio interview, he uses the stronger ACCOUNTING metaphor *there's no way of purging that debt...not in this life anyway.* This lexis is strongly reminiscent of Catholic texts, e.g. 'those who had not made satisfaction with adequate penance of their sins and omissions are cleaned after death with punishments designed to purge away their debt' (Vatican II, Apostolic Constitution on the Revision of Indulgences) (www.justforcatholics.org/a93.htm).
5. Lines are intonation units, after Chafe (1994) and du Bois et al. (1993). The ends of intonation units are marked with the following symbols:

   , continuing intonation contour;
   . final intonation contour;
   ? rising intonation contour;
   -- truncated (incomplete) intonation unit.

   The transcriptions also use the following conventions:

   ... marks a pause longer than one second, with the approximate time given in brackets;
   .. marks a pause shorter than one second;
   <X .. X> marks talk that was difficult to transcribe.
   Metaphor vehicle terms are underlined. (For details of the identification procedure, see Cameron 2003.)

6. It is important to note that metaphors identified in the transcripts did not have to be actively recognized as metaphorical by participants. They are required to have potential for metaphor that can be justified by the researchers, i.e. that the vehicle term has a basic meaning that contrasts with its meaning in this context, with the possibility of transfer of meaning from basic to contextual.
7. The processes described by these poets are not, of course, necessarily representative of all poets.

8. Some poets and artists (e.g. de Kooning) reject the possibility of finalized stability and find they must keep changing what they have produced.
9. Bloody Sunday and Bloody Friday were two particularly violent days in Ireland in 1972. On Bloody Sunday 27 civil rights protesters were shot by the British army; on Bloody Friday, the Irish Republican Army exploded 20 bombs across the city of Belfast.
10. Thanks to Elizabeth Sandie for directing me to this piece.
11. The idea of the 'seven-year apprenticeship', which dates back to requirements on craftspeople in the Middle Ages, is well-known among artists. Research studies, recently summarized in Gladwell's book *Outliers* (2008), show that expertise in an art form requires around 10,000 hours of learning and practice.
12. Clines, continuum, discontinuity: these are all metaphors from the domain of mathematics, where they describe relationships between variables. To posit a discontinuity implies that the relationship between variables changes dramatically at a particular point. Perhaps we need a change of metaphors.

REFERENCES

Bakhtin, M.M. (1981 [1935]) *The Dialogic Imagination*. Austin: University of Texas Press.

Bakhtin, M.M. (1986 [1953]) *Speech Genres and other Late Essays*. Austin: University of Texas Press.

Bois, J. du, Schuetze-Coburn, S., Cumming, S. and Paolino, D. (1993) 'Outline of discourse transcription' in J. Edwards and M. Lampert (eds) *Talking Data: Transcription and Coding in Discourse Research*. Hillsdale, NJ: Lawrence Erlbaum Associates.

Cameron, L. (2003) *Metaphor in Educational Discourse*. London: Continuum.

Cameron, L. (2007) 'Patterns of metaphor use in reconciliation talk'. *Discourse and Society* 18(2): 197–222.

Cameron, L. (2010) *Metaphor and Reconciliation*. New York: Routledge.

Cameron, L., Maslen, R., Todd, Z., Maule, J., Stratton, P. and Stanley, N. (2009) 'The discourse dynamics approach to metaphor and metaphor-led discourse analysis'. *Metaphor & Symbol* 24: 63–89.

Carter, R. (2004) *Language and Creativity: The Art of Common Talk*. London: Routledge.

Carter, R. (2007) 'Response to special issue of *Applied Linguistics* devoted to language creativity in everyday contexts'. *Applied Linguistics* 28(4): 597–608.

Chafe, W. (1994) *Discourse, Consciousness and Time*. Chicago: University of Chicago Press.

Charteris-Black, J. (2004) *Corpus Approaches to Critical Metaphor Analysis*. Basingstoke: Palgrave Macmillan.

Deignan, A. (2005) *Metaphor and Corpus Linguistics*. Amsterdam: John Benjamins.

Doty, M. (2007) *Souls on Ice* (www.poets.org/viewmedia.php/prmMID/15847).

Gladwell, M. (2008) *Outliers: The Story of Success*. New York: Little, Brown.

Lakoff, G. and Johnson, M. (1980) *Metaphors We Live by*. Chicago, IL: University of Chicago Press.

Lakoff, G. and Turner, M. (1989) *More than Cool Reason: A Field Guide to Poetic Metaphor*. Chicago, IL: University of Chicago Press.

Maybin, J. and Swann, J. (2007) 'Everyday creativity in language: textuality, contextuality and critique'. *Applied Linguistics* 28(4): 497–517.

Morson, G.S. (1998) 'Contingency and freedom, prosaics and process'. *New Literary History* 29(4): 673–86.

Morson, G.S. and Emerson, C. (1990) *Mikhail Bakhtin: Creation of a Prosaics*. Stanford: Stanford University Press.

Musolff, A. (2004) *Metaphor and Political Discourse: Analogical Reasoning in Debates about Europe*. Basingstoke: Palgrave Macmillan.

O'Driscoll, D. (2008) *Stepping Stones: Interviews with Seamus Heaney*. London: Faber.

Semino, E. (2008) *Metaphor in Discourse*. Cambridge: Cambridge University Press.

Steen, G. (2008) 'The paradox of metaphor: why we need a three-dimensional model of metaphor'. *Metaphor & Symbol* 23(4): 213–41.

Yeats, W.B. (1961) *Essays and Introductions*. London: Macmillan.

6

Metaphor, Creativity and the Experience of Pain across Genres

Elena Semino

Introduction

In this chapter I will reflect on the creative use of metaphor in different genres. I begin by clarifying my approach to the definition of 'metaphor', and of 'creative metaphor' in particular. I then go on to show, with reference to specific examples, that metaphorical creativity (a) can play an important role in different genres and (b) tends to have different manifestations and functions depending on the genre. As a consequence, I suggest that any assessment of 'value' or 'success' in relation to creative uses of metaphor needs to take into account the specific contexts in which they occur (including, as appropriate, co-text, situational context, socio-cultural context, addresser(s), addressee(s), as well as genre). I will be concerned specifically with the creative use of metaphor in relation to different aspects of the phenomenon of pain. My main examples are drawn from a novel, a doctor–patient interaction, and a scientific paper.

Defining 'metaphor'

Generally speaking, metaphor can be defined as the phenomenon whereby we talk and, potentially, think about one thing in terms of another. For example, in a novel included in the British National Corpus (BNC), the description of a character's predicament after sustaining serious physical injuries includes the phrase 'in the darkness of her pain'. Here the noun 'darkness' is used to convey the deeply unpleasant physical and emotional sensations that the

83

character is experiencing as a result of her injuries. In terms of the metaphor identification procedure proposed in Pragglejaz Group (2007), there is a contrast between the 'basic' meaning of the noun 'darkness' (i.e. 'lack of light') and its 'contextual' meaning, namely, the meaning that we are likely to attribute to the noun in the specific context (i.e. something along the lines of 'unpleasant physical and emotional sensations'). Furthermore, the contextual meaning can be understood in comparison with the basic meaning: the experience of pain and distress can be understood via comparison with the experience of being in a dark place. As a consequence, I regard 'darkness' in the quotation above as a metaphorically used word, or metaphorical expression (see Pragglejaz Group 2007 for a detailed exposition of this approach to linguistic metaphor identification).

Over the last few decades, Cognitive Metaphor Theory (CMT) has drawn attention to the presence of patterns of conventional metaphorical expressions in language, and has proposed that these expressions reflect conventional patterns of thought, known as conceptual metaphors. For example, Kövecses has noted a conventional tendency in language to describe negative experiences, and in particular negative emotions, in terms of darkness (e.g. 'He is in a dark mood'; Kövecses 2005: 25). This conventional tendency is seen as a reflection of conventional conceptual metaphors that Kövecses formulates as BAD THINGS ARE DARK and, more specifically, SADNESS IS DARK (ibid.: 25, 44). More recently, Kövecses (2008) has proposed a more specific conventional conceptual metaphor for pain which he expresses as PAIN IS DARK, and which is realized in language by expressions such as the one quoted above. In CMT terms, BAD THINGS, SADNESS and PAIN are 'target' conceptual domains which are conventionally talked about and conceptualized in terms of the 'source' domain DARK (as well as other source domains, such as DOWN and BURDEN). Cognitive metaphor theorists emphasize that conventional conceptual metaphors are often based in our bodily experiences (e.g. our sensorial and emotional experience of darkness), and that the choice of source domain affects our view of the target domain, typically by foregrounding some aspects and backgrounding others: seeing pain experiences as darkness has rather different implications from seeing them, for example, as a test to be passed. Within CMT, conceptual metaphors have a variety of linguistic manifestations, including for example similes (e.g. 'There was a pain like a red-hot brand in her chest', from the BNC), as well as metaphorical expressions as defined above. In addition, conceptual metaphors can be realized via other semiotic modes, such as visual images and gestures.

The experience of pain shares some, but not all, of the characteristics of typical target domains. Unlike target domains such as TIME, it is an embodied, accessible and familiar experience. Like target domains such as SADNESS, however, it is a private, diffuse, subjective and invisible experience. As such, it is often difficult to express in language, especially in cases where the pain is not caused by an immediate, visible, physical injury ('non-nociceptive' pain, such as that of migraine) and persists for a long period of time (chronic pain, such as some backaches). Although pain has only recently started to receive the attention of metaphor scholars (e.g. Lascaratou 2007; Kövecses 2008), it is recognized in the medical literature that pain sensations are often expressed in language via similes and metaphorical expressions (e.g. Schott 2004). In addition, pain is one of the many phenomena that scientists need to explain in order to find adequate treatments. As I show below, these explanations may involve models that rely on the creative exploitation of specific metaphorical source domains.

Defining 'creative' metaphor

In the previous section, I used the term 'conventional' in relation to linguistic and conceptual metaphor as if the notion of conventionality was relatively unproblematic. In this section, I consider the difficult issues involved in describing metaphorical expressions as conventional or creative/novel, and I suggest that a proper account of metaphorical creativity in language needs to involve a consideration of at least the following three dimensions or levels of analysis: (a) the uses of the individual word or multiword expression, (b) the co-text, and (c) broader patterns of systematicity in the relevant language, which may reflect conventional conceptual metaphors (a fourth, related, dimension will be introduced on pp. 97–9; see Müller 2005 and 2010 for a comparable approach to the analysis of creative metaphors in political discourse). Consider, for example, the use of the adjective 'sharp' in the following extracts (unless otherwise indicated, all examples are taken from the BNC):

Extract 1
Gardeners know the value of a really <u>sharp</u> knife for pruning as well as propagating.

Extract 2
'You want to play with knives, little girl, you learn how to use them, eh?' He advanced on her. She covered her face with both her hands and screamed. The door behind her suddenly opened and she was pushed against Rico, who staggered back. Noreen felt a <u>sharp</u> little pain on her right arm and looking down, she saw the blood.

Extract 3

The main symptom [of hiatus hernia] is heartburn – a <u>sharp</u> pain behind the breastbone.

Extract 4

She swallowed again and tried to ignore the terrible <u>sharp</u> pain that was twisting viciously into the side of her head.

In Extract (1) the adjective 'sharp' is used in what I regard as its most basic meaning: a physical property of solid objects that have a very thin edge or a pointed end (see Pragglejaz Group 2007 for a discussion of the basic meanings). In Extract (2), 'sharp' is used to describe the kind of pain sensation that results from being cut with an object that has a very thin edge (a knife, in this case). I regard this kind of use as metonymic, since the contextual meaning (i.e. that particular kind of pain sensation) is not understood via comparison with the basic meaning, but rather via a cause–effect association between the basic meaning and the contextual meaning. In Extracts (3) and (4), in contrast, 'sharp' is used to describe pain sensations that do *not* result from injuries inflicted by contact with sharp objects. The pain described in (3) is caused by acidity in the stomach while (4) is concerned with the kind of headache that is not associated with any physical damage at all. In both cases, the contextual meanings (i.e. those particular kinds of pain sensations) are understood via comparison with the basic meaning: pain that does not result from contact with external entities is described in terms of a property of objects that can inflict injuries associated with a widely familiar kind of 'nociceptive' pain. As a consequence, I regard the adjective 'sharp' as being used metaphorically in both (3) and (4).

Let me now consider the issue of creativity in relation to the metaphorical use of 'sharp' in Extracts (3) and (4).[1] I imagine that readers will intuitively agree that the metaphorical use of 'sharp' in both (3) and (4) is not at all unusual in English. These intuitions can be supported by consulting two kinds of sources: corpora and (ideally, corpus-based) dictionaries. In the 100-million-word BNC, 'sharp' is the thirty-fifth most frequent collocate of 'pain':[2] it occurs 26 times immediately before the word 'pain'. Twenty-one of these occurrences are similar to those in (3) and (4), amounting to approximately 4.5 occurrences out of 1,000 citations of 'sharp'. In her corpus-based work on metaphor, Deignan (2005: 40) recognizes that the boundary between conventional and creative linguistic metaphors is 'fuzzy rather than stark', but adds:

Nonetheless in the analysis of concordance citations, the difficulty of deciding on cases of innovative metaphor arises only rarely, because innovative metaphors are infrequent. Corpus frequencies can be used as a rough guide: any sense of a word that is found less than once in every thousand citations can be considered either innovative or rare.

Not surprisingly, the entry for 'sharp' in the *Macmillan English Dictionary for Advanced Learners* (which is based on a different corpus of contemporary English) includes, amongst others, a meaning of the adjective that is explained as follows: 'a sharp pain is sudden and severe'. In other words, there is ample evidence to suggest that the metaphorical use of 'sharp' in the last two extracts above is quite conventional.

A consideration of the co-text, however, reveals a difference between Extracts (3) and (4). In (3) the adjective 'sharp' is the only word that relates to sharp objects. The only other case of metaphoricity in relation to pain sensations in the extract is 'burn' in the noun 'heartburn'. This expression is also conventionally used to describe non-nociceptive pain, but involves comparison with a different type of cause of nociceptive pain than is the case with 'sharp'. As a consequence, the metaphoricity of 'sharp' (as I have described it) is likely to go unnoticed. In contrast, in Extract (4) the 'sharp' pain is further described metaphorically as 'twisting viciously' into the side of the person's head. The metaphorical use of these two words in relation to pain is less conventional than in the case of 'sharp'. The *Macmillan Dictionary* does not have a pain-related meaning for the verb 'twist', nor for 'vicious' and 'viciously'. The BNC contains one instance of 'vicious pain' (out of 851 occurrences of the adjective), but no similar uses of the adverb. Two forms of the verb 'twist' are used metaphorically in the corpus in relation to pain. This applies to 'twisted' (four instances out of 1,433 citations) and 'twisting' (two instances out of 582 citations, including Extract 4). However, the BNC contains no other extracts where 'sharp', 'twist' and 'vicious' co-occur in the description of pain. More specifically, the collocation of 'twisting' with 'viciously' in Extract (4) contributes to the portrayal of pain as a malevolent animate entity deliberately causing physical harm to the character. In addition, the action described by 'twisting viciously into' is prototypically associated with a pointed object, such as a knife, so that the metaphoricity of 'sharp' (and that of 'twisting' and 'viciously') is more likely to become obvious to readers. As a result, the occurrence of the three metaphorical expressions in the same clause results in a local pattern that can be regarded as a fairly creative description of the experience of a headache. In other words, the textual patterns formed by metaphorical expressions may be described as creative even if the individual words contributing to the patterns are used in fairly conventional metaphorical senses[3] (see also Carter 2004: 119–41; Müller 2005, 2010; Semino 2008: 42–54).

At a broader level, it is important to notice that, in English, non-nociceptive pain is not just conventionally described as 'sharp', but also, for example, as 'stabbing' or 'lancing'. Kövecses (2008) captures this general pattern by pro-posing the conceptual metaphor PAIN IS A SHARP OBJECT. He also notes more generally that 'pain is conceptualized metaphorically in terms of its potential causes'. Indeed, the conventionality of expressions such as 'burning/searing/ stinging pain' reveals a more general pattern whereby non-nociceptive pain is conventionally described in terms of a variety of causes of nociceptive pain. The relevant broad source domain has been variously named in the litera-ture as HARM, DAMAGE or DESTRUCTION. The more specific domains of ATTACK, AGGRESSION or TORTURE are also invoked in order to account for cases where the cause of pain is described as a personified attacker, as in Extract (4) above (e.g. De Souza and Frank 2000; Lascaratou 2007). In my view, the conven-tional patterns I have pointed out in this section are best captured in terms of a general conventional conceptual metaphor which can be expressed as (NON-NOCICEPTIVE) PAIN IS CAUSE OF PHYSICAL DAMAGE. The cause of physical dam-age may be an entity (e.g. 'knife', 'fire'), a property of objects (e.g. 'sharp', 'incandescent') or a process (e.g. 'stabbing', 'burning'). Whatever the specific formulation, however, this particular metaphorical tendency has a metonymic basis, as suggested by my earlier comments on 'sharp' (see Lascaratou 2007: 161–5 for a more detailed discussion).

Let me now introduce two more obviously creative descriptions of pain by chronic sufferers:

Extract 5

The pain was like a small garden rake over my eyes and top of my head, dig-ging in and scraping away. (Migraine sufferer quoted in a factsheet entitled 'Migraine: how to live with it', by the City of London Migraine Clinic (http:// ww2.migraineclinic.org.uk/wp-content/uploads/2009/07/migraine-how-to-live-with-it.pdf).)

Extract 6

Pain is a concept you can look at in so many different ways. It is like an apple which is rotten from the inside. There is the central core which is the centre of the pain – which is what it would be if it were in the spine – and it comes through and affects the skin. When you have severe pain it increases and increases, so you can imagine that apple going rotten and eventually that would take you up to the peak of the pain. (John Pates, quoted in Padfield 2003: 103)

In both extracts, simile is used to introduce a very specific source scenario for the experience of pain ('like a small garden rake', 'like an apple'). Each scenario is then further developed via at least some metaphorical expressions that are not conventionally applied to pain (e.g. 'scraping away', 'core', 'rot-ten'). These expressions can therefore be described as creative at the level of the use of the individual word or multiword expression. Similarly, in both extracts the local extension of, respectively, the RAKE and ROTTING APPLE source scenarios results in creative patterns involving several related metaphorical expressions (Extract (6) is also accompanied by photographs of rotting apples, but I do not have the space to discuss this here; see Deignan et al. forthcoming). The crucial difference between the two extracts, however, involves their relationship with broader metaphorical patterns in English generally, and, consequently, with potential conventional conceptual metaphors. The RAKE metaphor in Extract (5) can be seen as a creative exploitation of the conventional conceptual metaphor that I have expressed as (NON-NOCICEPTIVE) PAIN IS CAUSE OF PHYSICAL DAMAGE. What is creative in this case is the choice of a very specific object that is not normally exploited in metaphorical descriptions of pain ('a small garden rake') and of very specific actions involving that object ('digging in' and 'scraping away') (see Lakoff and Turner 1989 for a discussion of this kind of metaphorical creativity). In contrast, the ROTTING APPLE metaphor in Extract (6) seems to be much less closely related to conventional metaphors for pain, and could be regarded as involving a novel cross-domain mapping.

In conclusion, I have suggested that a discussion of creativity in relation to metaphor use needs to take into account, minimally, the metaphorical uses of individual words/expressions, the possible presence of local metaphorical patterns in the co-text, and the existence of broader conventional patterns in the language, which may reflect conventional conceptual metaphors. It is also clear from my examples that creativity in relation to metaphor cannot be approached in terms of clearcut distinctions, but is best seen as a matter of degree.

Metaphorical Creativity and the Phenomenon of Pain in Three Different Genres

In the rest of this chapter I will apply the approach to the analysis of metaphorical creativity introduced in the previous section to three specific examples: a description of a migraine attack from Ian McEwan's (2001) novel *Atonement*, a transcript of a medical consultation in general practice, and a scientific account of the phenomenon of pain in a scholarly journal. Although I am concerned with the creative use of metaphor in particular, the following general definition of creativity proposed by Sternberg and Lubart (1999: 3; also quoted in Carter 2004: 47) is relevant to my discussion: 'creativity is the ability to produce work that is both novel (i.e., original, unexpected) and appropriate (i.e., useful, adaptive concerning task constraints)'.

I will also build on recent work on creativity in language, and particularly on the view that creativity is widespread in language use but varies in both frequency and function depending on context and genre (Carter 2004; Carter and McCarthy 2004; Pope 2005).

Metaphor and the Pain of Migraine in Ian McEwan's *Atonement*

Chapter 6 of Ian McEwan's novel *Atonement* is entirely devoted to a migraine attack experienced by one of the novel's minor characters, Emily Tallis (see Semino 2008: 36–41 for a more exhaustive discussion of metaphor in this extract). Emily is the mother of the two female protagonists of the novel, and, at this point in the story, is trying to supervise the running of her large and wealthy household on an extremely hot summer day. The chapter begins with Emily retreating to her bedroom after recognizing the early symptoms of a migraine attack, and continues as follows:

> She felt in the top right corner of her brain a heaviness, the inert body weight of some curled and sleeping animal...It was important, however, not to provoke it; once this lazy creature moved from the peripheries to the centre, then the knifing pains would obliterate all thought, and there would be no chance of dining with Leon and the family tonight. It bore her no malice, this animal, it was indifferent to her misery. It would move as a caged panther might: because it was awake, out of boredom, for the sake of movement itself, or for no reason at all, and with no awareness. (McEwan 2001: 63–4)

The account of Emily's headache includes several metaphorical expressions that can be related to conventional patterns whereby pain is described as HEAVINESS ('a heaviness', 'weight') and SHARP OBJECTS or, more generally, CAUSES OF PHYSICAL DAMAGE ('knifing pains') (Kövecses 2008). However, Emily's pain is also metaphorically described in the extract in terms of an animal that is sleeping inside her head, but that could easily wake up and start moving around. While the animal is asleep, the pain is tolerable, but the animal's movements cause peaks of intolerable pain.

It is possible to relate this ANIMAL metaphor to a conventional variant of the CAUSE OF PHYSICAL DAMAGE metaphor for pain that involves attacks from animals (e.g. 'stinging pain', 'gnawing pain'), as well as to a conventional tendency to describe pain in terms of movement (e.g. 'shooting' pain). However, in my view, McEwan's particular ANIMAL metaphor is only loosely related to these conventional patterns, and is best described as highly creative in terms of all three levels of analysis I introduced earlier. At the word level, many of the expressions that realize the ANIMAL source scenario in the extract do not have conventional meanings to do with pain (e.g. 'curled and sleeping animal', 'furred creature'). In textual terms, the ANIMAL scenario is developed in considerable detail in the paragraph quoted above, and is then further exploited in the course of the chapter to describe the various stages of Emily's migraine attack, until she finally feels better:

> Feeling the black-furred creature begin to stir, Emily let her thoughts move away from her eldest daughter. (McEwan 2001: 65)

> It was beginning to fade, the presence of her animal tormentor, and now she was able to arrange two pillows against the headboard in order to sit up. (Ibid.: 69)

> And so Emily lay back against the pillow for another several minutes, her creature having slunk away, and patiently planned, and revised her plans, and refined an order for them. (Ibid.: 70)

Textually, therefore, the ANIMAL metaphor is locally extended at the beginning of the chapter, and then recurs throughout the rest of the chapter, thus contributing to its overall intratextual coherence (NB: the last extract quoted above is the final sentence of the chapter) (see Chilton and Schäffner 2002: 29). The metaphorical expressions involved in the textual development of the metaphor involve both some repetition (e.g. 'creature') and a considerable amount of lexical variation (e.g. 'black-furred', 'slunk away'). In addition, the ANIMAL metaphor is also combined at various points with a more conventional description of the pain as an aggressor carrying a knife.

At the conceptual level, McEwan's ANIMAL metaphor contrasts with conventional conceptual metaphors for pain in at least three important ways. First, the animal is not presented as aggressive: rather it is described as 'indifferent', bearing 'no malice' to Emily, and moving 'out of boredom' and 'with no awareness'. Second, there is no reference to physical damage caused by the presence of the animal. Third, the animal's movements are presented as slow, in contrast with more conventional metaphorical descriptions of pain in terms of rapid movement inside the body (e.g. 'shooting pain'). All this suggests that McEwan's metaphor is also highly original at the conceptual level.

Let me now reflect on the possible functions of McEwan's creative use of metaphor in this particular chapter of the novel, and on their implications for issues of evaluation. Emily's migraine attack does not correspond to a crucial moment in the novel's plot, and could therefore be described as a minor digression. However, it contributes to the characterization of the mother of the novel's two female protagonists, and may possibly generate some degree of emotive involvement with a character who is not otherwise particularly easy to sympathize with. The ANIMAL metaphor in particular has the crucial function of contributing to the conveyance of an experience (the pain sensations caused by migraine) that, like other subjective, impalpable experiences, is notoriously difficult to put into words. This has been famously (and some-what hyperbolically) pointed out by Virginia Woolf (see also Scarry 1987: 4):

> Finally, to hinder the description of illness in literature, there is the poverty of the language. English, which can express the thoughts of Hamlet and the tragedy of Lear, has no words for the shiver and the headache... The merest schoolgirl, when she falls in love, has Shakespeare and Keats to speak her mind for her; but let a sufferer try to describe a pain in his head to a doctor and language at once runs dry. (Woolf 2008: 102)

McEwan's challenge is, on the one hand, to give readers unfamiliar with migraine attacks the impression that they know exactly what such an attack feels like, and, on the other hand, to give readers familiar with migraine attacks what has been called an 'Aha! experience': the sudden (and pleasurable) realization that the writer has successfully put into words something that they have themselves experienced but never been able to express quite so successfully (Bühler 1982: 311; Margolin 2003: 285). The metaphorical descriptions employed by McEwan play a central role in achieving these possible effects, especially given the inadequacy of non-metaphorical language in the expression of pain sensations. In addition, McEwan's use of the ANIMAL metaphor could arguably be linked to one of the novel's central themes: in the same way as Emily is described as being at the mercy of an indifferent, bored creature, who moves 'for no reason at all, and with no awareness', the novel's protagonists are at the mercy of individual actions and global events that could be described as happening with little awareness and for no rational reason.

The richness and variety of the textual realization of the ANIMAL metaphor, its novelty at the conceptual level, and the multiple functions it can perform, suggest that the extract above is a particularly clear example of the kind of finely wrought and interpretatively rich metaphorical creativity that is highly valued in literary texts. In spite of its minor role in the novel, McEwan's description of migraine could, I would argue, become a 'classic' in the literary representation of pain. At the time of writing (seven years after the publication of the novel), the extracts I have reproduced above have been cited as evidence of McEwan's exceptional mastery of language in a number of scholarly articles, including a paper by a consultant neurologist writing on neurology and literature (Larner 2006). A search of the World Wide Web has also revealed several informal comments by readers on the aptness of McEwan's description of migraine:[4] 'A group member who has suffered from migraines pointed out that Emily Tallis's section contains the best description of migraines she has ever read' (http://waltham.lib.ma.us/blog/bookclub/?p=16). 'Emily, the Mother, suffers from migraine and the author's description of this is so amazing and believable' (www.booklore.co.uk/PastReviews/McEwanIan/Atonement/AtonementReview.htm#Jessica).

In other words, McEwan's creative use of metaphor in Chapter 6 of *Atonement* may prove to belong to the types of creativity that Carter (2004: 47) describes as potentially able to transcend historical and cultural boundaries:

> It is important to underline that some creative art can be of its time and some beyond its time; some creative art can be socio-culturally relative and some art universal; and some creative art can be valued by specific groups and some art valued by a wide range of groups from different human communities.

In the next section, I will turn to a more context-bound example of metaphorical creativity.

Metaphor and Pain in a Doctor–Patient Interaction

The conversational transcript I discuss below has been extracted from the 'Context-Governed' section of the spoken part of the BNC. According to the information provided by the compilers of the corpus, the conversation took place in a doctor's surgery in Lanark (Scotland), between 1985 and 1993. It involves three people: a male doctor, who at the time was in the 60+ age bracket; a woman aged between 25 and 34; and the woman's five-year-old son. All three participants are described as being speakers of Scottish English. The names I use below (Doctor Jones, Beth and Josh) are not the participants' real names.

The transcript of the interaction opens with greetings and continues with the doctor feigning exasperation at having to deal once again with the little boy, whom he jokingly addresses as 'monster'. Beth then clarifies that she has made the appointment for herself and explains her problem as follows (below I only underline the metaphorical expressions I am going to discuss):[5]

Beth	15	My bust again Doctor Jones.
	16	I'm having terrible pains in my chest.
	17	\<pause\> It's only the, the right one,
Doctor	18	Mhm.
Beth	19	that I have any pains in.
	20	Now I keep taking this Shelabruse it clears, and it <u>comes back</u>.
	21	You know how sometimes you get a lot of vein <u>running</u> \<-|-> <u>down</u> \<-|->
Doctor	22	\<-|-> Mhm.

Beth	23	your bust?
	24	Well it's <u>sinking in</u>, it, it <u>goes</u> <u>into</u> your grove.
Doctor	25	Mhm.
Beth	26	But it's still the same, but it's the pains that I got the last time that's gon-- it's like <u>sharp</u> pains that's <u>going round about</u>, just <unclear> the insides of the nipple.

In addition to describing her pains as 'sharp', Beth explains her problem by using metaphorically various expressions that have basic meanings to do with movement. This applies both to the description of her veins ('running down' her bust) and of her pain, which is presented as 'sinking in', 'go[ing] into' her grove, 'going round about' the inside of her nipples and 'coming back' when she stops taking medication. In the turns following the extract above, Beth wonders whether her pain may be due to the fact that she has put on weight, and adds that it has been going on for two months. The doctor, who, up to this point, has only produced backchannelling feedback, asks whether she is currently taking any medication, and the conversation continues as follows:

Beth	40	<-|-> It isn't, it's not a pain that's <u>there</u> all the time, Doctor Jones.
	41	It just <u>comes</u>.
Doctor	42	It just <u>comes</u>.
	43	Is it a <u>sharp</u> <-|-> sort of <u>shooting</u> pain?
Beth	44	<-|-> Very <u>sharp</u> <-|-> it's <unclear> as though something's <u>bursting</u>.
	45	You know, something's <-|->
Doctor	46	<-|-> Mhm.
Josh	47	<u>running</u>, it's like that. <pause dur="14">
Doctor	48	<voice quality: whispering>Right.

In this extract, Beth continues to describe the pain metaphorically in terms of presence in her body ('there') and movement into her body ('It just comes'). Doctor Jones repeats one of Beth's metaphorical expressions (line 42), and then asks her for more detail about the pain (line 43). His suggested description includes a conventional metaphorical expression for pain that has already been used by Beth ('sharp'), and another equally conventional expression ('shooting'), which has a basic meaning to do with movement (and which also happens to alliterate with 'sharp'). The latter expression is preceded by a downtoner ('sort of') that can be seen as functioning as a 'tuning device' or 'signal' of metaphoricity (Cameron and Deignan 2003; Goatly 1997: 168–97). In line 44, Beth repeats one of the doctor's descriptors, but precedes it with an intensifier ('very sharp') and then introduces, via a simile, a different metaphorical scenario ('as though something's bursting'). At this point, Josh intervenes with what appears to be his own contribution to the description of his mother's pain. His turn (line 47) includes one of the MOVEMENT metaphors that Beth has previously used in relation to her veins ('running, it's like that').

This part of the conversation is followed by some informal talk about an appointment Beth has previously cancelled, and more banter involving the little boy. Doctor Jones then explains what he has decided to prescribe to Beth:

Doctor	75	Two things Beth.
	76	I've given you something to try and take the swelling off your chest, and that should ease a bit of the pain but I've also given you er stuff to stop all this <u>bursting</u>.
Beth	77	Mhm.
Doctor	78	on the inside.
	79	So \<unclear\> now, I want you to use that for a full month, and come back up, and let us know how things are doing.
Beth	80	Will do.

The doctor refers to the medication informally as 'something' and 'stuff', and spells out that its effect should be 'to stop all this bursting on the inside'. Here, he repeats one of the expressions Beth has used earlier to describe her pain ('bursting'), but changes it from a verb to a noun. The consultation then ends with a few more turns of informal chat and final greetings.

At the word level, most of the metaphorical expressions I have underlined in the quotations above are used conventionally, albeit to different extents, in order to describe bodily sensations and changes in general (e.g. 'comes back'), and the experience of non-nociceptive pain in particular ('sharp', 'shooting'). 'Bursting' is arguably less conventional as a metaphorical description of pain than 'sharp' and 'shooting', but does occur twice in the BNC as a premodifier of 'pain' (out of 556 occurrences of 'bursting'). However, the BNC contains no instances of 'bursting' being used as a noun to refer to a process associated with pain. Hence, Doctor Jones's variation on the metaphorical description introduced by Beth can be described as displaying some degree of creativity at the word level. In the terms used by Carter (2004) and Carter and McCarthy (2004), the doctor's use of 'bursting' can be placed in the category of 'pattern re-forming choices' which include 'presentational uses of figures of speech' and 'open displays of metaphoric invention' (ibid.: 79). At the conceptual level, all the metaphorical descriptions of pain in the interaction can be related to source domains that are conventionally applied to bodily sensations generally and pain in particular, namely MOVEMENT (e.g. 'comes back'),

SHARP OBJECT/CAUSE OF PHYSICAL DAMAGE (e.g. 'sharp') and PRESSURE IN A CONTAINER ('bursting') (see Kövecses 2008).

It is at the level of textual patterns, however, that we can observe a kind of creativity that is particularly characteristic of conversation (see Carter 2004). Beth's choices of words result in patterns of related metaphorical expressions that can be observed both within and across her turns. Doctor Jones repeatedly responds by repeating or elaborating on the expressions used by Beth. Even Josh appears to respond and contribute to the metaphorical construction of Beth's pain as movement by using the expression 'running' in line 47, although it is not clear from the transcript whether he is trying to be helpful, mischievous, or both.

Building particularly on Carter (2004) and Cameron (2007), it is possible to describe the kind of creativity that results from participants' use of metaphor and to reflect on its functions and degree of success in the interaction (see also Tannen 1989). Carter (2004: 101) notes that 'patterns are always potentially present in language, and language users always have options whether or not to establish patterns, and, if so, what kinds of patterns to create'.

More specifically, he uses the term 'pattern-forming choices' for 'various forms of repetition' which interlocutors are unlikely to be conscious of, but which become obvious when analysing transcripts. Carter claims that, in such cases, 'the creativity grows from mutual interaction rather than from individual motivation' (ibid.: 102). In fact, the creation of linguistic patterns (whether conscious or unconscious) has not traditionally been described as 'creative' in relation to conversation, but has long been recognized as one of the types of linguistic creativity associated with literariness, and especially with poetic language (see Jakobson 1960; Leech 1969). Crucially, Carter also suggests that pattern-forming choices in spoken interaction are often made in order to 'create greater mutuality' among participants, i.e. to increase mutual understanding and intimacy.

In a study focusing specifically on patterns of metaphor use in reconciliation talk, Cameron (2007: 201) notes how the metaphorical expressions used by participants within one or more discourse event(s) can form 'emergent and evolving sets of connected metaphors' which she calls 'systematic metaphors'. These systematic metaphors may be related to the conceptual metaphors of cognitive metaphor theory, but differ from them in that they are generalizations from the linguistic metaphors used by specific individuals interacting in particular discourse contexts. According to Cameron, systematic metaphors can play an important role in the negotiation and reduction of 'alterity' among interlocutors, which may result from 'differences in social identity and affiliation, in socio-cultural history and in experience' (see ibid.: 199).

Cumulatively, the metaphorical choices in the conversation under analysis form patterns within and across turns that can be described as the creative result of cooperation among the three participants, and especially Beth and Doctor Jones. These patterns can be captured in terms of four main systematic metaphors *for Beth's individual experience of pain*: PAIN IS MOVEMENT INSIDE THE BODY ('going round about', 'shooting'), PAIN IS MOVEMENT IN AND OUT OF THE BODY ('comes back'), PAIN IS SHARPNESS ('sharp'), and PAIN IS BURSTING ('bursting'). These patterns of metaphor use seem to result from the participants' attention and appreciation for their interlocutors' choices of language, and a desire to show understanding and empathy by making similar linguistic choices. This makes an important contribution to the reduction of 'alterity' within the encounter. While the three participants in the conversation know each other well, they have very different positions in relation to the pain experience that is the motivation and main topic of the discourse event: Beth has direct, personal experience of the pain; the Doctor has expert knowledge of the causes of pain and its treatment; and Josh is likely to be familiar with the consequences of pain for Beth, and with her ways of talking about it. The way in which the three participants introduce, repeat and vary on one another's metaphors turns Beth's pain into a shared, intersubjective experience (at least to some extent), allows the expression of both physical sensations and emotional reactions, and helps to convey the Doctor's (and Josh's) understanding and empathy.

While the overall 'success' of the interaction (and of metaphor's role within it) cannot be properly assessed via an analysis of the transcript, I would suggest that the metaphorical patterns that are creatively co-constructed by the three participants play an important role in reassuring Beth that the reality and nature of her pain is acknowledged by the doctor (as well as by Josh), and that the medication she has been prescribed is appropriate. These patterns are also likely to reinforce the informal and relatively close personal relationship that Beth and Josh already seem to have with Doctor Jones, and to prepare the ground for similarly positive interactions in future. Indeed, a medical consultation is the kind of asymmetrical, transactional interaction which, according to the findings of Carter and McCarthy (2004), is not particularly conducive to creative linguistic behaviour. However, in this case, the patterns we have observed both reflect and contribute to a doctor–patient relationship that is much closer and more personal than is often the case in contemporary healthcare settings, at least in the UK.

Metaphor and Pain in a Scholarly Paper

My choice of examples in this chapter has not yet enabled me to point out two further important aspects of creativity in metaphor use, namely that: (a) speakers/writers may use metaphors creatively in order to challenge or subvert others' uses of metaphor, and thus express disagreements or negative attitudes; (b) metaphorical expressions may form creative patterns not just within individual texts and discourse events, but also intertextually, i.e. across different texts and discourse events. Both phenomena have been observed in the field of politics, for example, where particular metaphors (e.g. that of the 'Middle East Road Map') may be used in different ways by different people in different contexts, thus leading to intertextual chains of metaphor use involving both repetition and variation (see Müller 2005, 2010; Musolff 2004: 115ff.; Semino 2008: 81–5, 109–17).

The use of metaphor in science can also exhibit similar phenomena. This can be observed, for example, in a paper entitled 'Pain mechanisms: a new theory' (Melzack and Wall 1965), which appeared in the journal *Science*, and which has been described as 'the most influential ever written in the field of pain' (Rathmell 2006). In the first section of the paper, the authors point out the shortcomings of those accounts of pain according to which there are nerve cells in the skin that specialize in reacting to noxious stimuli, and that, when stimulated, automatically lead to pain sensations. These accounts are seen as representative of what the authors call 'Specificity theory', and their origin is traced back to Descartes's explanation of pain sensations, which relied on the metaphor of the 'alarm bell'. Descartes argued that the application of harmful stimuli to the body automatically causes pain, 'just as by pulling at one end of a rope one makes to strike at the same instant a bell which hangs at the other end' (Descartes 1644, quoted in Melzack and Wall 1965: 150). Melzack and Wall discuss a number of phenomena that are not accounted for by this view of pain and explicitly question Descartes's metaphor when they say that pain 'does not consist of a single ring of the appropriate central bell, but is an ongoing process'. As an alternative, they propose what they call the 'Gate Control Theory of Pain'. Within this theory, pain phenomena depend on complex interactions involving different parts of the spinal cord and the brain; more specifically, a particular area of the spinal cord (the 'substantia gelatinosa'): 'acts as a gate control system that modulates the synaptic transmission of nerve impulses from peripheral fibers to central cells' (ibid.: 975).

Some phenomena (e.g. excitement) that may occur around the same time as a noxious stimulus 'close the gate' in the substantia gelatinosa, so that no or little pain is felt. In contrast, pain is experienced when no other processes interfere significantly with the activity of the small nerve fibres stimulated by the noxious stimulus, so that the gate is 'open.'

In other words, the two theories differ, amongst other things, in terms of the central metaphor on which they are based (see Boyd 1993 on 'theory-constitutive' metaphors; Semino 2008: 125ff. on metaphor in science). The development and exposition of Melzack and Wall's new theory involves challenging the metaphor that underlies specificity theory, and proposing a new metaphor that provides a different account of the phenomenon of pain: within the 'alarm bell' metaphor, pain necessarily results from noxious stimulation of bodily tissues, while within the 'gate' metaphor a number of factors affect whether or not pain is felt when noxious stimulation occurs. A proper account of this kind of metaphorical creativity obviously needs to include a consideration of the metaphors that are established and conventional among the members of the relevant discourse community of scholars, and particularly in the texts they have produced as part of their scientific activity.

As Gibbs (1994: 173) has pointed out, scientific metaphors are 'made to be overused'. In order for a new metaphor to be regarded as successful, it needs to be adopted, or, minimally, accepted as relevant by other members of the relevant discourse community of experts (see also Csikszentmihalyi 1996). The success of metaphors such as Melzack and Wall's 'gate' can therefore be assessed, at least in part, by observing the extent of the intertextual chain it has originated. In December 2008, a combined online search for 'gate', 'pain' and 'theory' resulted in approximately 78,200 hits in Googlescholar (a search engine for academic publications), and approximately 9,660 hits in Googlenews (a search engine for news stories). This begins to suggest that Melzack and Wall's theory, and its central metaphor, have had considerable impact, not just in subsequent writing within the scientific community, but also in media texts produced for the general public. Interestingly, Melzack's most recent theory aims to account for an even wider range of pain phenomena via a new set of metaphors: in Melzack (1999, 2005), pain is described as a particular 'neurosignature' of a large and complex network of neurons that he calls the 'neuromatrix', and that he has further described as an orchestra that 'produces a single unitary sound at any moment even though the sound comprises violins, cellos, horns, and so forth' (Melzack 2005: 88).

Concluding Remarks

In this chapter I have attempted to support a number of claims in relation to the creative use of metaphor. On the one hand, I have shown that it is possible to provide a general definition of creativity in metaphor use that can be applied broadly to the analysis of metaphor in different genres. My analyses suggest that this definition needs to take into account at least *four* different dimensions: the uses of individual words or multiword expressions; the whole text or discourse event; previous relevant texts produced by the discourse community of which the speaker/writer is part; conventional patterns of metaphor use in the relevant language, which may reflect conventional conceptual metaphors. On the other hand, I have shown that the uses of metaphor that may be described as creative can vary considerably in terms of their textual manifestations, intertextual connections, and the extent to which they are co-constructed by different speakers/writers. I have also suggested that metaphors may be used creatively for a variety of reasons and in order to achieve a variety of effects, such as expressing an experience that is difficult to verbalize, showing understanding and empathy, proposing a new theory of a particular phenomenon, and so on.

I have therefore argued that the 'value' or 'success' of creative uses of metaphor can only be properly discussed in relation to the text and genre in which it occurs, and, more specifically, in terms of the specific goals of the speaker/writer, the characteristics of the genre, the relationship between speakers/writers and listeners/readers, and so on. The three main cases of creativity in metaphor use I have discussed (McEwan's ANIMAL metaphor; the collaborative pattern in the medical consultation; and Melzack and Wall's 'gate' metaphor) are all, I would argue, valuable and successful because, in Sternberg's terms, they are not just 'novel' but also 'appropriate' to the different tasks that the speakers/writers are engaged in. This plural and context-sensitive approach to (metaphorical) creativity does not detract from the appreciation of the creative achievements of acclaimed authors such as Ian McEwan, but enables the appreciation of the creative achievements of speakers and writers in a much wider variety of types of communication.

NOTES

1. I will not discuss other metaphorical uses of 'sharp', e.g. as a description of cleverness.
2. Collocates were calculated on the basis of mutual information and with a window span of one word on either side of the search string.
3. I do not have the space here to discuss cases where a conventional metaphorical expression is 'revitalized' as a result of the contextual relevance of its basic meaning (but see Goatly 1997: 276–7; Müller forthcoming; Semino 2008: 222–5).
4. This is in spite of the fact that McEwan has publicly declared that he does not suffer from migraine himself (Maria Bortoluzzi, personal communication).
5. Apart from changing the participants' names, I have preserved the transcription conventions used in the creation of the BNC (see Hoffman et al. 2008: 27ff.; www.natcorp.ox.ac.uk/). These include the division of the text into 'sentence-like' units, which are displayed on separate numbered lines. Readers can refer to the line numbers in order to assess the amount of text that has been omitted from my quotations. The symbol <-|-> indicates overlap.

REFERENCES

Boyd, R. (1993) 'Metaphor and theory change: what is "metaphor" a metaphor for?' in A. Ortony (ed.) *Metaphor and Thought*. Cambridge: Cambridge University Press: 481–532.

Bühler, K. (1982) *Sprachtheorie*. Jena: Gustav Fischer.

Cameron, L.J. (2007) 'Patterns of metaphor use in reconciliation talk'. *Discourse and Society* 18(2): 197–222.

Cameron, L. and Deignan, A. (2003) 'Combining large and small corpora to investigate tuning devices around metaphor in spoken discourse'. *Metaphor and Symbol* 18(3): 149–60.

Carter, R. (2004) *Language and Creativity: The Art of Common Talk*. London: Routledge.

Carter, R. and McCarthy, M. (2004) 'Talking, creating: interactional language, creativity, and context'. *Applied Linguistics* 25(1): 62–88.

Chilton, P. and Schäffner, C. (2002) 'Introduction: themes and principles in the analysis of political discourse' in P. Chilton and C. Schäffner (eds) *Politics as Talk and Text: Analytic Approaches to Political Discourse*. Amsterdam: John Benjamins: 1–41.

Csikszentmihalyi, M. (1996) *Creativity. Flow and the Psychology of Discovery and Invention*. New York: Harper Collins.

Deignan, A. (2005) *Metaphor and Corpus Linguistics*. Amsterdam: John Benjamins.

Deignan, A., Littlemore, J. and Semino, E. (forthcoming) *Figurative Language and Discourse Communities*. Cambridge: Cambridge University Press.

De Souza, L.H. and Frank, A.O. (2000) 'Subjective pain experience of people with chronic back pain'. *Physiotherapy Research International* 5(4): 207–19.

Gibbs, R.W. Jr. (1994) *The Poetics of Mind: Figurative Thought, Language, and Understanding*. Cambridge: Cambridge University Press.

Goatly, A. (1997) *The Language of Metaphors*. London: Routledge.

Hoffmann, S., Evert, S., Smith, N., Lee, D. and Berglund Prytz, Y. (2008) *Corpus Linguistics with BNCweb – A Practical Guide*. Frankfurt am Main: Peter Lang.

Jakobson, R. (1960) 'Closing statement: linguistics and poetics' in T.A. Sebeok (ed.) *Style and Language*. Cambridge, MA: Massachusetts Institute of Technology Press.

Kövecses, Z. (2005) *Metaphor in Culture: Universality and Variation*. Cambridge: Cambridge University Press.

Kövecses, Z. (2008) 'The conceptual structure of happiness and pain' in C. Lascaratou, A. Despotopoulou, and E. Ifantidou (eds) *Reconstructing Pain and Joy: Linguistic, Literary and Cultural Perspectives*. Cambridge: Cambridge Scholars Publishing: 17-33.

Lakoff, G. and Turner, M. (1989) *More than Cool Reason: A Field Guide to Poetic Metaphor*. Chicago: University of Chicago Press.

Larner, A. (2006) '"Neurological literature": Headache (Part 2)'. *Advances in Clinical Neuroscience and Rehabilitation*, 6(2): 37–8.

Lascaratou, C. (2007) *The Language of Pain: Expression or Description*. Amsterdam: John Benjamins.

Leech, G.N. (1969) *A Linguistic Guide to English Poetry*. London: Longman.

Margolin, U. (2003) 'Cognitive science, the thinking mind, and literary narrative' in D. Herman (ed.) *Narrative Theory and the Cognitive Sciences*. Stanford: CSLI Publications.

McEwan, I. (2001) *Atonement*. London: Jonathan Cape.

Melzack, R. (1999) 'From the gate to the neuromatrix'. *Pain Supplement* 6: 121–6.

Melzack, R. (2004) 'Evolution of the neuromatrix theory of pain. The Prithvi Raj lecture: presented at the third World Congress of World Institute of Pain, Barcelona 2004'. *Pain Practice* 5(2): 85–94.

Melzack, R. (2005) 'Evolution of the neuromatrix theory of pain'. The Prithvi Raj Lecture, presented at the third World Congress of World Institute of Pain, Barcelona, 2004. *Pain Practice* 5(2): 85–94.

Melzack R. and Wall, P.D. (1965) 'Pain mechanisms: a new theory'. *Science* 150(3699): 971–9.

Müller, R. (2005) 'Creative metaphors in political discourse. Theoretical considerations on the basis of Swiss Speeches'. *metaphorik.de* 9: 53–73.

Müller, R. (2010) 'Critical analysis of creative metaphors in political speeches' in G. Low, Z. Todd, A. Deignan and L. Cameron (eds) *Researching and Applying Metaphor in the Real World*. Amsterdam: John Benjamins: 321–32.

Musolff, A. (2004) *Metaphor and Political Discourse: Analogical Reasoning in Debates about Europe*. Basingstoke: Palgrave Macmillan.

Padfield, D. (2003) *Perceptions of Pain*. Stockport: Dewi Lewis Publishing.

Pope, R. (2005) *Creativity: Theory, History, Practice*. London: Routledge.

Pragglejaz Group (2007) 'MIP: a method for identifying metaphorically used words in discourse'. *Metaphor and Symbol* 22(1): 1–39.

Rathmell, J.P. (2006) 'Review of Wall and Melzack's Textbook of Pain, 5th Edition'. *Anesthesia and Analgesia* 102: 1914–15.

Scarry, E. (1987) *The Body in Pain: The Making and Unmaking of the World*. Oxford: Oxford University Press.

Schott, G.D. (2004) 'Communicating the experience of pain: the role of analogy'. *Pain* 108: 209–12.

Semino, E. (2008) *Metaphor in Discourse*. Cambridge: Cambridge University Press.

Sternberg, R.J. and Lubart, T.I. (1999) 'The concept of creativity: prospects and paradigms' in Sternberg, R.J. (ed.) *Handbook of Creativity*. Cambridge: Cambridge University Press: 3–15.

Tannen, D. (1989) *Talking Voices: Repetition, Dialogue, and Imagery in Conversational Discourse*. Cambridge: Cambridge University Press.

Woolf, V. (2008) *Selected Essays*, ed. David Bradshaw. Oxford: Oxford University Press.

7

Word Play across Languages and Cultures

R. Amritavalli and S. Upendran in Conversation with G. D. Jayalakshmi

[*The transcript extracts below come from a conversation between G. D. Jayalakshmi, at the time a freelance media consultant; and S. Upendran and R. Amritavalli, from the University of English and Foreign Languages in Hyderabad, India. Upendran and Amritavalli have built up a corpus of bilingual jokes, often based on puns and other forms of wordplay. They are being interviewed about this for an Open University course on The Art of English.*]

Amritavalli: OK. I think I should ask Upendran this one. Why did the Tamilian cow eat the door?

Upendran: Because it had the word 'pull' written on it. (Laughter)

Amritavalli: And 'pull' means grass. A Tamil speaking cow ate the door.

Upendran: Here's another one. Amrit, when would Mickey Mouse write the Ramayana?

Amritavalli: When he was a 'Valmiki'. (Laughter) When you stick him up on a wall as a poster I suppose.

Jayalakshmi: Now, the reference to that is the Ramayana was written by a man called Valmiki. And so – Val – wall – Miki – Mickey. That is what it is about. So this is really a serious cultural reference to knowing who wrote the Ramayana and also knowing what Mickey Mouse is about, you know. So it's quite interesting in the way that it spans history.

Amritavalli: Yes, perhaps that's right, yes. But certainly the Ramayana is very much present in the consciousness of these kinds of people who are making these jokes. They are all very well educated. They are also very culturally rooted people.

Jayalakshmi: That's right. And to the next one. Another erudite reference: Karl Marx.

103

Upendran: OK. What is the similarity between 'janmashtami' and communism? And the answer is Karl Marx.

Jayalakshmi: I think Amrit perhaps you should explain that one.

Amritavalli: Well what we do is, 'janmashtami' is the day we celebrate the birth of Krishna, one of our most favourite gods. And since he's a baby he walks into the house on little feet and we use our white powder to make marks of his feet entering the homes and 'karl' in Tamil means 'foot'. So the foot marks of the Lord are Karl Marx.

Upendran: Right. OK. Here's another one. What did the amoeba tell the chai wallah? The chai wallah of course is the guy who makes tea.

Jayalakshmi: You tell us.

Upendran: OK. The answer is 'suda poddiya'.

Jayalakshmi: That's beautiful. 'Suda' means 'hot' and 'poddiya' is 'please make it hot'. 'They make the tea hot'. And of course we know that amoebae have pseudopodia.

It's again that stretching of words and having sort of word images in your head isn't it?

Amritavalli: Yes, yes, very much so, yes. I think one of the first funny stories that I remember was a bilingual joke and that was told to me by my mother. It was a silly story about this little boy who went on crying, saying 'ching gum, ching gum', and in Tamil 'singhum', which is a lion, is often pronounced 'ching gum, ching gum'. And so this boy was taken to the zoo. He was taken to the circus and showed a lion and he still wouldn't stop crying and finally they asked him 'what do you want?' And he actually wanted chewing gum. (Laughter)

[...]

Jayalakshmi: Why do you think people actually say these jokes to each other? What is the reason? Is it, is it for example if you are in a formal context you can break the formality by becoming informal?

Amritavalli: Well maybe, that would go for telling any joke right? Any joke. But you see a joke – it creates a shared community and it also is born out of some kind of a tension. And many of these jokes are actually extended puns along two languages. So it creates a community because both of you have to know both these languages in order to understand a joke, and it's drawing on two aspects of your personalities. It's integrating them. And at the same time it's seeing a tension between those two personalities. It's laughing at them.

Jayalakshmi: They are devilishly clever, no?

Amritavalli: Yes indeed. They probably come to you from people who have been educated in English and who are also very comfortable in their own languages you know. Pulling two cultures together – we have already seen that in the Ramayana joke.

It's just a lot of fun you are having because you know more than one language, and the sounds of it – they are kind of playing two kinds of music in your ear.

Jayalakshmi: Do you think monolinguals miss out?

Amritavalli: I wouldn't know – I have been a multilingual all my life. I wouldn't know what it is to be a monolingual at all.

Upendran: You know, telling bilingual jokes requires a lot of creativity, whereas in the case of monolingual jokes it doesn't. Some amount of punning – yes. But in the case of bilingual jokes you really have to sit and think.

Amritavalli: And not only that – probably a lot of it is created on the fly and also forgotten on the fly. Like I'm sure in my home my kids, you know, they can talk about three or four languages like all of our kids do today. And they're all the time switching and, you know, making fun of each other, and there must be a lot of this happening which we don't even pay attention to or retain.

Upendran: That's true.

CREATIVITY ACROSS MODES, MEDIA AND TECHNOLOGIES

Introduction to Part II

Part II continues the broadly contextualized perspective on creativities developed in Part I, but extends the discussion, and frames of analysis, to encompass creativity across different communicative modes, media and technologies.[1] Chapters here take on these concepts in different ways, but generally highlight the interplay between verbal language and sound, music, orthography and layout, visual imagery, and movement; but also materiality and place – for instance, the texture of poetic forms on the page, performed or on screen. Significant here is the question of what contribution the idea of multimodality can make to an understanding of creativity in language.

In **Chapter 8** Mario Petrucci discusses a series of responses to Chernobyl. *Heavy Water: A Film for Chernobyl* has its roots in eye-witness accounts of the disaster, transcribed then published as a book in Russian, translated into English, rewritten by Petrucci as poetry published in two books which, in turn, formed the basis for the film. Petrucci sketches a narrative of this 'chain of transformations' across modes and media, languages and genres.

Petrucci writes as a physicist as well as a poet. He is passionate in his insistence that the precision of physicist and poet are not at odds, and that the specialist knowledge and technical expertise of the one and the specific techniques and insight of the other are complementary and mutually enriching. It is precisely his attempt in *Heavy Water* to combine emotional empathy with rational understanding, aesthetic responsiveness with ethical responsibility.

Petrucci provides insights into the compositional process – the possible effects of his choice of one English translation over another; his interpretation of scientific information as a physicist and poet; ethical/aesthetic dilemmas – should he 'rampage permissively in other peoples' sadnesses'? Production of the film involved collaboration and sometimes disagreement with others, as well as different representational choices – the order in which to present the decay series; the selection of actors/voices; the creative exploitation of combinations of modes (truncating a poem to allow visual imagery to take over). While such decisions affected the form of the film, not all were visible to the audience – the duration of the 'chain of decay' film segment being roughly equivalent to workers' permitted exposure to the reactor.

In **Chapter 9** Janet Maybin presents an analysis of letter-writing between prisoners on death row in the US and their pen-friends in Britain. Maybin argues that understanding this as a creative practice depends both on textual analysis and ethnographic awareness of the letter-writers' experiences. At the level of text, Maybin focuses on generic play, poetic citations and enclosures, metaphor and parallelism. These are related to the affordances of a particular communicative technology and practice – e.g. the chance to reread, to build textual references across successive letters, to add enclosures. They serve also to construct relationships, intensifying experiences and creating alternative imaginative worlds. Maybin identifies similarities and differences between such epistolary practices and other forms of communication, face-to-face and electronic.

Maybin sees creative episodes as dialogically constructed between letter-writers, and also as a highly contextualized practice: creativity here is not purely the product of an individual, nor the property of a technology, but emerges through the dynamics of a particular context, channel of communication and interactional activity.

Angela Goddard's interest, in **Chapter 10**, is in computer-mediated communication (CMC) – in this case chat between students engaged in a curricular activity. In CMC, and perhaps some other forms of written communication such as letter-writing, people and events are 'textualized' – i.e. represented entirely through texts – a process Goddard refers to as 'making worlds from words'. Her focus is on users' adoption of a range of creative textual strategies within this communicative context.

For Goddard, language creativity has to do with making new connections or combining elements in novel ways. She identifies instances of metaphor (particularly spatial – e.g. talking about a chat room as if it were an actual room, linguistically constructing pubs and bars), and intertextuality – citations that bring particular cultural resonances. Creativity also occurs in play with the visual form of words and their materiality – how they appear on a scrolling screen, their juxtaposition with animated icons. Such practices demonstrate users' exploitation of the CMC environment and their engagement with available communicative resources. 'Metamodality', the opportunity for simultaneous communication through different channels (writing, audio, video), has the potential for further types and levels of creativity.

Chapter 11, like 9 and 10, reports on a research study of creativity, but there is a shift in analytical focus. Whereas Janet Maybin and Angela Goddard foregrounded formal, textual creativity alongside creative practices (the latter more so in Maybin's chapter), Kate Pahl is primarily interested in process and practice. Pahl's study is educational – she looks at a primary school classroom in which children were engaged in a 'multimodal box' project. This came under the auspices of the British 'Creative Partnerships' initiative, one of the aims of which was to enhance the creativity of young people, raising their aspirations and achievements.

For the teacher in Pahl's study, the project involved a creative approach to learning, with children using their imagination to construct a particular environment – e.g. an ocean environment. Creativity is here linked partly to agency – to children making their own decisions about how they wanted to carry out the activity. For Pahl, drawing on Bourdieu's concept of *habitus*, it is also about improvisation and transformation – 'a shift from the regular and everyday to produce something new'. Pahl analyses the children's talk and their construction and adaptation of the physical and social environments in their boxes. The talk is seen as dialogic, in that it carries echoes of other voices in school and at home, which are then mapped back on to the making of the boxes. The boxes are changed through the children's talk and indeed are seen as an 'instantiation' of this talk. Creativity (improvisation, adaptation, transformation) is therefore evident across modes and across a range of activities.

In **Chapter 12** Michelene Wandor writes of her experiences as a literary author, writer of non-fiction, musician and also a teacher of creative writing. She discusses an example of her work, 'The music of the prophets' – unambiguously a poem in print, but which becomes a hybrid genre in performance with music and song. While Wandor considers the compositional process – the choices she makes for both publication and performance – she argues also that the actual process of composition remains invisible and ungraspable. By implication the self-reflection/commentary that is routine in creative writing classes becomes at least problematical (see also Chapter 24).

Motivations for the author's choice of one genre over another are equally hard to articulate, but Wandor does consider differences between modes and genres and the implications of these for her own work. For instance her aim of creating 'some new active relationship between words and music', in a series of 'music and words' performances and publication pieces, also caused her to challenge musical performance conventions.

In Chapter 2 the poet Patience Agbabi discussed the writing and performance of her poem 'Word'. In **Chapter 13** we include a further example of her work, an illustration from a collection of poems that brings together a poetic form – the sonnet – with a popular genre not normally considered poetic – the problem page. Agbabi here reconstructs the voices of (long-dead) poets writing their problem to her, as agony aunt. This also involves an adaptation to the sonnet form – the construction of prose sonnets. Creativity is evident in transformations of various sorts – blending two genres; reworking the sonnet form; sampling and recontextualizing others' words.

Part II concludes with an interview between Joan Swann and the storyteller Ben Haggarty followed by a transcribed extract from a storytelling performance with a brief analysis by Swann. Storytelling is an archetypally multimodal genre in which the storyteller draws on a range of communicative resources to construct a literary performance and engage the audience. The extracts provide a brief illustration of how this works in Haggarty's performance.

The chapters in this part continue to develop themes introduced in Part I – of language creativity as multiple, differentiated, a set of highly contextualized practices bound up with relationships and identities. Dimensions of creativity considered here include, once more, the formal properties of texts as well as processes of production (composition) and reception. A number of themes, however, receive greater attention:

- Though the term is not always used, most chapters foreground aspects of **multimodality** – the operation of creativity across different communicative modes. This may also include a focus on certain channels (e.g. auditory, visual) and technologies (e.g. print, handwriting, film). Examples include Goddard's discussion of language play alongside the visual form of words, Petrucci's reference to shortening a poem to accommodate visual information, Wandor's interweaving of music and the spoken word, Haggarty's exploitation of different modes in performance. In each case what is at stake is the communicative and creative potential of particular modes or combinations of modes.

- Creativity is therefore in part a response to the **affordances** and **constraints** of different modes (and channels and technologies): what they enable or inhibit. Maybin writes of the possibilities offered by letter-writing, Goddard of CMC, Wandor of music and words; Agbabi focuses particularly on creative composition in written form.

- Creativity is evident in **transformations** of various sorts – in Pahl, children's transformation of their multimodal boxes, Petrucci's 'chains of transformations' from personal accounts through poetry to film, Agbabi's transformation of texts and genres, the creation of an artful hybrid genre (problem page/sonnet). This is bound up with the creative potential of **intertextuality**, where words and utterances are refashioned (borrowed, stolen, sampled) and recontextualized.

- Creativity is also seen as **dialogical** – a term used explicitly by Maybin and Pahl, and implicit in other chapters. Dialogicality relates here to different, though related, phenomena: to speakers' and writers' co-construction of language use ('riffs' across a series of letters, children's collaborative talk and construction of boxes, collaboration between poet and film-makers); to the responsiveness that characterizes intertextuality (where an utterance creatively incorporates different voices); and to dialogue, or imagined dialogue, between a speaker/writer and audience (designing a film or performance for an audience).

- Concepts such as multimodality and the affordances of modes and technologies have implications for **aesthetic** judgements or judgements of **literary value**: these need to take account of the exploitation of modes/technologies along with other factors.
- However judgements by writers, film-makers and performers reflect not just aesthetic concerns, but also **ethical and practical concerns** (Petrucci's dilemma about profiting from misfortune, for instance), representing a further set of affordances/constraints.

NOTE

1. Mode, medium and technology are widely but not always consistently used in language studies. 'Mode' usually refers to a semiotic resource (cf. Kress and van Leeuwen 2001), though not always a fully worked-up system (e.g. verbal language, paralinguistic features of voice, gesture, music, clothing, moving imagery in film). 'Multimodal' here involves communication across modes (e.g. verbal language, characteristics of voice and gesture in face-to-face interaction; or verbal language, music and imagery in film). Sometimes spoken and written language are distinguished as modes. These are alternatively (and more consistently with the definition above) associated with different channels of communication (auditory, visual). 'Technology' refers to a means of communication – e.g. the vocal apparatus, pen/paper, print, film, 'new' technologies. 'Medium' is used to refer to some technologies (e.g. print media) but also in some usage it may overlap with or conflate one or more of mode, channel or technology (e.g. medium of writing, visual media).

REFERENCE

Kress, G. and Van Leeuwen, T. (2001) *Multimodal Discourse: The Modes and Media of Contemporary Communication*. London: Arnold.

8

Chains of Transformation: The Making of *Heavy Water: A Film for Chernobyl*

Mario Petrucci

Introduction

Made to commemorate the 20th anniversary of the disaster, *Heavy Water: A Film for Chernobyl* provocatively sets archived against fresh footage of the contaminated zone and relies, for its narrative thrust, primarily on first-hand experiences of the event rendered (somewhat unusually) through poetic monologue. Two contrasting extracts from the film act as a focus for my discussion: The Room, based on Svetlana Alexievich's published transcripts of eyewitness accounts, carries strong humanitarian and socio-political overtones, while Chain of Decay delivers a litany of standard isotopic data modified for rhetorical and rhythmic effect. I present the intertextual journey from source to film (and beyond) as a concatenation of transformed outcomes which raise, en route, not only aesthetic, ethical and pragmatic issues distinct to each stage, but also transformative implications for protagonist and audience alike. Intermediate textual states include prose translations from Russian to English and a film script challenged by poetic form. Adopting an experiential rather than a theoretical perspective throughout, I sketch a 'creative narrative' for the extracts. My commentary – stripped back to the barest of notes and accompanied by the artefacts per se – is intended as stimulant for further discussion. I close on a number of speculations on this process of creative transformation, including the question of 'hidden' transformations: namely, those alterations of mediation which subsequent transformers and analysts may not easily access.

113

Inceptions

Finnegas, an old man, had fished [for a salmon] for seven years in a certain pool, knowing that whoever ate this salmon would acquire all knowledge. At last he caught it and, rejoicing, gave his young apprentice (aptly named Finn) strict instructions to cook it just right and not, on any condition, to eat any of it. But, being a boy, Finn grew distracted, staring into the dark woods. The salmon got burned. A blister, the size of his thumb, rose on one side of the fish. Terrified of failing his master, Finn pressed a thumb against the blister, hoping to press it back in. The blister burst. Three hot drops of salmon oil dripped onto the boy's thumb, which – instinctively – he thrust into his mouth. And so it was that Finn, the boy – not Finnegas, the old man – gained knowledge. (Petrucci 2006: 254)

Deep in the winter of early 2002, I had something of a near-Finn experience. My salmon was Svetlana Alexievich's *Voices from Chernobyl* (as translated by Antonina Bouis). These remarkable women – editor and translator – had converted eyewitness accounts of Chernobyl into a juxtaposed textual narrative so effective that the voices of each speaker seemed to incarnate, unimpeded, on the ear. Wife and soldier; fireman, cameraman; peasant and teacher; the official and the child: common voices, uncommonly eloquent. Opening *Voices*, I didn't receive instant knowledge – but I was most certainly burned. A key testimony, for me, came from Ludmila Polyanskaya: 'Where are our intellectuals? Writers? Philosophers?' she cried. 'Why are they silent?' Initially, recalling Seamus Heaney's warning not to 'rampage permissively in other people's sadnesses', I was reluctant to pick up my own pen. Again, from *Voices*, Alexandr Renansky reassured me that art, like 'the plasma of an infected person, can serve to inoculate'. One way or another, I began to realize, we were all infected by Chernobyl. It continues to be active, to activate. I resolved, as far as I could, to listen. In fact, composing the long poem *Heavy Water* often felt like taking dictation. Those voices, that prise open your heart even as they shatter it, were profoundly insistent.

Heavy Water and *Half Life* followed: a diptych of books, two facets of a single extended poem. Later, in 2005, I received a call from Bethan Roberts at Seventh Art Productions, an independent film company based in Brighton. Phil Grabsky was interested in using the poem as primary material for a new film (ultimately, two versions of the film emerged, each designed for specific target outlets). That one call launched many months of collaborative challenge, often involving intense comparisons of thought, experience and action. As with any lived, creative experience, it's impossible to translate (or recreate) the detail of all that; but I can sketch the journey, employing some of its material artefacts (both published and privately archived) as signposts. Archives are, in fact, a crucial resource here, as published material, on its own, may not always reveal very much about the background transformations and processes that occurred. I'll focus on two poetic segments, derived from very different sources: 'The Room' and 'Chain of Decay'.

The Work(s)

Frame 8.1   Chains of transformation. One chain (as I experienced it)

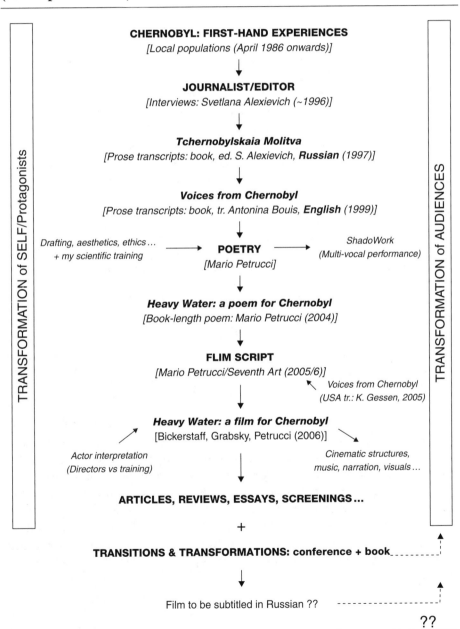

Hopefully, the 'creative narrative' of this particular Chain is self-descriptive. It's also simplified. For instance, there are many internal loops and linkages back (or 'feedbacks') where later aspects of the process have partly 'rewritten' earlier contributions to the project. I'm sure that reviews of the film, for example, have changed how I watch it and what I see in it; the making of the film itself, certainly, has permanently transformed how I read (and perform) the poetry.

During this work, decisions were based on intuition and previous working experience, tuning the eye and the ear at various cognitive and aesthetic levels and across the different media used. The ideas raised in this discussion (such as the Chain itself) are mostly after the event. Let me go further: in my experience, most modes of transformative creativity are not driven by theory or theorization, but are experiential in nature. My aim, then, is to use this Chain to focus on the tangible outcomes rather than the post hoc theory. I'm providing, as it were, the not-so-raw, created data.

There were also issues about the Chain having a distinctly ethical status. Transformations of text aren't necessarily, or perhaps cannot be, ethically neutral. Ethics and aesthetics are close cousins. Our aesthetic and intellectual choices – as editors, translators, poets, film-makers – do not control the reception of our created materials, but do ramify deeply into how the subject is understood by society, tending to activate different matrices of apprehension. The transformation of audiences *by* the artist's activity goes hand in hand with the transformation of self engendered in the artist *in* the act. And how do we value the desire of those who suffered Chernobyl to be (or not be) heard against the supposed duty of artists (collectively, if not individually) to offer something up on behalf of the neglected and excluded? My personal approach to this was a determination to listen creatively to the original protagonists rather than to deploy their experiences in service of my own ideas and imaginings. I concluded that certain forms of remembrance, or re-membering, constituted a civilizing act (upon my self as much as anyone else).

Finally, the form, detail and emphasis within the Chain will differ for each poetic segment under consideration (hence the plural 'Chains of Transformation' in the title). For 'Chain of Decay', for instance, the source material was of technical origin and already known to me from my studies in science: it didn't arise from (though its use may have been partly suggested by) my reading of *Voices*. Frame 8.1 therefore really serves as a generalized, summarizing template for discussion of the project as a whole; when dealing with particular segments of text or film, it must be re-established and reconsidered for each particular case and sometimes radically altered (or even abandoned) where necessary.

Frame 8.2   The Room. *Voices from Chernobyl* (the transcripts: Bouis translation)

---

116   VOICES FROM CHERNOBYL

hospitals all the time. The older boy, you can't even tell if he's a boy or a girl. He's bald. I've taken him to doctors and healers of all kinds. He's the smallest in his class. He's not allowed to run about and play because if anyone hits him by accident, he will start bleeding and may die. He's got a blood disease, I can't even pronounce it. I stayed with him in the hospital and thought, 'He's going to die.' Then I realized that I must not think that way. I cry in the toilet.

The Room → None of the mothers cry in the hospital rooms. They all cry in the toilets, in the bathroom.

   I come back looking cheerful. 'Your cheeks are getting rosier. You're going to get better.'

   'Mama, take me home. I will die here. Everyone here dies.'

   Where am I supposed to cry? In the toilet? But there's a queue ... and everyone there is just like me.'

One may note the underlined/highlighted text and see how it relates to the poetry (and the film). Indeed, it's fascinating to muse on how different my poetry might have been if I'd used Gessen's version of *Voices* as my source. Comparing the text of the poetry for 'The Room' with the source material (excerpted below) is as suggestive as it is illuminating:

> Where am I supposed to cry? In the toilet? But there's a queue ... and everyone there is just like me. (Bouis's translation in Alexievich 1999: 116; actually used for the poetry)

> Now where am I going to cry? In the bathroom? There's a line for the bathroom – everyone like me is in that line. (Gessen's translation in Alexievich 2005: 150; not used for the poetry)

'Only this queue for weeping' (line four of 'The Room') clearly owes its central noun to Bouis. I certainly have very different responses (as a writer as well as a reader) to the two translations, even accounting for the 'first love' of the order in which I found them (Bouis before Gessen). I wonder how my own line, at its very emergence, might have responded to Gessen's 'line'?

Frame 8.3   The Room. *Heavy Water* (the poetry)

THE ROOM

This hospital has a room
for weeping. It has no crèche.
No canteen. No washroom queue.
Only this queue for weeping.
No lost property booth. No
complaints department. Or
reception. No office of second
opinion. Of second chances. Its sons
and daughters die with surprise
in their faces. But mothers
must not cry before them. There is
a room for weeping. How hard
the staff are trying. Sometimes
they use the room themselves. They
must hose it out each evening.
The State is watching. They made
this room for weeping. No remission –
no quick fixes. A father wonders
if his boy is sleeping. A mother
rakes her soul for healing. Neighbours
in the corridor – one is screaming
It moved from your child to mine.
More come. Until the linoleum
blurs with tears and the walls
are heaving. Until the place can't
catch its breath - sour breath
of pine. And at its heart
this room.

(Petrucci 2004a)

Why am I drawn to poetry? Because, in poetry, language constantly falls short of experience – but miraculously so.

Frame 8.4   Chain of Decay. *Heavy Water* **(the physics; the poetry)**

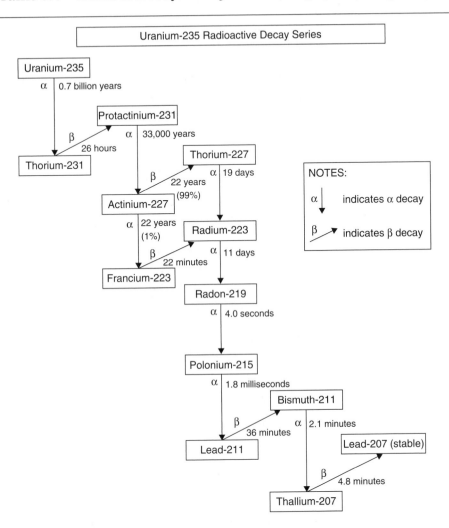

CHAIN OF DECAY

Lead 207   Stable
via beta and gamma radiation
Thallium 207 – 4.77 minutes
alpha radiation and x-rays
Bismuth 211 – 2.1 minutes
beta and gamma radiation
Lead 211 – 36.1 minutes
alpha radiation
Polonium 215 – 1.78 milliseconds
alpha and gamma radiation
Radon 219 – 3.96 seconds
alpha and gamma radiation
Radium 223 – 11.43 days
alpha and gamma radiation
Thorium 227 – 18.7 days
beta and gamma radiation
Actinium 227 – 21.77 years
alpha and gamma radiation
Protactinium 231 – 32,760 years
beta and gamma radiation
Thorium 231 – 25.52 hours
alpha and gamma radiation
Uranium 235
703.8 million years

(Petrucci 2004a).

I interpreted this Decay Chart dually – as a physicist as well as a poet. My understanding of the source material was heavily dependent on my training in science and my later role as a physics teacher. I was certainly able to transform/adapt the raw data to poetic purpose. The text I devised (almost a 'found poem', but not quite) aims for simplicity and clarity, but the data was edited in subtle ways to galvanize its rhetorical rhythm and drive. The decay series was also *inverted* in the poem (and film), so that we conclude with the atomic agent having an alarmingly long half-life. Importantly, I subjugated the logical movement of what appears to be simply raw data to an intended emotional impact. This 'local' rhetorical device is echoed macroscopically by the fact that I placed this segment near the end of the film, for maximum impact. It's also interesting to note how this short clip from the film is roughly equal to the permitted time spent shovelling graphite off the ruined roof of the reactor, one that translated (in many cases) to a fatal exposure.

Frame 8.5 Chain of Decay. *Heavy Water* (the film script; battle of the line breaks)

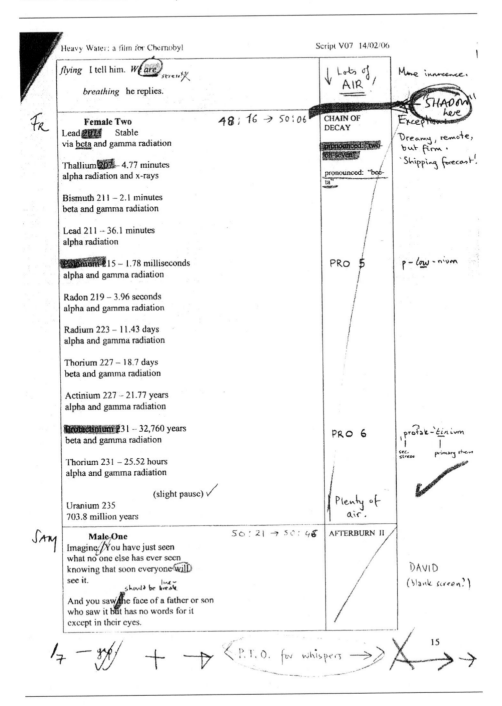

Heavy Water: a film for Chernobyl   Script V07 14/02/06

flying I tell him. We are ~~strength~~

    breathing he replies.

↓ Lots of **AIR** ↗

More innocence.

SHADOW here

Exception...

Female Two   48 : 16 → 50 : 06   CHAIN OF DECAY
Lead ~~207~~   Stable
via beta and gamma radiation

Dreamy, remote, but firm.
'Shipping forecast'.

pronounced two 'of seven'

Thallium ~~207~~ – 4.77 minutes
alpha radiation and x-rays

pronounced: "bee-ta"

Bismuth 211 – 2.1 minutes
beta and gamma radiation

Lead 211 – 36.1 minutes
alpha radiation

~~Polonium~~ 215 – 1.78 milliseconds
alpha and gamma radiation

PRO 5   p – low – nium

Radon 219 – 3.96 seconds
alpha and gamma radiation

Radium 223 – 11.43 days
alpha and gamma radiation

Thorium 227 – 18.7 days
beta and gamma radiation

Actinium 227 – 21.77 years
alpha and gamma radiation

~~Protactinium~~ 231 – 32,760 years
beta and gamma radiation

PRO 6   protak-'tinium
sec. stress   primary stress

Thorium 231 – 25.52 hours
alpha and gamma radiation

    (slight pause) ✓
Uranium 235
703.8 million years

Plenty of air.

Male One   50 : 21 → 50 : 48   AFTERBURN II
Imagine. You have just seen
what no one else has ever seen
knowing that soon everyone will
see it.   *should be line break*

DAVID
(blank screen?)

And you saw the face of a father or son
who saw it but has no words for it
except in their eyes.

FR

SAM

7 — yyy / ✝ → ⟨ P.T.O. for whispers →→⟩ ✗ →→

15

It's unusual for a film script to be primarily poem-driven. None of the creative protagonists had any significant previous experience of this, including the film directors themselves. Among our limited resource of precedents, Tarkovsky stood out for his style and creation of mood; also, various productions involving contemporary poets were studied for what we'd wish to avoid as much as what they demonstrated to be possible. I felt that too many films involving poetry either overwhelmed the text (it was almost impossible to follow the words for long periods whilst watching what was happening on screen) or deployed the visuals as merely illustrative (thus tautological) of the textual content.

We concluded, after much exploration and discussion, that our chosen deployment of *Heavy Water* (one which sought to emphasize the internalization of the text whilst exploiting the many subtleties of visual and textual interpenetration) was unlikely to be a well-established one, and that many of the outcomes couldn't be imposed *ab initio* but would have to be forged in the actual shooting and making of the film. That said, I've no doubt whatsoever that those early arguments and brainstorming sessions conditioned, profoundly, the many subsequent decisions concerning which poetic monologues should be used and what was captured (and how) on camera. We also headhunted actors very carefully indeed for their known ability to work sensitively with poetry (for instance, Juliet Stevenson's controlled yet very human immersion in character and David Threlfall's earlier renditions of Wordsworth for the BBC had been strongly noted). A decision was made not to show any of these speakers on film. I felt this would help to emphasize the text *as poetry* rather than reconstructed documentary and minimize any false personalization of the text.

The text of *Heavy Water* falls naturally into various monologues and utterances that may be broadly classified as voices, archetypes or 'roles'. These were recast for the film as:

Male 1:   official; Everyman; 'atom'.
Male 2:   male 'liquidator'; soldier; peasant; husband/father.
Female 1: local girl; young woman.
Female 2: female 'liquidator'; older peasant/wife/mother; girl grown up plus a narrating voice which focused on factual data and archive material.

During recording, directorial/poetic inputs acted so as to transform the actors' sense of what should be done (as acquired through training, learned technique, etc.).

In finalizing the script, there were some unexpected conflicts of form. There was intense disagreement about whether or not the line breaks were necessary for the script. One line of argument was that it was non-standard (which, actually, I thought was helpful to our cause) and that the actors would (and needed to) find their own pauses, stresses and caesurae. My position – which, as a poet, I felt I could not budge on (the only occasion, I believe, where non-negotiation occurred) – was that the line breaks were essential to distinguish the text from prose. For me, they were integral to how the meaning had been made and would be conveyed in the poem. As it turned out, the actors honoured them (to different degrees); but, in terms of the script at least, they were left in.

A final observation. Having completed my initial version of the script, it turned out we hadn't been studying the same versions of *Voices*. I began with (and, after I found Gessen's version, still preferred) Bouis's translation, while David Bickerstaff had the Gessen. I sometimes sensed our different interpretations of the witnessed accounts of Chernobyl could be put down to the variations between the two sources.

Frame 8.6 The Room and Chain of Decay. *Heavy Water* **(the film – two stills)**

Much was said and written during a conference at which I presented this material about the metaphor of creativity as an analytical lens. Well, at this stage of the project the idea of creativity through a lens became literal.

Excerpts from the film (for 'The Room' and 'Chain of Decay') show how poetic and filmic imagery commingled with music and other dubbed audio to generate unsettling or consolidating effects. A major issue here was (again) one of poetic line breaks and how they worked with/against filmic cuts.

Picking up on some earlier points about the reading style, many previous poetry films seemed unsure (or too sure) what to do with the speaker(s) or, worse still, suffered from over-zealous or 'stylized' acting in which (to be blunt and perhaps more than a little unfair) the working assumption seemed to be that poetry should always be presented to camera as an insufferably romantic or quasi-Shakespearean experience – a clear case of the performance of a text transforming it, as (whether or not we notice) it must always. Overcoming this 'mannered' quality in (some) actors' renditions of poetry was far from trivial. Our speakers were of the highest calibre, yet there were still certain infiltrations of training and technique – effectively, the actor 'translating' the text through learned and improvised methodologies of interpretation – that ran counter to our understanding of how the poem should be performed in this film.

'Chain of Decay' drew considerable (and often conflicting) discourse centred on precisely how that part of the sequence might be delivered. My own position on this was informed (not always usefully) by my long experience as a performer of my own work, and as co-founder of Shado Work, a group working with plural vocalization (more than one voice, often used non-sequentially) and experimental performance methods that give primacy to the textual content of the piece. Thankfully, this was not out of keeping with the shared opinion of the directors that the heightened language of poetry is potentially an agent of profound human transformation. It could provide, we believed, a penetrating experience of Chernobyl in its own right – not merely a secondary or substitute experience, nor even a parallel one.

Moreover, the ways in which visual (filmed) imagery and text-based imagery could combine forces (or, if handled poorly, compete) was an ongoing and energetic debate in the making of this film. An example of this was the way in which some of the poetry segments could be truncated (i.e. not read all the way through to the end) because, in various (and/or alternative) ways, the visuals were completing or substituting for the omitted textual content. This showed that the text, transposed to the visual medium and enmeshed there with a new set of semiotic codes, could exploit a new set of co-sensory pungencies. As a poet used to page and voice, this coexistence (and, to a degree, coeval evolution) of visual and aural forms felt like adding a third dimension to the familiar board version of chess.

Frame 8.7   The Room. Publication in *Interdisciplinary Science Reviews*

The artist and the self after Chernobyl   257

support, to empathy and sensitivity – to interfaces. Without that, nothing much is possible, however failsafe my machines may become, however persuasive or creative my organisational response may be. Nuclear energy is evidence of immense creativity; but creativity, we know, has its negative as well as positive incarnations, which come about through failing to engage the entire self. If we respond to Chernobyl personally, positively, only then can sustainable and sustaining collaborations and activities be discovered. I am not suggesting that, if we had Plato's philosophers running the Republic, material entities such as plutonium and nuclear bombs would be inconceivable. All I am saying is that this potency of self-response *is* very real and extremely present – at least potentially – in society. The fuller self of which I speak is not to be confused with a bigger ego; nor should it be dismissed as inappropriate (as it often is) in the context of pragmatics, organisations and communities. As Dostoevsky shows us, humans must have a point at which they stand against the culture and positively assert the self. Art provides interfaces: it can help us to access the self, assist us in transcending formalities so we can operate more powerfully than with intellectual efficiency alone. Art inoculates us against the temptation to short-circuit the self, which is what happens when we sink our responsibility and vitality entirely into the formal, the technical, the industrial response.

Mostly post hoc rationalizations, accretions, revisions. A systemization of thoughts and issues that don't always reflect the actual, lived, 'chaotic' experience of composing the poem. Useful, perhaps, as a means of consolidating and extending the transformational links in the Chain and for stimulating new Chains from any dangling ends.

Closing thoughts. Three cooler drops ...

Svetlana Alexievich's summarizing words, on the jacket sleeve of the Gessen version, demonstrates the creative plurality and plural responsiveness required and exemplified in every part of this project:

This is the way I see and hear the world: through voices, through details of everyday life. This genre – capturing human voices, confessions, testimonies – allows me to use all of my potential, because one has to be at the same time a writer, a journalist, a sociologist, a psychologist, and a priest. (Alexievich 2005)

At first glance, though, this sense of total involvement from the editor seems to run against the way in which many of the entries in *Voices* are entitled 'monologue', an attempt (perhaps) to intensify the sense of intimacy and courageous directness in the book that suits its material and approach. Indeed, it tends to give the impression that there'd been no editorial mediation, any interviewer (let alone interlocutor), at all. But to what extent were these testimonies conditioned or influenced through journalistic suggestion, editorial selection and so on? *Voices* doesn't dwell on how the contributors were prompted, or specify what questions (if any) were asked. Alexievich's agenda was, from what I can tell, utterly worthy; but it was an agenda nonetheless. Given all the multiple, interwoven subtleties of transposition, editing and translation, and the demonstrable shifts in emphasis and detail between the two English versions of Alexievich's original Russian text, shouldn't we include Alexievich and her translators as 'hidden mediators'? Not so hidden in the case of Gessen, whose approach to the text carries certain traits and interpretations I'd consider (arguably) as 'American'.

I'd have to include myself, too, among the 'hidden' mediators. So much of the process of creating a book occurs off and behind the page, in ways that are sometimes difficult to retrieve myself. There's probably another book to be written about that, concerning the complexly linked technical, aesthetic and poetic considerations that go into composing, arranging, editing and redrafting something like *Heavy Water* – the many mediations and transformations of consciousness that occur in and among these various overlapping processes. The facts are that 86 segments were composed, 82 of them over a period of just over two months, with afterthoughts aimed at filling 'gaps' perceived during the editing and rereading of the book and source materials. The construction of the book entailed an extended period of editing and reorganization (often involving outside readers), a major part of which involved attending to, and creating, a strong and suitable sense of formal construction across the pieces (including 'concrete' pieces which imitated the appearance of DNA). But, as ever, such facts are only the tongue-tip of the story.

My second point is to do with the ongoing metaphor, in this conference, of the creative lens. Whilst reading this, I first felt a tendency to consider 'lens' in the plural (creativity as multiple lenses) and, later, the urge to reject the metaphor altogether. The project I've been describing was an immensely complex, organic process. Even my own metaphor of a chain implies restraint, when actually I often found the process intensely fluid. I suppose a length of chain can have both of those qualities. Chains enable us to describe (i.e. fix) certain links, and suggest that there are constraints (or pressures) on what we do, which may be ethical (as discussed earlier), aesthetic (e.g. the etiquettes of, or when moving between, different forms) or practical (finance, time, TV timeslot, actor training and availability, anniversary deadlines, etc.). At the same time, chains can bend and flow, are also dynamic. But lenses are too mechanistic, too predictable and repeatable in their behaviour. Given the lens and the input, you can determine the output; making *Heavy Water* was about engaging with creativity where the outcomes (or even goals) weren't always known. Neither can the impact of the film on its viewers be entirely determined or controlled: they, too, are co-creators. Perhaps a better metaphor for creative transformations, then, would be mutation or some form of polymorphic moulting! Our central metaphors for creativity need (ironically) a little more precision as well as imagination.

And imagination brings me to my third and final thought. At this late stage of the *Heavy Water* project, now moving into analysis (articles and papers) and recycling (ongoing screenings, publishers' reprints), it might seem that imagination is barely implicated (beyond its role in advertising) with the near-automatic forms of cultural reproduction involved, but it still imbues every aspect of what happens next. If we respond to Chernobyl personally, positively, only then can sustainable and sustaining collaborations and activities be discovered with which to address it. In this process of being – and becoming – fully human, art and its various languages provide interfaces, helping us to access the self in ways that can transcend the formalities of institutions and socialized values. Imagination – and how that gets translated across cultural modes and media – allows us to operate more radically and powerfully than with intellectual efficiency alone. It's not only poetry that can get lost in translation across forms, but empathetic imagination too. To rewrite a line from Proverbs: 'Without imagination, the people perish'. And I wonder if that 'weeping room' was (in a sense) already there, as a Platonic potential or ideal, in the social and technical structures which led us to imagine nuclear power? Perhaps the film, the poem, the book of transcripts, the speech of eye-witnesses, their experiences of the accident, the 'accident' itself, were not exactly inevitable or predictable but nevertheless somehow pre-existent as a Chain of potential forms co-established with the blueprint for the reactor, potentials that (at least in part) drove those very transformations. Other Chains were also possible of course, other outcomes; but that particular possibility, the one that bloomed so tragically on the night of 26 April 1986, was – like all the others – latent, a kind of 'receiver' awaiting its actuality. Not all fish are edibly benevolent. We should be most careful where we direct our thumbs of creative imagination and to what ends we apply that sacred pressure.

Each object we create, whether fanciful or rooted in cast-iron physical-mathematical precepts, is an extension of our imagination ... Which is why the quantification of Chernobyl and its after effects, crucial as it is, can never become our sole aim. Chernobyl stands to remind us that knowledge is as much qualitative as quantitative. One of the chief outcomes of Chernobyl will be what we allow it to tell us about ourselves, as an expression of our negative imagination and its myths ... As John Steinbeck said, 'An animal which must protect itself with thick armour ... is on the road to extinction'. (Petrucci 2006: 258)

REFERENCES

Alexievich, S. (1997) *Tchernobylskaia Molitva. Moscow:* Editions Ostojie.
Alexievich, S. (1999) *Voices from Chernobyl,* tr. Antonina W. Bouis.
Alexievich, S. (2005) *Voices from Chernobyl,* tr. Keith Gessen. London: Aurum Press Dalkey Archive Press.
Bickerstaff, D., Grabsky, P., Petrucci, M. (2006) *Heavy Water: A Film for Chernobyl.* Seventh Art Productions (running time: 52 mins; www.heavy-water.co.uk).
Bickerstaff, D., Grabsky, P., Petrucci, M. (2006) *Half Life: A Journey to Chernobyl.* Seventh Art Productions (running time: 40 mins; www.half-life.org.uk).
Petrucci, M. (2004a) *Heavy Water (A Poem for Chernobyl),* 1st edn. Enitharmon Press.
Petrucci, M. (2004b) *Half Life (Poems for Chernobyl).* Heaventree Press.
Petrucci, M. (2006) '"Three hot drops of salmon oil": the artist and the self in the aftermath of Chernobyl'. *Interdisciplinary Science Reviews* 31(3): 254–60.

9

Intimate Strangers: Dialogue and Creativity in Penfriend Correspondence

Janet Maybin

Introduction

An important aspect of Bakhtinian theory which has captivated contemporary scholars is the idea that all utterances, spoken or written, are both a response to another voice or voices and, in their turn, are designed to invite a particular kind of response. On the surface this seems like common sense but at a more profound level Bakhtin is saying that this responsivity and addressivity in our use of language are fundamental to how we create meaning. From this point of view, meaning is not formed inside an individual head and then communicated to someone else, but occurs like a spark between people through the synergy between utterance and response, and through the cumulative crisscrossing chains of utterances and responses which link people together. This sparking of meaning itself could be seen as a creative act. It generates and sustains social relationships, mediated as these are through verbal communication, and it contributes to people's sense of self which emerges through their connections with others. I take this idea of meaning as an act of collaborative creativity as my starting point in this chapter and I shall argue that creativity in the sense of building relationship and extending the self can be intimately connected with language creativity at the level of text. Thus language form and language function are dynamically interconnected.

It is almost impossible to recover all the traces of responsivity and addressivity in examples of everyday talk: one would need a vast amount of contextual knowledge, as well as a history of dialogue between the people concerned. It is somewhat easier to find dialogic links in written literature, with its webs of intertextual connection and its self-conscious generic lineages.

In this chapter I shall discuss creativity in personal correspondence, a genre which has been traditionally viewed as quite close to talk. More specifically, I shall focus on penfriend correspondences which do, uniquely, provide a complete written record of the development of relationship between pairs of people who have never met, thus allowing us to trace the role of creativity within this context. Drawing on a corpus of correspondences between men on death row in the United States and their penfriends in England, I shall argue that the creative and playful language within their letters is intricately connected with the dialogic patterns of responsivity and addressivity across the correspondences which support the development of friendship between the pairs of penfriends.

The data on which this chapter is based come from questionnaire and interview research on the experiences of 162 individuals involved in death-row penfriend correspondences, including 59 prisoners scattered across 14 US death-row prisons (Maybin 1999), and the subsequent textual analysis of the beginnings of six correspondences (the first six to eight letters written by each individual involved, 80 letters in all). These correspondences were collected retrospectively from the six pairs of penfriends. In other words, the letters on which I base my analysis had all been written before the penfriends became involved in the research and gave me permission to use this material. These particular six correspondence relationships endured over at least a year (some substantially longer) and were valued positively by the letter-writers involved. As a penfriend myself, although not included in the data, I have had continuing contact with the death-row penfriend community over a number of years and have collected a considerable amount of background information about their experience. While the significance of creativity within these correspondences is strongly coloured by the specific circumstances from which they emerged, I would argue that they also provide a unique opportunity to trace on paper the role of creativity within the chains of dialogic connections across verbal relationship which are fundamental, as Bakhtin suggests, to the creation of meaning and significance in all human communicative activity.

Letter Writing as a Creative Practice

The creative potential of vernacular letter writing has long been realized. Letters can overcome barriers of distance and time, transforming absence into presence via the page, even beyond death (Altman 1982). They enable people to present a 'self', pursue and maintain relationships, and recreate and reflect on personal experience. A small number of recent ethnographic and historical studies suggest, in addition, that letters offer an outlet for emotions of tenderness and longing which cannot be otherwise expressed (Blythe

1993; Besnier 1995; Jolly 2006). Within the context of prison in particular, Wilson (1999) argues that letter writing and literacy creativity in general can play a fundamental role in helping prisoners to 'keep your mind'. Through language play, poetry, parody and the 'paraliteracy' features of letters, for example their visual form, design features and smell, she found that prisoners constructed a more personalized 'third space' (neither institution nor outside world), where, despite their circumstances, they could exercise some control over their lives.

In addition to these insights from historical and ethnographic studies, research on linguistic creativity in talk has suggested significant cognitive, emotional and interactive functions for creativity, some of which I shall argue also apply to personal correspondence. Linguists argue that speakers' use of puns and metaphors, repeated patterns of sound and rhythm and quotation, all serve to intensify cognitive and emotional experience, carry relationship work and create alternative imaginative worlds which enable them to break free of routine thought (e.g. Tannen 2007; Cook 2000; Carter 2004). I shall suggest below that the penfriends' use of language play and creativity in their letters contributed to the construction of a unique discursive world between each pair of correspondents. Like Wilson's metaphor of a third space these discursive worlds are emotionally and imaginatively intense, a form of escape from an untenable reality.

While the prisoners' situation and the particular motivations of people choosing to correspond with them clearly played a part in producing this intensity, it also seems to be related to the affordances of letter writing as a particular channel of communication within this context. Ironically, creativity and intimacy seemed to be actually facilitated by the barriers of time and space, and by the fact that the correspondents had no prior knowledge about each other's lives (Maybin 2006). There are parallels here with research into Internet relationships where visual cues and 'gating features' of face-to-face communication, like physical disparities, shyness or social anxiety, are also absent. In this context, there are apparently secure boundaries around disclosing inner feelings to a stranger who is not in a position to leak information to a mutual acquaintance (McKenna et al. 2002). Asynchronous computer mediated communication, like letter writing, provides time for reflection and the planning of disclosure, which is often met by a reciprocal expression of intimate feelings from the respondent. Correspondents consequently feel able to express their 'true self'. There is also more potential for the projection of the qualities of an 'ideal friend' onto a respondent, and belief in these idealized qualities often becomes a self-fulfilling prophecy (Bargh et al. 2002). The penfriends in my research echoed these findings from online research, with prisoners often reporting a sense of being able to share 'the real me' with their penfriend and correspondents from both Britain and the US reporting the experience of a kind of mirroring, as their experiences and feelings were reflected back to them by their respondent. This mirroring, they suggested, deepened their friendship and heightened their sense of closeness with their penfriend.

Creativity in the Text: Generic Play

The examples from letters quoted in this and the next section below come from the first six to eight letters from each side of the correspondences shown in Figure 9.1.

Death row	Britain
Richard, 36	John, 60, retired
Robert, 25	Kim, 29, housewife
Joe, 34, American Indian	Ruth, 50s, part-time teacher
Sam, 37, African American	Karen, 40s, freelance professional
Chris, 57	Patricia, 60s, freelance professional
Danny, 23	Meg, 60s, retired

Figure 9.1   Correspondents

Notes: Names are pseudonyms. Ages are taken from the questionnaire responses. Respondents (Caucasian unless indicated) reported particularly valuing interethnic friendships.

As a genre, letters are distinctly structured by their beginnings and endings, which are particularly significant for their communicative functions in a number of ways. Often formulaic, beginnings and endings affirm the nature of the epistolary relationship (the differences between 'dear' and 'dearest' in the address, for instance, or whether the letter concludes 'yours sincerely', 'all the best' or 'love and kisses'). Writers often refer to previous letters at the opening or future letters at the close, thus contextualizing the current letter within past and future correspondence, e.g. 'I received your letter last night, thank you for the postcard also... I'm pleased to hear you liked the little card see you make me smile, so I just want to pass this feeling back to you' (Sam, US, 5).[1] A typical ending refers to the act of closure, as well as to future correspondence. For example: 'Well, I guess I've run my head long enough and there's not much else going on with me here so I will close this letter for now so I can get it into the mail to you. I will be looking forward to your next letter. All my best to you and your family. Take care and write soon' (Joe, US, 6).

As in the example from Sam above, penfriends often started their letters, after the salutation, by noting the date when they had received their correspondent's last letter, and they also frequently included a calculation of the time it had taken to reach them. The delivery time is a matter of particular significance in a context where letters are sometimes read by prison authorities, can get delayed in the mail rooms and occasionally disappear. Especially in the early stages of a correspondence, writers were anxious to demonstrate that they had answered letters promptly or to explain and apologize for any delay. The business of dates and delivery times could also provide a source for playful exchange, as in the extracts below from correspondence between Richard and John. Richard and John frequently responded to each other's use of metaphor and language play, sometimes producing dialogic riffs which extended across a number of letters. Here, the openings of their letters are orientated towards the particular contingencies of this correspondence context, but also illustrate, at this early stage of the friendship, the shared dexterity and playfulness with language which was to become a distinguishing feature of this particular written relationship. Both men have a number of other penfriends, whom they sometimes mention in their letters:

> Dear John, I received your 5/19 letter today, which confirms my suspicion that our overseas mail is sent by cruise ship. Margaret's letters sometimes get to me in three days, but over a week both ways is usual. (Richard, US, 3)

> Dear Richard ... if the USA can put people on the surface of the moon, it ought to be capable of sending mail round the world expeditiously, I suppose, though logic does not often enter into the often esoteric behavior of bureaucratic government departments. (John, Britain, 3)

> Dear John, Thank you for your June 4th letter I received yesterday. Three days for mail to get to you, six days to me, the tail wind must blow from the US to the UK. (Richard 4)

> Dear Richard, 'Par for the course', the transit time of your latest letter: PM Jackson 12. 6 AM England 16.6. (John 4)

The joke, where the cruise ship becomes a metaphor for slowness, is collaboratively elaborated over four letters through its introduction (Richard 3) a contrast with rocket science (John 3), susceptibility to tail winds (Richard 4) and the mock official note invoking the 'transit time' of a ship's cargo delivery (John 4). In addition to illustrating the typically dialogical nature of penfriends' creative activity at the level of the text, this example also shows the progressive alignment which often emerged over a number of letters, as penfriends echoed and responded to each other. Here, Richard initiates the joke about the cruise ship in his third letter and extends it in his fourth, while John responds in letter 3 initially by a poke at the United States authorities and then, in letter 4, shifts more fully inside Richard's ship metaphor.

While openings reactivate the contact and the relationship, closings have the difficult function of managing the rupturing of the connection and of trying to ensure the continuation of the relationship over the space of time until the next letter arrives. This time is by no means empty in relationship terms, as the letter writers think about their correspondent, reread old letters and plan future letters. However, as the completion of a discrete communicative turn, letter endings in Western culture often express more explicit messages of affection than are conventional in other contexts, perhaps to compensate for signalling the cutting of the connection. Some penfriends said that the signing off was the first part of the letter they read, as the place where their penfriend's feelings towards them would be most clearly expressed. As well as expressions of affection, the endings of letters often included references to their correspondent's intimate social circle, as penfriends began to create a shared network of social connections, e.g. 'Give my best to your husband and my thoughts are with both of you and I hope everything goes okay for you' (Joe, US, 7). 'Tell everybody hi for me, and you take care' (Chris, US, 4).

Sometimes letter writers found creative ways of extending and elaborating this affirmation of their relationship, and its continuation, at the close of a letter. For instance, one British woman explained that she and her penfriend always concluded their letters with a written description of an imaginary hike or outing together, to a place they thought the other would enjoy (Open University 2006). This imaginary world, where they could walk side by side, provided an 'upbeat' ending, implying the continuation of the friendship beyond the bounds of the letter which was finishing and creating a shared experience which could be revisited and reimagined many times while waiting for future letters to arrive.

Poems, Metaphor and Parallelism

The reflective mirroring which correspondents often reported experiencing, as they picked up and gave back ideas and impressions of each other across a series of letters, was echoed by the patterning of creative uses of language within the text of the letters themselves. Projection and reflection were involved in collaborative joking, as in the letter openings from Richard and John discussed above. Other forms of interactive creative activity included the use of poems and poetic quotations, metaphor and parallelism (particularly in the rhythmic repetition of three-part lists), each of which is discussed below.

Penfriends often introduced quotations in their letters, from poetry, newspaper articles or religious writings. A quotation then became the focus for an exchange of ideas and expressions of judgement across a number of letters, providing scope for the discussion of different interpretations and setting up a joint reference point for the letter-writers' interactive exploration of personal beliefs and value positions. Richard and John provide a particularly rich example of the ways in which quotations could be recontextualized, elaborated, commented on and transformed (omitted text is indicated by a series of dots '...'):

> A co-worker told his mother who was worried about his health that he still goes fishing every Saturday. He told her the old prison saying; 'you can lock up our bodies, but you can't lock up our minds'. (Richard, US 4)

> I cannot find the quote from Oscar Wilde about his spirit being free when his body was imprisoned, but at the close of his De Profundis he writes 'All trials are trials for one's life just as all sentences are sentences of death ... Society, as we have constituted it, will have no place for me, has none to offer. But Nature, whose sweet rains fall on just and unjust alike, will have clefts in the rocks where I may hide, and secret valleys in whose silence I may weep undisturbed...' (John 4)

John goes on to quote a Bosnian cellist who had played Albinoni's *Adagio* at the site of a mortar bomb massacre:

> 'My father was a Muslim like my grandfather. But my nationality is music. Music is universal' he says with a smile. I like that '... my nationality is music'. It is almost on a par with my favourite quote, from Thomas Paine's The Rights of Man. 'My country is the world and my religion is to do good ...' (John 4)

> I love the quotes you send, and especially like Wilde's De Profundis quote. A popular version of it here goes: 'Nobody gets out of life alive'. I will also paraphrase the Bosnian cellist and Thomas Paine: My nationality is human, and my religion is friendship. Margaret sent me a quote from John Donne I had been looking for:
>
> > No man is an island each onto himself
> > Each is a part of the whole
> > Any man's death diminishes me
> > Ask not for whom the bell tolls, it tolls for me.
>
> If possible, could you please check the punctuation and form of that poem for me. Margaret is a dear friend, but punctuation is not her forte. (Richard 5)

Here, a number of related metaphors quoted from popular axioms, an essay, newspaper and poetry are passed back and forth. The image of the mind being able to transcend imprisonment in the popular axiom from Richard (4) is paralleled and elaborated by John (4) in his quotations from Wilde, and the Bosnian cellist and Thomas Paine's comments about identity. These ideas about a larger, all-embracing humanity are neatly encapsulated and brought back to the correspondence context by Richard (5): 'My nationality is human, and my religion is friendship'. He then goes on to express his alignment with John, in terms of language expertise, using the contrast with Margaret to highlight the men's affinity. The use of quotation and metaphor across these three letters generates a rich range of intertextual resources for interactional work and facilitates the discussion of difficult topics like imprisonment, justice and death. Both metaphor and quotation provide distancing mechanisms which are particularly useful when penfriends are still negotiating the beginning of a relationship. Metaphor involves indirectness and stimulates creativity through the semantic spaces opened up by the comparison. Quotation introduces a separate voice and value position into an utterance, providing writer and respondent with an outside reference point in relation to which they can more delicately negotiate their own positions than would be possible in a direct statement of personal belief.

It has been argued that poetic language is particularly amenable to decontextualization and reuse because of its foregrounding and framing effects (Bauman and Briggs 1990). In the letters, whole poems, as well as poetic quotations, provided a detachable, enduring, shared communicative resource which could be drawn on and reinvoked across the correspondence. Some prisoners included poems written by themselves, either as enclosures or incorporated into the body of their letters, and these were invariably commented on by their correspondent. For instance, Joe, who was half Cherokee, sent his penfriend Ruth a booklet of poems he had written, with his first letter. A recurring motif in these poems was the dream of one day returning to his people, e.g. 'I shall burst forth upon the world from behind mountains and trees/To resume my life of liberty'. While Ruth acknowledged the poems in her second letter, she also indirectly referred to them in her fourth letter: 'I imagine you to be a soul of the open spaces'. In her fifth letter, in the course of commenting on how his case was progressing, she referred indirectly to a line in one of his poems, 'I am like a bird in a cage', in her comment: 'any intimation that the caged bird will fly free again makes me very happy'. The memorability and potential for recontextualization provided by poetic form means that Ruth can intensify her expression of hope regarding the outcome of Joe's case by laminating a response to a poem sent with his first letter onto her response to news about legal processes in his fourth letter. Ruth's response serves both to accept and to value the feelings and identity that Joe presented in his poems, and also to mark the continuing, consistent nature of their relationship over time by invoking a past point in its history and bringing this to bear on the present. Thus the correspondences and the relationships they generate become knitted together through a network of criss-crossing dialogic links, which stretch back across previous letters.

The exchange and recycling of quotations and whole poems provide a vehicle in these letters for feelings which are not usually expressed so directly in face-to-face talk, where limitations of memory and 'embarrassment and shame', as one prisoner expressed it, would normally preclude such extended poetic activity. While some letters included more poetry than is usual in speech, however, this was not true of all the correspondences which I examined. For instance, Sam and Karen's first 12 letters only included one poetic quotation from Karen (letter 4), to which Sam failed to respond. What might be termed the seeds of poetic language, on the other hand, were fairly common. For instance, Sam frequently used metaphor, e.g. 'all my life I've ran against the wind so this struggle is nothing new to me' (3), 'in my mind I can hear your voice' (5). Karen also produced her own metaphors, especially as the correspondence got going, e.g. 'you wouldn't let yourself be "bought"' (5), 'I need to spend some time knuckling down and doing some work' (6). She also, on two occasions, quoted Sam's metaphors back to him (the only occasions in which she quoted any language from his letters). In his second letter, Sam had responded to her descriptions of overseas travel by writing: 'you give me a chance to learn without spending a dime to go anywhere so I guess you can say I'm getting a free ride' (Sam 2). Karen replied: 'as you seem interested in "free rides", I'm sending you a copy of the report' (3). In his fifth letter, Sam commented: 'it hurt me because they don't seem to care, or is it they forget how to care after so many years of pain?'. Karen responded: 'I suspect it's because it is one of their few pleasures after, as you say, "so many years of pain"' (6).

This kind of progressive echoing and mutual alignment can also be found in the penfriends' parallel use of three-part lists, e.g. 'I write to you because sometimes I'm scared, and lonely, and I need a friend' (Danny 4), 'I did not love, like or respect him' (John 2). In some cases, the interactive use of these was very striking. For example, three-part lists were only used once each by Joe and Ruth in their first six letters, but this single reciprocal use coincided with the moment of 'opening up' which penfriends often reported experiencing once trust had been established in the correspondence. This opening up on the side of the prisoner often involved revealing details of their conviction, despite the fact that they were expressly instructed by their lawyers never to discuss this on paper. In her seventh letter Ruth wrote: 'I am always your friend, now, tomorrow and for ever'; and Joe's response included an answering three-part structure: 'I was arrested and charged with murder, kidnapping and robbery'. While these two statements might not seem immediately connected at a literal level, the patterns of relationship found within the penfriend correspondences suggest that the structural echo signified a specific response: Ruth's strong expression of friendship prompted a disclosure from Joe which, if Ruth still accepted him as a friend, could take their relationship to a deeper level.

In contrast, in the correspondence between Chris and Patricia three-part lists were a recurring feature of Chris's writing style, e.g. 'I am tired of reading books, police reports and trial transcripts' (2), 'we talk, lift weights and play cards' (4), 'added stuff, deleted some things I didn't really like and corrected lots of words' (5). Patricia also starts using three-part lists from her third letter onwards: 'Her house is full of children, animals and a fair amount of mess' (3), 'one can always hope for clouds, or stars, or even birds' (4), 'trials and pardons and so forth' (5). While I cannot incontrovertibly claim that letter writers like Patricia (and Karen, who echoed Sam's imagery) are drawn into specific language patterns by their penfriend, it is certainly the case that particular kinds of forms predominated in particular correspondence relationships, suggesting a kind of interactional convergence at the level of linguistic structure similar to that which has been observed in the telling of stories among women friends (Coates 1996), the 'format-tying' in children's interactive talk (Goodwin 1990) and the use of accent (Giles and Coupland 1991).

Conclusion

The textual analysis suggested that each correspondence developed its own distinctive creative profile, varying from the rich range of metaphoric play in the letters between Richard and John, through Sam and Karen's focus on metaphor (with no use of three-part lists and only one quotation) and Chris and Patricia's abundance of parallelism, to a correspondence between two other penfriends, Robert and Kim, where there was virtually no use of creative language at all. At the formal level, I would suggest, the penfriends, consciously or unconsciously, echoed the foregrounded use of creative forms in each other's letters. To paraphrase Tannen's comments on conversationalists, this dialogic creativity drew them into a kind of rhythmic ensemble, producing an aesthetic experience of coherence, an emotional sense of connectedness and intellectual and emotional insight. It is perhaps significant that Robert and Kim's correspondence, unlike the others quoted in this chapter, was not sustained beyond the first year.

While creative language use in the letters shared some characteristics with creativity in spoken language, for instance the echoing of formal structures and the use of metaphor, it also had its own distinct characteristics, in particular the quotations from poetry (and I did not find any use of punning at all, in the 80 letter corpus). As a literacy practice, the penfriend correspondences had their own particular affordances and opportunities for creativity, both at the level of the text and in relation to the art of written relationship. I have suggested that there are interesting parallels to be drawn between the letter writers' experience of relationship using this oldest of communicative technologies, and the recent experiences of online Internet correspondents. The processes of mirroring and projection that the penfriends described in their questionnaire responses and expressed through their collaborative uses of creative language are also facilitated through a particular configuration of circumstances and technology.

The use of creativity which has been the focus of this chapter is not part of the high art of poetry, drama or the epic novel, but an intrinsic aspect of vernacular exchange. As Mukarovsky (1970 [1936]) points out, any object can carry an aesthetic function, foregrounded to a greater or lesser extent in particular contexts; and many linguistic items lie on the border between art and communication. Some letters are carefully crafted; they are reread and redrafted before sending, sometimes in ornately decorated envelopes. In order to understand how creativity within personal correspondence generates and organizes the ties between the letter writers, I have shown how creative language served expressive and interactional purposes, and also generated a dialogically patterned network of connections across the correspondence which contributed to its overall coherence and sustained the relationship it supported. In circumstances where communication with the outside world is largely limited to the written word it is striking how rich the resources of written language are, and how resourceful letter writers can be in overcoming barriers of time and space to create imaginative and emotionally intense, mutually rewarding relationships with strangers.

NOTE

1. Numbers refer to the chronological sequence of each writer's letters.

REFERENCES

Altman, J. (1982) *Epistolarity: Approaches to a Form*. Columbus: Ohio State University Press.

Bargh, J.A., McKenna, K.Y.A. and Fitzimmons, G.M. (2002) 'Can you see the real me? Activation and expression of the "true self" on the Internet'. *Journal of Social Issues* 58(1): 3–48.

Bauman, R. and Briggs, C. (1990) 'Poetics and performance as critical perspectives on language and social life'. *Annual Review of Anthropology* 19: 59–88.

Besnier, N. (1995) *Literacy, Emotion and Authority: Reading and Writing on a Polynesian Atoll*. Cambridge: Cambridge University Press.

Blythe R. (1993) *Private Words: Letters and Diaries from the Second World War*, 2nd edn. London: Penguin.

Carter, R. (2004) *Language and Creativity: The Art of Common Talk*. London/New York: Routledge.

Coates, J. (1996) *Women Talk: Conversation between Women Friends*. Oxford: Blackwell.

Cook, G. (2000) *Language Play, Language Learning*. Oxford: Oxford University Press.

Giles, H. and Coupland, N. (1991) *Language: Contexts and Consequences*. Milton Keynes: Open University Press.

Goodwin, M.H. (1990) *He-said-she-said: Talk as Social Organisation among Black Children*. Bloomington: Indiana University Press.

Jolly, M. (2006) 'Sincerely yours: everyday letters and the art of written relationship' in J. Maybin and J. Swann (eds) *The Art of English: Everyday Texts and Practices*. Basingstoke: Palgrave Macmillan: 280–92.

Maybin, J. (1999) 'Death row penfriends: some effects of letter writing on identity and relationships' in D. Barton and N. Hall (eds) *Letter Writing as a Social Practice*. Amsterdam: Benjamins.

Maybin, J. (2006) 'Death row penfriends: configuring time, space and self'. *Auto/Biography* 21(1): 58–69.

McKenna, K.Y.A., Green, A.S and Gleason, M.E.J. (2002) 'Relationship formation on the internet: what's the big attraction?' *Journal of Social Issues* 58(1): 9–31.

Mukarovsky, J. (1970 [1936]) *Aesthetic Function, Norm, and Value as Social Facts*, tr. M.E. Suino. Ann Arbor: University of Michigan.

Open University (2006) Recorded interview in *E301 The Art of English*.

Tannen, D. (2007) *Talking Voices: Repetition, Dialogue and Imagery in Conversational Discourse*, 2nd edn. Cambridge: Cambridge University Press.

Wilson, A. (1999) '"Absolute truly brill to see you": visuality and prisoners' letters' in D. Barton and N. Hall (eds) *Letter Writing as a Social Practice*. Amsterdam: John Benjamins.

.   look im over here: Creativity, Materiality and Representation in New Communication Technologies

Angela Goddard

Introduction

This chapter follows Koestler's well-known definition of creativity as making new connections by bringing together existing elements in a new way:

> The creative act does not create something out of nothing, like the God of the Old Testament; it combines, reshuffles and relates already existing but hitherto separate ideas, facts, frames of perception, associative contexts. (Koestler 1976: 644)

By this definition, the history of computer mediated communication (CMC) has been one of rapidly escalating creativity, as converging technologies produce ever new hybrids. However, it is no easy matter to decide where an individual's creativity begins and that of the communication tool itself ends. For example, after browsing some different books on Amazon, the online bookstore, I am offered a link to view 'the page you have created': opening the link displays an attractive arrangement of the books I have browsed. I have done nothing: I am offered the flattery of creative authorship as part of Amazon's marketing strategy, enabled by the data-handling potential of its software – a kind of machine-driven bricolage fuelled by the online shopping behaviour of my 'data double' (Haggarty and Ericson 2006: 4). To judge users' creativity, we need to understand the nature of the communication environments they are in. Only then can we hope to assess how individuals use the available resources (termed 'communication constraints' by Sellen and Harper 2001) for their own communicative purposes.

Herring's (2004) review of how approaches to analysing the language of CMC have changed during the previous decade traces an increasing focus on the individual user. In terms of creativity, an earlier interest in theatrical set pieces, such as real-time, online performances of Shakespeare (see for example Danet et al. 1995), has given way to the study of everyday task-based engagements with CMC. The title of Herring's (2004) paper, 'Slouching towards the ordinary', sums up this shift of perspective; the title also, of course, hints at a loss of technological innocence in moving away from the rather utopian early studies of cyberspace.

A focus on the 'ordinary' can be seen in Goddard (2003, 2005), which involve corpora (36,000 words in total) of 'interactive written discourse' (IWD), a label coined by Ferrara et al. (1991) to describe online 'chat'. Both corpora represent the linguistic output of students working together online in real time to complete tasks, a different group in each case: Goddard (2003) reports on students working on an international module, with a mix of UK and Swedish students; Goddard (2005) reports on a UK-only module. The task given to the international group was to compare research findings on aspects of language and culture, while for the UK-only group the task involved discussion of particular language-based topics. There were approximately 60 students enrolled on each of the modules. In both cases, the chatlogs were supplemented by face to face interviews with the participants. The 'chat' tool used can be seen in Figure 10.1.

Metaphorized Spaces

Both corpora show a range of linguistic strategies that, in formalist paradigms, have often been associated with literary texts. For example, participants regularly used metaphor to construct the nature of the 'spaces' they were in.

The metaphorical concept of the chatroom tool as a 'room' was certainly in place in public discourse (such as software advertising) by 2003; in addition, in the studies referred to here, participants were offered spaces explicitly called 'rooms', identified via different colours. It can be argued, then, that the metaphor of being in a space was normalized for them, requiring no particular individual creativity. Even so, it is interesting how consistently both groups maintained usage of what I have termed 'metaphorical deictics' (Goddard 2003): locational or directional pointers that metaphorize spaces as tangibly bounded. For example, 'in'/'here' and 'out'/'there' are regularly used by participants in both groups to locate immediate domains and those beyond their reach, respectively, even though there are no such real dimensions. So,

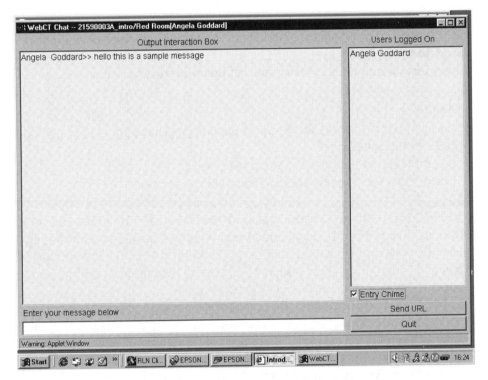

Figure 10.1   The WebCT chat tool used in Goddard (2003) and (2005)

while questions such as 'is there anyone in here?' or 'is anyone coming in?' express the idea of the speaker's immediate vicinity, other examples, such as 'anyone there?' and 'is there anybody out there?', refer to unknown spaces beyond the boundary of the speaker's room.

Sometimes, the deictic terms are employed very knowingly, to play with ideas about the materiality of the medium. For example, in the following exchange, the participants use deictic terms to question the very idea of indexicality in virtual spaces:

Sample 1

Al>there you are

Anne>no, I'm not there, I'm here

while in the example below, a participant plays with the idea of writing as a spatial indicator of presence:

Sample 2

RyanS> .   look im over here

The examples above are all from people using English as their first language; but below, Helene, a Swedish participant, co-constructs the room as a physical space with visual sight-lines. The asterisks work as a form of stage direction, indicating non-verbal behaviour and paralinguistic effects:

Sample 3

(Helene is told to ignore Dave, one of the UK participants)
Helene>*ignoring dave*
Dave>Please speak to me!!!! *crying in a corner*
Helene>Oh, sorry were you here dave? didn't notice you ...

Participants in both groups also elaborate the idea of getting to the chatroom as having involved a journey, commenting on others having possibly 'got lost' along the way, and on having had to 'go looking' for them. To summarize, participants' language choices serve to textualize the physicality of their environment – in other words, to embody their authors.

As well as metaphorizing the IWD tool as a space with physical dimensions, participants also construct those spaces linguistically as particular types of rooms or events. For example, there are constructions of pubs and bars in both sets of data: in the UK–Swedish group, one participant asks another whether she had been 'bounced' after finding herself suddenly outside of the chatroom; while in the UK-only data, one male participant playfully challenges another to a virtual fight:

Sample 4

RyanS>mr [1] are you threatening me
Devin>Yes mr [2] that is exactly what i'm doing
RyanS>come on you and me outside

The lack of visibility inherent in online spaces allows participants to play with different social and institutional roles. One type of play frequently employed by the UK students within their own groups is to ventriloquize the voices of authority figures – for example, teachers and parents. While Sample 5 suggests a classroom context, Sample 6 textualizes the home environment:

Sample 5

Andrew>Come on children lets talk about work

Sample 6

Ryan>oi clean your room
Rebecca>stop it and tidy up!

While UK students clearly found the subversive potential of inhabiting institutional voices pleasurable, these kinds of exchanges do not feature at all in the international data – presumably because of fears of having such roles taken seriously and not seen as play at all, but rather as assertions of power. The same lack of 'translatability' affects many other culturally embedded phrases, such as the following:

Sample 7

Joanne>hello hello hello

This construction is difficult to explain, even to some speakers of English (for example, speakers of English beyond the UK). It is the voice of the stereotypical English village policeman, a stock figure from countless fictional portrayals in light comedy routines. Although the phrase is curiously antique, particularly coming from young speakers now, it is quite well suited to the cyberspace context. For it articulates a whiff of suspicion of others and what they might be getting up to under cover of darkness (in other words, the invisibility of the IWD situation). An equally 'antique' voice is used by a participant to express the disappointment of being stood up in a chatroom:

Sample 8

Glyn>I came, I saw, and no one turned up

Phrases such as those in Samples 7 and 8 can be seen as classic pieces of refashioned cultural material, linguistic fragments which carry with them enough of a trace of their history of use to make them readily usable, but which also have sufficient vagueness to make them usefully plastic in their application. Both are examples of 'intertextuality', which, by Kristeva's definition, is 'the transposition of one (or several) sign-systems(s) into another', producing a new speaking position (Kristeva cited in Moi 1986: 111).

The voices being discussed here offer evidence of Bakhtin's (1981 [1935]) idea that language is heteroglossic or 'multiply voiced' because it is ideologically saturated with meanings from previous contexts of use: 'the word in language is half someone else's ... Language comes to us already populated – overpopulated – with the intentions of others' (ibid.: 293–4).

With reference to the definition of creativity at the start of this chapter, if texts are always intertextual and interdiscursive – producing, as Bakhtin suggests above, a kind of historically derived conversation that is beyond the control of individuals – then there are questions here about the extent to which individuals ever 'own' the texts they produce. For some interactional sociolinguists, such as Scollon (1998), it is the very indeterminacy resulting from there being no purely original texts or fixable voices that provides a creative space where participants can be resourceful in their negotiations of identity.

Putting the 'Real' Back into Real-time

The metaphorical strategies referred to above represent what Lakoff and Johnson (1980) term 'ontological metaphoricity' – that is, talking about something abstract as if it were concrete. Actually, the examples show something more complex than that: participants are talking about something that is concrete in the real world (such as a pub) as if it is still concrete when it is, in fact, virtual at the point of their interaction. The fact that computer games and other elaborate simulations such as Second Life have made this idea more familiar shouldn't distract us from recognizing the essential creativity of making worlds from words.

As well as textualizing people and events, the language of real-time writing is also substance itself, of course – material which appears, fills the screen, and disappears as interactions proceed. In the studies discussed here, the chatroom tools used had no sound (apart from a door chime, alerting participants to new entrants: see Figure 10.1) and there were no webcams, so the only visual aspect was the writing itself. However, it is clear that this seeming aridity did not prevent the participants from finding and mining a rich seam of materiality for playful purposes, a phenomenon which has been well observed (for example, see Danet 2001).

The materiality of writing in Goddard (2003, 2005) is expressed in a number of different ways. One of those ways is shown when participants engage in seemingly endless opening and closing routines, pointing up the essential linearity of the written medium. Elsewhere I have called this strategy 'broken record' (Gillen and Goddard 2003):

Sample 9

Laura>hey. sorry i am late, this is group nine isn't it?
RyanS>hi there
Laura>hello
RyanS>welcome
Rebecca>hello laura
RyanS>hi
Laura>hello
RyanS>hello laura
Laura>hello
Rebecca>hi

RyanS>h
Laura>hello
RyanS>.....
Rebecca>h
Laura>hello
RyanS>zzzzzz

Clearly, a static chatlog, which is a record of what the participants have left behind rather than the interaction itself, cannot easily do justice to the experience of an episode like this. There is of course much work involved here for the analyst, just in reading the chatlog and distinguishing the serial ordering of the lines from their sequential relationships (see Garcia and Jacobs 1999 on the disrupted nature of turntaking in this environment). But as a general starting point, analysts need to have experienced the medium they are studying in order to appreciate the communication constraints of the environment. As evidence of this need, it would be difficult to understand the episode above (and therefore appreciate it as play) without having had some experience of screen scrolling in populated chatrooms where participants post little and often (the average line length in the chatrooms Werry 1996 researched was six words). And only then can metalinguistic commentary such as the line below be properly understood – a participant cries out at his loss of control over the interaction, because of the scrolling rate:

Sample 10
David>help, someone for the love of god help me, stop the madness, pleaseeeeeeeeeee

The materiality of writing also comes to the fore not just in the fact of its appearance and disappearance, but in how it appears. In the example below, Alex responds to a participant who asks whether anyone is going on an exchange to the USA:

Sample 11
Alex>I would considerit
Andrew replies:
Andrew>considerit is not oneword
Alex then comes back with:
Alex>ItsanewmoneysavingschemefromMcDonalds

Reading these lines together post-event, in the chatlog, does not express the comical surprise that would have ensued as this brief interaction unfolded, line by line:

Alex>I would considerit
Andrew>conseiderit is not oneword
Alex>ItsanewmoneysavingschemefromMcDonalds

A similar 'problem' attaches to the following, where a complex pattern of sounds and symbols, woven through intertextual media and cultural references, would have gradually built, then tumbled into anticlimax, before the participants' view:

Sample 12
Glyn>your name has been added to the list you will not see another sunrise andrew
RyanS>the blair twitch project
Alex>So your a twitcher then Andy
RyanS>smack my twitch up
RyanJ>the wicked twitch of the west
RyanJ>or wirral

Speech and Writing in Cyberspace

Although these participants illustrate well the complexity of grapho-phonemics and textual representation, language use in CMC contexts is often represented apparently unproblematically as if it were speech. Certainly, some new forms of communication (such as Instant Messenger) appear to be marketed as essentially interpersonal, via labels such as 'chat' and 'buddy' lists. But academic linguists have also characterized CMC in problematic ways. For example, despite acknowledging that CMC cannot be accounted for by combining traditional binary speech/writing classifications, Crystal (2001) coins the term 'Netspeak' for CMC. Labels such as 'chat' and 'netspeak' would be of peripheral importance were it not for the fact that 'speech' and 'writing' are far from transparent concepts, so individuals operate with sets of rather hidden assumptions about their salient characteristics. For example, Goddard (2005) reports that a senior academic learning and teaching expert suggested online 'chat' in WebCT, a wholly written medium in the sense of being composed at a keyboard (see Figure 10.1), would benefit students who were better at speaking than they were at writing (see Goddard 2004 for a fuller discussion of models of speech and writing).

Although some academic sources do not label the language of CMC as explicitly as Crystal, their descriptions of CMC communication constraints are very revealing. For example, the idea of CMC as disembodied communication is at the core of the comments below. The default model seems to be face-to-face communication (i.e. spoken language), but with CMC lacking the physical embodiment of speech. This is then viewed as liberating because all the attitudinal encumbrances that regularly attend embodied interactions are removed – accent prejudice, gender and racial stereotyping, and other factors linked with acoustic and visual embodiments of 'difference': 'the most important criterion by which we judge each other in CMC conversations is one's mind rather than appearance, race, accent, etc.' (Van Gelder 1990: 130). 'Those from different cultures engaging in computer-mediated conversations do not occupy a common physical space, so they are not bounded by any particular set of cultural rules' (Ma 1996: 177).

This curiously free-floating medium where minds meet in a kind of cultural no-man's-land has CMC as a cool, rational communication operated at a remove; and yet CMC literature is awash with reports of angry outbursts (termed 'flaming' – see for example Turnage 2007). What seems to be overlooked in comments such as the quotations above is the potential for words to be a powerful vehicle for ideology, for conveying both individual identities and also deeply embedded cultural assumptions and positions. Furthermore, seeing CMC communication as lacking the kind of non-verbal cues carried by speech downplays all the ways in which writing as physical material has paralinguistic properties: Street (1988) claims writing is often seen mistakenly by linguists as 'autonomous' in this way, when everything from typeface to paper quality, let alone the relationship between writers and readers, and the context of the composition, contribute to a negotiation of meaning which is highly situated.

A different view of how language works in CMC is offered by the computer scientist Stone (1995), who challenges any simple idea of 'presence' as a physical, face-to-face phenomenon, preferring the notion that a sense of force or effect can come in a number of different ways. Summarizing the idea of presence as an impression of agency, Stone focuses scholarly attention on the work readers do to interpret the symbols they are given. Framing her views in terms of communication bandwidth, she suggests that 'narrow bandwidth' communication (e.g. computer-based communication in its present form) can produce a more intensive experience of engagement – a more heightened sense of 'presence' – than the 'wide bandwidth' variety (i.e. face-to-face interaction):

> The effect of narrowing bandwidth is to engage more of the participants' interpretive faculties...Frequently in narrow-bandwidth communication the interpretive faculties of one participant or another are powerfully, even obsessively, engaged. (Stone 1995: 93)

Multimodality

Since the era of chat tools like the WebCT room (see Figure 10.1), synchronous writing environments such as MSN (Microsoft message network), like many other CMC tools, have gone multimodal – offering visual links using webcams, sound from voice tools, and galleries of animated icons to enhance the real-time writing. In these new environments, communicators need to understand the constraints of the medium and exploit whatever is available, but they also need to be aware that interlocutors might have a different array of communication tools from themselves.

To exemplify the above, consider the chatlog in Figure 10.2, which is taken from an MSN dialogue between myself and my great-niece, Alice.

While Alice had a webcam, I didn't, so she was writing to me and communicating via the camera as well. Some lines only make sense with that knowledge – for example, Alice's 'do you like my nails?', my 'put him on I haven't seen him for ages', and my 'excellent stroke action' (in response to Alice miming her swimming moves on camera). Although I don't have a webcam to project my image to Alice, I use animated icons in response to some of her comments and actions: for example, I send her the wink 'heart' as a temporary closing move; 'lots of laughing' in response to Alice's laughter on camera and her written 'hahahahaha'; and 'kiss' at the final closing point. You could see these animations as my strategy to reciprocate the moving images she is offering me.

My comments above are evidence of my earlier note that analysts need to have experienced the environment they are studying, not necessarily in the sense of having been part of the interaction, of course, but certainly in order to read back into the chatlog what must have been part of the original experience. For example, when the wink 'heart' is sent, a big pink heart fills the screen, then splits into little hearts that flutter down the screen; while this is happening, the computer speakers produce a pulsating sound, to match the visual throbbing of the heart(s) on the screen. In getting a sense of the original text, the timings on the chatlogs are helpful, but the written lines of the chatlog cannot do justice to the multimodality of the interaction, in the same way that a transcript of speech cannot represent the whole experience of talk. In thinking about creativity, we need to make sure we have the original text in our sights, and not a one-dimensional representation that is then creatively 'performed' by the analyst.

Alice, at nine years old, is managing a very complex communication environment with some ease. She writes responses to an adult who, like many adults in adult–child interactions, takes a rather unfair number of turns (four turns in lines 5–8), and she makes an orderly arrangement of her responses to

11/03/2007	18:13:05			You have accepted the invitation to start viewing webcam.
11/03/2007	18:13:24	Alice	Angela	hello
11/03/2007	18:13:33	Angela	Alice	'elo!
11/03/2007	18:13:40	Angela	Alice	hey i can see you!!
11/03/2007	18:14:06	Alice	Angela	be back in half an hour got to hav t
11/03/2007	18:14:39	Angela	Alice	what are you having for t?
11/03/2007	18:14:46	Angela	Alice	waving at you too!
11/03/2007	18:15:08	Angela	Alice	what is your badge?
11/03/2007	18:15:19	Angela	Alice	is it for swimming?
11/03/2007	18:15:50	Alice	Angela	roast and we are having lamb and roasted beetroot mmm delicious
11/03/2007	18:16:10	Alice	Angela	its a pirates in the carribean one
11/03/2007	18:16:17	Alice	Angela	coo lovely! we are having a chicken...oh!
11/03/2007	18:16:27	Angela	Alice	ok have a good dinner - see you later!
11/03/2007	18:16:42			Angela sent the wink "Heart"
11/03/2007	18:17:08	Alice	Angela	see you in alf an our
11/03/2007	18:17:13	Angela	Alice	bye bye!
11/03/2007	18:17:39	Alice	Angela	see you in 30
11/03/2007	18:17:59	Alice	Angela	twiddle do do do
11/03/2007	18:43:10	Alice	Angela	hello r u there?
11/03/2007	18:43:30	Angela	Alice	hello, that was a quick dinner!
11/03/2007	18:43:46	Alice	Angela	how long was i?
11/03/2007	18:43:56	Angela	Alice	only about 20 minutes
11/03/2007	18:44:22	Alice	Angela	holdon heres josh he wants you to see him
11/03/2007	18:45:10	Angela	Alice	whose hand is that?
11/03/2007	18:45:21	Alice	Angela	do you like my nails?
11/03/2007	18:45:31	Angela	Alice	very nice, better than mine!
11/03/2007	18:46:18	Alice	Angela	they are glued on french manicure
11/03/2007	18:46:25	Angela	Alice	tricky
11/03/2007	18:46:45	Angela	Alice	difficult to pick your nose then
11/03/2007	18:48:00	Alice	Angela	i dont pick my nose anyway
11/03/2007	18:48:26	Angela	Alice	oh sorry of course not
11/03/2007	18:48:41	Alice	Angela	hahahahaha
11/03/2007	18:52:58			Angela sent the wink "Lots of Laughing"
11/03/2007	19:03:19	Angela	Alice	where is your bro' then?
11/03/2007	19:03:25	Alice	Angela	josh wants a wii
11/03/2007	19:03:33	Angela	Alice	a wii?
11/03/2007	19:03:48	Angela	Alice	put him on i haven't seen him for ages
11/03/2007	19:04:20	Alice	Angela	nintendo wii new playstation thingy
11/03/2007	19:04:35	Angela	Alice	hi josh!
11/03/2007	19:05:00	Angela	Alice	you've grown up a bit! hello grandad!
11/03/2007	19:05:15	Angela	Alice	grandad has grown up a lot!!
11/03/2007	19:06:11	Alice	Angela	hes 61 in 6 days!
11/03/2007	19:06:22	Angela	Alice	i know! soooo old!!
11/03/2007	19:06:44	Alice	Angela	nannys 62!
11/03/2007	19:06:52	Angela	Alice	i am taking him out for dinner, nanny as well
11/03/2007	19:07:28	Alice	Angela	yes i know!
11/03/2007	19:07:38	Alice	Angela	very lucky boy
11/03/2007	19:08:07	Angela	Alice	want to go swimming when i come down?
11/03/2007	19:08:33	Alice	Angela	yes please!
11/03/2007	19:08:50	Angela	Alice	is there a good swimming place?
11/03/2007	19:08:50	Alice	Angela	im in grade 5 level 10
11/03/2007	19:09:04	Angela	Alice	excellent stroke action
11/03/2007	19:09:04	Alice	Angela	waterside
11/03/2007	19:09:07	Angela	Alice	ok
11/03/2007	19:09:58	Angela	Alice	i'd better go and have my dinner now
11/03/2007	19:10:27	Alice	Angela	oh how long will u be?
11/03/2007	19:10:29	Angela	Alice	see you next weekend then
11/03/2007	19:10:48	Angela	Alice	not sure because i watch a TV programme on a sunday night as well - 24
11/03/2007	19:11:04	Alice	Angela	when will we go swimmnig?
11/03/2007	19:11:32	Angela	Alice	you'd better talk to grandad about his plans for the wekend, we will need to fit in with him and nanny
11/03/2007	19:12:20	Alice	Angela	ill go and tell them every thing youve said
11/03/2007	19:14:47	Angela	Alice	ok. see you later! bye bye!!!!
11/03/2007	19:15:17	Alice	Angela	bye angela
11/03/2007	19:15:24			Angela sent the wink "Kiss"

Figure 10.2   MSN chat

the many questions I fire at her. She moves easily between the keyboard and the camera; in the absence of sound, she offers me a 'song' in writing (twiddle do do do) while she has her tea. She accomplishes openings, pre-closings and closings with considerable expertise. In a context where children's communication skills are often disparaged, and particularly where new technologies are blamed for supposedly falling standards of literacy, Alice is showing creative writing skills that would surpass many of her older, more traditionally 'literate' relatives in this environment.

Metamodality

In Alice's future education or, indeed, workplace, she may encounter a more formalized version of the MSN or social networking environment she uses in her leisure time at home. Figure 10.3 represents a virtual classroom tool, where users are offered opportunities to interact in multiple ways, simultaneously.

Participants can write to each other via the text box, while also speaking and listening via headsets, interacting non-verbally via the webcam and

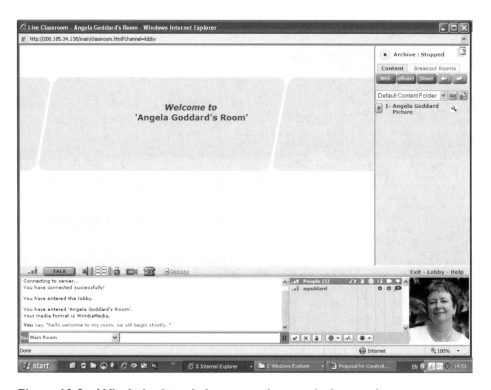

Figure 10.3   Wimba's virtual classroom (www.wimba.com)

the icon gallery, and communicating in a range of ways in the presentation area (including giving presentations, sharing documents and sites, and creating joint plans and drawings). The room owner can set a range of different communication constraints, from limiting the ability of the invitees to speak, to enabling them to take over the presentation role, with several points of affordance and limitation in-between.

In a multimodal tool such as this, the ability to exploit one mode of communication would not make an individual a creative communicator, in fact, quite the reverse. Neither would it make any sense to research the way one mode or another was used, as the modes of communication are intertwined: what A or B says in the text box might be triggered by a previous oral exchange; a diagram in the presentation area might be explained by voice and responded to via an emoticon. An individual's choice of mode will also be influenced by the repertoire available to others, as some people will have webcams and others not, some might have microphones and others not, and so on. This is not dissimilar to the way speakers might choose a lingua franca in multilingual situations.

The ability to be creative in an environment such as this virtual classroom relies on participants not just handling multiple systems running alongside each other, but handling systems that are interwoven – not so much multimodality, as *metamodality* (see Lemke 1998).

Research which focuses on one communicative element of an environment such as this won't be in a position to capture the way the communication works. Fortunately, a significant aspect of the world of new media – archiving (Gane and Beer 2008) – allows the collection of data which preserves its authenticity. In Figure 10.3 the archiving button is clearly visible and, when toggled, records all aspects of the environment as it unfolded in real time. There is now real potential, then, for collecting and analysing this kind of data in a way that does justice to the complexity of its production and to the creativity of its producers.

NOTES

1. Surname removed.
2. Surname removed.

REFERENCES

Bakhtin, M.M. (1981 [1935]) *The Dialogic Imagination*, ed. M. Holquist, trs C. Emerson and M. Holquist. Austin, TX: University of Texas Press.

Crystal, D. (2001) *Language and the Internet*. Cambridge: Cambridge University Press.

Danet, B. (2001) *Cyberpl@y: Communicating Online*. Oxford and New York: Berg.

Danet, B., Wachenhauser, T., Cividalli, A., Bechar-Israeli, H. and Rosenbaum-Tamari, Y. (1995) 'Curtain time 20:00 GMT: experiments in virtual theatre on internet relay chat'. *Journal of Computer Mediated Communication* 1(2) (http://jcmc.indiana. edu/vol1/issue2/contents.html).

Ferrara, K., Brunner, H. and Whittemore, G. (1991) 'Interactive written discourse as an emergent register'. *Written Communication* 8(1): 8–34.

Gane, N. and Beer, D. (2008) *New Media: The Key Concepts*. Oxford: Berg.

Garcia, A. and Jacobs, J. (1999) 'The eyes of the beholder: understanding the turn-taking system in quasi-synchronous computer-mediated communication'. *Research on Language and Social Interaction* 32(4): 337–67.

Gillen, J. and Goddard, A. (2003) 'Medium management for beginners: the discursive practices of undergraduate and mature novice users of internet relay chat, compared with those of young children using the telephone' in M. Bondi and S. Stati (eds) *Proceedings of the Annual Conference of the International Association for Dialogue Analysis*. Niemeyer: TFC Bingen: 219–30.

Goddard, A. (2003) '"Is there anybody out there?": creative language play and literariness in internet relay chat (IRC)' in A. Schorr, B. Campbell and M. Schenk (eds) *Communication Research and Media Science in Europe*. Berlin: Mouton De Gruyter: 325–43.

Goddard, A. (2004) '"The way to write a phone call": multimodality in novices' use and perceptions of interactive written discourse' in R. Scollon and P. Levine (eds) *Discourse and Technology: Multimodal Discourse Analysis*. Washington: Georgetown University Press: 34–46.

Goddard, A. (2005) 'Being online: linguistic strategies, involvement and interactive written discourse (IWD)'. University of Nottingham, unpublished PhD thesis.

Haggerty, K. and Ericson, R. (eds) (2006) *The New Politics of Surveillance and Visibility*. Toronto: University of Toronto Press.

Herring, S. (ed.) (1996) *Computer-mediated Communication: Linguistic, Social and Cross-cultural Perspectives*. Amsterdam: John Benjamins.

Herring, S. (2004) 'Slouching toward the ordinary: current trends in computer-mediated communication'. *New Media and Society* 6(1): 26–36.

Koestler, A. (1976) 'Association and bisociation' in J.S. Bruner, A. Jolly and K. Sylva (eds) *Play: Its Role in Development and Evolution*. London: Penguin: 643–9.

Lakoff, G. and Johnson, M. (1980) *Metaphors We Live by*. Chicago: University of Chicago Press.

Lemke, J. (1998) 'Metamedia literacy: transforming meanings and media' in D. Reinking, M. McKenna, D. Labbo, and R. Kieffer (eds) *Handbook of Literacy and Technology: Transformations in a Post-typographic World*. New Jersey: Lawrence Erlbaum.

Ma, R. (1996) 'Computer-mediated conversations as a new dimension of inter-cultural communication between East Asian and North American college students' in S. Herring (ed.) *Computer-mediated Communication: Linguistic, Social and Cross-cultural Perspectives*. Amsterdam: John Benjamins: 173–85.

Moi, T. (1986) *The Kristeva Reader*. New York: Columbia University Press.

Scollon, R. (1998) *Mediated Discourse as Social Interaction*. Harlow, Essex: Longman.

Sellen, A. and Harper, R. (2001) *The Myth of the Paperless Office*. Cambridge, MA: MIT Press.

Stone, A.R. (1995) *The War of Desire and Technology at the Close of the Machine Age*. Cambridge, MA: MIT Press.

Street, B. (1988) 'Literacy practices and literacy myths' in R. Saljö (ed.) *The Written World: Studies in Literate Thought and Action*. Berlin, London and New York: Springer-Verlag: 59–71.

Turnage, A.K. (2007) 'Email flaming behaviors and organizational conflict', *Journal of Computer-Mediated Communication* 13(1): article 3 (http://jcmc.indiana.edu/vol13/issue1/turnage.html).

Van Gelder, L. (1990) 'The strange case of the electronic lover' in G. Gumpert and S.L. Fish (eds) *Talking to Strangers: Mediated Therapeutic Communication*. Norwood, NJ: Ablex: 128–42.

Werry, C.C. (1996) 'Linguistic and interactional features of internet relay chat' in S. Herring (ed.) *Computer-mediated Communication: Linguistic, Social and Cross-cultural Perspectives*. Amsterdam: John Benjamins: 47–63.

Improvisations and Transformations across Modes: The Case of a Classroom Multimodal Box Project

KATE PAHL

Introduction

This chapter takes as its focus the study of one teacher's creative practice in the classroom. The study was from a longer project looking at creativity in the classroom, funded by Creative Partnerships. Creative Partnership in the UK was an initiative designed to enhance:

- the creativity of young people, raising their aspirations and achievements;
- the skills of teachers and their ability to work with creative practitioners;
- schools' approaches to culture, creativity and partnership working;
- the skills, capacity and sustainability of the creative industries.
  (www.creative-partnerships.com/)

Creative Partnerships has been positively evaluated and was particularly noted for its impact on pupil's motivation and learner agency (Ofsted 2006). I was funded to study the impact of a group of artists called 'Heads Together' on a small infants' school in South Yorkshire. I was particularly interested in how the teachers in the school took hold of creative practices within their teaching. As part of the research project, I interviewed all the teachers and teaching assistants and found out about their approaches to creative learning. One of the teachers, Mrs B,[1] invited me into her year 2 (six–seven year olds) classroom in order to watch an action research project she was conducting. She wanted to evaluate a creative approach to learning, which involved the making of imagined environments, using shoe boxes. The children were to work in twos or threes, collaboratively, to create panoramic environments using craft materials and to place animals appropriate to the environment within the boxes. Mrs B was taking from the original Creative Partnerships project a focus on the creative learning of the children, particularly a focus on the children's agency. She had been very impressed by the possibilities for creative learning that ensued when the children were given a choice about what they wanted to do: 'it was a big eye opener for me, that they were so capable at deciding what they wanted to learn and what they wanted to do in that session and in that project' (interview with Mrs B, November 2005). Mrs B's focus for her action research project was how this way of working could create opportunities for collaborative talk in the classroom. At her invitation, I then decided to spend one spring term coming in on a weekly basis to record the making of the boxes. Subsequently, I was invited back into the classroom, for the following spring term, to record the making of the boxes for a second time, and to see how the next intake of children made sense of this activity.

Multimodality and Creativity

Creativity in educational settings has been associated with risk taking, possibility thinking and has focused on the importance of the 'unexpected outcome' (Craft 2000, 2002; Jeffery and Craft 2004; Jeffery 2006; Burnard et al. 2006). In this study, I investigated the talk that surrounded the making of the children's boxes, here seen as multimodal texts. I focus specifically on the transformations of meaning across modes, particularly across from talk to a multimodal text and back again.

Communication can be realized in a number of modes (Kress 1997) including linguistic, visual and three dimensional, tactile and gestural. I explore here how the linguistic and visual interrelate. Flewitt (2008) used the term 'multimodal literacies' to signal how literacy practices seep across modes and how meaning cannot be limited to one mode. I describe the co-creation of meaning across modes, and I locate creativities in those transformations and transitions. In this analysis, I draw on the work of the New Literacy Studies that presents the concepts of 'literacy events' and 'literacy practices' to describe observable occurrences where reading and writing has a role (events), together with the sometimes unobservable, taken for granted *practices* that are drawn on when the event takes place (Barton and Hamilton 1998; Street 2000). I consider ways in which the concept of 'multimodal events' and 'multimodal practices' can also be drawn up to look at the making of multimodal texts (Street 2008). The study was a classroom ethnography, that is, it involved close analysis of linguistics and multimodal practices in one classroom, over time, with an attention to meaning, cultural processes and practices and researcher reflexivity (Bloome et al. 2004).

Returning to the idea of creativity as something connected to wider possibilities, to unexpected outcomes, I consider a particular proposition that creativity can be considered in relation to moments of *improvisation*. The concept of improvisations implies a shift from the regular and everyday to something new. Therefore, I needed to consider the regular, everyday ways of being and doing. I looked to practice theory, from Bourdieu, to describe acquired and settled dispositions that can be observed within practice (Bourdieu 1977, 1990). Bourdieu focused on *habitus* as a word to describe everyday texts and practices, as described here in relation to the Algerian context of the Kabyle in the 1950s. Bourdieu said of the Kabyle child:

> Whether in verbal products such as proverbs, sayings, gnomic poems, songs or riddles or in objects such as tools, the house or the village, or in practices such as games, contexts of honour, gift exchange or rites, the material that the Kabyle child has to learn is the product of the systematic application of a small number of principles coherent in practice. (Bourdieu 1990: 74)

While the children I watched came from a different cultural context, I was interested in how they responded to existing ways of doing and expressing things, their *habitus*. I explore what happens when children improvise upon a settled textual reality and make changes in this setting, either within a multimodal text or within the accompanying talk. I will relate these improvisations to the teacher's ways of being and doing in the classroom, her *pedagogic habitus* (Grenfell 1996). Grenfell identified the *pedagogic habitus* as being the ways in which teachers made sense of what they absorbed in the field of the classroom. I was able to observe shifts in the way the children responded and then changed and improvised upon what the teacher suggested. My argument here is that creativity as observed within classrooms can be seen as a kind of improvisation upon this *pedagogic habitus* that can lead to what Craft and Jeffery (2004) describe as 'the unexpected outcome'.

Methodology

This slice of data comes from right at the end of the two-year project in which I became interested in how children realized their ideas within multimodal texts. I watched the making of these texts for two hours a week during the spring term of 2006, and then watched the same project unfold, with the same teacher but different children, in the spring term of 2007. My aim was to record the making of the boxes, using digital cameras and audio tape, together with fieldnotes and interviews with the children about the boxes after they were made. Background data were also collected in the form of in-depth interviews from all the teachers in the school about their experiences of the Creative Partnerships intervention project. The methodology for the study included:

- interviews;
- participant observations written up in the form of fieldnotes;
- audio-taped data;
- photographic evidence;
- the teacher's notes on the project.

The resulting dataset included about 100 photographs from both years, and detailed observations of classroom practice, together with follow-up interviews with selected groups of children from both years. I analysed the data by looking specifically at the relationship between their talk and their multimodal texts, and by combing the data for patterns which showed both similarities and variations from the original plan by the teacher, Mrs B. I was interested in when the children deviated from the plans they had originally made for the boxes, and how they carried out their plans in relation to their interests at the time. As I looked closely at the children's talk, I considered how it related to specific moments of multimodal meaning making. As this talk was collaborative, and often involved up to three children, the boxes themselves could be understood as being creations of three separate individuals. Untangling these threads and presenting the data in relation to individual children uncovered moments where children's voices carried other voices, and held different experiences, from home and school. These echoes of other voices, which I called 'dialogic' from Maybin's (2006) work, were then mapped back on to the making of the boxes.

Children's Voices in Multimodal Texts

In a previous article (Rowsell and Pahl 2007) I argued that it was possible to view children's identities and their ways of being and doing as being 'sedimented' within their multimodal texts. In this chapter, I argue that, if children's voices and concerns can be considered as being realized within multimodal texts, a richer account of creative meaning making can be developed that has implications for educational work with children's language and literacy. I look at how the children's ways of doing and being, their dispositions, in Bourdieu's (1990) terms, acquired over time within home settings, could be discerned, sedimented within this text and then animated and turned into a narrative that reflected their social life and concerns. In my analysis of this, I argue, from Maybin (2006), that children's talk has a dialogic, intertextual quality, echoing others' voices and drawing on many other conversations and concerns. I consider the question of what happens when we apply this analysis to the multimodal text as well as to the talk. Can the object itself carry a fluid, dialogic element, including signalling shifts in meaning? The making of the box and the creation of meaning as it resided within the box gave the children's talk a further material dimension. The box itself instantiated some of this talk, and watching the process of making enabled me to see how this was constructed both within the talk and within the box, each speaking to the other. The box itself then appears more fluid, less a solid, created object, but an object with a history that has shifted in the process of its making. Its meaning is also contested and the narratives the children produced animated different parts of the boxes they created.

I will present two contrastive instances of practice. One, from the first year of the project, was described by the teacher as an example of creativity, being an instance of successful problem solving in the material world. The second example is an account of the way the box construction created a new set of narratives that crossed domains and led to new ways of being and doing in the classroom – an improvisation on the *pedagogic habitus*.

The Box Project: Year 1

When the teacher introduced the box project to the children, she encouraged them to look at what her previous class had done and point out aspects of how they had created the boxes. She also researched her own practice in creating opportunities for the children to make choices about the art they created. In her own taped notes, which she then wrote up, she recorded herself as pointing this out to the children, concerning one box made previously:

> Mrs B: Can you see the paint effects? They have used dark blue, and little light blue splodges to create the splashes. They tried out different ways to create a waterfall, and then decided in the end to use paint.

The children encountered many challenges concerning the actual realization of their vision. One pair, who were making an ocean environment, struggled to realize their visions. They were trying to get seaweed to stand up and also to get paint to stick to acetate to create a see-through effect:

Kate (researcher): Can you just explain to me what you are doing?

Emma: I am testing the masking tape to see if paint will stick to it.

(Fieldnotes, 20 February 2006)

Here, Emma adopts an almost scientific evaluative approach to her material problem-solving using the term 'testing'. However, as she worked she announced to me:

Emma: I don't think that is going to work.

Kate: Why not?

Emma: Because it is all bubbling up.

The girls continue to struggle with making the box do what they want it to. Later on in the same session, Emma said to me:

Emma: The seaweed's going um pretty well. Instead of putting it in the middle of the box we decided to put it in the back of the box.

So, it's going all well but the problem with our animals is that they won't stand up.

(Ibid.)

The box was coming together, and at the end of this discussion Emma says:

Emma: It looks like a good effect, the bubbles – all the fishes swimming here...

Echoing Mrs B's focus on the effects of the boxes, and on trying different solutions to material problems, the girls are working with Mrs B's *pedagogic habitus*, with her focus on the children testing, trying out, to create unexpected effects. Problem solving was the focus of the teaching. When I returned to talk to the two girls, they had thought of a solution, which was to mix glue with paint:

Sophie: First we got a box and my partner was Emma. Secondly we painted our box and then we added some things to it. My partner tried to make seaweed and we couldn't. We tried everything we could think of and then teacher Mrs B had a bolt of lightning and she thought of something and we did it but we haven't tried it yet but I think it will work. I hope so.

Emma: Because we tried some see-through crunchy tissue paper, and that didn't work, we wanted it to stand up and it didn't.

Kate: I remember.

Emma: And then we tried...

Kate: Sellotape?

Sophie: What was it, for the seaweed? We did Blu-tack.

Kate: Blu-tack!

Emma: We did Blu-tack to stick it down, well that's when we thought of the acetate and Mrs B thought of the acetate. We didn't know how to stick it up for itself, because we wanted it to look real, so we...

Sophie: Then we painted like the acetate and stuck it to the box.

Emma: But we needed to put glue into it because um paint would just peel off.

(Fieldnotes and tape, 20 February 2006)

Figure 11.1   Image of box

The created box has a translucent quality. The seaweed is represented at the back, and it is see-through. The box was presented as an example of a triumph over materially problematic conditions. The focus was the multimodal text as a site of creativity in relation to materiality within the box and how to create the 'good effect' of the seaweed standing up. The *pedagogic habitus* created by Mrs B was focused on creative problem solving in the material world. The account of creativity was focused on that ability to problem-solve. However, in the second year, the focus was less on the making of the boxes, and more on their meaning.

The Box Project: Year 2

In the second year, the box-making activity was resumed in the spring term and I came in to watch. I focused on particular groups of children, representing about half of the total classroom of 24, about 12 children consisting of four groups of three: two boys' groups and two girls' groups. I was looking at how the children made sense of the teacher's instructions and their multimodal text making in relation to their talk. In the discussion below, I focus on the work of three girls, Coral, Savannah and Taylor, who decided to take the ocean as their starting point. I watched the girls paint the box and then create a small hill using newspaper and masking tape. Slowly this box hill took shape (see Figures 11.2 and 11.3)

Figure 11.2   First stages of box

Figure 11.3   Hill with masking tape on it

The girls' plan for the hill was that they would paint over it:

Savannah: Here we are going to paint over the masking tape so it makes it look like/
Taylor: /We are going to put some fish in the seabed.

(Tape, 13 March 2007)

Figure 11.4 shows the hill covered with paint.

Figure 11.4   Box with paint

As it took shape, the creatures within it became animated:

Savannah: We could put the dolphins, we could put the dolphins.
Taylor: We could put the light in there because it makes it light.
Savannah: Because the fish will swim into there anyway (higher pitch).
Taylor: No they could swim, the dolphins could be peeping through there couldn't they (pause). It's gonna have to be ripped a bit like that.
Savannah: No the dolphins sleep there, Taylor, it can't be like that.
Taylor: Yes that's where the dolphins sleep.

(Ibid.)

The hill is transformed into a place where the fish can swim into, a bit like an aquarium. The rip in the hill enables a discussion about the possibility for the hill to act as a bedroom, out of which the dolphins could be peeping through. After some discussion with Savannah who is keen to make the hill a bedroom for the dolphins, Taylor concedes the point, while describing the dolphins as 'peeping through', much as girls peep through curtains when they wake up in the morning.

As the vision emerges in the taped discussion, aspects of the box come alive. Here Savannah and Taylor are talking about how they have transformed the box into a school:

Taylor: And we have made a bit of a school up haven't we?
Savannah: Yeah well the school we should have made it up by now, but we are
              going to make it now, we are going to make it up over there.

(Ibid.)

The talk between the girls began to emerge in relation to the final box, as a place of play, where the dolphins slept, and also a school (see Figure 11.5).

Figure 11.5   Finished box

At the end of the project, I invited the girls to discuss the box with me. This discussion took place in a quiet moment during breaktime. Most of the information was volunteered, with a very small amount of initial questioning from me. The girls began a story that then described the complexities of the meanings within the box environment. All three were present at this discussion with me – whereas the earlier discussions had involved just Taylor and Savannah, being in the middle stages of the project. Coral was now back, and her words often echoed the driving narrative from Savannah and Taylor:

Kate (researcher): Are you the ones that had a dolphin school?
Girls: Yeah! A dolphin school.
Coral: Because the mummy is going to take the baby to school.
Kate: I love this.

Taylor: Yes, that's right, it's really close. Because it only lives down here (pause). We did the jellyfish, er one's the sister, one's the brother, one's the baby and one's the mum.

Coral: That's the baby.

Taylor: Yeah and that's the sister and that's the brother and that's the other big sister.

(Taped discussion, 17 April 2007,
opening section lines 21–48)

This opening discussion presents an image of a family, including a sister, a brother, a baby and a mum, all described as residing in the box. The girls were prepared to view the dolphin school in relation to the different sea creatures that were within the box:

Taylor: Because the dolphins are going first and then they are all going different ways.

Savannah: And then the jellyfish, then…

Taylor: Then the starfish.

Savannah: No then, jellyfish, oct…er sea turtle, jell … er starfish.

But these creatures also have human characteristics and traumas:

Coral: We did 'em all in different places so then one can be wi' each baby.

Kate: I love this. This is just brilliant. What I love is that you have got these children. And these families you have got the starfish family and the dolphins.

Savannah: The daddy's died.

(Ibid., discussion lines 65–76)

Savannah's comment that the daddy's died (which has echoes of the film *Finding Nemo* which also involves an absent parent and a trauma of loss) comes in at the end of a long discussion as to who pairs off with each child. Each of the animals is to go in line, and each has its own child attached. Savannah is uncertain as to which of the animals goes first. The children spent a lot of time determining the way in which the animals were to be ordered. The key determinant for the girls' decision to make their box environment a dolphin school was the material quality of the hill, here described as a rock, that enabled the action to take place:

Taylor: We did the school because um we just wanted to make, well we decided that we wanted it to be a rock, but then we changed us mind to put it to a school because there's a door.

(Ibid., lines 107–10)

The decision to make the rock into a door for the dolphins to emerge from then created the imaginary space of the dolphin school. When I analysed these sequences, finding patterns across the talk and the boxes as I saw them in the images, I found that, in some cases, the talk was realized within the multimodal text. For example, in the earlier discussion, Taylor had said to Savannah:

Taylor: No they could swim, the dolphins could be peeping through there couldn't they (pause). It's gonna have to be ripped a bit like that.

(Talk, 13 March 2007)

This decision to make the hill have a rip so that there was a door for the dolphins to go in created an affordance for the subsequent play. Shells were used not to denote the ocean but to lead the play back to the imaginary school:

Savannah: We did some shells so then they can pretend they are paper and pencils.

(Taped discussion, 17 April 2007, line 91)

The box remains stable as an ocean environment, but then has immense possibilities for play both as a home, where the dolphins sleep and the daddy dies, and as a school. The box is an instantiation of dialogic talk in which a number of possibilities are present. The box is a home, where you can sleep, and, at the same time, the box is a school; and the children describe a world where the dolphins go to school and learn to read and write:

Taylor:	Um the big shells are for writing on and the little ones are for the pencils.
Kate:	Oh for the pencils?
Coral:	Twenty-four shells on there (starts counting 1 2 3 4 5 6 7 8 9 10 11 12 13). Sound of coughing. Coral has been off sick.)
Coral:	1234 (counting)
Savannah:	They don't all go to school.
Taylor:	Yeah?
Savannah:	The babies don't.

(Ibid., lines 93–101)

While Taylor pursues the *school* idea, Savannah, whose initial vision involved the dolphins sleeping in the hill, continued to pursue the *home* theme of the babies, who obviously cannot go to school. However, each girl also backs up the other's vision for the box. Savannah provides the idea of shells used for paper and pencils and Taylor provides an account of the family at home. Coral suggests that the baby's mummy was the teacher, thus mingling both home and school. Their voices mingle in the created multimodal text. The box then carries both home and school meanings within it. The girls describe their scenario to me while, at the same time, arguing about it:

Savannah: That's the playground you come in/
Coral: /One jellyfish is the teacher.
Savannah: No no no no no no no no the dolphin is the teacher.
Coral: Yeah and that's the baby's mummy was the teacher (pause) because she weren't.
Taylor: Because she weren't last.
Coral: I know.
Taylor: She was born first and then that then that then that then that then that then that then that then that then ... that that that!

(underlining indicates strong emphasis; ibid., lines 111–18)

This final discussion, which came at the end of the dolphin school discussion, was a focus for the girls, who listened to it over and over again, laughing at the interchange about whose turn it was to go first above.

Analysis and Concluding Discussion

When I came to reflect on how this data could help illuminate a discussion of creativity, I decided to separate out the processes involved in the improvisations and transformations that occur around the meanings within the box:

Stage 1	*Stage 2*	*Stage 3*	*Stage 4*	*Stage 5*
Pedagogic habitus instantiated in multimodal text	Children shifting the meaning to create the idea of a 'home'	Improvisation through creation of 'school'	New thread comes through – Savannah's vision of the home	Taylor's vision of the school; Coral's mummy is the teacher
Fish in seabed	Dolphins sleep inside the hill	The dolphin school	The family at home	The family go to school
Following teacher instructions – fishes are just fishes	Dolphins are asleep in the hill (Savannah) and peep out from the hill (Taylor)	We are going to make it up over there (Savannah)	We did the jellyfish, er one's the sister, one's the brother, one's the baby and one's the mum	Um the big shells are for writing on and the little ones are for the pencils

In a way that is reminiscent of the girls' stories in Steadman's (1983) study of working-class girls writing in *The Tidy House*, one narrative within the dolphin school text is the question of what birth order the children occupy and how this birth order then dictates their relationship to school and home. One of the aspects of the analysis was realizing how complex the thread was, that the three voices of the meaning-makers intertwined, went apart and then came together within the multimodal text which acted as a trace of these decisions. The text's improvisatory quality comes from the complex meanings that are inscribed within the box. Unlike the year 1 girls, who focus on how to solve problems in the *material* world, these girls are focusing on how to solve problems in the *social* world, connected to birth order.

Returning to Emma and Sophie, who solved the problem of the seaweed that couldn't stand up in year 1 of the research project, it is clear that creativity can be associated with inventiveness, with a focus on craft and solving material problems in new and unexpected ways. In year 2, the girls imbued their box with a set of intertwined and connected stories, thus animating the box in a new way. The process of analysing this data made me realize that if a definition of creativity focused on improvisation of the *habitus*, then moments of transformation – when the meaning maker does something different with the expected text, within a set of structures and dispositions built up over time – can be pinned down and focused upon. This understanding of the *habitus* can be built up through classroom ethnography, and can be identified within texts, practices and discourses. Longitudinal classroom ethnography can unravel these instances of practice and consider them in relation to existing discourses, ideologies and practices.

In some instances, these will be different and competing. The field of play, in this case the classroom, can be understood as crossed with different discourses, ideologies and practices. In this example, the teacher, Mrs B, carried one conception of creativity, that of profiling learner agency and inventiveness in material practices, into her practice. She built up the *habitus* of creating boxes over many years, and then profiling learner agency and decision making in relation to the boxes. Her initial focus was on ways of solving creative problems within the material world of the box environments.

However, the children brought in diverse discourses, ideologies and practices into the field of the classroom. In the case of the dolphin school, I concluded that the girls were improvising, and their improvisation was on the form and function of the boxes themselves. While in year 1, the girls were able to improvise on the *material* form of the box, in year 2 they improvised upon the *meanings* inscribed into the box. This improvisation was connected to the material affordance of the box (the hill where the dolphins slept) as well as to the imagined lived realities instantiated in the talk. By looking at the multimodal event (the creation of the box) together with the multimodal practice (the box project looked at over two years) the improvisations upon the practice emerge. Creativities can be associated with these deviations and digressions that can be extended and developed across modes and across domains of practice.

NOTE

1. I would like to thank Sally Bean for her generosity in sharing her creative teaching with me.

REFERENCES

Barton, D. and Hamilton, M. (1998) *Local Literacies: Reading and Writing in One Community*. London: Routledge.

Bloome, D., Carter, S.P., Christian, B.M., Otto, S. and Shuart-Farris, N. (2004) *Discourse Analysis and the Study of Classroom Language and Literacy Events: A Microethnographic Perspective*. London: Routledge.

Bourdieu, P. (1977) *Outline of a Theory of Practice*, tr. R. Nice. Cambridge: Cambridge University Press.

Bourdieu, P. (1990) *The Logic of Practice*, tr. R. Nice. Cambridge: Polity Press.

Burnard, P., Craft, A. and Cremin, T., with Duffy, B., Hanson, R., Keene, R., Haynes, L. and Burns, D. (2006) 'Documenting possibility thinking: a journey of collaborative inquiry'. *International Journal of Early Years Education* 14(3): 243–62.

Craft, A. (2000) *Creativity across the Primary Curriculum: Framing and Developing Practice*. London: Routledge.

Craft, A. (2002) *Creativity and Early Years Education*. London: Continuum.

Flewitt, R. (2008) 'Multimodal literacies' in J. Marsh and E. Hallett (eds) *Desirable Literacies: Approaches to Language and Literacy in the Early Years*. London: Sage: 122–39.

Grenfell, M. (1996) 'Bourdieu and initial teacher education: a post-structuralist approach' *British Educational Research Journal*. 22 (3): 287–303.

Jeffrey, B. (ed.) (2006) *Creative Learning Practices: European Experiences*. London: Tuffnell Press.

Jeffrey, B. and Craft. A. (2004) 'Creative teaching and teaching for creativity: distinctions and relationships' *Educational Studies* 30(1): 77–87.

Kress, G. (1997) *Before Writing: Rethinking the Paths to Literacy*. London: Routledge.

Maybin, J. (2006) *Children's Voices: Talk, Knowledge and Identity*. Basingstoke: Palgrave Macmillan.

Ofsted (2006) *Creative Partnerships: Initiative and Impact*. Ofsted. (www.ofsted.gov.uk/Ofsted-home/Publications-and-research/Browse-all-by/Education/Leadership/Management/Creative-Partnerships-initiative-and-impact).

Pahl, K. (1999) *Transformations: Children's Meaning Making in a Nursery*. Stoke on Trent: Trentham Books.

Pahl, K. (2007) 'Creativity in events and practices: a lens for understanding children's multimodal texts'. *Literacy* 41(2): 86–92

Rowsell, J. and Pahl, K. (2007) 'Sedimented identities in texts: instances of practice'. *Reading Research Quarterly* 42(3): 388–401

Steadman, A. (1983) *The Tidy House: Little Girls' Writing*. London: Virago.

Street, B.V. (2000) 'Literacy events and literacy practices: theory and practice in the new literacy studies', in M. Martin-Jones and K. Jones (eds) *Multilingual Literacies: Reading and Writing Different Worlds*. Amsterdam: John Benjamins.

Street, B.V. (2008) 'New literacies, new times: developments in literacy studies', in B.V. Street and N. Hornberger (eds) *Encyclopedia of Language and Education, vol. 2: Literacy*. New York: Springer: 3–14.

12

Hybridity in the Mind and on the Page: Genre, Words, Music and Narrative

Michelene Wandor

> This is the story of dreams
> of promised lands
> and broken promises
> of prophecies and of the music of dreams

My long poem, *The Music of the Prophets* (Wandor 2006a), exists in a number of forms and media. In print, it is an extended 'narrative' poem, structured to interweave chronology, figurative moments and themes. For poetry readings, I select and link sections to create a live performance-narrative. Combined with music (of which more later), it is a script for a different sort of live performance, involving me (words and viola da gamba) and a singer. This last is hard to characterize precisely: it's not conventional dramatic performance, not a straight poetry reading or a conventional chamber concert. In print it is permanent, in performance it passes on the air and ear as you see and hear it. It is, in many senses, a hybrid:

> This is the story of two people
> the story of two peoples
> the story of two men

The impetus for *The Music of the Prophets* was the anniversary of the resettlement of the Jews in England, in the mid-seventeenth century. I received a grant from the European Association for Jewish Culture. I've written/performed a number of words/music pieces, and I can only devote the time to them with a commission of some kind. The process involved extensive research – into the history of the Jews in England, Oliver Cromwell and revolutionary England, Menasseh ben Israel and the history of the Jews in Holland. I collected music, which included pieces by John Hingeston, Master of Oliver Cromwell's Musick, along with some John Dowland (earlier in the seventeenth century), Purcell (later), and some from the Henry VIII Songbook (a century earlier):

> Menasseh ben Israel
> and Oliver Cromwell
> sit in the coffee house
> as ordinary as
> a merchant banker
> an insurance underwriter
> a broker
> a musician
> a journalist

As I researched these pieces, I began writing and playing. I moved from words to music, explored within each mode, always aware of the discreteness of each process, and of the need to combine them. However, I have no way of being certain of the order in which all these happened. Everything is constantly in my mind, even when I am working on one single element. There is synchronicity, and there is discreteness, and everything you have just read is very, very post hoc. Even if I had made notes as I worked, recording the 'process' as it seemed to be happening, these would only be very approximate, and could never catch its innerness – *inscape*, perhaps, to borrow rather freely from Gerard Manley Hopkins. I 'think' performance and publication, and I structure and pace with an awareness of the ways in which music and words create different and complementary rhythms:

> a small coffee cup
> delicate bone china
> thick black Turkish coffee

There has to be an overall, cumulative narrative. A series of narratives, rather, which are told in poetic, rather than prose fiction tropes, even where they convey factual information. These parts of the overall 'story' build, and are interspersed with more contemplative, evocative (poetic?) sections. At the same time, music intersperses and underlays the words. Narrative, pace and rhythm are of different kinds in music, poetry and prose fiction. In the end, no description of this kind can do more than whet the appetite to see the performance and/or read the poem. This is still a post hoc blurb, as it were.

I choreograph everything before rehearsals; each piece of music is performed in its entirety at some point in the programme, and I also fragment elements to underlay some of the words. There is a script – a complex cut-and-paste of words and music. The final, performed version (and the words for subsequent publication) is clean, cleared of all uncertainty – a small number of pages, relative to the amassed notes, fragments, drafts, writing, crossings out, scribbling, rewriting. While some people might find these fascinating, they are – in an important sense – irrelevant, superseded by the complete piece, towards which all thinking and writing tends. This is not merely my own feeling about my work. There is a broader, more general issue at stake here. Literary scholarship is fascinated by drafts of manuscripts, marginalia, the writing and rewriting of famous, canonic works. Such documents command high prices from university archives. The fascination with handwriting – the sheer messiness of composition – has a real symbolic value: by looking at handwriting, seeing crossed-out words, scribbles, we might seem to be getting 'closer' to the person, to what he or she was actually thinking at the time. But we are not. All it can really do is show that, empirically, T. S. Eliot (say) crossed out one word and substituted another. He may have been thinking about shopping (did he go shopping?), he may just have not 'liked' that word at that moment, he may have changed his mind, but couldn't be bothered to change the word back. We will never know. Even if he tells us in a memoir, we do not know whether he is telling the truth. Or, even, indeed, if that 'truth' is knowable.

No writer can really know, because (*pace* everything post- and pre-Freud, and *pace* Horatio) there is always more in the mind than we can ever know. We know how wide the gap can be between intention and execution (between synopsis and realization, as it were). To have what the mind and transformative labour of writing has produced in the completed poem, novel, story, play, is the greatest privilege we can have. This is what we still call the 'text', even with the challenges of literary/cultural theory. Because the imaginative mode of thought – which is what produces imaginative writing – is invisible: it takes place in the mind. We think. We imagine. Material is sought and brought into the mind; material arrives unbidden in the mind. Material is processed invisibly in the mind. We apply our interests, skills and understanding of conventions, and we produce the evidence of what has gone on in the mind: the material artefact: the writing. The book. The poem. The drama:

> This is the story of two people
> the story of two peoples
> the story of two people
> and coffee

coffee is the alchemy which turns life into gold and treasure
coffee tastes like home

coffee is good for the soul

do Jews have souls?
is there coffee in the afterlife?
your afterlife or mine?

There is a literary phenomenon which might appear to contradict this. This is the preface, which belongs to academic and/or non-fiction books. Here the book's thesis might be summarized, the argument presented, and sometimes an account of the practicalities (and difficulties) of the process explained. In biography, there might be acknowledgement of the support of interested parties, the sources of the material (letters, etc.), perhaps how hard it was to get hold of them, or why someone withheld permission for them to be quoted. Such introductory material can be enlightening about the circumstances accompanying the writing, and help to bolster the certifiable validity of the work – its empirical justifications, as it were. However, it will not be an account of the thinking or writing and rewriting process – of the inner workings of the author's mind:

Had we but world enough and time
this leisure, Cromwell, were no crime
we would sit down, drink our coffee
and pass our friendship's day

Nevertheless, people continue to be fascinated by the 'creative' process in the arts. Where does this new thing, which did not exist before, which is (in some way, even when pastiched) different from everything which existed before, come from? To ask a historian 'Where do you get your inspiration from?' might sound insulting, as if he or she hadn't put in years of hard work before writing a book. 'What interests you about the French Revolution?' might be equally silly, since the very existence of the book is predicated on the fact that the event is interesting or important, and an assumption that there may be new material, new arguments, new interpretations. And yet, at poetry or fiction readings, the same questions recur with dreary (I am afraid to say!) regularity: 'Where do you get your inspiration from?' 'Who is your favourite author?' (as if that means you want to imitate him or her). 'Do the characters write themselves?' 'Who are your influences?' While each of these questions might be interesting to deconstruct, they all home in on attempts to grasp the ungraspable, the intractable, the invisible. I suspect the real subtext to these questions is: 'How do you do it? If you tell me your secret, then I will be able to do it.'

> thou, by the Thames' side
> should'st rubies find: I, by Holland's flat tides
> should speak and write

Perhaps I could be accused of falling into the same trap: by saying that the process is unknowable, I might be read as saying that the imagination is ruled by mysterious forces, mystical processes, magical spirits, the genius which we all desire, and which seems so elusive. The cliché that creative writing can be 'taught' but not 'learned' is based on the assumption that 'genius' is either there or not – unpredictable, incomprehensible and infinitely desirable. However, the matter of 'genius' (a soubriquet which can apply to all kinds of human endeavour, not just literature) is a diversion from what is really important in creative writing as it is in creative writing pedagogy:[1]

> theologians may explain the world
> our job is to change it

This brings us back to practical matters of genre choice and narrative. I write prose, poetry, drama – as well as reviewing and writing non-fiction. Many professional writers similarly combine and cross genres. Our raw materials are language; different contexts demand different intellectual/mind approaches, and different deployments of language to suit different conventions. The advent of theories of the text have not intrinsically altered this. Despite (perhaps more easily because of?) semiology, it is still perfectly possible (indeed, necessary) to delineate the differences between prose fiction and poetry. We can talk about how language is used differently (literal versus figurative), how meanings and associations accumulate differently (narrative links spelled out versus narrative connections suggested). I argue that all students and teachers of creative writing need this bedrock of knowledge, understanding and practice in different genres, in order to know why they gravitate or opt for any particular one. What makes someone prefer to write poetry, rather than stories? Why do some people lean towards writing drama, where everything is created through dialogue?

I am not at all sure I can answer these questions satisfactorily in relation to myself. I read long books, fiction and non-fiction. At school I was gripped by seventeenth-century poetry (including Shakespeare), and, later, the linguistic density of Hopkins and early twentieth-century modernism and imagism. I love performance, and at one point wanted to be an actress. I have recently finished my first novel, and it is interesting that it has taken me so long to get round to it. I did co-write a novel with Sara Maitland, some twenty years ago. I have written four long, elaborate, non-fiction books. Short stories and poetry may have fewer words, but that doesn't make them 'easier'. In the past few years, I have also written long poems. Perhaps the distillation of imaginative intensity appeals to me as much as does constructing longer non-fiction books: these have been impelled by arguments I have with dominant ideas and practices. I have written books about post-war theatre and gender, and, in addition to the creative writing book already cited, I have written *The Art of Writing Drama* (Wandor 2008a).

Choice of genre is likely to be made on the basis of individual predilection, circumstance, understanding or curiosity. In my case, my choices of genre depend (except for short poems and, occasionally, stories) on who is commissioning me. If it is radio, it will be drama; if an academic publisher, it will be a work of non-fiction. Of course, I make pre-choices about whom I approach for what, but, in principle, any 'idea' or subject can be channelled into any genre:

> This is the story of dreams

This has consequences in terms of any consideration of 'narrative'. At the most superficial level, everything has narrative: every piece of writing is constructed with order and sequence, chosen and developed. Cause and effect may be more or less explicit. Whatever the resonances of intertextuality, each piece of writing only has one beginning and one end. Every piece of writing, as Rob Pope (2005: xv) has succinctly pointed out, is 'all middle'. Our dominant assumptions about narrative (from which narratology takes its cue) come from prose fiction. The dominant English-language fictional mode is still realism. Linear concepts of cause and effect, expressed over some sort of time scale, in some kind of order and sequence, create a narrative, a story, in which events succeed each other in a kind of logic which results from our cognition of time, events and their several causes. The concept of cause-and-effect in structuring fictional narratives is paramount, whether defined by psychology, character or certain fictional tropes – e.g. the imperatives of the detective story, the gothic thriller, the popular romance. This is also the case, even where the structure itself plays with chronology – flashbacks, flashforwards, games with tenses and points of view. There is always some sort of narrative, even if it has to be de- or reconstructed retrospectively:

> This is the story of dreams
> of promised lands
> and broken promises
> of prophecies and of the music of dreams

In music, the 'logic' of any narrative is determined by imperatives which are technically different from those of verbal language. These derive from the musical systems in operation in any given composition. Modal music established a hierarchy of harmonies, which was modified by diatonic music. Both hierarchies established certain expectations to do with excursions round a dominant key. There is no narrative in music in the sense that we use the term in relation to language, where 'meaning' is the driving imperative. Music is not representational (except insofar as it might imitate other sounds) and is thus not 'about' anything, except itself. Music is thought to 'convey' different (emotional/mood) associations, but this is culturally relative. For example, in Western culture, funerals are accompanied by slow-moving music, in a low tessitura – in other cultures the music might be fast and high. So musical 'narrative' and meaning is culture and convention-specific. Programmatic titles (popular from the nineteenth century onwards) may gear us into an associative link, but cannot 'make' the music 'tell a story'. We can impose any story we wish onto any piece of music. Attempts in the eighteenth century to construct dictionaries of emotional affect (e.g. G major is a happy key) were contradictory and constantly challenged by the realities of actual compositions and interpretations of them. Music, while it is internally entirely regulated by time and timing (rhythm), does not make explicit references to time. It is not deictic in the sense that prose narrative is: things take place *somewhere* at *some time*, involving *specific* people/characters/ human agents:

> This is the story of two people
> the story of two peoples

My involvement with Renaissance and baroque music has been an extremely exciting one. Although words and music are notionally combined in opera (fictional narrative in words, against musical arcs), musicians generally handle verbal language very crudely indeed, where they might write their own libretti (though I would exclude from this assertion composers of stage musicals – Stephen Sondheim, for example). The language of musical criticism tends to be either technical (Schenkerian) or metaphorical and vaguely 'descriptive', full of emotional tugs and hooks. In order to explore or understand this better, as well as hone my performance skills, I went to a conservatoire in London for five years, as a (very!) mature student.

This training augmented my skills and expanded my artistic production. I made – composed – wrote – developed a series of seamless music-and-words performance and publication pieces: researching Salamone Rossi, Jewish composer in early seventeenth-century Mantua. I wrote a poem ('Writing Salamone Rossi') (Wandor 2006b), which wove between the pieces of music, seamlessly, with a chitarrone (bass lute) playing chords under the poem (which I read, as well as playing in the ensemble). Audiences were not given a chance to applaud, and we stayed onstage throughout, much as the cast of a play would. I had come to dislike the bittiness of concert convention, with musicians trotting on and off, taking bows between pieces, dressing up in evening clothes, checking out the audience to see where their friends were sitting. I wanted to create a new active relationship between words and music, and to challenge some musical performance conventions. My experience with drama and the fourth wall was a powerful influence here, where the notion of illusion, collusively understood by both performers and audience, lends a great frisson of excitement to the experience on both sides of the footlights.

I then researched, wrote, performed (and published) three programmes with long 'narrative' poems: 'Plain and Fancy', on the life, work and times of Benvenuto Cellini; 'The Marriage of True Minds: Shakespeare and the Dark (Jewish?) Lady of the Sonnets'; and one on early seventeenth-century London and the life and presence of Emilia Lanier (Wandor 2006b).[2] The most recent of these is *The Music of the Prophets*.

Working with music enabled me to move between different kinds of narrative. In *The Music of the Prophets*, I was under no obligation to write a straight historical narrative: he did this, and then this happened, and then they went there. I could dip in and out of the evocative, the atmospheric, keeping the larger chronology of real historical events ticking over, and creating a tension which was not resolved until the end (what happened next?). I could divert into a bit of biography, explore contemporary images, quote in a concealed (intertextual) way, by making other people's phrases my own, and I could use repetition or refrain. Here, as tropes, music and words met as similar devices used in different artistic discourses (poetry/music):

> a small coffee cup
> delicate bone china

Repetition and refrain are extremely interesting. They provide reassuring touchstones in ballads, for example, and yet, while the same words recur, each time they appear, the words have different resonances because each time the context/narrative is somewhere else, has moved on. I used repetition and refrain at appropriate points in the poem and in the performance piece – but I wouldn't dream of either trying to explain exactly why I chose these moments or suggesting how they should be 'read'. This is the task of the reader/audience, using whatever critical or aesthetic apparatus they bring with them to the experience:

> coffee tastes like home

No matter how much noise is made by post-modernism about the fragmentation of realist representation, linear narrative continues to dominate prose fiction and drama. Emotional/thematic narratives dominate the lyric poem. I don't want this to be read as if I am advocating realism as the best or only form, or rejecting it as a form of illusory bourgeois representation. Both these positions are fairly meaningless, since form *of itself* does not exist. There is, if you like, good realism and there is bad realism, and critical discourse engages with value judgements. What I am saying is that whatever genre or form one writes in, cause-and-effect tropes frame one's thinking. The very nature of language – the word, with letters in a certain sequence, the sentence, with certain ways of making meaning – is predicated on this, even when it is flouted. coffee is good for the soul:

> do Jews have souls?
> is there coffee in the afterlife?
> your afterlife or mine?

Enough post hoc. Enough words ABOUT, rather than the thing itself. Please read my poetry. Please see or listen to my plays. I'm off to play some music. Or read a book. Or.

NOTES

1. See Wandor (2008b) for a fuller analysis of the assumptions behind creative writing pedagogy.
2. A Poetry Book Society recommendation.

REFERENCES

Pope, R. (2005) *Creativity: Theory, History, Practice*. London: Routledge.
Wandor, M. (2006a) *The Music of the Prophets*. Todmorden: Arc Publications.
Wandor, M. (2006b) *Musica Transalpina*. Todmorden: Arc Publications.
Wandor, M. (2008a) *The Art of Writing Drama*. London: Methuen.
Wandor, M. (2008b) *The Author is Not Dead, Merely Somewhere Else: Creative Writing Reconceived*. Basingstoke: Palgrave Macmillan.

13

Mature Poet Steals: Sonnet as Problem Page

PATIENCE AGBABI

[A poet tells how she got through writer's block by reading a Milton sonnet and writing back to it through a genre borrowed from tabloid journalism. The eventual result was a whole series of poetic 'Problem Pages'. Here she invokes and sports with T. S. Eliot's proposition that 'mature poets steal' (Eliot 1920).]

The primary reason I revisit Milton's Sonnet XVI is that it gives me strength when I'm blocked. I think: Milton clearly agonized over losing his sight (he wrote another sonnet about it), and he was totally blind when he wrote *Paradise Lost*: whatever it is, get over it and get back to your writing desk. I also applaud the line 'And that one talent which is death to hide', interpreting the word 'talent' for its current rather than biblical meaning. It reminds me that if you've got a gift, use it or you'll be in reverse gear, heading for a crash. What interests me personally in this sonnet is what happens in the cross-over between the octave and sestet: 'But patience to prevent/That murmur soon replies'. Patience is anthropomorphized. It was only when I reread the poem on this particular occasion that another meaning leapt out at me: that Milton's patience subliminally inspired me, Patience, to become an agony aunt, to reply to dead poets.

'My Light Is Spent' was a direct response to Milton's agony over his blindness in his sonnet. It was also a response to his aims for *Paradise Lost* before he wrote it. To get more of a feel for Milton, as a character and as a writer, I reread the introduction to my edition. This quoted an extract from one of his essays, which epitomized Milton's ambition 'to imbreed and cherish in a great people the seeds of virtue and public civility'. I decided that rather than précis or pastiche this, I'd *sample* it. Not only would I hybridize form: I'd also hybridize content. So I sampled the quote and then added biographical detail at the beginning of the sentence, making it long and ponderous to sound more authentically Miltonic. I deliberately ended his problem page letter with a short sentence for contrast and as a punchline, since Milton was also renowned for not having luck with women. It was, of course, a nod to our contemporary problem pages that deal exclusively with matters of the heart.

For my response, in this case – and then with all the other letters to poets that followed – I 'pretended' I was indeed a real literary agony aunt who'd just received the letter and genuinely wanted to help. I got quite emotionally involved: it really hit me how harrowing it must have been as a writer to have such high ambitions and lose one's sight before they were realized. Of course, we have *hind*sight and know that Milton more than realized his ambitions, but as agony aunt I had to respond as spontaneously as I could. Although all my answers underwent several rewrites, they did not dramatically change:

> WHEN I consider how my light is spent,
>   Ere half my days, in this dark world and wide
>   And that one talent which is death to hide
>   Lodged with me useless, though my soul more bent
> To serve therewith my maker, and present
>   My true account, lest he returning chide,
>   'Doth God exact day-labour, light denied?'
>   I fondly ask: but patience to prevent
> That murmur soon replies, 'God doth not need
>   Either man's work or his own gifts; who best
>   Bear his mild yoke, they serve him best, his state
> Is kingly. Thousands at his bidding speed
>   And post o'er land and ocean without rest:
>   They also serve who only stand and wait.'
>   (Milton 1992 [1673]: 427–8)

MY LIGHT IS SPENT

Dear Patience, I am a middle-aged, respected, white, male poet, neoformalist yet reformist, who is losing his sight, and therefore losing sight of his poetic vision, whose ultimate aim is to implant and cherish in all people the seeds of virtue and public civility.　Not writing is death but to write in perpetual darkness is also death. And I lack companionship with women.

I wish more poets shared your ambition. Poetry has long been afraid to admit it wants to change the world. Invest in a dictaphone that transcribes. You may begin to compensate with your other five senses, especially your sixth sense, insight, that will rekindle love of writing.　And women.

(Agbabi 2008)

REFERENCES

Agbabi, P. (2008) 'My Light is Spent', one of a series of fourteen 'Problem Pages' in her *Bloodshot Monochrome*, Edinburgh: Canongate: 36. [The others are responses to sonnets by Surrey, Shakespeare, Wroth, Smith, Wordsworth, Keats, Barrett Browning, Hopkins, Frost, McKay, St Vincent Millay, Brooks and Jordan.]

Eliot, T.S. (1920) *The Sacred Wood: Essays on Poetry and Criticism*. London: Methuen.

Milton, J. (1992 [1673]) Sonnet XVI, from *The New Oxford Book of Seventeenth-Century Verse*, ed. Alastair Fowler. Oxford: Oxford University Press: 427–8.

14

Stories in Performance

BEN HAGGARTY WITH JOAN SWANN

[The extracts below come from an interview with the storyteller Ben Haggarty. They are followed by an illustrative analysis by Joan Swann of a sequence from one of Ben's stories.]

Interview Extracts

On 'Stitching Together' Stories

When you re-tell a traditional tale you tell it in your own words and in your own way... so if I tell a long wonder tale, a fairy tale, I'll read six or seven different variations of it... and because the events are modular there is a great fun to be had stitching together the modules in possibly a new or novel way.

[As an example, the 'witch baby' story is based on a well-known tale type:] 'The Search for the Land of No Death'. The bulk of the story is from the Romanian Gypsy story which was collected on the title 'The Red King and the Witch', but I also put in a bit from Arthur Ransome's *Old Peter's Russian Tales* where there is a story about 'Prince Ivan, the Witch Baby and the Little Sister of the Sun', plus various other motifs are in there so that's a very composite piece of work.

On Language

The work that needs to be done is the translation of material into communicative language. You can see something in your mind's eye and you have to select and describe, and it's very, very fast. And sometimes when you've got a strong rhythmical piece of performance... you hit a sentence and you realise that you can suddenly go alliterative. I've told [the 'witch baby' story] very many times so in a sense some of that has settled down into a script but it was never written – it's been evolved through repetition. You get a piece of alliteration which was 'her iron shod hoofs found firm footing on the farthest shore', and that just came one day and it stayed ... it's after this great pulsing 'and they swam and they swam and they swam, until her iron shod hoofs found firm footing on the farthest shore' ... it's got meaning in it, it's got sound in it, it's got poetry, it's got a strange geography – what is the farthest shore? – it's metaphorical, it's a nice sentence to punch ...

On Performance, and Audience

And then there is a performative element which is volume, which is gesture which is the sculpture, the use of the space, the interaction ... when adult faces go like children's faces it's quite extraordinary ... they are taken to this strange world which is there but not there ...

One's very aware of monitoring what is happening and making adjustments, so you know the clock is there and you are watching the clock and you're – OK, they are enjoying this, I can milk it a little bit, but ooops, I've done it too much, I'm going to really pay for that now because I took up three minutes that I didn't have and now I have to rush through another piece – and all the way through you've got this sort of director voice going on in your mind, arranging what's happening.

The best image really is as if one has a very long ear and eye, sitting out there in the audience and you're watching yourself with a fraction of delay ... you need to know what you've said, you need to see how it's going down and you need to see the faces.

... actually what you're trying to do is make people's eyes rotate in a pit like those old dolls with weighted eyes which would roll back in a rather sinister manner. We want people to look at the story inside their minds ... we want to allow the space there so that the audience can bring something of themselves to it. And this effort to listen means that they are paying quite expensively for this experience so there is an engagement which is very delicate.

A Performance of the 'Witch Baby' Story

The story is a long and winding narrative, lasting about 50 minutes, performed to a class of primary school children. A prince, having seen his baby sister transform herself temporarily into a ravenous witch, sets off on a quest to find the land where death can't reach him. His sister devours other family members before pursuing him.

The brief extract transcribed below comes from an early point in the story when the prince first sees his sister, in witch form, speeding past him to get to the palace kitchen.

The transformation of the witch baby

<u>With her teeth like iron axe blades, with her fingernails like razor blades</u> **yaahh** she flew past his head, **yaahh** she flew along the corridor, **yaahh** she flew down the stairs, **yaahh** she flew along the corridor, **yaahh** she entered the kitchen, <u>she stood in front of that larder door and she wrestled it off its hinges and then she stared at the food</u> **yum, yum**. And with <u>her iron teeth she scoffed, scoffed, scoffed, scoffed, scoffed all the food and then smash, smash, smash, smash, smashed all the plates</u> and then **yaahh** she flew out the kitchen, **yaahh** along the corridor, **yaahh** up the stairs, **yaahh** along the corridor, **yaahh** past his head, did three somersaults and turned back into ever such a sweet little baby sister.

Note: plain text shows Ben, as narrator, recounting the story; **bold** indicates where he takes on the voice of a character, using direct speech; <u>underlining</u> indicates where he visually embodies a character.

Ben builds up a terrifying picture of the witch – his initial description ('with her teeth like iron axe blades, with her fingernails like razor blades') is emphasized visually in his embodiment of the character (her facial expression, posture, gestures, etc.; see Figure 14.1). He uses a repeated clause structure (*she flew [preposition] [noun phrase]*) to depict her movement through the palace and, in reverse order, her return journey. Clauses are uttered rapidly, punctuated by a repeated screeching *yaahh* uttered in the witch's voice and accompanying darting hand gestures indicating the witch's movement. In the kitchen Ben again takes on the witch's body to represent her activity (*she stood...*, *wrenched... and stared*), and *yum, yum* is uttered in the witch's voice (Figure 14.2). The repeated *scoffed* is accompanied by hand-movements as the witch crams food into her mouth, and *smashed* by rapid downward gestures as the witch lays waste to the kitchen. The transformation of the witch back into a baby is marked by a shift into a gentle and melodic voice as Ben indicates the child doing tumbling somersaults into her cot (Figure 14.3).

As he recounts the narrative and represents characters, Ben also monitors his audience. Sometimes, as the witch, his gaze moves away from the audience (e.g. in Figure 14.2 his *yum, yum* is uttered with gaze to the left, towards the food in the larder). But in embodying characters Ben often, simultaneously, keeps half an eye on the audience (Figure 14.1) and he also faces them more directly as narrator – e.g. in pointing to the baby in her cot (Figure 14.3).

Figure 14.1 Ben as the witch: 'With her teeth like iron axe blades'

Figure 14.2 Ben as the witch: 'Yum, yum'

Figure 14.3   Ben representing 'ever such a sweet little baby sister'

Monitoring and responding to the audience is not incidental to the narrative, it is woven into the story fabric. The skill and artistry of the storyteller resides in their ability to orchestrate semiotic resources to construct the characters, places and events that make up the story and secure the audience's involvement in the story world.

For more on Ben Haggarty's work, visit the Crick Crack Club website at www.crickcrackclub.com/CRICRACK/TELLUKAF.HTM. For a fuller analysis of this and other stories, see Swann, J. (2009) 'Stories in performance' in J. Maybin and N.J. Watson (eds) *Children's Literature: Mapping the Field*. Basingstoke: Palgrave Macmillan.

CREATIVE INTERPRETATIONS: RESPONSE, READING, REWRITING

Introduction to Part III

This part shifts attention to the creative nature of response and interpretation, ranging from the acts of reading and rereading to those of critique and rewriting. Always in the background is the question of what it might actually mean for someone to write *in their own 'write/right'* – find or make *their own 'voice'*? Or are we always required to speak and write 'another's words in one's own language', as Bakhtin puts it (Bakhtin et al. 1994 [1929]: 52)? The 'dialogic' nature of creativity was considered in the previous part. Here we extend the notion of creative 'response' to the concept of *re-creation* in general. For if all human creation is not from nothing (*ex nihilo*) but from something or someone else (*ex aliis*, say), then we should be prepared to attach the prefix 're-' to all sorts of activities (re-vision, re-membering, re-construction, say) and *re*-cognize and *re*-configure our notion of creativity accordingly. Re-posed in this way, the creativity question has less to do with the 'new' or 'novel' as such and is much more a matter of distinguishing what is done 'afresh' from what is simply done 'again'. All the contributors that follow, and some elsewhere in the book, offer their own ways of framing and responding to these questions.

Part III opens with a film director's view of how the anticipation of wide differences in audience response fundamentally affects a film's conception and construction. From before formal planning to after first showing, G. D. Jayalakshmi 'was intensely conscious of [the] likely twofold audience' of her *Arranged Marriage* (2003), which was made to be shown in both Britain and India. The film treated a sensitive subject that might be known in outline and more or less stereotypically by most mainstream Western audiences but would be known immediately, personally and with fine nuances by many members of an Indian audience. Awareness of this informed decisions on everything from choice of actors, setting and music to pacing of action and delivery of

189

dialogue. It also extended to the recasting of the script during shooting and last-minute changes when switching between the native language (Kannada) and the lingua franca (English). Such adjustments reach to the very core of what actually gets said and shown; and they clearly endorse an essentially Bakhtinian view of the 'addressivity' and 'response-ability' – in short the *dialogic* nature – of discourse: 'the two-sided word that is framed in anticipation as well as response' (Bakhtin et al. 1994 [1929]: 48–60).

The creative as well as critical dynamics of a strongly theorized and closely analytical reading of a pair of purely verbal texts are explored in **Chapter 16,** Peter Stockwell's 'Authenticity and Creativity in Reading Lamentation'. Plotting possible and likely responses to two elegies translated into English from Polish, he argues that for all the inevitably idiosyncratic and more or less culture- and period-specific variations in interpretation that particular readers and readings may produce, there are nonetheless some broadly describable and even precisely definable cognitive parameters in which certain kinds of reading experience can be placed. These may not be universal or unanimous; but they are more or less commonly accessible and can be consistently modelled. Particular attention is drawn to the kinds of 'text-world' that may prompt and sustain either *sympathy for* or *empathy with* the figures projected by these two poetic texts; also the kinds and degrees of *authenticity* that may be attributed to a particular experience and 'invested in' when a reader identifies with the persona of the writer. 'Reading naturally', it is argued, invites the cooperation of a reader in the creation of a quite specific and in some ways peculiarly unique world, even while responding to ostensibly the same words.

The more overtly pragmatic and collaborative dimensions of reading are traced in **Chapter 17** in Joan Swann's empirical and ethnographic study of the dynamics of reading groups. While the reading of agreed books is obviously the chief rationale and, in every sense, 'pre-text' for reading groups, their chief mode is more or less spontaneous face-to-face conversation. Text in hand or on the table, they are mainly about the dynamics of talk 'as members collaboratively co-construct textual interpretations'. Typically, such talk about books is punctuated by 'a pattern of excursions out into discussion of a range of personal and social issues' and then back to the novel at issue (for novel it usually is). This, too, is therefore a deeply dialogic and highly contextualized kind of face-to-face group encounter that has something distinct from – as well as much in common with – other, differently mediated and more or less constrained modes of verbal exchange treated in this collection: Maybin on letter-writing, Goddard on electronic chat-rooms and messaging, Pahl on classroom interaction (Chapters 9, 10 and 11). The chief things that are 'created' by such exchanges – always with different materials and media and never with the same forms, functions and effects – are therefore opportunities for the creation of personal identity and social relationship, not just textual interpretation. In the case of reading groups this is openly a matter of ongoing negotiation. The aims and procedures, like the texts, are much less 'set' than those familiar in the literature and language classes of formal education. They emerge more directly from the social dynamics.

Issues of personal expression, social role and identity are also well to the fore in the two chapters that follow: one concerned with the reader as judge; the other with the poet as editor. Together, like many of the other pieces in this section, they remind us that it is crucial to distinguish creative and critical *roles* within the ongoing process of reading and writing, rather than to separate these off as utterly distinct *persons* with quite distinct objects. One person may assume many roles at different times, if not simultaneously. If this rather obvious truth is borne in mind, then much of the anxiety about whether a person is 'critical' *or* 'creative' can be avoided: it is as about as odd as asking whether someone is a 'reader' *or* a 'writer'. In fact it is often better to talk of dynamically interdependent as well as reciprocally defining *critical–creative roles* and *reading–writing processes* (with orders reversed – *creative–critical*, *writing–reading* – for differences of emphasis).

Bearing all this in mind, Jane Spiro's 'Reader Response and the Formulation of Literary Judgement' (**Chapter 18**) and Fiona Sampson's 'Practical Measures: Poet as Editor' (**Chapter 19**) afford rich insights into creativity and/as criticism and writers-who-read (and vice versa); also, more specifically, into the nature of poetic taste and literary value. Spiro looks at the various criteria adopted by a wide range of people (including professional writers, teachers, editors and 'leisure readers') when asked to be 'judges' of unidentified poems by an equally wide range of writers (from a Nobel prize-winner to students in a creative writing class). These criteria range from notions of popular appeal and educational efficacy to literary prestige and immediate interest. Significantly, though notions commonly associated with 'literature' and 'literariness' are widely invoked (to do with complexity, ambiguity, patterning, imagery, and so forth), they are applied very variously and often with diametrically opposed valuations: the same feature may be seen as striking or mannered, successful or strained. In such terms a Nobel prize-winning poet may get as much of a mauling from fellow professionals as do amateurs in the field.

Comparison with Sampson's contribution on poetry editing is both revealing and salutary. Where Sampson sees herself as cultivator and custodian of a certain idea of poetry and poetic value with posterity – or rather, futurity – in mind, many of the judges examined by Spiro either cannot agree with one another or cannot be consistent in the basis for their judgements. Some broad convergences and commonalities are discernible; but there are also awkward inconsistencies and catastrophic reversals. For Sampson, however, such a chaotic and potentially confusing state of affairs might well be seen as an 'egalitarian, post-value model' as well as a 'post-literary' one; it represents 'the death of value, in which every opinion is equivalent'. Set resolutely and resourcefully against this, she sees her own role as editor of *Poetry Review*, one of the main UK poetry journals, as that of maintaining 'a sense of the persistence of the literary beyond the death of value'. To underwrite this, she uses the time-honoured images of the 'garden' of poetry and of the editor as gardener/cultivator, also of previous writing as the 'compost' from which fresh writing will spring if tended properly. This may seem a long way from Spiro's vision of a substantial lack of agreement and a welter of different ends in view: reading 'as a creative writing teacher'; 'as a poetry editor'; 'for enjoyment'. But if it is remembered that in both cases we are talking about different *roles* and *activities*, with different *aims* in different *contexts*, then we may agonize less about matters of absolute and fixed value (who is *most* creative) and get on with addressing issues of variable valuation and relative fitness for purpose (creative *for what*).

This engagement with critical reading and creative writing is picked up in Rob Pope's 'Rewriting the Critical–creative Continuum: 10x ...' (**Chapter 20**). This traces versions of the biblical 'Ten Commandments' from its openly plural beginnings (the commandments are often more or less than ten and not always commands, depending which source text one reads) through successive moments of translation, adaptation and parody. These bring us to the contemporary 'Ten Commandments' of the Underground, Banking, Jamming (the improvised jazz kind), and much else. The piece opens with 'Ten Commandments of Critical-creative Interpretation', which the present reader is invited to rewrite as she or he sees fit; and concludes with 'Ten Dos and Don'ts of Creativity' gathered from 'experts' in creativity of one kind or another (including many of the contributors to this volume). There are excursions into parodic versions of the 'Decalogue' by Clough, Bierce and Auden along the way; also some expressly multimodal and multimedia takes on the topic, courtesy of Hollywood film and Lego toys. These are materials and activities that explore the critical–creative continuum as process and in action.

The topics of interpretation, adaptation and translation are picked up again in Rukmini Bhaya Nair's contribution on 'Reading a Hindi Poem' (**Chapter 21**). This explores the complex of linguistic meanings, poetic conventions and cultural understandings that are needed to appreciate a *doha* (two-line verse) written by a fifteenth-century Indian poet. While Bhaya Nair is able to describe the characteristics of the *doha*, and its historical and cultural context, she concludes that its meaning needs to be 'instinctively *sensed*, not explicated'. Whereas performance is what, in Agbabi's phrase in Chapter 2, 'elevates' poetry; here, to recall the words of Robert Frost, poetry is still what 'gets lost in translation'.

A final poetic 'A–Z of Textual Re-creation' rounds off the section, and reprises many of its key terms in a playful way.

Issues that recur in this section and connect, implicitly or explicitly, to those in the rest of the book therefore include:

- the idea that we had better conceive of **creating and criticizing** as complementary or competing but never absolutely separable activities, and that, for example, 'creative artist' and 'literary critic' or 'textual analyst' are *roles* that may be assumed by one person at different times (with difficulty at the same time) as well as by different people;
- the corresponding idea that **reading and writing** are often better conceived as distinct yet interdependent points on a continuum, and that the precise point one comes into it and how, whether as (receptive) *subject* or (active) *agent*, depends on the form, function and context of the discourse in play as well as the aims in mind and ends in prospect;
- a particular focus on the literary judgements made by various kinds of reader (including 'leisure readers' and those who read professionally), as this prompts us to review our conceptions of **aesthetics** and **literary value**;
- overall, a deepening and broadening realization that creativity is – creativities are – **multiple** and **differentiated**, deeply **contextualized** and endlessly involved in **transformations** (metamorphoses, shape-shiftings) – though in any given and remade instance we will always be inclined and may well wish to stress the **singularity** (or peculiarity) and sheer **newness** (or mere **novelty**).

REFERENCE

Bakhtin, M., Medvedev, P. and Voloshinov, V. (1994) *The Bakhtin Reader: Selected Writings of Bakhtin, Medvedev, Voloshinov*, ed. P. Morris. London: Arnold.

15

The First Three Minutes: Seducing the Audience in *Arranged Marriage*

G. D. JAYALAKSHMI

In 2003, I wrote and directed a short film called *Arranged Marriage*. The story was about Shashi, a second generation British Indian young woman who is sent to India by her parents so that her grandparents can use the arranged marriage system to find her a suitable husband.

Throughout the making of this film and its reception, I was intensely conscious of its likely twofold audience. First, I hoped that it might play theatrically in Britain – and in the event, it did. It was taken up by Cine-UK and exhibited as a short film before *Whale-Rider* and *Calendar Girls* in all their Cineworld cinemas. So there was a Western mainstream audience, irrespective of colour and ethnicity. Such an audience knows that Indians have arranged marriages, but does not necessarily know the mechanism – either in its generality or in the subtle nuances – by which 'girl meets boy'.

A second audience was the one in India. The film needed to be authentic in portraying the practice of arranged marriages, so that an Indian audience would find the action credible, but at the same time depart from routine enough to gain and hold their interest.

So, in the opening sequence of the film, just three minutes long, I had to ensure that a mainly white British audience could understand a process that is culturally alien to them without losing an Indian audience that might get bored with a didactic opening. I began with the title itself. This was the straightforwardly descriptive 'Arranged Marriage' to ensure that a British audience would know from the beginning what was going on; an Indian audience would have grasped this at once no matter what the film had been called. I hoped the Indian audience would eventually come to see that the title is not quite as straightforward as it seems: a marriage is indeed 'arranged' by the end of the film, but not in the way that custom and tradition would lead them to expect. However, it remains true that, as the film opens, the main purpose of the title is simply to tell a British audience what the film is about.

When I wrote the script, I decided that Shashi would see three boys before she objected to the whole process. (Prospective brides and grooms in India are 'girls' and 'boys', regardless of age or experience of life.) The encounter with the first boy would be set up elaborately so that the Western audience understood the basic system of arranged marriages. The one with the second boy would be quicker and the last one would be the quickest of them all. The Western audience in some senses was in the same shoes as Shashi. Neither of them really knew what was in store. So, the Western audience discovers the arranged marriage system along with her.

Film is very unlike the written word, with many more tools at the director's disposal. Words in the form of dialogue are of course very important. But there is also the visual medium of shot sizes and shot transitions, tracking and panning, cutting and so on; there is also the aural medium of music and other incidental sounds. In addition, actors bring their own presence. There are innumerable ways to communicate non-verbally – pauses, facial expressions, bodily demeanours, ways of walking and so on – and all these come together making the acts of communication complex. No one of these elements creates meaning on its own, but when they are all put together in a naturalistic film, they try to represent lived reality on the screen, in a way that the audience can accept and identify with.

The beginning of a film is crucial to a film-maker – and especially so in a short film. It introduces the characters and setting and it also sets the tone for what is to follow. The visual element is probably the one that most film-makers concentrate on, not least because of the logistics of setting shots up. Even before anyone has arrived on set, the director has to know what kind of shots he or she intends to use – lenses, film stock and equipment such as dollies and cranes have to be ordered in advance. So the visual dimension is one that the director takes into consideration early on.

The first few visuals in a film lead the audience into the story and plot lines. My film begins with the grandfather, the grandmother and Shashi buying flowers in a South Indian market on their way to the first boy's house. While the grandparents are dressed in traditional Indian attire – he is in a dhoti, kurta and a South Indian headgear called pètè and she is in a bright silk sari – the heroine wears a smart pair of trousers and shirt. Visually, this establishes some of the parameters I wanted to set. I wanted the audience to be at least subliminally aware of the difference in value systems. In wearing more traditional clothes and in being so resplendently comfortable in them, the grandparents are obviously operating within a system that they know very well. Shashi, on the other hand, appears to be alien to a system that she should rightfully be an heir to. Although her clothes are well tailored, I would expect an Indian audience to judge that she is not dressed appropriately for the encounter. Hopefully they would wonder if this was deliberate on her part, and be intrigued about how she will handle other aspects of the process that is about to begin.

But I am not so sure about a Western audience. I doubt if the clothes are so significant to them. They would of course be aware of the contrast between the grandparents' and the granddaughter's clothing, but they might assume that this was purely generational. I think that the beginning has a slightly different meaning for them. They are probably more interested in the exuberance of the market. They can see the colours, the people, the flowers, the different fruits and vegetables, the mounds of green banana leaves, yellow turmeric and red kumkum. It is set up as exotic, as 'the other'. And it is this otherness that they will come to explore as the film progresses.

The film opens with the camera tracking down from sky and green leaves, through a busy street onto the market. We see the grandparents buying flowers. Shashi hangs back a little. Throughout this sequence, she walks behind them. She is more hesitant and does not stride with the same sense of purpose that her grandparents have. But neither does she walk demurely the way a traditional Indian bride would. Her gait comes across as being 'ever so slightly awkward' and 'just that bit uncomfortable'. So visually, I was trying to give a hint of something 'not quite right'. The film then goes on to explore how these relationships pan out. Thus even before anybody has actually said anything, I wanted to convey that there are two world values in operation here.

The very first words spoken in the film set up a clash of these two different world orders. The grandmother, with her fruit thaali, is an upholder of tradition. When they arrive outside the first boy's house, both grandparents smooth their clothes out, preparing for the important encounter ahead. Shashi, on the other hand, stands still and quiet, though with a palpable air of unease and resentment. This is how I had written the scene:

EXT. RESIDENTIAL STREET IN BANGALORE – CONTINUOUS
At one house they stop. Ashok studies it, checks with a piece of paper he is carrying, and nods. They walk up the driveway and pause at the door while Bhanu adjusts her sari and casts a critical look over Shashi.
BHANU: You should be in a sari. There are proper ways of doing this ...
Shashi's eyes flash, but before she can reply, Ashok intervenes, quiet and conciliatory.
ASHOK: Hmm. Let it be.
He rings the bell, and immediately the door is opened.

But what happens in the film is slightly different. When the grandmother says, 'You should be in a sari,' the grandfather scolds her in Kannada, the language spoken in Karnataka where the film is set. He says, 'i:g hel ye:n prayo:jna:?'[1] meaning 'What is the point of saying this now?' Then he eyes Shashi up and down, accepts her for being different and says, 'Hmm, let it be.'

An Indian audience will recognize many elements in these exchanges. First, there is the relationship between the grandparents. They are open and free with each other, not afraid to bicker even at important times. Their relationship will easily survive such small irritations. Second, the grandmother is stricter and more openly critical of her granddaughter's lack of respect for the occasion. The grandfather, although equally disapproving (as can be seen by his looks and the slight shake of his head), is more indulgent towards Shashi. The ease with which the grandparents move between Kannada and English adds to the air of naturalism in the film, but it will also convey subtle messages about relationships to the Kannada-speaking audience. By talking in Kannada to his wife, Ashok is at least partially excluding Shashi from the exchange, not scolding Bhanu too openly in front of their granddaughter, or conveying to Shashi that he is more prepared than Bhanu to tolerate her inappropriate clothing.

Although the Western audience may not understand the exact words spoken by the grandfather to his wife, I expect them to get the gist of what is being said through the non-verbal clues. The pointed angry look by the grandmother, the quick flash of anger on Shashi's part, the interruption by the grandfather as he scolds his wife and then looks Shashi up and down before pronouncing her just about suitable – these set up the relationship between the three central characters. It should be obvious right from the start that the grandmother disapproves of Shashi's behaviour; and although the grandfather is more indulgent towards her, his word is the word of authority.

Then the door opens and Shashi and her grandparents go in. It is time to set up the central conflict that will be played out in the houses of the three boys that Shashi visits. The bone of contention has to do with where Shashi will sit.

I have always been struck by the unquestioning display of patriarchy in Indian culture on occasions like these. The men take it as their automatic right to sit on chairs while the women are offered a straw mat on the floor. The Indian women in the film (Shashi's grandmother and the boy's mother) think nothing of it – this is the tradition and this is how it has always been. But Shashi stands hesitantly wondering what to do, especially as there is actually an empty seat. The grandfather gestures to her that she should sit on the mat. Reluctantly, but unwilling to go against her grandfather, she sits down. Shashi's hesitation before sitting down and the obvious discomfort it causes her (both physically and emotionally) is invisible to the other Indians on screen. Silently, the film has set up a tension between two cultures.

Then the first father starts asking her questions. Shashi makes an effort to be polite and indeed deferential to someone from the older generation. She answers all the questions the father puts to her, even if all her answers are monosyllabic. But when a 'boy' of her own age replicates the treatment, she is quick to put him in his place:

> The father turns to Shashi and smiles.
> FIRST FATHER: So ... Tell me, you have studied at university, isn't it?
> SHASHI: Yes.
> FIRST FATHER: You have now graduated?
> SHASHI: Yes.
> FIRST FATHER: With a first degree only?
> SHASHI: Yes.
> The father nods to the boy indicating that he should take over.
> FIRST BOY: In which subject or subjects?
> SHASHI: Would you like me to send you my CV?

Shashi's British 'otherness' comes out forcefully when she asks the final question. First of all, no prospective Indian bride speaks on such occasions, except to answer questions. She certainly never asks questions of her own. Shashi's sharpness here is shocking – she is instantly identified as someone who cannot be trusted to fit into a prospective family.

Secondly, Shashi has a strong Edinburgh accent. This choice was deliberate – the actor playing Shashi is not Scottish – as we wanted to highlight her Britishness. The actor's normal RP accent would not have been enough to do this. Many Indians from or in India have RP accents – including Shashi's father in the film and the actor who plays the part. By giving her an Edinburgh accent, we are deliberately emphasizing her difference.

And this difference is also shown in her choice of words. 'CV' is a British term. In India, a curriculum vitae is called a biodata. It was interesting that when we were shooting the film we had to explain the meaning of CV to some of the Indian actors, who had not come across it.

I have often wondered if Indian audiences have understood that line, especially when said with such a strong Edinburgh accent. Whether they have got the exact meaning or not, the implications of her actions are there for all to see. The Indian audience will suddenly see Shashi's defiance of the unquestioning acceptance of the arranged marriage system. If they laugh, this is rueful laughter at themselves as much as at the situation on the screen. For a mainly white British audience, the humour will be more straightforward. But it also sets up something else that is important – when a young girl marries an Indian, she does not marry just the person. Rather she marries into a whole family and their entire way of life.

The music in the film contributes to the mood being set up. I am delighted to have had a number of South Indian viewers compliment me on the use of music. The film begins with the score of a traditional, well known hymn to Lord Ganesha – *Vaataapi ganapathim bhaje.* We Hindus pray to Ganesha at the beginning of anything auspicious. So starting the film off with this music signals the start of an important and almost holy endeavour for Shashi and her grandparents.

It also had a similar meaning for me as a film-maker. This was the first 35 mm short film I was shooting and it was meant to be the prelude to a much longer feature film that I was putting together. So, it was an invocation to Lord Ganesha, asking him to keep an eye on this film and hopefully on other films to follow.

Once Shashi and her grandparents leave the first boy's house, the music changes. It turns into an insistent drum beat – a beat that seeks to convey the fall in status for Shashi's grandparents, their indignation and, at the same time, a triumph for Shashi. These come across through the music, the single file walk down the street where the grandfather strides down with the grandmother nearly running to catch up and a more confident Shashi walking behind. The cross tracking shot enables the audience to catch a small smile of glee on Shashi's face.

This encounter makes Shashi bolder. When they go to the second house, she actually instigates conversation. She is learning to play the system. Instead of waiting for questions to be thrown at her when she sits down, she asks for a chair. This is comical but deadly serious:

> As before, Bhanu and the mother sit down on the mat, but this time Shashi is prepared.
> SHASHI: Could I have a chair, please?
> Stunned silence for a moment. Then her grandparents speak together.
> BHANU: (fierce whisper) Sit down!
> ASHOK: (determinedly casual) Shashi, please sit down. You will be more ... more comfortable.
> SHASHI: No, I think I'd be more comfortable on a chair, actually ... if that's all right with you.
> Silence as everyone tries to comprehend Shashi's bad behaviour. Shashi smiles sweetly:
> SHASHI: I'll get one if you tell me where ...
> The boy is the first to recover. Flustered, he stands up.
> SECOND BOY: I'll get you a chair.

The boy rises from his seat to get her a chair. It is above all the look on his face – his total incomprehension of a girl like Shashi, his shock that she has asked his mother for a chair and his final polite resignation when he gives in to a woman who is after all a guest in their house – that brings about the comedy in the scene. So, irrespective of the writing, the humour comes from the actual performance of the piece. The non-verbal interactions like the sweet smile on Shashi's face when she asks for a chair, the shock on the boy's mother's face, the quiet looks exchanged, the grandfather's embarrassment when he looks down – these are what make the piece funny. And they set up the final scenario well.

The walk at the end of seeing the second boy is swift. I did not want to linger when the point is to build tension – see what Shashi does next or what the grandparents do to thwart their naughty granddaughter.

Figure 15.1   Shashi and her grandfather

Outside the front door, the grandfather speaks straight to Shashi. He tells her that she simply must not ask for a chair. He is a man used to authority, and so is confident that she will respect him. The audience, though, will have realized by now that Shashi is far from happy with the arranged marriage system, even if they do not yet know all her reasons, personal as well as general. They realize that she will not put up with it submissively. So the question is, what will Shashi do next? This is what happens:

As before, Ashok and the THIRD BOY are taking their place on the arm-
chairs. Shashi and Bhanu stand and wait, Shashi smouldering with resentment as she watches the men sit. The THIRD FATHER goes to the stairs and
shouts up:
THIRD FATHER: Eh! They have come!
Suddenly Shashi has an idea. Her eyes light up, she glances around her, then
she steps over to the only vacant armchair and sits down.

And the final walk, shot in close-up, shows the grandfather walking in grim
thoughtfulness, the grandmother turning back to look daggers at Shashi and
the almost convincingly innocent smile on Shashi's face. This was designed
to bring the entire sequence of visits to boys' houses to a satisfactory conclusion. Shashi has won, at least temporarily. But what will happen next?

So, in a short opening sequence like this, the film-maker has to use all
the tools available – language, gestures, non-verbal communication, camera
angles, the pace of editing and finally music – to create an introduction that
will allow everyone to understand what is happening and to want to know
what will happen next. It is particularly gratifying when a British audience
laughs at something so simple, and in British terms so unremarkable as a
young woman sitting down on a vacant chair. It suggests that the culture of
arranged marriages, and the tensions between the countries and the generations, have been successfully established.

NOTE

1. Kannada has its own script, but the transcription here uses a system in common use in
   India to represent the language in Roman script.

16

Authenticity and Creativity in Reading Lamentation

Peter Stockwell

Methods and Metaphors

It has long been a common understanding that reading is an active process, and that the literary work is the rich outcome not only of an author's productive creativity but also of the receptive creativity of a readership. In spite of a great deal of introspective exposition and poetic expression, however, a systematic account of how texts and readers interact to create literary works has only recently emerged. On the one hand, a stylistic tradition has become increasingly adept at applying the insights of linguistics to the patterning of literary texts, and, on the other, an empirical approach to the activity of reading has emerged with both psychological and sociological roots. Together, these traditions have developed into a cognitive poetics that is equally sensitive to stylistic texture and interpretative significance (see Stockwell 2002, 2009a; Semino and Culpeper 2002; Gavins and Steen 2003; Brône and Vandaele 2009).

This collision of disciplines allows for a valid and systematic account of that most difficult of objects of investigation: literary reading. Because literary reading is a form of self-consciousness, in which subjectivity itself is shaped, the observer's paradox familiar in social science is potentially disastrous. Direct empirical methods of investigation instantly alter the nature of reading. Triangulating towards this dynamic subjectivity is the only means of gaining an insight into the reading process that aspires to more than a poetic gesturing. Validity is gained firstly by an open, evidential and principled analysis of textual patterns, secondly by adapting models that have been empirically tested in comparable disciplines, and thirdly by matching the organizing concepts closely with the concerns of natural readers. Taking this last point, for example, involves examining the ways that natural readers (that is, non-academics) describe their own interpretative processes, and then developing analytical approaches that correspond with these conceptualizations. Such an analytical account is then produced in accord with the first two dimensions: psychological plausibility and textual evidence.

For example, in a study of online book-group discourse (Stockwell 2009a), it was quickly apparent that there are three general conceptual metaphors that are consistently used by natural readers to describe their own literary experiences:

- reading as transportation;
- reading as control;
- reading as investment.

The first is the most popular form of expression, accounting for roughly half of all examples. People say things like 'I really got lost in this after the first few pages' and 'Persist with it and it will carry you off.' This conceptual metaphor has been studied closely by the psychologist Richard Gerrig (1993) as a form of readerly identification. The second conceptual metaphor underlies statements such as 'It's gripping stuff' and 'I couldn't put it down' (see Gibbs 2002 for a discussion). Both of these conceptual metaphors are bidirectional: the reader is transported or transports the fiction, the reader controls the reading or is controlled by it. Both might be seen as a specification of a more general conceptual metaphor: READING IS A JOURNEY. The third organizing metaphor – reading as investment – has been relatively neglected, perhaps because of all three it tends to be used mostly for describing emotional or aesthetic experiences: 'By the end I was emotionally drained but rewarded by it,' 'It rewards your effort with a great payoff at the end,' 'Well worth the investment – emotional and financial!' 'You get more out of it on each reading,' and so on. In this chapter, then, I will sketch out an investment model of reading on cognitive poetic principles in terms of text worlds, and I will use it to illuminate the subtle difference between two aspects of readerly identification: sympathy and empathy. This will also allow me to discuss the notion of authentic experience in literary reading and demonstrate how creativity is central to any engagement with literary works, especially emotionally charged ones.

Emotional Investment and Cognitive Stance

When readers talk of their successful involvement in a literary work in terms of investment, there is an (often unconscious) *idealized cognitive model* (Lakoff 1987) underlying their thinking. For illustration, a schematized conceptual net can be drawn (Figure 16.1) to represent the most common factors and processes that are implied in readerly investment, where the currency of investment is time, emotional engagement and intellectual effort.

The key elements of the semantics of investment here are represented by the boxed flowchart objects from the initial presumption of an ownership of resources, which are transferred elsewhere, where those resources are put to work. This part of the process (through the double-arrows) is the investor's primary activity; the return on investment (the single arrow looping back) represents marginal profit. Associated with these key elements are the other sketched concepts: the individual's investment instantly becomes a social fact; the investment is initially a monetary loss; the investment itself is an effort. Other connotations of investment are the notions of risk and faith originating back with the investor, the flow of capital and trust which are forward-looking and anticipatory, and the basic notion of an improvement in the capital which returns the future-view back to the investor's present. In literary terms, a readerly sense of your own investment commits a reader to the elements drawn out in this schematic representation. Your own involvement and identity is figured as a matter of resources that are owned and are available to be invested. Engaging with a literary work involves a potential loss, and thus a personal risk, which can be understood as either wasted time (a linked metaphor of TIME/ATTENTION IS MONEY) or as opening up the reader's personality as a form of vulnerability. The reader's personal resources (your

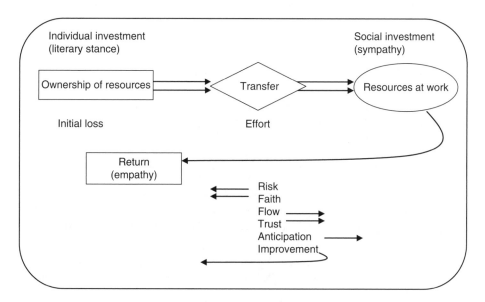

Figure 16.1   A conceptual net for investment

emotional engagement) are put to work: the process is regarded as effortful. The whole experience is motivated by the expectation that a greater emotional and aesthetic payoff will return on the initial investment. Sympathy (a feeling *for* another personality) is extended, and if the investment loop pays off, then the reader experiences an empathetic response (a feeling *with* the other personality).

The individual investment by a reader involves the adoption of a literary stance upon an initial engagement with a literary work (by contrast, for example, a reader approaching the text simply as a piece of data for analysis, or as a comprehension passage in a language test, and so on, would not be adopting a literary stance and it is highly unlikely that any strong emotional engagement would occur). However, this engagement itself then opens up a social domain, in the sense that the work is the creative discourse of an author and is available for reading and discussion in the world. An individual emotional investment in a literary experience therefore implicitly becomes a matter of social investment. From the viewpoint of the initial reading, a sympathetic relationship is instantly opened up. Since the conceptual metaphor is a financial one, we can turn to economic theory where 'emotional capital' is the theorized form of 'sympathy' (deriving from Bourdieu's 1972 notion of 'social capital'). This stands in contrast to 'intellectual capital' or 'knowledge'. Returning to literary reading, both informational value and aesthetic value are thus viewed as related forms of capital that can be transmitted, shared and put to productive work. The first part of the process (a reader regarding an emotionally charged domain) is sympathy, and the completion of the investment cycle as a return on the investment is a more closely identified and self-modifying sense of empathy. The argument drawing on the blended economic and literary metaphor is that sympathy is primarily a social phenomenon and empathy a more individual and intimate one, though of course they often cannot be so sharply delineated in practice.

Under application to literary reading, the most obvious way of accounting for subjective positioning across fictional boundaries is by drawing on *text world theory* (Werth 1997, 1999; Gavins 2007). A reader adopts a cognitive stance (a general readiness for discourse which might encompass a literary stance), which is imagined and expressed deictically: deictic relationships are established, linking the reader and other personalities (speaking voice, focalizing narrator, characters). The deictic dimensions of language are those aspects which delineate relationships between personalities, on the basis of locating person, time and place, and also in terms of social and textual positioning: for example by personal pronouns, adverbial locatives, spatial demonstratives and verbs, social naming conventions, and so on (see Stockwell 2002; McIntyre 2007). The beauty of text world theory is that it is cognitively plausible but retains a strong text-driven, stylistic grounding.

A world, in this model, is a deictically defined space with participants. At the top, discourse, world level (the 'real world'), an actual reader creates a text world on the basis of the literary text created by an actual author. This text world is built by the reader in his or her mind as a rich world representation that is used as the medium of the literary experience. Entities existing in the same world are participants, and other entities in other worlds are characters: worlds are only directly accessible (knowable) to participants in them. Within the text world, further departures from the deictic location can be made, creating one or several embedded world-switches. These switches are triggered by modalizations, negatives, metaphors, flashbacks, flashforwards, speculative or hypothetical states, direct speech and other narrative switches, or reorientations in spatial location. For example, if poor characters in a text world present an imagined altered state in which they were rich, a world-switch is created in which they *are* rich, and the reader keeps track of this other state as an embedded speculative world. Negations demonstrate this very clearly. The famous phrase 'Don't think of an elephant' creates an elephant (in a switched world) whose relationship to the text world is that it doesn't exist – but the readerly sense that it positively doesn't exist, rather than never having been mentioned at all, is captured by the theory. All of these world shifts are enacted stylistically.

In the investment framework, sympathy is modelled as a distance from the readerly stance, which would involve a text world creation and a reader imagining a situation across one or more world boundaries. The feedback loop that produces empathy as a return on investment indicates a shift back, as a result of the mapping, towards a realignment of the readerly stance. I will show some examples of this below. It is plain from this model that there is a direct relationship between perceived effort invested and the degree of empathy felt, with the stylistic patterns of the literary work serving as a multiplier in the process. In terms of text world theory, sympathy involves a reader in the discourse world observing a character in a text world and his or her world-switches; empathy, by contrast, involves a bidirectional transworld mapping between the discourse world reader and the character in the embedded worlds.

As a means of demonstrating this argument, I have collected (for other purposes) a body of literary texts that are highly successful at eliciting an observable emotional response in readers, ranging from a verbal description of being moved to the physical observation of crying in an audience (see Stockwell 2009a, 2009b). A large proportion of these literary works are concerned with grief and loss, and they form part of the major and ancient tradition of the poetry of lamentation. Suter (2008) points to very early examples such as the Sumerian *Lament for Ur* – about the destruction of the city – and the Old Testament *Book of Lamentations* of Jeremiah (from 2000 BC and 500 BC respectively). Laments also feature strongly in the classical Greek and Roman traditions, and the elegy is a consistent thread throughout English literature from the tenth-century poem *The Wanderer* through post-Renaissance examples in Shakespeare, Donne and Dryden, and persisting right into our contemporary period.

In this chapter, I will explore two laments by the great sixteenth-century Polish writer, Jan Kochanowski (1530–84). His sequence of 19 laments (or *Threnodies – Treny* in Polish) is regarded as one of the greatest achievements in Slavic poetry and a revolutionary turn in European Renaissance literature (see Welsh 1974). Published in 1580, the *Treny* were criticized for casting in elegiac form a lament on the death, not of a great statesman or holy person, but the poet's own two-year-old daughter Urszula. They mark a shift in the poet's own voice, too, moving from his early stoical work to this more personal and emotional writing. To modern readers, the laments are contemporary-sounding and moving, and carry a human voice out of history and into the present moment. I will read the poems in their English translation by Dorothea Prall (1920). Though two recent versions by Stanisław Barańczak and Seamus Heaney (1995) and Adam Czerniawski (2001) have brought Kochanowski to Western eyes again, I prefer the earlier translation. The original Polish laments appear at the end of the chapter, though it is important to note that my arguments are made largely in relation to the English versions.

Lamentation: in Sympathy

'Lament VII'
Sad trinkets of my little daughter, dresses
    That touched her like caresses,
Why do you draw my mournful eyes? To borrow
    A newer weight of sorrow?
No longer will you clothe her form, to fold her
    Around, and wrap her, hold her.
A hard, unwaking sleep has overpowered
    Her limbs, and now the flowered
Cool muslin and the ribbon snoods are bootless,
    The gilded girdles fruitless.
My little girl, 'twas to a bed far other
    That one day thy poor mother
Had thought to lead thee, and this simple dower
    Suits not the bridal hour;
A tiny shroud and gown of her own sewing
    She gives thee at thy going.

> Thy father brings a clod of earth, a sombre
>   Pillow for thy last slumber.
> And so a single casket, scant of measure,
>   Locks thee and all thy treasure.

It seems to me that this poem can be said at the very least to create a feeling of sympathy in most readers. In terms of text world theory (see Figure 16.2), the poet Jan Kochanowski speaks to the modern-day reader in the joint discourse world (DW). Though we are separated by time, space and culture, this direct communication is the basis for the reader's creation of the main text world (TW). In that imaginary deictic space, a counterpart father begins by addressing his daughter's clothes. Throughout the whole of the rest of the poem, the TW father's address remains bounded within that text world.

The diagram makes it clear at a glance that the main narratological and aesthetic technique in the poem is one of deictic displacement. The father cannot initially bring himself to address his dead daughter, and so he asks a question of her clothes, a metonym for her and an emblem of his sense of loss. His question, rather than assertion, might also be seen as a similar, echoic sort of avoidance strategy. The daughter, in fact, does not exist at all in the main text world: she is displaced, at two removes from the reader, inaccessible to us and only accessible ontologically by the text world father. In fact, the 'daughter' character in the embedded world-switch (WS1) is dead, and

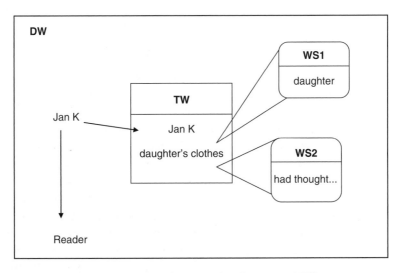

Figure 16.2 Broad text-world diagram for 'Lament VII'

Notes: WS1: world-switch 1; WS2: world-switch 2.

the father's memories of her alive are a further displacement (not drawn here) into the past of his recollection.

Also not drawn in the broad representation of Figure 16.2 are the numerous negations that create fleeting world-switches repeatedly across the first two-thirds of the poem. The negations 'No longer', 'unwaking', 'bootless', 'fruitless' and 'suits not' all create their referents in displaced world-switches, leaving what I have elsewhere called *lacunae* (Stockwell 2009b), a tangible sense of felt absence remaining in the text world. Further at this microscopic textual level, the simile 'like caresses', as a mini-metaphor, also operates as a fleeting world-switch to a world of actual caresses, underlining again that, back in the text world in which that WS is embedded, the father has lost his child's soft touch.

In parallel with these patterns of displacement, all grammatical agency that would perhaps normally be attached to the father is assigned elsewhere, though in most cases the deflection is strongly suggested. For example, it is the trinkets and the dresses that 'touched her like caresses', rather than the father. They are addressed as 'you' and they receive the main verb in the interrogative 'draw my mournful eyes'; it is they who 'clothe her', strongly implicitly rather than him; they 'fold her ..., wrap her, hold her' rather than him. The 'hard, unwaking sleep has overpowered' her. The poem begins with the father (actually only his mournful eyes) as passive, and he is so deflected from any agency that he disappears grammatically, until the abstraction 'sleep' (another displacement, a euphemism for death) takes the main verb ('has overpowered'). This is followed by a mere existential verb ('muslin and ... snoods are') asserting an absence ('bootless'); and in the next line the existential verb itself is elided altogether (the 'girdles [are] fruitless'). All of these semantic and grammatical lacunae serve to place the girl's lost life and lost future into the reader's consciousness only as felt absences, displaced away in distant world-switches.

The pattern is brought to explicitness in the next four lines (drawn in Figure 16.2 as WS2), in which the never-to-be-realized lost future is captured in an embedded future-in-the-past – 'one day thy poor mother had thought to lead thee' – with a further complicating world-switch into the mother's belief-world ('thought'). Again, the diagram only draws the broad representation of this as WS2, though it is textually composed of several embedded world shifts away from the immediate text world level. For example, there is a spatial shift 'far other', a temporal shift 'one day', the aspectual shift of 'had thought' and the belief shift of 'thought', and the whole is embedded in a metaphorical shift linking the girl and her 'treasure' as a dowry that her mother no longer possesses – she is 'poor' in the financial as well as the sympathetic sense.

These lines mark a shift in the address form that is more direct: 'My little girl ...'. If I could animate Figure 16.2, this could be represented by the displaced address of the TW father towards his WS1 daughter being assimilated into his TW frame of reference. This would have brought the father–daughter relationship relatively closer to the deictic level occupied by the reader at the top of the discourse world, but the closeness is undermined immediately by the shift of the DW poetic voice into a third-person form: 'Thy father ...'. The 'clod of earth' stands as a further metonym for the father's sense of his own inarticulacy, powerlessness and numbness. The poem ends with the daughter as the passive recipient of agency, and the agent is finally the casket.

Overall, the poem keeps a distance between the reader and the poetic persona. The poet's viewpoint is turned inward, and the embedded world-switches serve only to remove the focus of the poem further away from the reader. Ontologically, the reader observes the rich texture of the father's grief, but does not participate in it, and this structural deictic marking stands as a correlate for the emotional distance too. The poem begins with the poetic persona addressing the girl's belongings, and then moves further away with an address to displaced switched worlds. Only at the end does the present, continuous commentary seem to return to the discourse world, as if the poem ends as a lament spoken at the graveside, but the reader even then is figured as an onlooker, a witness rather than a participant. The poem closes itself off at this present moment.

My argument is that all of these patterns allow the reader to create a strong sense of sympathy (a feeling *for* the father's loss), but they maintain a level of inaccessibility and distance that leaves the emotion in the social sphere rather than anything more intimate – the reader's sympathy is extended to the right of the investment model in Figure 16.1, but there is no exponential return. Of course, the poem's power lies also in its enactment of this emotional restraint: grief being stopped up by rhetoric. And the poem in itself is still a moving and human expression of loss and grief. Viewed in comparison with Kochanowski's 'Lament XII' below, however, there is a contrastive sense of the inclination towards sympathy rather than full empathy.

Lamentation: in Empathy

To modern minds (at least to mine), 'Lament VII' above is less emotionally involving than 'Lament XII' below. I am arguing in this chapter that the former evokes sympathy and the latter evokes empathy, though both relationships are moving and involving in their own right. Of course, it may be that I am reacting relatively adversely to the stoicism, the financial metaphor and the historically situated treatment of a girl as a potential bride with a dowry and a measure of virginity as 'treasure' in 'Lament VII'. These are all culturally alien to me, or at least only accessible through an act of sympathetic imagination. By contrast, the following lament later in Kochanowski's sequence evokes a deeply affecting empathy, I think:

'Lament XII'
I think no father under any sky
More fondly loved a daughter than did I,
And scarcely ever has a child been born
Whose loss her parents could more justly mourn.
Unspoiled and neat, obedient at all times,
She seemed already versed in songs and rhymes,
And with a highborn courtesy and art,
Though but a babe, she played a maiden's part.
Discreet and modest, sociable and free
From jealous habits, docile, mannerly,
She never thought to taste her morning fare
Until she should have said her morning prayer;
She never went to sleep at night until
She had prayed God to save us all from ill.
She used to run to meet her father when
He came from any journey home again;
She loved to work and to anticipate
The servants of the house ere they could wait
Upon her parents. This she had begun
When thirty months their little course had run.
So many virtues and such active zeal
Her youth could not sustain; she fell from weal
Ere harvest. Little ear of wheat, thy prime
Was distant; 'tis before thy proper time
I sow thee once again in the sad earth,
Knowing I bury with thee hope and mirth.
For thou wilt not spring up when blossoms quicken
But leave mine eyes forever sorrow-stricken.

Here, instantly, there is a first person confession in the first two lines, but in the course of those lines the speaker claims the generality and universality of his own thoughts, abstracting and negating himself ('no father'), and abstracting and idealizing his daughter ('a daughter ... a child'). This sudden personal outpouring is instantly stopped up in the next two lines, as the speaker and his wife are turned into the third person ('her parents'), and the large central section of the poem then sets out a character sketch that might be that of an ideal child but is too realistic to be idealized. In contrast to the religious and social conventionality of 'Lament VII', here the girl is drawn in similar conventions ('discreet and modest'), but as a child and not as an anticipated bride. The past tense makes for a straightforward narrativized description that fills the main body of the poem, with a fixed regard towards the daughter. A simple text world diagram (see Figure 16.3) can represent the simplicity of this at a glance.

In contrast with the first lament, there are no broad world-switches here, and therefore a more direct relationship between reader and daughter, deflected only through the discourse world speaker. Where the embedded world-switches in 'Lament VII' were only character-accessible and thus distanced from the reader, here in 'Lament XII' the reader creates out of the text a participant-accessible text world. Instead of observing the poetic speaker's grief, the reader is invited to occupy the same ontological space, and participate in it. This feeling *with* the father in the discourse world is empathy.

The poem intensifies this directness in the way it closes. A few lines from the end, following the balanced, line-ending list of good attributes, the line is broken 'upon her parents'. And again a few lines later (and in the Polish original), 'ere harvest'. As it is uttered, this phrase is a literal marker of time, but in the rest of the line it shifts as a reader must read it retrospectively as a metaphor which is then extended across the end of the poem ('I sow thee once again'). The girl is addressed directly as 'little ear of wheat', the tense shifts to the present, then to the unrealized future ('wilt not spring up'), and then to the actual future ('leave mine eyes forever sorrow-stricken'). And the first person intimacy, pushed aside after the first two lines by the focused regard towards the daughter, returns directly at the same time as the syntax of each

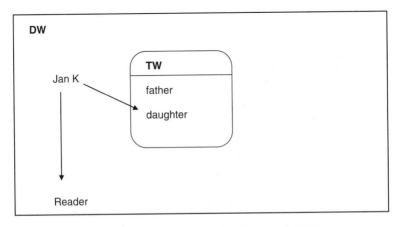

Figure 16.3 Broad text-world diagram for 'Lament XII'

line runs over into the next. The iconic emblem of the flow of grief could not be more marked. The intensity is all the greater for the extended distraction that is the descriptive main body of the poem, that has delayed and delayed the final release of grief.

In some literary experiences, the investment of emotional work correlates with effort expended: you get more out when you put more in. In 'Lament XII', the investment of emotional engagement is all too easy, deceptively simple and direct, and the poem returns with a strongly empathetic and – paradoxically – rich sense of loss.

Authenticity and Attenuation

An objection can be made that such vicarious literary grief, even when made intensely empathetic, is not the same as real-life grief, not even when the grief is real for the author. Of course at a literal level this is true. However, both sympathetic and empathetic connections with discourse participants are created by readers out of language events and are text-driven. In his cognitive grammar, Langacker (2008: 536–8) points out that *all* language representations involve some sense of simulation, in that they are not literally the thing they represent. This means that all expressions are more or less *attenuated* from the objective reality. Authenticity – or at least the readerly sense of authenticity – is a matter of the perceived degree of attenuation. My argument in this chapter is that Kochanowski's laments seem minimally simulated, minimally attenuated, and 'Lament XII' in particular is the most ontologically direct. This is not to say that the creative engagement of the reader is identical to the actual grief of the authorial persona, but the degree of attenuation, because of the stylistic patterns I have sketched out, is so slight as to be barely perceived inauthentically at all.

The conclusion can only be that simulated literary feeling and genuine nonliterary feeling are both authentic, but are different in the degree of apparent attenuation. Kochanowski's laments are of course highly wrought artistic objects, but their skill lies in their seeming directness of voice. Literary and genuine emotions are both represented to consciousness, and both involve similar physically moving effects. In this chapter, I have outlined very briefly two patterns in which this attenuation can be realized. Both require as a prerequisite of reading the adoption of a cognitive stance that is deictically defined relative to the participating speaking consciousness. My argument is that the willing disposition of taking up and creating this stance is the first and inevitable step in an emotional investment in the other person's feelings.

Original Polish Texts of the Laments

'Tren VII'

Nieszczęsne ochędóstwo, żałosne ubiory
Mojej namilszej cory!
Po co me smutne oczy za sobą ciągniecie,
Żalu mi przydajecie?
Już ona członeczków swych wami nie odzieje -
Nie masz, nie masz nadzieje!
Ujął ją sen żelazny, twardy, nieprzespany ...
Już letniczek pisany
I uploteczki wniwecz, i paski złocone,
Matczyne dary płone.
Nie do takiej łożnice, moja dziewko droga,
Miała cię mać uboga
Doprowadzić! Nie takąć dać obiecowala
Wyprawę, jakąć dała
Giezłeczkoć tylko dała a lichą tkaneczkę;
Ojciec ziemie brełeczkę
W główki włożył. - Niestetyż, i posag, i ona
W jednej skrzynce zamkniona!

'Tren XII'

Żaden ojciec podobno barziej nie miłował
Dziecięcia, żaden barziej nad mię nie żałował.
A też ledwe się kiedy dziecię urodziło.
Co by łaski rodziców swych tak godne było.
Ochędożne, posłuszne, karne, niepieszczone,
Śpiewać, mówić, rymować jako co uczone;
Każdego ukłon trafić; wyrazić postawę,
Obyczaje panieńskie umieć i zabawę;
Roztropne, obyczajne, ludzkie, nierzewniwe,
Dobrowolne, układne, skromne i wstydliwe.
Nigdy ona po ranu karmie nie wspomniała,
Aż pierwej Bogu swoje moditwy oddała.
Nie poszła spać, aż pierwej matkę pozdrowiła
I zdrowie rodziców swych Bogu poruczyła.
Zawżdy przeciwko ojcu wszytki przebyć progi,
Zawżdy się uradować i przywitać z drogi,
Każdej roboty pomóc, do każdej posługi
Uprzedzić było wszytki rodziców swych sługi.
A to w tak małym wieku sobie poczynała,

Że więcej nad trzydzieści miesięcy nie miała.
Tak wiele cnót jej młodość i takich dzielności
Nie mogła znieść; upadła od swejże bujności,
Żniwa nie doczekawszy! Kłosie mój jedyny,
Jeszcześ mi się był nie zstał, a ja, twej godziny
Nie czekając; znowu cię w smutną ziemię sieję!
Ale pospołu z tobą grzebę i nadzieję:
Bo już nigdy nie wznidziesz ani przed mojema
Wiekom wiecznie zakwitniesz smutnymi oczema.

REFERENCES

Barańczak, S. and Heaney, S. (eds and trs) (1995) *Laments, by Jan Kochanowski*. New York: Farrar, Strauss and Giroux.

Bourdieu, P. (1972) *Outline of a Theory of Practice*. Cambridge: Cambridge University Press.

Brône, G. and Vandaele, J. (eds) (2009) *Cognitive Poetics: Goals, Gains and Gaps*. Berlin: Mouton de Gruyter.

Czerniawski, A. (tr.) (2001) *Treny: The Laments of Kochanowski*. Oxford: Legenda.

Gavins, J. (2007) *Text World Theory*. Edinburgh: Edinburgh University Press.

Gavins, J. and Steen, G. (eds) (2003) *Cognitive Poetics in Practice*. London: Routledge.

Gerrig, R. (1993) *Experiencing Narrative Worlds: On the Psychological Activities of Reading*. New Haven: Yale University Press.

Gibbs, R. (2002) 'Feeling moved by metaphor' in S. Csabi and J. Zerkowitz (eds) *Textual Secrets*. Budapest: ELTE: 13–28.

Lakoff, G. (1987) *Women, Fire and Dangerous Things: What Categories Reveal about the Mind*. Chicago: University of Chicago Press.

Langacker, R. (2008) *Cognitive Grammar: A Basic Introduction*. Oxford: Oxford University Press.

McIntyre, Dan (2007) 'Deixis, cognition and the construction of viewpoint' in Marina Lambrou and Peter Stockwell (eds) *Contemporary Stylistics*. London: Continuum: 118–30.

Prall, D. (tr.) (1920) *Laments, by Jan Kochanowski*. Berkeley: University of California Press.

Semino, E. and Culpeper, J. (eds) (2002) *Cognitive Stylistics*. Amsterdam: Benjamins.

Stockwell, P. (2002) *Cognitive Poetics: An Introduction*. London: Routledge.

Stockwell, P. (2009a) *Texture: A Cognitive Aesthetics of Reading*. Edinburgh: Edinburgh University Press.

Stockwell, P. (2009b) 'The cognitive poetics of literary resonance'. *Language and Cognition* 1(1): 25–44.

Suter, A. (ed.) (2008) *Lament: Studies in the Ancient Mediterranean and Beyond*. New York: Oxford University Press.

Welsh, D. (1974) *Jan Kochanowski*. New York: Twayne.

Werth, Paul (1997) 'Conditionality as cognitive distance' in A. Athanasiadou and R. Dirven (eds) *On Conditionals Again*. Amsterdam: Benjamins: 243–71.

Werth, P. (1999) *Text Worlds: Representing Conceptual Space in Discourse*. Harlow: Longman.

17

How Reading Groups Talk about Books: A Study of Literary Reception

Joan Swann

Introduction

Reading groups have become an important cultural phenomenon in Britain, the US and several other countries. As the journalist Kieran Falconer comments, 'reading might be a solitary experience but it is one we want to share' (*The Guardian*, 30 January 2009). Reading groups (or book groups or book clubs) regularly meet in members' houses, in pubs or restaurants, in bookshops, workplaces, schools or prisons, or more recently online to discuss contemporary fiction and sometimes more established canonical literature. My focus in this chapter is on the nature of this discussion: the way reading groups talk about books. I believe this has to do with creativity in language in two respects: first, groups are engaged in the interpretation of archetypally creative texts – loosely, print literature; second, the interpretive process, in which groups discursively construct literary readings, may itself be seen as creative. This interest in everyday literary reception – in the literary interpretations provided by 'ordinary' readers, as opposed to critics and academics – also parallels a more established interest in the production of creative episodes in everyday discourse evident in some other chapters in this volume, a point I refer to towards the end of the chapter.

The focus on readers and reading in this chapter is shared by that of Peter Stockwell in Chapter 16, but there are important differences. Stockwell's interest is in cognitive poetics (Stockwell 2002). The emphasis in this tradition is on the construction of cognitive models that map aspects of literary interpretation. Evidence for these models however usually derives from textual analysis: textual analysis by the researcher produces an 'ideal' reading (and an ideal reader) that informs theories of literary reception. Some cognitively motivated studies rely just on the analysis of texts. Other studies draw on empirical evidence of the responses of 'real readers', in this case largely in experimental or quasi-experimental contexts (see e.g. the papers in van Peer 2007). Stockwell's chapter is interesting in that the cognitive 'investment' model of reading that he outlines derives from metaphors evident in the discussions of 'real readers' in a naturally occurring environment – an online reading group – rather than an experiment. However, the work on reading group discourse that I discuss below differs from this study in that it sees naturally occurring reading activities as of interest in their own right, not simply as a potential window on cognitive processes.

A number of studies, in recent years, have begun to look at literary discourse in everyday contexts – for instance, Daniel Allington's (2007) study of slash fiction; Bethan Benwell's (2009) account of the reception of diasporic fiction; and Katarina Eriksson and Karin Aronsson's research on school 'booktalk' (Eriksson 2002; Eriksson and Aronsson 2004). These studies focus on discourse as a site for interpretive activity – an opportunity to catch reception, or one type of reception, on the hoof in particular reading contexts.

The study that I report on here[1] has focussed on *what* reading groups talk about – the interpretations they provide of books under discussion; and also on *how* they construct these interpretations – in particular, how literary activity is a dialogic process, interwoven with the social and interpersonal demands of group interaction and the kinds of reader identities that are negotiated by participants. In the sections that follow I shall look at three illustrations of this interpretive process: the negotiation of interim readings that develop over time; the co-construction of readings between participants; and the orientation towards aspects of participants' identities.

Reading over Time

> When you read them it's very private isn't it – it's your thing, so then when you do turn up at the book club and people start talking about it – I mean most of the time I think my opinion or what I thought about the book will change during the discussion, or maybe not change but it will certainly be – you know, lots more will be added to it.

Reading is often thought of as a private encounter with a text, with reading-group discussion being an opportunity to report and reflect on this. However, reading-group discussion is not simply talk *about* reading: it constitutes one of a series of readerly acts that may also include individual private reading, rereading in the light of discussion, consultation of other readings such as published reviews, or writing up notes or reviews. Textual interpretations are responsive to prior readings, reconstructed and recontextualized across this process. They are not settled, but always susceptible to change in new interpretive contexts. In interviews, group members report that discussion, in particular, affects their earlier interpretations (changing, adding to or perhaps reinforcing these). Analysis of the discussion itself reveals more closely the sequential development of readings as these are collaboratively co-constructed within the interaction. For instance, in one group's discussion of language in Anne Enright's *The Gathering*, an initial reference to the language as 'extremely crude' is further developed over three and a half minutes and balanced with an alternative view of language as 'very seductive and lyrical' to give a blended and more considered interpretation – the language is both 'crude' and 'sublime' (Swann and Allington 2009).

The Co-construction of Readings between Participants

We are a pretty talkative group, and after almost five years we know each other pretty well, so any inhibitions have disappeared!

Literary talk itself – the way this is done – is necessarily contingent on patterns of conversation management that characterize informal interaction, as readings are collaboratively developed between participants and closely embedded in social and interpersonal processes. The extract below, from a discussion of Muriel Spark's *A Far Cry from Kensington*, shows how the topic of class in the novel is developed by two reading group members I refer to as Lynne and Jenny (these are L and J in the transcript; 'Sev' is short for 'several speakers')[2]:

```
1    L    The   other   question   actually    Relatively
          eh I had about this book is is        slow,
          (.) whereas I think it is very        measured
          evocative of the time in my view      speaking
          (.) it seems to me also to be         style
          very evocative of a of a class
          <mmh> (.) you know <mmh> and eh
          the kinds of things that happen
          to her the places that she worked
          and and (.) even her ability you
          know not to have to work you know
          f- for you know she didn't not
          having to find a job immediately
          <mmh> no- that
```

kind of thing was kind of just
struck me that she was (.) she was
representing eh mmh (.) I don't
know (.) upper working class lower
middle class kind of life=

2   J   =kind of lower middle class   Slow speech
cos they <u>lived in real modest</u>
<u>circumstances</u> <mmh> you know
hot plates in the room <mmh>
and things like that the sort of
thing that we would all go 'oh   takes on
<u>lord</u>' at now (.) and um (.) on the   alternative
other hand there was that kind   voice
of (.) the girl had the telephone
put in
[(by the father)

3   L   [Yeah so that [was funny
4   Sev   [mmh
5   L   but when I got here in 68 most
people didn't have telephones
either so that that didn't strike
me as
unus[ual you know

6   J   [we didn't have a phone until
1976

7   ?   yeah
8   ?   <u>no</u>   Slightly
extended
– agreement

9   J   when I paid for it

Note: see the Appendix for transcript conventions here and below.

Lynne draws a parallel between her new topic – class – and the group's earlier discussion of the 1950s, both by direct reference ('The other question ... etc.') and by parallelism: in the same way as the book is 'very evocative of the time' it is 'very evocative of a class'. The pauses indicate a fairly measured speaking style and, as is usual in informal talk, there are hesitations and some false starts – Lynne has the floor to herself apart from minimal responses (here indicating attention and interactional support) but she is constructing her ideas as she speaks. Lynne suggests the novel is representing an upper-working-class or lower-middle-class lifestyle. Jenny continues this point, arguing that it is lower-middle class. Both speakers display a degree of tentativeness: Lynne's 'kind of just struck me', 'I don't know'; Jenny's initial 'kind of'. Such mitigation, in which speakers hedge their views, is common across our reading groups. In an earlier paper, (Swann and Allington 2009) my colleague Daniel Allington and I interpret this sort of activity in terms of face work (Goffman 1955) where speakers need to respect the face of fellow group members who may evaluate or interpret the same books differently.

Jenny's argument is supported by a hypothetical appeal to the views of others in the group ('we would all go "Oh lord"'). In her use of reported speech here, Jenny draws on voice quality and intonation to represent and animate her speakers.

In turn 5 Lynne's interpretation of an event in the novel – the installation of a phone – draws on her own experience: it wouldn't have been unusual not to have a phone at this time. This is recognized by others and leads into a series of personal recollections. Later, in bringing the discussion back to class in the novel, another speaker, Theresa (T), uses anaphoric reference ('the whole class thing') to link to the earlier discussion:

```
51      T     I guess with the whole class thing     Turn
              because it was something that's you     begins
              know because William was a um (.) he    after a
              comes he ca- she's quite surprised      five-second
              that he comes from a very (xxx)         pause
              <mmh> background <mmh> and <mmh>
              (.) you know he was a scholarship
              boy and stuff like that <yeah> which
              is quite interesting
```

These extracts show how speakers manage their discussion – in this case of social class, but the broad patterns identified here apply also to other topics and to discussion in other groups: interpretations are a dialogical accomplishment, jointly constructed, with speakers appealing to shared recollections, citing others' voices and building on one another's ideas within and across topics while also attending to the management of interpersonal relations.

The following extract, from another group discussion, provides a somewhat different and slightly more complex illustration of this process. This second group meets in a pub. It consisted originally of four male friends who had been meeting for a drink for several years and then decided to discuss a book occasionally. A female partner of one of the men began attending more recently, and two additional female partners are attending this meeting. The group is discussing the Egyptian novel *The Yakoubian Building* by Alaa al Aswany.

1	R	The Koran says you can have an abor-	
		tion if I twist the rules a bit <yes>	
		and it's entirely cynical and you	
		wonder if that Al <u>Aswany</u> is is a	<u>i.e. book</u>
		Christian name	<u>author</u>
2	Sev	(xxxxxx)	
3	R	Aswany means coming from Aswan	
4	M	it's also a very bad	
		[(hand at scrabble)	
5	R	[but I don't know-	
6	M	look he's got six 'a's in his name-	
7	R	yes (he's gonna) but if he's a	
		Christian (.) it puts a different	
		light on it doesn't it (.) I don't	
		know if he's a Christian	
8	M	so is this a funny spelling of	
		Al- (xxx)	
9	R	it's not Allah it's not no no it's	
		a different 'l' and it's a differ-	
		ent 'a' there's no 'h' Al Aswan Al	
		Aswany means	
10	?	from [Aswan	
11	R	[the person who comes from Aswan	
12	M?	but he's a [genuine person though	
13	R	[it's not it's not	
14	R	yeah yeah but I just wonder if he	
		himself is a Christian	
15	S	does anybody know how the	
		[book (was received	
16	C	[<u>he</u>'s a dentist	<u>i.e. author</u>
17	S	in Egypt)	
18	R	he's a dentist but is he Christian	
19	D	<u>he might be a Coptic dentist</u>	<u>humorous</u>
			<u>tone</u>
20	R	<u>he could be a Coptic dentist</u>	
21	D	do the Coptics come from Aswan	
		(xxx)	
22	R	the Co- the Copts come from all over	
		Egypt	
23	D	(but) what what is it here that makes	
		you think he's Christian	

The group has been discussing the novel's depiction of corruption in Egyptian society, including religion. This leads Rob (R in the transcribed extract) to speculate whether the author is a Christian. Other speakers raise different topics – the meaning and spelling of the author's name, including a jocular reference to Scrabble; a topic raised at turn 15 that is not taken up here, though the speaker, Sally (S), returns to it later; the fact that the author is a dentist. One point of interest here is the management of these different topics and, in particular, the interactional work carried out by Rob, who seeks to pursue his own topic (is the author a Christian?) while also, concurrently, contributing to topics raised by others. I have retranscribed the extract in Figure 17.1 in two columns, and with less detail, to illustrate this process more clearly.

Here Rob's utterances are represented in bold text, and those of other speakers in plain text. The 'Christian' topic development is shown in the left-hand column, and other topics in the right-hand column. While pursuing his own topic, Rob also hops across to respond to questions raised by other speakers in the discussion of other topics, until Dan (D), initially humorously, links Rob's 'Christian' topic with Chris (C)'s reference to the fact that the author is a dentist ('He might be a Coptic dentist') before asking Rob more seriously what makes him think the author is Christian.

Rob has lived and worked in Egypt, where the book is set, and much of his time throughout the interaction is spent providing information on events in the novel, the Arabic language and Egyptian culture. This is often in response to questions addressed to him by other speakers. Explanations occasionally occupy lengthy speaking turns running over one or two minutes – something that is otherwise uncharacteristic of this group's interactional style. Rob enjoys a marked but temporary status in the interaction, speaking and being oriented to by others as someone with expertise. This is made explicit by another speaker, Mike (M), who is about to visit Egypt and tells Rob, in a slightly laughing voice, 'we must have another tutorial before we go to Cairo'.

Rob's expertise constitutes an interpretive resource, invoked by Rob and by other speakers and drawn on in the construction of literary readings. This affects what is said and how the talk is structured. This process may also be analysed in terms of identity construction, as a potential aspect of Rob's identity is temporarily foregrounded and enacted (oriented to and performed) by participants. Particular identity categories may also be more explicitly invoked in discussion of characters and events in the book – a point I illustrate in the following section.

Is the author a Christian?	Other topics
The Koran says you can have an abortion if I twist the rules a bit and it's entirely cynical and you wonder if that Aswany is a Christian name	
	(xxxxxx) Aswany means coming from Aswan It's also a very bad (hand at scrabble) look he's got six 'a's in his name-
but if he's a Christian it puts a different light on it doesn't it I don't know if he's a Christian	
	So is this a funny spelling of Al (xxx) It's not Allah it's not no no it's a different 'l' and it's a different 'a' there's no 'h' and Al Aswany means the person who comes from Aswan But he's a genuine person though Yeah yeah...
...but I just wonder if he himself is a Christian	
	Does anybody know how the book (was received in Egypt) He's a dentist
He's a dentist but is he a Christian He might be a Coptic dentist He could be a Coptic dentist Do the Coptics come from Aswan (xxx) The Copts come from all over Egypt But what is it here that makes you think he's Christian	

Figure 17.1　Is the author a Christian? Column transcript

Aspects of Participants' Identities

> When you read you have a relationship with the novel, related to your life and what's happened to you, and that comes out.

The extracts below come from a reading group that meets in a prison, organized by the prison librarian. This is an all-male prison but the librarian is female. The group has been reading *The Worms of Euston Square* by William Sutton. There are 11 reading-group members at the meeting, including the librarian. On this occasion the author is also present. We were not able to audio-record this discussion, so the extracts below are not verbatim transcripts but are based on notes made by two researchers at the meeting. While they give a good idea of the topics that were discussed, they do not include any of the interactional detail evident in the transcripts above. In the notes, B is the librarian; C, D, E, F and G are other reading-group members.

Just before the first extract (turns 24–26), there has been some discussion of characters in the novel, then at turn 24 Geoff (G) refers to the character of a librarian at the British Museum. After some discussion of other characters, the prison librarian returns to this at turn 55:

24	G	... and the resourceful librarian absolutely resourceful, absolutely resourceful, absolutely resourceful
25	E	nuff respect
26	G	I thought she got a raw deal [...]
55	B	Where did the character of Ruth [librarian] come from? ((laughter))
56	G	she sacrificed so much
57	E	the bit that tickled me was when (xxx)
58	F	that tickled me too
59	B	I have a complaint, actually 'he bought a cape to cover my dowdy library clothes' ((reads from book)) ((laughter)) [...]
62	C	I was a bit upset that she never had a trendy assistant. ((laughter))

63	G	I worried about her. She found out so much. Did she have a hidden agenda?
64	D	That set off alarm bells.
65	C	And that bit about confidentiality – there's no confidentiality in libraries. ((laughter))
66	B	I haven't told security what you've been reading.

There is a great deal of humour in this extract, evident in laughter from participants. At turn 55, it is the prison librarian herself who asks about the librarian in the novel, and who later (turn 59) complains about this character's 'dowdy library clothes'. At turn 62 Chris (C), who refers to the absence of a 'trendy assistant', is someone who works as an assistant in the prison library. His later humorous reference to the lack of confidentiality in libraries (turn 65) is capped by the librarian in turn 66. The humour comes from the blending of the text world of the novel (here constructed in interaction between readers[3]) and aspects of the discourse world (the 'here and now' in which interpretations of the novel are created). This allows readers humorously to link the depiction of a character (or in one case the absence of a character) and aspects of their own identity that become salient in this context – either in ironic references to themselves or in mutual teasing of one another (turns 65–6). There are similar occasions in other discussions where reference to a character or event in the novel calls up, and provides an opportunity for working on, aspects of a participant's identity. Here, then, it's evident that literary activity is not simply contingent on the social and interpersonal activity that characterizes spoken interaction (so that issues of face, for instance, affect the construction of interpretations). Literary activity itself may be brought into service – humorously in this case – to invoke participants' identities and construct relations with others.

Discussion

> Readers read for someone and for some purpose, they do not just 'read' in a vacuum. (Hall 2009: 334)

It's possible to make a connection between the study of literary reading (the reception of 'creative' texts) and work on creativity in language that has a greater focus on production. My own interest in 'ordinary readers' parallels an interest amongst many language scholars in the creative language produced by 'ordinary' speakers and writers – in this collection, for instance, Elena Semino's study of metaphor across genres, Lynne Cameron's discussion of 'prosaic creativity', Angela Goddard's work on language use in new communication technologies, and Janet Maybin's account of the dialogic creativity evident in personal letters.

In both cases research may be seen as contributing to a process of 'democratisation' (cf. Carter 2004) in which instances of literary, or literary-like, activity in everyday discourse are recognized and acknowledged. Reading-group activity itself has been seen as legitimizing everyday literary interpretations. For instance, a commentary on reading groups in the British newspaper *The Guardian* cites a claim from the literary scholar John Sutherland that 'people are reclaiming the right to read from pointy-headed academics' (Higgins, C. *The Guardian*, 12 February 2005). And Jenny Hartley's (2002) survey of reading groups suggests that, while reading groups do not want to be academic authorities, neither are they fazed by authority. In a neat turning of the tables, the study of reading-group discourse suggests that an activity sometimes positioned against academic discourse is itself worthy of academic attention.

I mentioned earlier, in the introduction to this chapter, that the study of interpretations of literary texts by 'real readers' has sometimes taken an experimental or quasi-experimental approach. Geoff Hall (2008, 2009) cautions against this relatively decontextualized approach to reading. Reading groups, by contrast, provide a naturally occurring laboratory in which a habitual literary practice may be studied (cf. Allington and Swann 2009; Swann and Allington 2009). The extracts above, for instance, show reading being done in context and to a purpose. Reading here is seen as:

- Interim, not settled (readings may develop and change over time).
- Contingent upon the interactional context in which this occurs (adapted to the routines and requirements of informal interaction; embedded within particular sets of social and interpersonal relationships; calling up shared recollections of prior events).
- Dialogic, both in the sense that readings respond to (revisit and recontextualize) earlier readings, and that they are sequentially developed and co-constructed between participants.
- Functional/strategic – participants are not simply doing a literary activity, they are doing something with this (e.g. managing relationships; playing; foregrounding and working on participants' identities).

This view of reading as interim, contingent, dialogic and strategic contrasts with a relatively stable and decontextualized conception of reading that is implicit in much experimental and/or cognitively oriented work (i.e. when a particular reading of a text or textual extract is identified). It does however have something in common with studies of language creativity (the production of creative episodes) that, similarly, view this as contextualized and locally strategic (as in the chapters in Parts I and II of this volume).

Recognizing and paying attention to the literary interpretations of ordinary readers does not suggest that these are as good as (or for that matter better or worse than) those of professional readers such as critics and academics. In fact the approach I have outlined does not seek to evaluate the literary quality of particular interpretations. Here again there are parallels with the production of creative (literary-like) language – for instance, with Semino's argument (see Chapter 6) that the success of metaphor may only be assessed in relation to the context in which it occurs (the genre, goals of the speaker/writer, relationships between speaker/writer and listener/reader, etc.).

In the same way, everyday and professional readings cannot be judged according to the same criteria, as they are doing different things. In the study of reading groups readers mention, variously: the transformative potential of discussion; the value of collaborative processes of interpretation in which meanings are shared and other readers may be drawn on as a resource; the stimulus provided by literary discussion for discussion of other topics; the social value of talking about books with friends and colleagues. A contextualized approach to the study of everyday literary reading, with its focus on local interpretive processes, would also need to take account of such local sets of values, suggesting that it is pointless to seek to evaluate ways of reading, or particular readings, outside the context in which these are produced.

Appendix: Transcription Conventions

The following conventions are used in the transcripts above:

(.)	Brief pause.
<mmh>	Minimal response that does not constitute a separate turn, and where it is not possible to identify the speaker.
=	Latching, a turn that follows immediately after another with no perceptible gap.
[Aswan [the person	Square brackets mark the start of overlapping text.

(hand at scrabble)	Brackets indicate some uncertainty in transcription.
(xxxx)	Unclear text that could not be transcribed.
<u>Aswany</u>	Underlining indicates text that is commented on in the right-hand margin.

NOTES

1. The study is entitled The Discourse of Reading Groups (2008) and was funded by the British Arts and Humanities Research Council (AHRC). Researchers were Joan Swann, Kieran O'Halloran and Daniel Allington. We are grateful to the reading groups who participated in this research and to the AHRC for their support. For information on the project, see www.open.ac.uk/dorg/index.shtml.
2. All participants in the study are referred to by pseudonyms.
3. The 'reader' in Chapter 16 seems to be an individual construct in which an individual (ideal) reader interacts with a text, but here the text world of the novel is jointly constructed between readers.

REFERENCES

Allington, D. (2007) '"How come most people don't see it?": slashing *The Lord of the Rings*', *Social Semiotics* 17(1): 45–64.

Allington, D. and Swann, J. (2009) 'Researching literary reading as social practice' in Allington, D. and Swann, J. (eds) *Literary Reading as Social Practice*. Special Issue of *Language and Literature* 18(3): 219–30.

Benwell, B. (2009) '"A pathetic and racist and awful character": ethnomethodological approaches to the reception of diasporic fiction' in Allington, D. and Swann, J. (eds) *Literary Reading as Social Practice*. Special Issue of *Language and Literature* 18(3): 300–15.

Carter, R. (2004) *Language and Creativity: The Art of Common Talk*. London: Routledge.

Eriksson, K. (2002) *Life and Fiction: On Intertextuality in Pupils' Booktalk*. Linköping, Sweden: Linköping University Press.

Eriksson, K. and Aronsson, K. (2004) 'Building life world connections during school booktalk'. *Scandinavian Journal of Educational Research* 48(5): 511–28.

Goffman, E. (1955) 'On face-work: an analysis of ritual element in social interaction', *Psychiatry* 18: 213–31. Reproduced in Hutchinson, J. and Laver, S. (eds) (1972) *Communication in Face to Face Interaction*. Harmondsworth: Penguin Books.

Hall, G. (2008) 'Empirical research into the processing of free indirect discourse and the imperative of ecological validity' in Zyngier, S., Bortolussi, M., Chesnokova, A. and Auracher, J. (eds) *Directions in Empirical Literary Studies*. Amsterdam: John Benjamins.

Hall, G. (2009) 'Texts, readers – and real readers' in Allington, D. and Swann, J. (eds) *Literary Reading as Social Practice*. Special Issue of *Language and Literature* 18(3): 331–7.

Hartley, J. (2002) *The Reading Groups Book: 2002–2003 Edition*. Oxford: Oxford University Press.

Peer, W. van (ed.) (2007) Special issue of *Language and Literature* on Foregrounding (2)16.

Stockwell, Peter (2002) *Cognitive Poetics: An Introduction*. London/New York: Routledge.

Swann, J. and Allington, D. (2009) 'Reading groups and the language of literary texts: a case study in social reading' in Allington, D. and Swann, J. (eds) *Literary Reading as Social Practice*. Special Issue of *Language and Literature* 18(3): 247–64.

18

Reader Response and the Formulation of Literary Judgement

Jane Spiro

Introduction

Contemporary readers will acknowledge the volatile nature of reader taste. We are ready to agree that notions of literary quality 'mutate along with the cultural evolution of a society' (McDonald 2007: 23). Yet we are also able to identify easily the guardians of our literary tastes: the publishers, journals, prizes, literary appointments that determine what is mainstream and successful. Whilst, at a theoretical level, we might as readers believe in a democracy of taste, it is these yardsticks of success that direct our notions of quality. As readers, we are invited to believe that the slush pile separates the worthy from the less worthy. But would the poets and poems that have achieved visibility be valued more highly than those which have not, if stripped from their context? Is there a coherent notion as to what constitutes poetic quality? And do the amateur and the professional always fall on opposite sides of this divide?

   This chapter enters the debate by setting side by side, anonymously, poems by major poets, small press poets and creative writing students. Eight readers, all with a professional or lifelong connection with poetry, were asked to rank these poems. No background information was offered by which to prejudge their reading. The study offers cautious answers to the three questions above, and in so doing unravels reader perceptions of 'poetic quality', exploring how readers rationalize their intuitive judgement of what they like and do not, and how far these perceptions correlate with the prestige or otherwise of the poet.

Poems, Readers and a Purpose for Reading

The Poems

The eight poems included: two from students practising creative writing in an undergraduate class; two unpublished poems from participants in poetry workshops; two poems, one published in a small press and the other self-published; two poems from mainstream publishers, including one by Wislawa Szymborska, a Nobel prizewinner for poetry. To minimize the variables the poems were between 10 and 25 lines in length. One poem out of the eight included a consistent A B C B rhyme scheme, but otherwise none of the poems adopted traditional forms, nor belonged to a discernible 'school' or genre of poetry such as 'language' or narrative poetry. Six out of the eight poems dealt with aspects of nature – birds, animals, the natural world. These choices were made in order to isolate features of judgement which were not type, genre, content or school-specific. In addition, relatively obscure poems and poets were chosen, to ensure readers would not be able to recognize authors.

The Readers

Eight readers were invited to respond to the texts. Four of the readers had a professional connection with poetry, four did not. The readers can be grouped as follows:

- Two readers had been teachers of creative writing and poetry. One of these readers had in addition judged a national poetry competition and is also a published poet.
- Two readers had edited a poetry journal. Both these readers are in addition published poets.
- Four readers (termed 'leisure readers' below) had no professional connection with poetry, but were self-acclaimed and lifelong readers of poetry.

Richards (1978: 310–11) cites immaturity and lack of reading as factors in the judgement of his informants in the practical criticism exercise described in the book that introduced 'practical criticism' as a method. These readers, in contrast, represent the informed adult reader, with evolved views about literary quality that shape their professional judgements and reading preferences.

The Purpose of Reading

The readers were asked to respond to the poems on the basis of their own relationship with poetry. In each case, they were invited to divide the poems into three ranked groups. These rankings matched those with which they would be professionally or personally familiar:

- A excellent; B competent; C unacceptable (the creative writing teachers/ competition judge);
- accept; shortlist; reject (the poetry editors);
- I like this poem; I'm not sure; I don't like this poem (leisure readers).

The readers were invited to make this first ordering rapidly and intuitively. However, once this was complete, they were asked to review their choice and write brief explanatory notes rationalizing their decisions.

Analysing the Poems as Literary Text

The section that follows invites you the reader to experience the poems in the same way as the informants of this research study. They are presented in the same format, with the poet remaining anonymous. As with the informants of this study, you are invited to consider where would you place each poem on a spectrum of like/not sure/dislike (accept/reserve/reject), and what would be your reasoning for doing so?

1. 'The Common Finch'
One way of looking
is to listen.

Finches, look at finches
heartening drabs of cranberry
which the dictionary calls 'any small
seed-eating passerine bird of the family
fringillidae'

Finches are a reminder
of things fierce and delicate,
small creatures which congregate on the thinly strung
wires which connect
our buildings,
and sing to each other

Small creatures that sing to each other

2. 'fish out of water'

Heron
Statuesque grace
Sleek tension
Elastic readiness
Stands seawater body high Speckled camouflage Near invisible
Delicate wind Feathers ruffle A sideways shift Orange red beak
Rigid Expectant
Circular eye taut in preparation
Ready to diffract water

Lightningfastspeedshockofthestrike
Neckheadbeakinsideoutsidewaterinaflashofmovement

Sight strains to catch up
Back to sculpture mine
Breath out
Vice grip
Fish twists
Head, tail squirm in waterless space
Eye blink joins a single gulp

Dysfunctional journey of airborne fish continues

fish out of water power of the heron its stillness

3. 'Could have'

For copyright reasons it has proved impossible to reproduce this poem here. An electronic version can be found at http://justajutsa.blogspot.com/2005/05/wislawa-szymborska-could-have-poem.html. For full bibliographic details, see p. 244.

4. 'Desolution'

Blue as ice but not cold, no
Sea green but not wet, this
Deep abyss bright, bright as mist –

My whole past flashed past last
Time I surfaced, guess it's still
Up there careering about
Or, lifeless raft, rocked land,

Sits like some dumb microland
Gulls use, let them: I float down –

Look! It does not drown!

5. 'Captivity'

And suddenly I am the falling bird
peppered with your words,
a flurry of feathers,
wheeling down from blue
to waiting earth,

Suddenly, without warning,
I am the prisoner on the run
felled by your fire
splattered like a cartoon cat
against a wall.

I was the hare cavorting in the sun,
my flapping ears attuned to joy
until you spoke,
whose legs fold, who knows
she is undone.

6. 'Prophecy'

A seer writes with a broken icicle
around the circumference of a melting lake,
a seeing sentence short as winter:
a prophecy on our landscape.
He warns of summer's hot heart
whose deadly beam will burn
skin, scale, fur, bone
and all the open faces of flowers;
our air laced with fly-away poisons.
The eleventh hour now known,
the twelfth too late to unhappen.

7. 'Summer of '92'

It was in the Summer of 1992
When so much depended on my Mother's approval
To go for a walk and enjoy this beautiful day.

We walked up the hill of the Chemin du Gachet
And there at the peak we saw Monsieur Dupont, the Farmer
of Fainex.

He waved at my mother and asked if I wanted to feed his
white chickens

I ran towards the birdcage, so excited.

And beside the cage, were two of the farmer's dogs
playing away
They ran toward a red wheelbarrow where they found
and drank collected rain water left from yesterday.

8. 'An Alternative Last Duchess'
The Duchess didn't love him
She loved his name
So he wanted her painted
The Duke went insane

He told me 'paint her now
Before she is dead'
I wanted to show beauty
But instead my brush was led

He said she had cheated
I asked 'who's to blame?'
He held 'She's a beast
Who I need to tame!'

So I painted the Duchess
I gave my best try
Little did he know?
That the lover was I.

As reader, your response to these poems will draw on a complexity of possible values, notions and specific literary features. Amongst those features of 'literary value' that may or may not have shaped your interpretation are: semantic density – the capacity for a text to work at several levels (Carter 2005); metaphor as 'special ability to evoke deep emotional responses and elevate the human spirit' (Gibbs 2008: 209); engagement with the subject matter itself (as in the Richards exercise); vocabulary choice or syntax; line breaks and enjambement as the most visual distinction between prose and poetry; use of specific poetic strategies such as patterning in sound, rhythm and rhyme; proximity or otherwise to 'everyday' language; the capacity to surprise. What may also have emerged in your first encounter was a sense of which were, according to you, the preferable/publishable poets and which were not. You might like, now, to match these interpretations beside the information below.

Poem 1: Cralan Kelder, 'The Common Finch'
In Kelder (2006). Poem 1 was published in a small press of writers living in Berlin.

Poem 2: Stanley Pelter, 'fish out of water'
In Pelter (2008).

Poem 3: Wislawa Szymborska, 'Could have'
In Szymborska (1998). A poem by the Nobel prizewinning poet, Wislawa Szymborska, translated from the Polish.

Poem 4: Libby Houston, 'Desolution'
In Houston (1999).

Poem 5: 'Captivity'
Unpublished poem from creative writing participant Christine Koutilieri.[1]

Poem 6: 'Prophecy'
Unpublished poem from creative writing workshop participant Caroline Ashley.

Poem 7: 'Summer of '92'
Unpublished student poem.

Poem 8: 'An Alternative Last Duchess'
Unpublished student poem.

Analysing Reader Response

Figure 18.1 lists the poems in order of writer experience. The number of entries in each category will offer a rapid visual summary of reader response and these are subdivided into three kinds of reader:

L   'leisure' reader (4 people);
T   creative writing teacher/judge (2 people);
E   poetry editor (2 people).

Figure 18.1 shows firstly the lack of consensus in response, even between the professional readers. For example, the two editors differed in their response to each one of the eight poems. In all eight cases, the literary teacher/competition judges differed from at least one of the poetry editors. Three out of the eight poems were accepted by one editor and rejected by another; and in none of the eight readings did the editors agree on their responses.

There is also an interesting lack of consistent relationship between the poem's 'scoring' and the poet's writing status and experience. 'Desolution', written by a successful mainstream published poet, scored less well as a first choice than 'Summer of '92', by a student embarking on writing poetry for the first time. 'Captivity', an unpublished poem shared at a writing workshop,

Poem	Authorship	I like this poem (L); A grade (T); accept (E)	I'm not sure (L); B grade (T); shortlist (E)	I don't like this poem (L); C grade (T); reject (E)
Summer of '92	Student	L T	L L T E	L E
An Alternative Last Duchess	Student	L L L	E	L T T E
Captivity	Workshop	L L L T T E	L E	
Prophecy	Workshop	L L E	L L T T	E
fish out of water	Self-published	L L L	T E	L T E
The Common Finch	Small press	L L E	L T T	L E
Desolution	Mainstream poet		L T E	L L L T E
Could have	Mainstream poet/ Nobel prizewinner	L L T T E	L L	E

Figure 18.1   Reader response to the eight poems

was the most popular in the set, and equally valued by both professional and leisure readers.

In justifying their choices, it is possible to identify poetic characteristics raised by several readers. However, these characteristics elicited opposing responses in different readers: text patterning of various sorts evinced excitement in one reader and resistance in another; responses to ambiguity and imagery were expressed in different ways and with different levels of enthusiasm. Thus, whilst poetic characteristics may inform literary judgements and may distinguish writing along a cline of literariness (Carter 2006), it is not possible to determine whether, or how far, such characteristics correlate with reading enjoyment in isolation from other factors. Also evident in the reader responses were concepts such as authenticity, engagement with content, believability and 'relatability' of the content. How can analysis really arrive at any objective measure of these? Yet clearly there are dangers in arriving at notions of poetic quality which do not take account of what experienced readers actually value.

Tolerance of Ambiguity

Two leisure readers explicitly disliked ambiguity as a feature: 'I like less or am uncertain about poems that to me felt either too worked on and contrived, or poems that seemed a bit pretentious'; 'they were alluding to "bigger" enigmatic things without making anything clearer. What's the pleasure in a poem if it just asks a question?'.

The poem identified as most ambiguous ('Desolution') was the least popular with both leisure and professional readers. None selected this as a poem they liked or would accept for a journal. Comments about this included: 'I like the flow of the language but I don't understand this!'; 'I wasn't sure what was going on so didn't find the imagery so effective'; 'I feel it is too deliberately obscure to satisfy'.

In contrast, four readers (L x 1, T x 2, E x 1) agreed on the intriguing ambiguity of 'Could have' by Szymborska. This was described by readers as 'fluctuating and breathless' 'thrilling' and revealing 'the complex nature of simple language'. The language was both opaque enough to be intriguing, yet simple enough to convey meaning. 'I had a moment of not being sure with this poem, but re-read it and decided I really liked all those near-miss ideas' (L). However, one of the literary editors put this poem in the reject pile: 'I don't know what's going on'.

Response to Text Patterning

Some readers were explicit in stating that patterns within the text did not impact on their reading enjoyment: 'Don't think I was particularly influenced by metre, word patterns or rhyme in liking' (L); whilst another reader cited this as a factor in making a positive choice: 'deft combination of sight and sound' (E).

'Summer of '92', which includes long final lines that are rhymed *playing away/yesterday*, evoked a reaction: 'I don't like the rhyme in the last stanza for some reason' (T), although the same reader enjoyed the simplicity of style and subject matter earlier in the poem. 'An Alternative Last Duchess', with its rhyming stanzas, was described by the competition judge as 'too tricksy' (T).

'fish out of water', which is set out long and thin on the page rather like the heron it describes, was noted by one leisure reader: 'I like the shape of the poem on the page'. This reader also liked the running together of words (*Lightningfastspeedshockofthestrike*) to reflect the speed and motion of the heron. Three of the leisure readers enjoyed the patterning in this poem and felt it elicited 'brilliantly' the movement, speed and shape of the heron. Yet this same linguistic patterning and precision was felt to be mechanical by the creative writing teacher. The structure adjective/noun, followed by the subject/complement structure, seemed to him mechanical: 'I would advise to list a little less and develop a sense of continuous voice'. The term 'mechanical' was used by both professional and non-professional readers critically; for example where a poetic device such as rhyme seemed to be used irresponsibly or with a 'jingle-jangle effect'; or where a pattern seemed to be used repetitively while 'not saying much'.

The Affective Qualities of Poetry

For the leisure readers, the core quality that made a poem enjoyable was the capacity: 'to make my heart thrill in a moment of recognition: kindred spirit, a moment of time stopped, irony' (L). 'Captivity' was selected by three out of four of the leisure readers on the basis of its emotional impact: 'I think this poem expresses brilliantly the sudden shock of critical words' (L). By the same token, the poems which created distance were deselected. This distance might be created simply by the use of a pronoun which excludes the reader: 'I felt distanced from this poem because the seer is *he*' (L; referring to 'Prophecy'); or the distance might be created by a lack of mood-setting language ('Summer of '92') or, for one reader, a sense of insincerity: 'the words don't set any mood for me and the quote and end repetition killed the thing dead' ('The common finch'). 'Could have', which derives its power explicitly from linguistic paradoxes and ambiguities, was rejected by one of the two poetry editors: 'it seems too clever and detached, which undermines the mystery, the joy, the passion?'.

The Role of the Image/Metaphor

The capacity to create an image was mentioned by several of the readers. One wrote of a dispreferred poem: 'does not convey a strong image'. Here the preferred poem was 'fish out of water', which describes rather than invites a symbolic or metaphorical reading. For this leisure reader, the term 'image' meant the capacity to convey a clear picture without ambiguity: 'captures the tension and movement of a heron catching a fish'. Yet this same quality was rejected by one of the judges/teachers: 'just descriptive – doesn't go anywhere'.

Other readers mention specifically their enjoyment of imagery in the precise literary sense of simile or metaphor. 'I liked the imagery of the finches being *drabs of cranberry*' (E). 'Desolation' was appreciated by the creative writing teacher who enjoyed the symbolism of gull/drowning person and the movement in imagery between surface and depth.

The Subject and Content of Poetry

As suggested earlier, the common thread in six of the eight poems was an attention to the natural world, yet some drew on natural imagery more ambiguously or symbolically than others. Thus, it was interesting to note the readers who commented on the importance of subject matter. One leisure reader preferred the poem about the heron in 'fish out of water' to 'The common finch' because 'I like poems about nature anyway'. The heron was popular as a subject and determined the preference of three of the leisure readers: 'I'm always thrilled by a glimpse of a heron and this poem helps to explain why'.

Other specific references to content included the childhood memories in 'Summer of '92' as a specific factor in enjoyment; and the 'icily described prediction' of global warming in 'Prophecy', admired by one of the poetry editors.

Lexical Choices

Two professional readers identified cliché as a negative – 'avoid clichéd subject and phrasing', whilst this same feature in 'An Alternative Last Duchess' was described by a leisure reader as 'simple language' and a factor determining enjoyment. The professional readers were also critical of the archaisms in 'Prophecy' and 'An Alternative Last Duchess'. A key factor in merit, suggested by one of the editors, was the linguistic discipline of 'Prophecy': 'every word counts, nothing wasted, and beneath the lyrical strength there is a vital message'.

Coherence

The creative writing teacher was the only reader in this group to mention coherence as an issue in evaluation. Here, specifically, comments included coherence of poetic voice in terms of line length, stylistic consistency and clarity of the authorial voice: 'would advise to work on coherence of form'.

Echoes of Other Work

Where readers were reminded of other writers or genres, they were invariably positive. For example, Szymborska's 'Could have' was described by the creative writing teacher as 'Beckett-esque', and the poetry editor notes in his marginalia that this is like Miroslav Holub. Both highly appreciated the poem and placed it in their top category. Similarly, the editor wondered whether 'The Common Finch' was by Ruth Padel, and also selected it for his journal. Again, one of the poetry editors identified 'Summer of '92' as having a '*faux naif*' quality. This, he goes on to explain, would be acceptable in a 'young poet, or an older poet just starting out' but 'if it is an established poet attempting to revisit the world of childhood by reinventing him/herself in this mode of expression, then I'm not so sure'. Verbal echoes, or affiliation to a school or style of poetry, seem to invite the reader here to question writer intention and authenticity.

Reading for Different Purposes

Reading as a Creative Writing Teacher

One creative writing teacher felt strongly that the academy's concern should be with process and not with product. To arrive at a complete judgement, the teacher/reader thus needed to take account of 'reflection, analysis, comparison' and not product alone. The teacher approached the text as negotiable and fluid, rather than final. In this reading exercise, the teacher recorded his sense of the difference between reader as mentor and reader as judge; between writing as process and writing as end-product. The judgements are offered with the proviso that principled reflection would make a difference to rank order, and that these judgements appear partial and incomplete as a result.

In contrast, the second creative writing teacher (who had also judged poetry competitions) described an intuitive preference for 'poems I want to read again – poems which allow the reader to breathe'. This reader stated also the search for 'authenticity – a reason why the image or idea is there' and dispreferred poems which were 'mechanical or tricksy'. Decisions were made on the basis of these two articulated values.

Reading as a Poetry Editor

One poetry editor offered rapid and precise judgements in the form of ticks and crosses on each text and amendments to typos. The poems otherwise are not annotated. 'fish out of water' and 'Summer of '92' 'seem like an exercise' and 'Desolation' 'has an odd title'– and these three are excluded from the shortlist. The editor choices included 'The common finch' for its 'deft combination of sight and sound', 'Could have' for its coherence, and 'Captivity' for its interesting final image: 'whose legs fold is good'. The pattern of reading suggests brisk decisive judgement, possibly without the benefit of rereading.

The second editor chose, in contrast, 'Prophecy' (unpublished workshop poem) – 'the only poem in the list that I would mark for definite inclusion'. This reader was irritated by ambiguity of content, cliché, linguistic dullness and experienced this with the other seven poems.

Reading for Enjoyment

The leisure readers were more likely to focus on affective factors such as mood, rapport and sense of distance. They described the poetry they liked as *powerful, complex, convincing, thrilling,* and poetry they didn't like as *obscure, worked, contrived, pretentious, routine.* The greatest indictment against poetry was its capacity to confuse and obscure meaning. Unilaterally the readers did not trust the poet who seemed to 'deliberately obfuscate'.

On Judging Literary Judgement

Whilst this study was extremely small scale, it still offers tentative answers to our opening questions:

Would the poets and poems that have achieved visibility be valued more highly than those which have not, if stripped from their context? The aspiring poets whose poems had not yet been shared outside private writing workshops ('Captivity' and 'Prophecy') were valued just as highly as the published poets. One editor rejected the Nobel prizewinner Szymborska in favour of one of these unpublished workshop poems, for example.

Is there a coherent notion as to what constitutes poetic quality? There was no consensus in the way the readers judged and selected. There was indeed a shared language in articulating literary judgements: ambiguity, imagery, musicality, rhythm, rapport, sense and content, were points covered by most of the readers. However, each of these were judged differently. Some readers sought clarity, others ambiguity; some used imagery to mean metaphor, others used it to mean visual snapshots. Some valued simplicity, others mistrusted it.

Do the amateur and the professional always fall on opposite sides of this divide? The findings suggest that 'amateur' and 'professional' are not clear indicators of how work will be read and perceived. The former at best is capable of work that is indistinguishable from the highly experienced and prolifically published; and vice versa. Thus we need to review again the wall of protection that separates the developing poet from the fully developed. Readers are able to find the former just as effective as the latter – in all the different ways in which they articulate effectiveness.

This study tentatively opens up new questions about the blurring of the edge between creative writing 'on the ground' in poetry workshops and classes, and creative writing in the publishing houses. Publishers and poetry presses might need to reconsider the slush pile and the rapidity of response to the apparent newcomer. It might be that the 'creative writing class', far from dumbing down our reading expectations, is allowing readers to become writers; and in so doing is requiring us to think again about who and what we value when we read and why.

NOTE

1. All unpublished poems are cited with the writers' permissions.

REFERENCES

Bourdieu, P. (1984) *Distinction: A Social Critique of Judgement and Taste*. Cambridge, MA: Harvard University Press.

Carter, R. (2005) *Language and Creativity: The Art of Common Talk*. London: Routledge Falmer.

Carter, R. (2006) 'Is there a literary language?' in Goodman, S. and O'Halloran, K. (eds) *The Art of English: Literary Creativity*. Basingstoke: Palgrave Macmillan/Open University: 84–8.

Culler, J. (1981) *The Pursuit of Signs*. London: Routledge and Kegan Paul.

Gibbs, R. (2008) 'Feeling moved by metaphor' in Carter, R. and Stockwell, P. *The Language and Literature Reader*. London: Routledge: 209–18.

Houston, L. (1999) *Cover of Darkness*. London: Slow Dancer Press.

Kelder, C. (2006) *Bordercrossing Berlin. The English Literary Magazine* 20(3).

McDonald, R. (2007) *The Death of the Critic*. London: Continuum.

Pelter, S. (2008) *insideoutside*. Self-published collection by Stanley Pelter.

Richards, I.A. (1973) *Practical Criticism: A Study of Literary Judgment*. London: Routledge and Kegan Paul.

Szymborska, W. (1998) *Collected Poems 1957–1997*, trs Stanislaw Baranczak and Clare Cavanagh. Boston: Harcourt.

Widdowson, H. (2000) 'Extracts from Critical practices: representation and the interpretation of text' in Goodman, S. and O'Halloran, K. (eds) *The Art of English: Literary Creativity*. Basingstoke: Palgrave Macmillan/Open University: 30–7.

19

Practical Measures: Poet as Editor

Fiona Sampson

[A poet and editor of a national poetry review talks about the creative and critical nature of literary editing in terms of 'organic' and 'vegetable' aesthetics.]

I've an instinct that literary – and perhaps other – aesthetics might be more usefully seen, not as a grid of criteria which we can drop over every text and its reception, but as something like organic outgrowths from key moments in the life of a text. These moments probably include each occasion on which it's read. It's also conceivable that such 'outgrowths' might cease to have an active relationship with their own places and moments of origin and acquire an independent existence: for example as critical texts, ideas or literary reputations. What would this be like? Well, whenever I come across the term 'organic', my symbol-forming imagination makes an association with the vegetable kingdom. Thus, whatever is intrinsic is usually associated, in my mind, with contingency and decay. Let me widen this thought a little. Working in just the same way, the word 'germane' has always reminded me of the 'germinal'. The seed at the heart of each word – in each 'germ' – is a map of a particular nature. *Naturally*, the map it draws is specific. Being intrinsic, for the germane, means being local, made-to-measure.[1]

This cluster of intuitive ideas about what 'organic' outgrowths of literary aesthetics might be contradicts many of our shared intuitions about how literature works: intuitions having to do with the authority and persistence of the text itself. Let me give an example of what I have in mind. The way that I experience the words of a Pauline Stainer poem as polished beads on a string has everything to do with a private triangulation between the note-beads of her namesake's *Crucifixion*, the rounded double vowels of her name (*au, ai* and the double trace of *ie*), and the perfected images (often religious) and vocabulary of her short verses (see, in particular, Stainer 2003). From this circumstantial soil grow occasions when I've published, reviewed or taught on Stainer as a vivid miniaturist. Although her poems are delicate, exact, even hieratic, it has never occurred to me to hear them as whispered or misty. And my generative logic here is so personal that it can't be described as either right or wrong. But my approach falls away from the absolute in another sense, too. Someone who picks up his or her Saturday paper and reads a review I've written knows nothing about this (personal) starting point. Let's assume that 'someone' is a graduate student, a stranger we'll call Xenia. Xenia puts Sampson's review on file. When she comes to write up her thesis on contemporary women poets, she'll take Sampson to task, arguing that there's a great deal more flexibility in Stainer's syntax than the beads-on-a-string model acknowledges. My review will mulch down into a footnote, and X – what secret root does *she* send down into Stainer? – will publish her thesis as a book, which one day a young reader wanting to know more about that terrific poet Pauline Stainer, just encountered, will shut with a sense of irritated disappointment, since of course it falls short of *her own* Stainer.

If I succumb to the predictable and use the term 'vegetable' instead of 'organic', I add – to the original idea of aesthetics as spontaneous organic outgrowth – some sense of a necessary, and *useful*, cycle of obsolescence. Something flourishes, decays and becomes the soil in which the new grows. A continuing calendrical cycle. This does not give me licence to read sloppily. It does make me a Heraclitean critic, a pragmatist of flux as much as of fiery literary brilliance. Aesthetics – shared ideas about what is 'literary' – aren't just creative in the sense that they're *made*. They also spring from and inform moments of specifically literary creation. I've always been aware of the 'falling-free' (*not* free-fall) of literary matter. It's a deposit; a humus out of which I, like most poets, write. The sense of a *culture* of literary activity going on (there goes another of those vegetable terms) – that there are other readers and writers 'out there', working away, passionately opinionated about what they're doing, whether or not as each other's bitter rivals – is itself the container that makes individual writing *make sense*. It is what allows literary writing to happen. It wouldn't occur to me *not* to read literary ephemera, such as poets' letters – Elizabeth Bishop's, Ted Hughes's, Amy Lowell's – or essays by poet-critics like Sean O'Brien, Don Paterson and, in the US, Donald Hall or Christian Wiman. But here I'm drawn up short by my use of the double negative. Why have I written *wouldn't occur to me not to*? I'd like to claim this isn't just routine defensiveness. In the fruitful fuzziness of the double negative I can make out a trace of the way in which plurality, a good mix in the soil, allows for healthy growth.

My next-door neighbour has a traditional, immaculate vegetable garden. In fact, his long cottage plot is entirely given over to vegetables. They are *organic*, but they float on a bed of good husbandry. The American critic Ira

Sadoff says that 'poems require acknowledgement and integration of their literary antecedents because poets compose in a medium that makes reference to their linguistic as well as personal experience' (2009: 4). Another way to say this is that all poets read before writing. Yet another way might be that it's not enough to play the Furniture Game in a workshop – *if I were a vegetable, I would be a slender juicy cucumber* – in order to produce a poem. Taking part in poetry, rather than in such cousin-activities as song-writing, therapeutic journal-keeping or cabaret, means acting in relation to a field of existing practices, both historical and contemporary. To squeeze the metaphor, gardeners don't destroy last year's work when they weed the same row again. Rather the reverse. Indeed, the link between 'compost' and 'composition' – and the tension which marks 'de/composition' – are fruitfully present at the etymological and semantic levels too.

I seem to be saying, then, that there's a healthily ephemeral aspect to literary culture. Confusingly, though, my generation was brought up on what might be called 'aspirational modernity'. In the last fling of the brief welfare state, we Generation X-ers were taught that history was a story of progress. Doubtless our parents and teachers, having survived much of what the twentieth century did to itself, had to believe the worst was over. Only the events of the twenty-first century have untaught that lesson. One thing is entailed by another not because it's better but simply because *it has been produced* – as bad actions produce lousy outcomes. So it's taken us a long time to understand that literary history, too, need not be seen as a story of technical improvement and continual escape from limitations. Things change because change is necessary, and inevitable. Iambic pentameter is neither ethically nor aesthetically superior or inferior to free verse. It's simply what came along in, inter alia, early modern Europe. In practice, just as lots of reading washes off, so do most drafts of a poem – or of a magazine. I always feel moved and implicated by the long, late poems of D. H. Lawrence, which enact their own 'Try again. Fail again. Fail better'. (Isn't it interesting that Beckett used this construction and in more than one place?) Among the exactest and most exacting contemporary examples of this kind of poetry-as-process is Jorie Graham's *Overlord* (2005), a collection dealing with the Normandy landings, and by extension war in general, where the poem's struggle to make meaning, if not sense, is staged through her representation of parallel processes of prayer.

A poem or a book of poems, even a magazine, moves towards its own wholeness, shedding debris as it goes. It's not quite like a space probe shedding booster-rockets as it races out of the earth's atmosphere. It's not, either, quite like waiting for tomato flowers to set as fruit. But if we still believe in the category of the literary – that some poems and stories are *the real thing* – then we *do* believe in progress *within the life story* of each individual poem, story, magazine and book. We believe, in short, that the writer *aims to* make a particular kind of something. Thus, working as an editor also means work-ing *with the aim of* creating the best possible publication from the material available. The ideal text is latent not within some purely abstracted editorial intention but within the given textual material. And yet at the same time we must believe – if we're not to be crippled by grandiosity, hubris or a sense of impotence – that all participation in these activities, in whatever comes before the desired goal, *is itself* literary work. The narrative of progress, in other words, has to nestle down inside the writing or editing process – and fall away from the act of reading. What makes this possible is the sense of the equal contingency of each of these stages in the text's life-cycle, rather than its finished performance.

We therefore need to cultivate – again in the richest and fullest sense of the term – a kind of modest immodesty, where each draft, reaction or note is a display of creativity, and where none is a moment of aesthetic legislation. To put it Stein's way: 'a rose is a rose is a rose', whether wild, single, double, wind-blown or in bud. That chaos of forms, which lasts from the last to the first frosts each year and often best suggests ideal rose-ness from a distance, is a fruitful model in which apparent *approximation* overlays essential *iden-tity*; where apparent ephemerality is in fact persistence through change; of chronological trajectory within unitary identity.

Differing aesthetic criteria emerge at differentiated moments in the life-cycle of a literary text. A single poem may satisfy mouth and ear when read aloud, play the crowd-pleaser in a festival, afford a critic an easy, uncluttered speed-read, and prove semantically rewarding upon study. In other words, aesthetic criteria for literary identity *are* contingent as well as momentary. Every poet and novelist has had the experience of being 'interpreted' by a reviewer or scholar who extrapolates metaphoric meanings which, while they don't conflict with our authorial intention, were certainly not already present in it. And it's precisely the temporary nature of such individual literary crite-ria which gestures towards a continuing, and in that sense generative, quality which can be called 'the literary'. For the literary text is *both* the repeated 'occasion' on which the text's completed self performs itself *and* the ongoing 'life-cycle' through which it arrives at that point of performance. It knows – and shows – what kind of work went into the making of it.

NOTE

1. Even if DNA does rely on huge chunks of repeated code and does codify the ability to recognize others of the same species: still, a seed-head will only grow its *own* cornstalk, not another.

REFERENCES

Graham, J. (2005) *Overlord*. Manchester: Carcanet.
Sadoff, I. (2009) *History Matters: Contemporary Poetry on the Margins of American Culture*. Iowa City: University of Iowa Press.
Stainer, P. (2003) *The Lady and the Hare*. Newcastle-upon-Tyne: Bloodaxe.

20

Rewriting the Critical–Creative Continuum: '10x...'

ROB POPE

> There is neither a first nor a last word, and there are no limits to the dialogic context (it passes from the limitless past to the limitless future). Even the most ancient meanings, originating in dialogue of long-past centuries, can never be stable (once and for all completed, finished) – they will always change (be renewed) in the course of the following and future development of the dialogue. (Mikhail Bakhtin)[1]

When does a reading of a text become a rewriting of it – and that in turn become another and another till it is almost a different text entirely? How far is a full response necessarily 'creative' as well as 'critical', and are these terms complementary rather than opposed? What can we learn about processes of textual transformation by actively participating in them ourselves, while also observing what others have done with notionally 'the same' texts previously? Where does the matter of 'value' come into all this – whether absolute or relative, for 'use' or 'exchange' – and how do we engage with the ongoing activity of revaluing? This is the cluster of open-ended questions that informs the analyses and activities that follow. The chapter revolves around versions of the biblical Ten Commandments and turns upon a 'critical–creative' axis. I will critically examine some translations, adaptations and parodies of the Ten Commandments for the insights these offer into ongoing processes of textual transformation; and I will show how these have been – and still may be – used creatively as prompts and frameworks to make all sorts of texts, 'commandments' and otherwise. The latter are basically generated according to the formula '10x' where 'x' means whatever you want it to.[2]

The best way into the method, as well as the substance of the present piece, is to engage with what I have here recast as the 'Ten Commandments of Critical–Creative Interpretation'. These serve both to cue the chief canonical text and topic featured and to clarify the methodology in play. You may or may not agree with them. You may not think they are all 'commandments' or 'ten'. The crucial thing is to respond with marks or remarks of some kind.

Prelude: Ten Commandments of Critical–Creative Interpretation

1. In reading texts we rewrite them – in our heads if not on the page.
2. Interpretation *of* texts always involves interaction *with* texts.
3. Interaction *with* texts necessarily entails intervention *in* texts.
4. Translation fully grasped is a form of transformation, never mere transference. All writing and reading is a form of 'translation' – from one set of wor(l)ds to another.
5. One text leads to another and another and another – so we had better grasp texts intertextually (in the spaces between) and transversally (in their movements across).
6. Our own words are always implicated in those of others – so we had better grasp our selves interpersonally through dialogue: voicing dissent as well as assent, and thereby joining in the ongoing 'conversations' we variously call Culture, History, Life ...
7. Because textual *changes* always involve social *exchanges*, you can't have the one without the other – and one another. Perhaps we should therefore think in terms of *ex/changes* and talk of transformative dialogues that are as interpersonal as they are intertextual.
8. *Responding* fully and being *responsive* are responsible acts. Perhaps we should therefore talk about the *responsibility* of 'response-ability' too, of actively *answering* as well as being *answerable*.
9. *Creating* involves recombining as well as replacing. *Criticizing* can be a constructive as well as a destructive activity. *De*-construction, therefore, is best realized through *re*-construction; just as thoroughgoing *critique* comes out as radical *re-creation* – taking apart to put together differently. 'Creative' or 'critical', these are the differences that make a difference.
10. That is why *interpretation* can be done through acts of 'creative' *performance* (as in dance, music and drama, and all kinds of adaptation) as well as through 'critical' *commentary* (as in the essay, analysis or review). For we are all in various ways or at different moments performers *and* commentators, adopters *and* adapters, critics *and* creators. We are all operating on the *critical–creative continuum*; though each of us does so distinctly, in our own times and on our own terms.[3]

Whether you respond negatively or positively to the above commandments is important but in a way incidental for present purposes. (Paradoxically, if you agree completely and wouldn't change a single word, they are wrong. But if you disagree with them completely and would change the lot, they are right.) Much more important is that you produced a response at all, possibly in your head but preferably in writing or talk: marks, remarks ... the odd word or phrase, note or query ... a sentence or three ... perhaps a full-scale counter-proposal. To explore these processes further and to engage with the critical–creative continuum through a text that is in every sense 'canonical', we now turn to previous versions of the Ten Commandments – biblical and otherwise, chiefly in English but also in film and plastic. In the event, these turn out to be many more and fewer than 'ten' and often very different from 'commandments'.

'Originals'? Translation, Adaptation, Parody and Formula

I will look at just a tiny sample of the thousands of versions of the Ten Commandments that exist. These survive in ancient languages ranging from Aramaic and Hebrew to Greek and Latin and are current in just about every modern language, and in many major varieties currently spoken and written on the Earth. But these few examples should be enough to substantiate the general point about textual transformation involving kinds of rereading and rewriting, and will help underwrite the observations on critical–creative interpretation offered above.[4] They also, together, serve to cue some 'Commandments of Creativity' that follow. The texts featured are readily and conveniently distinguishable as 'translations', 'adaptations' or 'parodies'; but the fact that these conventional analytical categories invariably break down under pressure is part of the fascination of dealing with particular instances rather than generic types.[5] The term 'formula' (in this case the transformative procedure '10x → new text') is offered to help catch the apparently mechanical yet richly generative nature of such a resilient and adaptable text-type/topic/schema (also to avoid such triplication of terms).

The first and most crucial thing to observe about the text of the Ten Commandments in the Old Testament (even in the oldest extant sources) is that there is no single 'original'. It exists in three versions in two books (Exodus twice and Deuteronomy) and by definition none of the surviving manuscripts is the original because that, they tell us, was carved in tablets of stone twice (one deliberately broken, the other now lost) and given by God to Moses on Mount Sinai. The second thing is to recognize that these are indeed very different versions, written by different hands at various moments between the tenth and seventh centuries BCE, and that their relative authority is far from fixed or agreed. We also do well to recall that 'Bible' comes from the Greek *biblia* (books, plural): it is made up of two Testaments (Old and New) and many books, some of them judged apocryphal, all with various origins and purposes in a wide range of genres (from tables of tribal law to erotic love lyrics). Here, for example, is the first full specification of the commandments initially delivered to Moses, as described in Exodus 20:2–8 (verse divisions omitted). In the subsequent story this is the copy 'which Moses didst break' and God replaced; in the history of Biblical transmission this part of Exodus is ascribed to an anonymous writer conventionally identified as 'E', operating between 922 and 722 BCE. For present purposes, reference will be made to the Authorized (King James) version in English (1611), itself produced in part by committee and drawing heavily on earlier versions in English, notably one by Tyndall that was initially banned and burned in Britain:[6]

> I am the LORD thy God which have brought thee out of the land of Egypt, out of the house of bondage. Thou shalt have no other gods before me. Thou shalt not make unto thee any graven image, or any likeness of any thing that is in heaven above, or that is in the earth beneath, or that is in the water under the earth. Thou shalt not bow down thyself to them, nor serve them; for I the LORD thy God am a jealous God, visiting the iniquity of the fathers upon the children unto the third and fourth generation of them that hate me. And shewing mercy unto thousands of them that love me, and keep my commandments. Thou shalt not take the name of the LORD thy God in vain; for the Lord will not hold him guiltless that taketh his name in vain. Remember the Sabbath day, to keep it holy.

This text may be contrasted with the version of the commandments as they next appear a few chapters later, in Exodus 34:12–18 (ascribed nowadays to another anonymous writer identified as 'J', who operated between 844 and 722 BCE):

> Take heed to thyself, lest thou make a covenant with the inhabitants of the land whither thou goest, lest it be for a snare in the midst of thee: But ye shall destroy their altars, break their images, and cut down their groves: For thou shalt worship no other god; for the LORD, whose name is Jealous, is a jealous God: Lest thou make a covenant with the inhabitants of the land, and they go a-whoring after their gods, and do sacrifice unto their gods, and one call thee, and thou eat of his sacrifice: And thou take of their daughters unto thy sons, and their daughters go a-whoring after their gods, and make thy sons go a-whoring after their gods. Thou shalt make thee no molten gods. The feast of unleavened bread shalt thou keep.

Clearly, though the latter claims to be 'the words that were on the first [tab-let]', these two versions are substantially different, both in overall emphasis and detail. While the first is initially framed in terms of divine delivery 'out of the land of Egypt, out of the land of bondage' (reserved to a later mention in the other), the second is centrally concerned with not going 'a-whoring' (not mentioned at all in the first). Further, while the first is initially centred on the self-characterization of the addresser ('I ... the Lord thy God', repeated), the second is firmly addressee-centred on 'thou' throughout. As for the com-mandments themselves, not only does each list only very vaguely approximate to the other in terms of topic (and hardly at all in wording), it is sometimes very difficult to distinguish the reduplication, qualification or glossing of a point from the main thrust of a specific commandment. In terms of impera-tives alone (both positive and negative – 'thou shalt/not', etc.), the first text contains five while the second contains eight. The dramatic situation and the arithmetic get even more complicated if we add in the other primary locus for the commandments in Deuteronomy 5, currently ascribed to an anonymous writer identified as 'D', reckoned to be operating *c.*622 BCE.

The basic biblical point will be clear enough. The so-called Ten Commandments are largely a retrospective construct superimposed on a mass (even mess) of narrative frames, speech acts and lexical variation. The neatness of subsequent abstractions may be doctrinally clear and didactically convenient; but it is a drastically reduced simplification of the many and vari-ous biblical sources it claims as its authority. Indeed, whether there are five, ten or more commandments, and how far they are grammatically 'command-ments' (i.e. imperatives) at all, very much depends on who is looking where and what they are counting. The broader 'canonical' point, to do with cul-tural transformation realized through kinds of rereading and rewriting, may be clear too, at least at the level of its foundations with a classic and culturally central case. The myth of a single 'originary' moment as the scene of writing is powerful and persuasive in the stories we tell ourselves about the process of literary creation. But the compositional reality is much messier and more protracted, and often involves many more hands and minds than one. The biblical record of transmission is characteristic of the larger cultural picture; it is rehearsed in miniature with virtually every piece of sustained writing that goes public, all the way through from notes and drafts to editing and performance or publication.[7]

This kind of divided authority involving multiple versions is common with canonical texts of many kinds. The four versions of Christ's life in the Gospels and the various recensions of the Koran and its associated com-mentaries, additions and apocrypha are other examples from religions of the book. From English literatures of the book we have the two earlier quarto and later folio versions of Shakespeare's *Hamlet*; the three (and more) versions of Wordsworth's *The Prelude*; Joyce's *Ulysses* as initially serialized and subsequently published whole, twice and differently; and so on. Time and again, the one turns out to be many. What look like particular points can also be seen as parts of a wave. In this respect the notion of a critical–creative continuum resembles wave-particle dynamics. Now you see it – now you see them!

At this point we turn to the differently complex and even more contentious afterlife of the Ten Commandments, not just as biblical source but more generally as cultural resource. Below are two later versions of the Ten Commandments in very different kinds of English. They hover between 'translation' and 'adaptation' in that they attempt to transfer the core biblical meanings even while radically transforming them, the one by reduction, the other by elaboration. The first is in a form of Kanaka Pidgin English produced by a missionary in Queensland, Australia (1871). The second is in a kind of streetwise New York American English produced by a prison chaplain in the late 1960s (both are taken from Crystal 2005: 516–17):

Australian Kanaka Pidgin

Man take one fellow God; no more.

Man like him God first time; everything else behind.

Man no swear.

Man keep Sunday good fellow day belong big fellow master.

New York prison chaplain

You shall have no other gods before me ... Means God's the leader – nobody, but nobody, man, gets in the way. This is the top. He is Mr. Big, real big.

You shall not make for yourself a graven image ... This means no making things that look like God in the craftshop at the settlement house. No worship things like rabbits' foots and lucky dice and, damn it, dolls.

You shall not take the name of the Lord your God in vain ... It means knock off the swearing or you better watch out.

Before leaving versions of the Ten Commandments as such, brief mention will be made of two 'limit' – or, perhaps better, 'liminal' – cases of translation as it tends towards adaptation. Both involve changes of material and medium drawing on contemporary communications technologies: one (newer) into a plastic construction toy accessed visually on a computer screen through the web; the other (older) into strips of celluloid accessed initially though synchronized light- and sound-projection in a cinema. What I refer to are, respectively, *The Brick Testament, The Ten Commandments in Lego,* by Brendan Powell Smith (2001; see www.bricktestament) and *The Ten Commandments* as Hollywood epic film (1956), directed by Cecil B. DeMille and starring Charlton Heston as Moses. In medium and material these may seem a long way from the written word of 'the good book'. Then again, so were those uttered by God and carved in tablets of stone on Mount Sinai.

All these fundamental changes in material, medium and historical moment have profound implications for what is judged to be valuable, why and for whom. A pointed way of putting this is in terms of which of the historically available senses of 'original' is felt to apply: 'original' meaning 'going back to the origin, most ancient' (its dominant sense up to the mid-eighteenth century) or 'original' meaning 'never been done before, most novel' (the currently dominant sense).[8] In the former (older) sense, the Ten Commandments carved in stone was 'original'; in the latter (newer) sense, the Ten Commandments cast in plastic is 'original'. Perhaps we had better, therefore, see 'originality' in the fullest and most flexible senses – critically and creatively, theoretically and practically – as the product of a constantly shifting and perpetually unresolved tension between 'old' and 'new': harking back to some purportedly mythic ('earliest') origin in previous materials and conditions while striving towards some original ('latest') realization in contemporary materials and conditions. So it may well be that the most complexly and enduringly 'original' act of re/production remains open to the claims of both.

To see how such a triple-faced 'originality' – picking up past models and turning them to present purposes with an eye to the future – plays out in another moment and material, I will turn back the pages (literally) to a highly influential nineteenth-century instance of the Ten Commandments in manuscript and print. This is 'The Latest Decalogue' by Arthur Hugh Clough (1819–61), first published in print a year after his death, though apparently circulated in manuscript before. The poem is here quoted in its entirety (Clough 1987: 51):

> Thou shalt have one God only: who
>   Would be at the expense of two?
> No graven images may be
>   Worshipped, except the currency:
> Swear not at all; for, for thy curse
>   Thine enemy is none the worse:
> At church on Sunday to attend
>   Will serve to keep the world thy friend:
> Honour thy parents: that is, all
>   From whom advancement may befall:
> Thou shalt not kill, but needst not strive
>   Officiously to keep alive:
> Do not adultery commit:
>   Advantage rarely comes of it:
> Thou shalt not steal: an empty feat,

When it's so lucrative to cheat:
Bear not false witness: let the lie
    Have time on its own wings to fly:
Thou shalt not covet, but tradition
    Approves all forms of competition.

Loosely speaking, this is a 'parody' in the sense that it is an imitation with humorous or critical intent; but it does not poke fun at the Bible. Rather, it uses the 'ten' framework of the Decalogue along with the tell-tale signature of the Authorized version's archaic formula 'Thou shalt not' to point up the distance and difference between the received forms of ancient religious authority and the relatively hollow substance of Victorian pseudo-morality. 'The Latest Decalogue' is therefore strictly satiric rather than parodic; and it is 'mock-biblical' in that it uses biblical forms and norms as a foil to set off current abuses – not to 'mock' the Bible as such. These were qualities that doubtless recommended Clough's poem to Ambrose Bierce, the witty and scandalous American writer of *The Devil's Dictionary* (1911). He drew on it freely for his own poem on the subject in the entry on 'Decalogue'. The following lines illustrate his debt to Clough, including the use of the couplet to point out the antitheses; they also catch Bierce's jauntier tone and more scurrilous manner:

Thou shalt no God but me adore:
    'Twere too expensive to have more…
Kill not, abet not those who kill:
    Thou shalt not pay the butcher's bill.
Kiss not thy neighbor's wife, unless
    Thine own thy neighbour doth caress.
Don't steal; thou'll never thus compete
    Successfully in business. Cheat.

The mock-definition of 'decalogue' with which Bierce prefaces his poem is just as freebootingly iconoclastic. This may well be adopted (and here adapted) to introduce most of the modern uses of the Ten Commandments motif that follow.

Decalogue, *n.* A series of commandments, ten in number – just enough to permit an intelligent selection for observance, but not enough to embarrass the choice. Following is the revised edition [are the revised editions] of the Decalogue calculated for this meridian [these meridians].

So saying, with Bierce's help, we move from the Ten Commandments as specifically biblical textual source to a 'series of commandments, ten in number' as general cultural resource. This is what I term a 'formula', as already mentioned, so as to signal its essentially generative and dynamic capacity. 'Formula' in this sense can be broadly aligned with what Bakhtin in his later work terms a 'chronotope': a shifting cultural 'space' (*topos*) that moves with the 'time' (*chronos*) (Bakhtin 1986; also Morris 1994: 180–7). In the case of the 'ten commandments' as a '10x' formula, what we typically witness is the transformation of a holy and solemn text into a profane or comic one. The overall trend – with Clough then Bierce occupying slightly different cultural-historical space-times between – can be plotted on a trajectory ranging from 'canonical classic' to 'carnivalesque gesture' (to pick up another of Bakhtin's central concepts; see Morris 1994: 194–244).

To illustrate this, we can extend the formula a further 40 years to another 'space-time'/chronotope, W. H. Auden's 'Phi Beta Kappa' poem for Harvard University in 1946. For there, in his poem called 'Under Which Lyre – A Reactionary Tract for the Times' (Auden 1966: 221–6), we are treated to a 'Hermetic Decalogue' that openly lambasts or subtly skewers a whole host of academic orthodoxies. Some of these are pointedly contemporary and others are more perennial. Thus we are instructed 'Thou shalt not': 'be on friendly terms/With guys in advertising firms'; 'answer questionnaires/Or quizzes upon World Affairs'; 'write thy doctor's thesis/On education'; 'sit/With statisticians nor commit/A social science'. Auden concludes with the modest, mocking injunction to 'Read *The New Yorker*, trust in God;/And take short views'.[9]

A question necessarily arises as to the value, and by extension the ongoing revaluing, of particular instances. How far is the specific textual transformation not only novel and effective in its own terms and times, but also capable of extending to and affecting those of others? Perhaps it even prompts yet further transformations ... and so on and so forth, each time not just again but potentially afresh. Some such question must be put to any text insofar as we wish to connect its immediately perceived value to its potentially enduring capacity for ongoing acts of revaluing. It is a question that converges on and cuts across whatever we conceive to be at the core of our aesthetics and ethics, poetics and politics. Some such question can be put to the texts that follow, as to those above. They are extracts from just a couple of the many contemporary instances of the Ten Commandments formula plucked from the Web one afternoon late in the first decade of the twenty-first century.

THE TEN LONDON TRANSPORT COMMANDMENTS

2. Thou shalt have thine Oyster Card in thine hand when thou reachest the ticket barrier, and not stand there, rummaging through thine bag for five minutes, like a tool.

3. Thou shalt talk quietly, or not at all, on thine mobile phone when on the bus – nobody else wants to hear who Emma did last night or how much Liam spent on his sodding shoes.

4. Thou shalt not press the 'open' button on tube doors as this is the mark of the tourist.

8. Thou shalt not duck, dive or bomb. And shalt most certainly not heavy pet. (http://london.fridaycities.com/transport/conversations)

THE TEN COMMANDMENTS OF JAMMING [i.e. improvisation]

I   Thou shalt not ever forsake the beat.

II Thou shalt arrange thyselves in a small circle so that thou mayest hear and see the other musicians ... Thou shalt play softly when someone lifteth the voice in song, when playing harmony, and when thou knowest not what thou is doing.

IX Thou shalt not, by thine own self, commence noodling off on a tune the other musicians know not, unless asked or unless thou art teaching that tune, for it is an abomination, and the other musicians will not hold thee guiltless, and shall take thee off their computer lists, yea, even unto the third and fourth generation.

X   Thou shalt have fun and play well.
(www.Guitarseminars.com/ubb/Forum1)

Broadly comparable yet inevitably different examples will turn up if you do a search today – whenever that may be. For example, tapping in 'Ten Commandments of ...' on the day I am revising this part (3 June 2009) produced everything from 'The Ten Commandments of Good Business Practice' to 'Ten Commandments of Sexual Joy'; but it also threw up 'The Eleventh Commandment of Golf' and 'Ten Questions of Judaism'. In fact the only common denominator in these four titles is 'of'! Indeed, if one recalls that even the biblical Ten Commandments are neither consistently ten in number nor grammatically imperative then it will be realized that formulae are a logically 'fuzzy' category characterized by something like Wittgenstein's notion of 'family resemblances': members of a family may broadly resemble one another but there may be individual members who share virtually no visible characteristics. Bakhtin's 'chronotope' is a necessarily fuzzy concept too. He wrestled with the definition of it over many years; but it never kept still for the simple fact that he – along with others – was always seeking to define it from another time-space with respect to different generic materials (for discussion, see Morris 1994: 18–21).

By extension, supposedly 'personal' preference and immediate perspective cannot and should never be banished from the reckoning. For instance, on reflection, I realize that I selected the two examples featured above (the 'Transport Commandments' and those of 'Jamming') because I sometimes travel on the London tube and because I play guitar. So I could readily recognize the references (e.g. 'Oyster Card', a renewable pass) and relate to the experiences (for instance, someone 'noodling off' on a tune of their own). Other people would doubtless pick up other instances of '10x' texts that they found particularly relevant and interesting to them. Such peculiarities of response are not to be ignored or played down. They help constitute whatever we mean by 'individuality' and 'idiosyncrasy'. To pass them over in favour of the blandly generalizable and universally available is to miss much of what makes each of us 'me'.

Postlude: Ten Commandments of Creativity?

To demonstrate what a formula can do experimentally – not just be analytically – we shall look at a 'Ten Commandments' activity undertaken at one of the symposia on which the present book is based. The session in question (attended by around 40 academics at the Open University in September 2007) was mainly devoted to a review of some of the materials presented earlier in this chapter. These also helped to set up the activity that now follows. As before, the best way to get the most out of this is to try it yourself before reading on.

Commandments of Creativity	
In order to be creative thou shalt	*In order not to be creative thou shalt*
1................................	1................................
2................................	2................................
3................................	3................................

Below are some responses to compare with yours. They can be read down or across for a variety of effects.

In order to be creative thou shalt	*In order not to be creative thou shalt*
1 Avoid regimes but know their procedures	1 Love epaulettes
2 Take risks	2 Be too busy
3 Believe in omelettes	3 Believe in unbroken eggs
4 Get a 'room of one's own'	4 Always do what you are told

5 Take from the goods given thee and make something new of thine own	5 Be a copycat from generation unto generation and hold all others are too
6 Seek the approval of those you respect	6 Please yourself alone
7 Question and challenge what is assumed	7 Uncritically follow rules and roles
8 Keep your senses open at all times	8 Rely on your rationality
9 Spend considerable portions of the night awake – having first fallen sound asleep	9 Get a job you dislike but which pays a persuasive amount of money
10 Do it!	10 Not!

It is important to emphasize that the above Commandments of Creativity are simply a selection (mine) from over a hundred supplied by some 40 participants. And, yes – by deliberate design not by magic or chance – they now make exactly ten of each. It is also important to note that some responses sought to exceed or subvert the formula, and with it the constraints of the task as such. These included 'In order to be creative thou shalt not use commandments at all. But how about question and exclamations?!' and 'What's all this Biblical stuff got to do with creativity in the 21st century?'. There was also an extended offering by three people working as a group: 'Thou shalt begin by replacing "creative" – which is more trouble than it's worth – with a choice of words such as "imaginative" and "innovative" and "playing around" and "arsing about" and any others that suit you'. Interestingly, all these last responses, awkward and 'uncooperative' though they may seem, are arguably just as responsive and responsible as those which agreed to 'play the game' as set. It is also a moot point whether 'thinking outside the box' is a more or less critical and creative activity than thinking 'inside it'. Perhaps we had better reconceive both, in the fullest and most flexible sense, as 'thinking *through* the box'. In any event, people seem to benefit from some kind of 'box' (ongoing constraint – formal or functional, arbitrary or otherwise) to get and then keep going. This leads us, almost finally, to three closely connected negations of negations:

- no creativity without constraint;
- no reading without rewriting;
- no value without revaluing.

Present readers are invited to posit the corresponding positives as they see fit and feel moved. The writer only appears to have the last word: the reader always has the next.

NOTES

1. These notes were amongst the last that Bakhtin made the year before his death: they include the revisions (in brackets) he made in 1974 of an article that he first drafted around 1940 with the title 'Towards a Methodology of the Human Sciences'. The translation (mine, which differs from that of Holquist 1990: 39) is of the Russian text published in the posthumous collection under the title (not Bakhtin's) *The Aesthetics of Verbal Creation* (1979: 373, 409). In its openly annotated and differently translated form(s) as well as in what it said, says and will continue to say at various moments in various contexts, this epigraph expresses in miniature the gist of the present chapter.

2. This piece relates in general to early Reception Aesthetics, Reader Response and, latterly, Cognitive Poetics; for which see respectively Holub (1984), Bennett (1995) and Stockwell (2002). It especially draws ideas and inspiration from Jacques Derrida ('difference/deferral' and 'counter-signing'; e.g. Derrida 1994), Gilles Deleuze and Félix Guattari ('difference and/as repetition' and 'multiplicity', Deleuze 1994; 'lines of flight' and 'the rhizome', e.g. Deleuze and Guattari 1988) and Mikhail Bakhtin (for 'response-ability/answerability' and 'chronotope' as well as 'dialogic'; see Bakhtin 1986 and Holquist 1990). More or less practical precursors and fellow-travellers include Robert Scholes on 'textual power' (Scholes 1985, 1998), Jerome McGann on 'radiant textuality' (McGann 2002) and Ben Knights on 'active reading' (Knights 1992; Knights and Thurgar-Dawson 2006). My own work along these lines is crystallized in the technique 'textual intervention' (Pope 1995) and the concept 're…creation' (Pope 2005); also the notions of 'Englishing', 'matrix' and 'transversion' (e.g. Pope 2009a, 2009b, 2010). All these ideas were in mind in the writing though not all of the terms will appear in the reading; many crop up cryptically in the 'Ten Commandments of Critical-Creative Interpretation'. For further discussion and examples of academic discourse in critical-creative genres, see Currie (2001) and Sheppard (2008).

3. Various versions of this, all different, have appeared previously. This is the fullest to date.

4. The text of the Authorized Version and the general information on the Bible are drawn from Carroll and Prickett (1996). An essential reference on the rewriting of the Bible is Boitani (1999).

5. Each of these areas is rich in work relevant to 'reading as rewriting'. For example, for *translation*, see Lefevere (1992) and Bassnett (2005); for *adaptation*, see Stam (2005), Hutcheon (2006) and Sanders (2008); and for *parody*, see Hutcheon (1985). An attempt to embrace all these processes in terms of the concept 'tranversion' is to be found in Pope (2010).

6. See the 'General Introduction' in Carroll and Prickett (1996).

7. For powerful arguments along these lines, on specifically biblical and mythically foundational texts in general, see Chauvin (2005) and Wunenberger (2005).

8. See *Oxford English Dictionary entry for* 'original' and Pope (2005: 57–60).

9. This kind of thing happens with many culturally prestigious texts that gain common currency. Quickly cued by brief, immediately recognizable formulae, they prove endlessly productive as vehicles of critique, comic and otherwise, or simply for passing amusement. Hamlet's 'To be or not to be'; Descartes's 'I think, therefore I am'; Nietzsche's 'God is dead' – along with the Bible's 'In the beginning …' or 'Blessed are the …' – are all formulae in this sense. They come easily to mind as clichés and stereotypes, and thereby offer readily shareable resources for developing, and perhaps refreshing, a wide range of materials in catchy and coherent ways. For workouts with many of these, see Pope (1995: 31–45).

REFERENCES

Auden, W.H. (1966) *Collected Shorter Poems*. London: Faber and Faber.

Bakhtin. M. (1979) *Estetika Slovesnovo Tvortchestva (The Aesthetics of Verbal Creativity)*, eds C.G. Botcharov and A. Averintstev. Moscow: Iskustvo.

Bakhtin, M. (1986 [1953]) *Speech Genres and Other Late Essays*, eds C. Emerson and M. Holquist, tr. Vern McGee. Austin: University of Texas Press.

Bassnett, S. (2005) *Translation Studies*, 3rd edn. London: Routledge.

Bennett, A. (ed.) (1995) *Readers and Reading: A Critical Reader*. London: Longman.

Bierce, A. (1911) *The Devil's Dictionary*. New York: Doubleday.

Boitani, P. (1999) *The Bible and its Rewritings*, tr. A. Weston. New York: Oxford University Press.

Brecht, B. (1964) *Brecht on Theatre*, ed. and tr. J. Willett. London: Methuen.

Carroll, R. and Prickett, S. (eds) (1996) *The Bible, Authorised King James Version*. Oxford: Oxford University Press.

Chauvin, D. 'Bible et Mythocritique' in Chauvin, D., Siganos, A. and Walter, P. (eds) (2005) *Questions de mythocritique: dictionnaire*. Paris: Imago : 41–50.

Chauvin, D., Siganos, A. and Walter, P. (eds) (2005) *Questions de mythocritique: dictionnaire*. Paris: Imago.

Clough, A. (1987) *Arthur Hugh Clough: Selected Poems*, ed. S. Chew. Manchester: Carcanet.

Crystal, D. (2005 *The Stories of English*. London: Penguin.

Currie, M. (2001) 'Criticism and creativity: poststructuralist theories', in Julian Wolfreys (ed.) *Introducing Literary Theory*. Edinburgh: Edinburgh University Press.

Deleuze, G. (1994 [1968]) *Difference et repetition*, tr. P. Patton. New York: Columbia University Press.

Deleuze, G. and Guattari, F. (1988 [1980]) *A Thousand Plateaus*, tr. B. Massumi. London: Athlone.

Derrida, J. (1992) *Acts of Literature*, ed. and tr. D. Attridge. London and New York: Routledge.

Derrida, J. (1994) *Acts of Literature*, ed. D. Attridge. New York: Routledge.

Finnegan, R. (1992) *Oral Traditions and the Verbal Arts*. London: Routledge.

Holub, R. (1984) *Reception Theory: A Critical Introduction*. London: Methuen.

Holquist, R. (1990) *Dialogism: Bakhtin and His World*. London: Methuen.

Hutcheon, L. (1985) *A Theory of Parody*. New York and London: Methuen.

Hutcheon, L. (2006) *Adaptation*, London and New York: Routledge.

Knights, B. (1992) *From Reader to Reader: Theory, Text and Practice in the Study Group*. Brighton: Harvester Wheatsheaf.

Knights, B. and Thurgar-Dawson, C. (2006) *Active Reading: Transformative Practices in English Studies*. London and New York: Continuum.

Lefevere, A. (1992) *Translation, Rewriting and the Manipulation of Literary Fame*. London and New York: Routledge.

McGann, J. (2002) *Radiant Textuality*. New York: Palgrave.

Morris, Pam (ed.) (1994) *The Bakhtin Reader: Selected Writings of Bakhtin, Medvedev, Voloshinov*. London: Arnold.

OULIPO (1973) *La littérature potentielle*. Paris: Gallimard.

OULIPO (1981) *Atlas de littérature potentielle*. Paris: Gallimard.

Pope, R. (1995) *Textual Intervention: Critical and Creative Strategies for Literary Studies.* London and New York: Routledge.

Pope, R. (2005) *Creativity: Theory, History, Practice.* London and New York: Routledge.

Pope, R. (2009a) '"Curriculum", "National", "English" ...? A critical exploration of key terms with some seriously playful alternatives'. *English in Australia* 43(1): 29–35.

Pope, R. (2009b) 'English and creativity' in J. Maybin and J. Swann (eds) *The Routledge Companion to English Language Studies.* London and New York: Routledge.

Pope, R (2010) 'Rewriting texts, transforming culture' in C. Cottenet, J.-P. Murat and N. Vanfasse (eds) *Transforming Culture: Essays in Textual Exploration.* Cambridge: Scholars Press.

Sanders, J. (2008) *Adaptation and Appropriation.* London and New York: Routledge.

Scholes, R. (1985) *Textual Power: Literary Theory and the Teaching of English.* Binghampton: Yale University Press.

Scholes, R. (1998) *The Rise and Fall of English: Reconstructing English as a Discipline.* Cambridge, MA: Harvard University Press.

Sharples, M. (1999) *How We Write: Writing as Creative Design.* London: Routledge.

Sheppard, R. (2008) 'Poetics as conjecture and provocation'. *New Writing: The International Journal for the Theory and Practice of Creative Writing* 5(1): 3–26.

Stam, R. (2005) *Literature through Film: Realism, Magic and the Art of Adaptation.* Oxford and New York: Blackwell.

Stockwell, P. (2002) *Cognitive Poetics: An Introduction.* London: Routledge.

Wunenberger, J.-J. (2005) 'Création Artistique et Mythologique' in D. Chauvin, A. Siganos and P. Walter (eds) *Questions de mythocritique: dictionnaire.* Paris: Imago: 69–84.

21

Reading a Hindi Poem: Lost in Translation?

Rukmini Bhaya Nair

Extract from 'The Interior of Words', a Plenary Lecture delivered at the Creative Arts Program for gifted incoming students joining the National University of Singapore.

Supposing I recite a couple of lines of poetry to you in Hindi:

> *Bara hua to kya hua, jaise per khajoor*
> *Panthi ko chaya nehi, phal lage ati dur!*

These lines are by the famous fifteenth-century Indian poet called Kabir and every schoolchild in India would probably know them. Yet here in Singapore, when these Hindi words are uttered, what you hear is simply a facade of sound. All you are offered is an 'exterior' – the unfamiliar phonemes and syllables of this foreign language: Hindi. But the interiors of meaning, the internal resonances, are lost to you, because you do not know this language. So the first simple observation to make when we are investigating words is that they are made up of an exterior of *sounds*. But several other elements – scripts, gestures and the body language of the speaker – also make up the exteriors of words. An unfamiliar script, for instance, creates a visual barrier of external patterns around the poem:

> बड़ा हुआ तो क्या हुआ जैसे पेड़ खजूर
> पंथी को छाया नहीं फल लागे अति दूर

In this particular instance, my own gestures and body language, even my clothing (a sari), as you hear me speak, create other external 'shells' around the words we are discussing. The point I'm making is the basic one that, confronted simply with the exteriors of words such as sounds and script and so

265

forth, people are lost – lost in translation. Readers of poetry need more; they need *meanings*, they need to understand the cultural contexts in which words are produced before they can respond to words. For poetry deals not just with dictionary meanings but with meanings embedded in culture, soaked in social contexts that constitute the 'interiors' of words – that is why it is so especially vulnerable to being destroyed in the process of cultural transfer. Now if I go further and translate the meaning of these mysterious Hindi lines, they would turn out to be something like this:

So what if you are as big and proud as a date palm tree?
It offers no shade and its fruit is as far away as can be!

Such a rough-and-ready translation would not, however, do either, because one is then likely to think 'Hey, this doesn't seem to be great poetry, does it? It sounds boring and old-fashioned and not particularly musical to boot!' So it's clear that 'bare meanings' are inadequate, too, if one is to really 'get' a poem. Consider, for example, a rough word-for-word translation from the Hindi into English:

बड़ा	हुआ	तो	क्या	हुआ	जैसे	पेड़	खजूर
big	be	so	what	be	like	tree	date-palm

पंथी		को		छाया	नहीं	फल	लागे	अति	दूर
traveller/bird		(objective case)		shade	none, fruit	seems	very	far	

Here, we have perforce to take into account the patterns of syntax as well. Hindi word order typically follows a subject-object-verb (SOV) structure unlike English where the standard word order is subject-verb-object (SVO). How in the world can we cross over from one language pattern to the other without loss? And then there is semantics! In Kabir's couplet, for example, there is a sophisticated quasi-pun. This involves a classical 'minimal pair' in the first word of the second line: *panthi* means 'traveller' and *panchi* means 'bird'. Both interpretations make amazing sense, and this ambiguity is another source of creative delight for the reader/listener in the original language – but which especially hard to carry over in translation.

Paradoxically, then, the whole vast external world of culture seems to constitute part of the 'interior' of words. If you know, for example, that this couplet was composed in the fifteenth century by a low caste weaver, some of its subversive potential may be more easily accessed. You begin to see that, in writing couplets like this, Kabir was, among other things, challenging the upper caste gentry of his time by comparing them to the way in which a date-palm tree stands out tall and remote in a landscape. The rich remained aloof from the common populace, exactly like the date palm, offering neither shelter nor shade nor succour. For a fuller understanding, you may also need to know the metrical patterns of Hindi and how Kabir's language employs the simple idiom used by the poor rather than the Sanskritized language of the higher castes and the economically privileged. In fact, literary historians today regard Kabir and other poets like him as spearheading an important social revolution, known as the 'Bhakti Movement', which sought to free poetry and language from their 'ownership' by the elite classes of India. But trying to *explain* all this is terribly tedious; it seems to militate against the very spirit of poetry. The unique combinations of sound and sense, or exteriors and interiors, that make up a poem have, it appears, to be instinctively *sensed*, not explicated. This, indeed, is one of the most difficult problems for many today who write in English: how does a writer convey the specific, local flavours, the details of historical context and the mixed cultural metaphors of those who live in Singapore or Delhi or Zanzibar using this remote 'world-language'?

22

An A–Z of Textual Re-creation

ROB POPE

Afresh not just again – all aesthetics, all plural

Becoming

Critical-creative – or creative-critical – any way

Differences that make a differance, dynamics of dialogue,

Energy, enthusiasm and, in the Event, the

> emergence of evolution
>
> emergency of revolution

Folding the one into, around, and out of another to make a many – a manifold

Genius of place and time, plant, animal, even machine, and person

Happy! (unhappy, mishappy, perhappy ...?) A healing, handy too

Inspire (perspire expire) ...

> imagine image unseen
>
> invent, intervene
>
> ideally idiosyncratically.

Just a joke? Or jumping for jouissance!

Kinetic: the movement in movies, the motion in emotion,

Laughter, learning, life and, oh yes, of course, language-and-or-as-literature

Metamorphic stuff – metaphoric, mythic, magic, and much more MORE! Encore!! – the

Now, the New or

Old Original?

Play the games of your lives – the politics of poetricks

Quanta become Qualia

Re-creating the response

significantly **S**ingular.

Techniques and txologies that transl8, trans4m – some say tranSEND –

Unconscious become conscious, uncanny made canny and

                                                     Vicey-Versey

                         vibrations <<< visions

           vortices <<< voices

Worlds within words, Words without worlds, whirled without end, yet allways

X-perimenting, -ploring, -periencing, -pressing (add your own) – Xcessive, Xtreme?

Yes. Y not

Zenith to Zeno and Zero – zebras for sure – just time for some

               ZZZZZZZZZZZZZZZZZZZZZZZZZZZs

                  and then
                  back again
                 continuously
                 doing differently
               extra … ordinarily
               f r e s h   lines

Introduction to Part IV

In this concluding part we pick up persistent issues and point to the emergence of fresh agendas. It is in the nature of debates on creativity that the one cannot be entirely disentangled from the other: what is old and continuing has a habit of prompting or providing a platform for what is new and disruptive. Some of the questions that arise may therefore have a deceptively familiar look to them: Is 'creativity' a specifically modern concept – and 'genius' an enduring one? Is 'literature' still a culturally central term and, if not, where and how are we to ground alternative aesthetics (plural)? How are literary 'canons' formed and what does it take to become a 'classic', ancient, modern or otherwise? Institutionally, what is the impact of Creative Writing on studies (and Departments) of Literature and Language? How does language blend with other sign systems and modes of communication and expression to create fresh ways of saying, seeing, being and becoming? There continue to be no once-and-for-all answers. But there are some fresh and important ways of posing the problems and responding across a wide range of activities, inside and outside the academy.

In 'The Production of "Creativity"' (**Chapter 23**), Daniel Allington revisits the specifically modern and Western notion of the concept. If we are going to talk of creativity, he suggests, then let's recognize that it is 'produced' – and by extension 're-produced' – as a result of social interaction in a particular moment, 'not essentially a thing' at all. Further, he argues that both 'populist' and 'elitist' conceptions of creativity tend to reify it in their own images and thereby appropriate it for their own agendas. These (re)productions of 'creativity' then get superimposed retrospectively in specifically 'modern' ways with 'innovation as the basic narrative principle'. What gets studied as a 'set' text or instituted as a 'classic' in a 'canon' therefore tends to be the result of a more or less deliberate act of 'forgetting'. Shakespeare, for instance, has arguably a huge amount in common with his immediate precursors and contemporaries (Kyd, Marlowe and Webster); but it is the perceived individual differences and supposed innovations that tend to be accentuated. Allington compares this with arguments over when zombies in films first began to run rather than stumble – and the obsession with who exactly is to be credited for it. This too attests to a specifically modern (and Western) preoccupation with creativity framed in terms of innovation and individualism, as well as property.

'In Defence of Genius' (**Chapter 24**) is a vigorous critique by Guy Cook of what he sees as the current preoccupation with 'ordinary', 'common' and 'democratic' creativity. He places his own position towards the 'extraordinary' end of the spectrum, explaining that 'what I shall mean by "extraordinary creativity" are creative artefacts, acts and ideas which are perceived as qualitatively different and superior to others'. Cook specifically takes issue with the editors of the present volume, and targets a number of implications that he sees as following from their basic positions. These he casts – and contests – as a number of flawed propositions: for example, that conceptions of 'genius' are often elitist and sexist and *therefore* cannot be universal; that creativity is ubiquitous and *therefore* cannot be special; and that the production of works of literature is often collaborative and *therefore* cannot be an individual attribute. While he broadly accepts the premises, he cannot accept the inferences. He concludes that 'there are no reasons I can find in the current debate to undermine the validity of the claim that there is ... extraordinary creativity, unequally distributed among a very few individuals, to the great benefit of the rest of us'. His piece may be read both as a corrective and a complement to some of the ideas expressed in this volume. It also chimes with some of the views expressed by Cameron (Chapter 5) and Sampson (Chapter 19), as well as Allington and (Jon) Cook in the present section.

In the following chapter (**Chapter 25**), the novelist and academic Graeme Harper offers a summary gesture that extends to many of the creative practitioners in the book. He emphasizes the many processes and 'actions' involved in what he terms the 'habitat homo sapiens' that, ideally, is 'Creative Writing' as an institution. While he acknowledges that the 'end' of the process, as aim and outcome, is indeed a text, what the writer constantly engages with are partial ideas for texts, notes, drafts – in T. S. Eliot's phrase, 'visions and revisions'. Indeed, invoking Heidegger, it is the sense of the writer involved in a sense of 'being there' and, more tentatively, of 'becoming' (something, someone else) that for Harper characterizes the creative process. He therefore deliberately cuts across both the 'Hermeneutic Circle' beloved of some phenomenological theorists and the schematic model of 'reflective practice' much favoured in creative arts education: practice followed by reflection followed by revised practice followed by critical commentary. Harper insists that the 'whole thing' is much more partial and unpredictable, experiential as well as experimental. In this respect his views resonate with some of those expressed and exemplified by Wandor (Chapter 12) and Agbabi (Chapter 2).

All this, clearly, presents a profound challenge when it comes to the practicalities of the rapidly burgeoning and increasingly deep-rooted subject that is 'Creative Writing' in education. Harper was one of the national committee responsible for the drafting of the first 'bench-marking' statement for Creative Writing in UK Higher Education; and he is an adviser on the current introduction of the subject at 'Advanced Level' in UK, post-16 secondary education. He concludes by offering insights into the drafting of criteria and principles designed to help generate such a *'habitus'* and way of student knowing, becoming – even while recognizing the pressures of predominantly outcome-driven and end-assessed examinations.

In 'Three Reflections on Creativity and Writing' (**Chapter 26**), Jon Cook takes a distinctly philosophical and literary look at the nature of creative language. He begins by establishing a background in which 'spontaneity and improvisation' are fully recognized as 'language's own curious powers of inventiveness'. In the foreground he then gradually draws attention to instances of 'language on display': the kind of utterance and text that openly 'displays language's inventiveness', that artfully stages the verbal act and does not just communicate a meaning. The perspectives opened up by Cook therefore supplement as well as complement those offered by contributors earlier in the book: the shift between conversational accessibility and poetic difficulty in the early and late poetry of MacNeice (Brown, Chapter 3); the differing, 'prosaic' and 'poetic' functions of metaphor in dialogue and verse (Cameron, Chapter 5); the connections and distinctions between the metaphorical treatment of 'pain' in the discourses of prose fiction and professional medicine (Semino, Chapter 6). Significantly, Cook's emphasis is not so much on the kinds of trope and device routinely identified as 'literary' by formalists (imagery, sound-effects, deviation, etc.) – important though he recognizes these to be in localized ways. Rather, he is concerned with the creative deployment of character, narrative, perspective and situation; shifts in world view rather than word-play alone (compare Stockwell's specifically cognitive poetics in Chapter 16).

Focusing on writers who wrote and thought in different genres at different moments (Kleist, Merleau-Ponty, Wittgenstein and Wallace Stevens), Cook insists on an understanding of verbal creativity that is cultural and historical as well as aesthetic. He also models a sophistication and complexity of approach that precludes appeals to the usual binaries (extra/ordinary, un/common, un/familiar). In their place he makes claims – and demands – for discriminations amongst kinds of 'creative language' (and by extension critical thinking) that differ in function and strategy, not just form and style. In effect he offers to reconfigure the language-literature-creativity debate on freshly philosophical and aesthetic lines.

In 'Creativity Looks at Language' (**Chapter 27**), Ruth Finnegan offers a critical review of many of the contributions to the book. Our introduction here to Finnegan's chapter will also be used as an occasion to draw together many of the book's main strands; some of the others are woven in above. Observing that 'it is not just "creativity" that has now become problematic but also "language" and, by the same signal, "literature"', Finnegan goes on to triangulate fresh grounds upon which the work in this volume is helping to lay foundations for further work or gesturing to adjoining sites and related projects. First is the emphasis upon 'the processual, the emergent, the experiential rather than the fixed text'. For references to 'process', both in the artefacts and events studied and the apparatus of study, are ubiquitous in the present volume; while the notion of creativity, especially co-creativity, 'emerging' and being 'emergent' also recur regularly in many different modes and contexts: in the work of Maybin on letter writing (Chapter 9); Swann on the dynamics of reading groups (Chapter 17); Pahl on classroom interaction round a box (Chapter 11); and Petrucci on the gradual composition of his series of poems on Chernobyl and its eventual transformation into a film (Chapter 8). Appeals to 'experience' are also frequent and expressly modelled in terms of empathy and sympathy by Stockwell (Chapter 16).

The second dimension unfolds naturally from the first. Finnegan welcomes 'the current zest for performance and practice' in so far as it leads to 'enhanced sensitivity to the performed, experiential, actively-manipulated dimensions of creativity'. This resonates with Finnegan's own early and abiding interest in oral tradition and performance (e.g. Finnegan 1992). Immediately and palpably performance-based pieces featured and discussed in the current volume include Agbabi's 'Word' (Chapter 2), Wandor's 'Music of the Prophets' (Chapter 12) and Haggarty's energetically physical and vocally virtuosic telling of the 'Witch baby' story (Chapter 14). In their emphasis upon bodily or musical as well as verbal modes of expression, these lead us directly to the third dimension of Finnegan's preferred perspective. For this she draws attention to the compound visual-verbal-musical 'texts' (and oral-aural-ocular textures) that are articulated in action in the film by Jayalakshmi and that based on Petrucci's poems (Chapters 15 and 8); also the electronically mediated, webcam and icon-supported MSN exchanges featured by Goddard (Chapter 10). To these may be added work on the staged presences and multimediated youth identities of the Hong Kong Cantopop group featured by Lin (Chapter 4). Their linguistically hybrid and sometimes proto-verbal lyrics are only a part of the overall design and effect.

All of these materials and accounts tend to underscore Finnegan's contention that 'it is not in the verbal alone that creativity can be found, but in the interplay of language with other modes'. Further – potentially much further – the vision that Finnegan gestures to in the conclusion of her review stretches way beyond the debate about 'continuities between "everyday" and "literary" language'. To this, she insists, 'we must surely now add the equally fascinating and debatable continuities between language and the broader galaxy of arts'. These, she suggests may be roughly – if inadequately – signalled by 'such notions as (among others) music, gesture, dance, image, graphics, movement, material, sound or touch'. Nowadays, as many pieces in the present volume attest, these are also likely to be multimedia as well as multimodal and involve blends of actual and virtual community.

The 'Epilogue' (**Chapter 28**) closes the book but keeps its contents wide open. Ronald Carter looks back as well as forwards across creativity debates in and around language and literature. This entails precisely the kind of retrospective–prospective scanning that seems to be essential when attempting to grasp the old–new dynamics that characterize this field – these fields – of activity. His parting remarks are therefore offered by way of open invitation, in anticipation of responses to come, as well as in summary of what has already been achieved.

REFERENCE

Finnegan, R. (1992) *Oral Traditions and the Verbal Arts*. London: Routledge.

23

The Production of 'Creativity'

Daniel Allington

Reifying and Critical Approaches to 'Creativity'

My position in this chapter is that there is no such thing as creativity. I mean this in two senses. First, creativity is not an object: not something that can be looked at from different angles, conceived in different ways. It is a concept, which is to say that – unless one subscribes to Plato's theory of Forms – it has no existence apart from its own history as a concept. This history is recent and largely Western.[1] Attempts to contrast 'Western conceptions of creativity' or 'post-Romantic conceptions of creativity' with their opposites are, on this understanding, attempts to contrast tautologies with oxymora; one might as well contrast Christian and non-Christian conceptions of Original Sin. Second, creativity is not an objective property: not something that can be present in or absent from particular people, acts, texts, utterances, etc. It can only be ascribed, which is to say that it is always a function of social interactions that – often retrospectively, and always provisionally – produce particular people, acts, texts, utterances, etc. as creative or non-creative. This is the approach that I call 'critical'.

The concept of creativity is closely related to the concept of discovery; to some extent they are counterparts, with creativity supposed to happen in (although not only in) what we call the arts, and discovery supposed to happen in (although not only in) what we call the sciences. Scientific findings are commonly referred to as discoveries, not creations, but the concept appears to operate similarly. Nonetheless, there is a sense in which 'discovery' is the special name that we give to creativity in the sciences. Thus: 'creativity can lead to new scientific findings, new movements in art, new inventions, and new social programmes' (Sternberg and Lubart 1999: 3). The concept of creativity is also related to the concept of genius. The latter has a substantially longer history than the former, and much appears to have been transferred between the two, although each is sometimes regarded as the explanation of the other. The word 'genius' is sometimes used to refer to a supposed ability and sometimes to something supposedly displayed in actions (as in the phrase 'stroke of genius'); confusingly, the same goes for 'creativity'. Both concepts have been reified by some experimental psychologists; for example, creativity has been described as a 'factor' accounting for genius (Eysenck 1995: 83). To return to the argument of the previous paragraph, the critical approach is the rejection of such reifications. Two approaches to creativity and genius that do not reject them are described in the following paragraph.

The first I shall call the populist approach. Recent applied linguistic research into creativity – that is, the research tradition exemplified by Ronald Carter's *Language and Creativity: The Art of Common Talk* (2004) – has, as Alastair Pennycook writes, 'democratised creativity', exchanging the Romantic view that creativity is the preserve of the 'lone genius' for the view that 'we're all at it' in our 'everyday language use' (2007: 583). 'Ordinary language', we are therefore told, 'is far from ordinary' (Carter 2004: 85). The second I shall call the elitist approach. This is an older tradition, and begins with interest in the older concept of 'genius'; Francis Galton's *Hereditary Genius* (1869) is perhaps the defining work. It is elitist firstly because it assumes that eminence in literature, science and other fields results from innate characteristics possessed by a minority of individuals, and secondly because it lends itself to grand schemes of quasi-fascistic social engineering, such as Galton's own proposal to 'improve our race ... by granting diplomas to a select class X of young men and women, by encouraging their intermarriages and by promoting the early marriage of girls of that high class' (1901: 162), or Colin Martindale's suggestion that, to produce a 'creative society', we should 'minimise rules and control and maximise freedom and individuality', but only amongst the 'middle and upper classes', since 'the proportion of eminent creators coming from the lower class is and always has been extremely small' (1994: 193). As for the populists' anti-elitism, however, it relies on terminological fiat. What has been called the 'democratic endeavour to restore and revalue creativity as a common property of virtually all human beings' (Carter 2004: 49) seems to be accomplished, in other words, by using the word 'creativity' in an idiosyncratic way – for instance as a new term for what Roman Jakobson (1960) called the 'poetic function' of language and claimed was manifest in any communicative act. This means that the populists cannot engage – let alone win arguments with – the elitists: what the populists refer to as 'creativity' when they make statements to the effect that 'we're all at it' is not what elitists refer to when they make statements to the effect that 'creativity is a rare trait' (Martindale 1999: 137).

How, then, to understand 'creativity'? Since it is essentially a Western concept, I shall regard what Carter refers to as the understanding of creativity found 'within "Western" traditions of thought' (2004: 48) as overwhelmingly the most significant.[2] This understanding is that 'originality becomes *bona fide* creativity only when it is ... recognised, accepted, and valued as such both by the community peers of the creative individual and by the guardians of the particular artistic or scientific domain in or with which the creator works' (ibid.). Something like this understanding is shared by most of the elitist camp. But while elitists assume the evaluations of peers and experts to index an objective property of the individual to whom credit for the evaluated is given,[3] this assumption can be argued to be 'fundamentally flawed by a naivety about the relationship between facts and values' (Battersby 1994: 226). This chapter precisely concerns that relationship; its critique is directed neither at elitists nor at populists, but at creativity itself – which is to say, at 'the ideology of creation' (Bourdieu 1993b: 76).

'Making up Creativity'

The link between the words 'creative' and 'original' is recognized by Carter (2004: 26), together with the consequent implication that what is creative must be 'new and innovative' (ibid.). Although Carter suggests that 'the most salient etymological meaning of "original" is of *going back to* an original, perhaps divine, creative beginning' (ibid., emphasis added), it should be recognized that the 'original', in this sense, is *at* the beginning, and does not go back anywhere. Moreover, when this sense of 'original' is used in the arts, it is in relation to a *copy*: it is not the original that goes back to the beginning, but the copy that harks back to the original. That which shall come to be copied, and which (being new and innovative) is not itself a copy, is an original in two senses, and this is perhaps the ideal for a work of Western art: 'that ... from which something springs, proceeds, or is derived' (*Oxford English Dictionary*, 2008 revision: 'original', sense A.1a), where the springing, proceeding or derivative 'something' is an artistic tradition, and where, as Franz Marc put it, 'traditions are beautiful – but to create, not to follow' (quoted in Webster 1999: 444). To be original in this double sense is by definition to have come to be valued, since imitation is (as the saying goes) the sincerest form of flattery. And given that creativity implies valued originality, this would seem a paragon case. It also provides a parallel with the sciences, since the great scientific discoveries are those on which subsequent work is taken to rest (indeed, one collection of scientific classics is entitled *On the Shoulders of Giants* (Hawking 2003)).

Something very close to this is argued by Derek Attridge in *The Singularity of Literature* (2004). He defines originality (in contrast to 'mere novelty') as 'entailing a particular kind of difference from what has gone before, one that changes the field in question for later practitioners' (ibid.: 36). Attridge relates this to Kant's conception of ' "exemplary individuality", a type of originality that, as a product of genius, provides both a pattern for methodical reproduction by future artists lacking in genius ... and ... a spur to future geniuses for the further exercise of exemplary individuality' (ibid.). He illustrates this with the example of Wagner as just such an original creator (i.e. Kantian genius): 'The music of Schoenberg could not have immediately followed the music of Bach, since Bach does not make Schoenberg possible; Wagner, however, does' (ibid.: 39). But this reveals the problem of 'originality'/'creativity' as a model of cultural change, since it must surely strike us as a little simplistic. It is certain that Schoenberg's works could not have been composed in the eighteenth century. But how can this be *explained by* the work of a single nineteenth-century composer? The theory that an artwork is a singular creative act demanding a singular creative response – whether from an artist like Schoenberg or a critic like Attridge – would appear to reproduce the charismatic view of creation and re-creation debunked by Bourdieu (1993a).[4]

A different theory is provided in Thomas Roberts's *Junk Fiction* (1990). Roberts argues that mass market paperbacks offer replicated structures in which variations can be detected by those who are extensively familiar with the genres in which they are written; he argues that 'genres ... are (or rather, include) traditions of formulas that are mutating, formulas that are evolving' (ibid.: 225). He suggests that the pleasure of reading works 'by genre' is in the perception of variations from formulae and of the evolutions of formulae which result. Double-sense originality might thus consist in the production of variations that become formulaic, but this is not quite accurate, since aspects of a changing formula may be adopted without any explicit sense of *copying an original*: it is only where a particular work is singled out as having been the source of some particular feature that such terms become meaningful. The writer of the television series *Dead Set* (2008) provides an interesting example:

> Proper zombies can't operate a door handle or climb a ladder. Toss one a Rubik's Cube and it'll bounce off his thick, moaning head. All they do is walk around aimlessly, pausing occasionally to eat survivors.
>   Except they don't walk these days. They run. Zombies started jogging in 2002, when *28 Days Later* came out. OK, so technically they weren't zombies in that movie – being still alive, albeit infected – but from that point on, it was difficult to return to the old-school shambling George Romero zombies of yore. They're dumb and they can run? Brilliant. (Brooker 2008: 4)

This account establishes (one particular aspect of) *28 Days Later* as original in the double sense: as a respect in which that film *does not copy* earlier works in the formula, and in which it *is copied by* later works (including *Dead Set*).

It might be thought to be a long way from made-for-(cable)-TV, serialized zombie flicks to the literary canon, but part of Roberts's argument is that *all* literature has always been written in this way, even where that is no longer remembered, as in the case of works that have outlasted their genres (i.e. of those works now known to us as classic or canonical). An important implication is that people who read works in genres with which they are not familiar will tend to *misread* them: 'inevitably they see the features that distinguish the stories in this genre from the stories in other genres; experienced readers are focusing on what distinguishes this story from other stories in the same genre' (Roberts 1990: 214). Something like this is suggested by Marcel Proust in the following:

> I had not then read any real novels ... The narrative devices designed to melt to pity, certain modes of expression which disturb or sadden the reader, and which, with a little experience, he may recognize as common to a great many novels, seemed to me – for whom a new book was not one of a number of similar objects but, as it were, a unique person, absolutely self-contained – simply an intoxicating distillation of the peculiar essence of *François le Champi*. (Proust 1996 [1913]: 47)

Thus, the respects in which the naive reader considers works to deviate from formulae he or she knows will often be respects in which those works conform to formulae he or she does *not* know – which is to say, to past deviations that had, by the time of writing but unbeknownst to the reader, themselves become formulaic. Watching *Dead Set* in a world where the horror genre had been forgotten, we might be astonished at how different it seems from the works we know, little suspecting – like the Proustian narrator in his youth – that the uniqueness of *the work we see* will be the product of its similarity to *works we have not seen*. In a world where the only other work of horror still remembered happened to be (say) *Alien Dead* (1980), we might conclude that *Dead Set* had 'copied' this 'original' in some respects (with regard to which it could equally well be said to have 'copied' other works unknown to us) whilst 'being original' in certain others (with regard to which, of course, precisely the same thing could be said). What the writer of *Dead Set* would be likely to see as his *real* innovation – the parodic use of 'reality TV' conventions – might still be perceptible under such circumstances, or it might simply be lost among all the seeming innovations that a more knowledgeable viewer would recognize as old hat.

One might suggest that this is the inevitable condition for readers of canonical literature – doomed to credit to its writers the deviations of other writers long forgotten. It is under such circumstances that 'double-sense' originality can most easily arise, since the canon presents us not with a confusing mass of more-or-less similar, more-or-less different works that resemble (and do not resemble) one another in countless, tiny ways, but with a relatively small number of monumental works whose differences and similarities seem clearer. Of course, this means that creativity is an illusion born of forgetfulness. But that is my point: that creativity is not a natural relationship to an independently existing tradition, but an evaluational relationship to a tradition retrospectively produced in the form of a narrative (such as the screenwriter's narrative above, in which the zombie formula is seen to be altered by the creative originality of *28 Days Later*). Indeed, creativity is the tradition-narrative's key plot device, as well as the main provider of its cast and chronology: Attridge comes close to recognizing this in his comment that 'histories of art, of music, of literature, almost always take innovation as their basic *narrative principle*' and 'often put names and dates to moments of breakthrough: Abbot Suger using pointed arches for his cathedral church at St Denis; Walt Whitman writing English verse without regular metre; Albrecht Altdorfer painting landscapes lacking in human figures or narrative; Buddy Bolden improvising trumpet solos in New Orleans' (2004: 38). These examples all show how double-sense originality comes into being: that which has become formulaic is traced back to the point at which it was deviant and identified with a work or *oeuvre* that is pronounced the model for all successive work that accepts the former deviation as formulaic.

Nonetheless, I depart from Attridge at his implication that creative 'moments of breakthrough' between formulae really exist, and merely await the acknowledgement of their true names and dates: 'the list of such moments would grow longer if we possessed more historical knowledge (a circumstance which would no doubt also serve to demolish many of our cherished examples)' (ibid.). Artistic breakthroughs can, I would argue, be compared to Thomas Kuhn's (1962) 'unpredictable' scientific discoveries – i.e. discoveries that could not have been predicted from accepted theory before they were made – since the question of whether a deviation is going to be important for a future stage in the history of art (i.e. by becoming formulaic) and thus count as a breakthrough can only be settled once that stage has been reached. And, as Kuhn recognized, the trouble with unpredictable discoveries is that if people do not know what they are looking for, then what precisely has been found may not immediately become apparent, greatly confusing questions of priority: one cannot be said to have 'discovered' what one does not know oneself to have found, but knowing-what-one-has-found is not an absolute. Kuhn uses the example of oxygen: relatively pure oxygen was produced decades before it was 'discovered' (as is usually said) by one of four possible candidates at some time in the 1770s. But each of these four understood that-which-he-is-said-to-have-discovered in terms that have now been rejected, so the question of whose understanding of oxygen was adequate enough to constitute a discovery becomes a matter of retrospective definition, not past fact. Thus, Kuhn writes that 'the sentence "Oxygen was discovered" misleads by suggesting that discovering something is a single, simple act unequivocally attributable, if only we knew enough, to an individual and an instant in time' (ibid.: 762). Can the initiation of a new architectural style be an event more stable and certain than the discovery of a chemical element? I think not: the question is not whether Abbot Suger and his architects were the source of the idea to put pointed arches in a church, nor even whether St Denis was the first church to have any pointed arches – two questions whose answering requires only information (whether or not that information is available in practice) – but rather *why* it is that the construction of pointed arches in the choir of a church with a Romanesque facade should be considered the beginning of the Gothic style of architecture. And this is not a matter of information about the past, but of how the history of architecture is to be written: of how we are to narrate the apparent rise, from the twelfth century onwards, of a new style in ecclesiastical architecture. The 'creativity' of Abbott Suger and his architects is thus not an event in time, but a crux in a narrative of change over time.[5] We might compare Christine Battersby's pragmatic definition of the work of genius as that which 'marks the boundary between the old ways and the new within the tradition' (1994: 226). And in this, it is very important to emphasize the active role of retrospection. Thus, Simon Schaffer talks of discovery as something that is *made up* in the practice of historiography:

> Discoveries are made up in the course of making the disciplinary histories of specific scientific practices. The process of making up a discovery involves specifying its author, its location, and, most important, its content ... this account of discovery within the functioning of social networks distracts our attention from the tedious debates about the distinction between discovery and invention, between sciences and arts. (Schaffer 1994: 16)

The cultural equivalent of this 'making up' of discovery – a making up (or production) of creativity – can be understood as a process that begins with the production of candidate artworks, literary texts, etc., and proceeds with their winnowing down to a canon of 'major works'. The production of distinctions between art and mere painting, between literature and mere writing, has been analysed by Pierre Bourdieu by analogy with religious belief: 'at the very source of the art-work's existence' there is a 'miracle of transubstantiation' (1993c: 259). This 'transubstantiation' is, he argues, a function of 'the entire set of social conditions' (ibid.) that produce 'belief in the value of art and in the artist's power of valuable creation' (ibid.: 260) – recall the centrality of *valuedness* to creativity – and thus 'make possible the character of the artist as a producer of the fetish which is the work of art' (ibid.: 259).

Bourdieu shows that writers compete with writers, artists with artists, publishers with publishers, galleries with galleries, critics with critics, etc., for the prize that is *shared belief* in the value of the specific works they have authored or endorsed – and how, by competing, they collude in the (re)production of belief in the value of art and literature *in general*.[6] Since it is only what Bourdieu calls the 'consecrated' works (i.e. those most prestigious in artistic circles; another religious metaphor) that are remembered in the long term, future generations are always left with a fragmentary picture of past culture. I would thus argue that, just as the relationship of 'copy' to 'original' is often a simplification projected upon the lacunae of cultural memory, so the singularity of works remembered may arise from non-remembrance of works that would allow us to see them as non- (or at least, not-quite-so-) singular. Preserving the work of one 'creator' in isolation from the less-valued work of his or her contemporaries may in turn produce further value through a sort of feedback process: the work will seem more singular (and therefore less copy-like), and – being remembered – may come to be considered to have been 'copied' in subsequent remembered works (and, of course, may be copied indeed). The creator and his or her creations can thus be seen to be produced as such through a complex of social actions that also produces (and assumes) belief in 'creativity' (or an antecedent concept such as 'genius').

Consider the canon of Romantic poetry, familiar from any number of anthologies and lecture series. This is comprised not of the whole roster of British versifiers of the late eighteenth and early nineteenth centuries, but of a scant handful of 'great' names (Blake, Wordsworth, Coleridge, Keats, Byron and Shelley; Burns, Clare and a few others at a pinch). Each of these names represents not just a body of works, but a singular creative essence to be related and rerelated to its predecessors, contemporaries and successors. If we see what has come to be remembered as 'great poetry' in context of what has come to be remembered as 'minor verse', however, the picture changes. When Keats is read alongside the largely forgotten Della Cruscan poets, for example, many similarities become clear, and so Jerome McGann can (iconoclastically) write that Keats is 'in an important sense ... the greatest representative of the Della Cruscan movement, as the attacks and criticisms of John Wilson Croker, Wordsworth, Byron, and, later, Matthew Arnold show very well' (1993: xx). But Keats is not often read alongside the Della Cruscans, since they are so very far from canonical as usually to be regarded (when at all) as an embarrassment. Thus, characteristics of the largely forgotten Della Cruscan movement come to be seen as characteristics of its sole representative in the canon, and, together with those characteristics that might once have served to distinguish that representative from Robert Merry and the rest, contribute to his production as one of a small handful of creative contemporaries (Blake, Wordsworth, etc.), maximally different from one another. This can be seen in the following excerpt from an undergraduate seminar, in which a lecturer responds to a point raised by a student:

> S: I kind of find with Keats that . ehm . it was almost like he was sitting . watching this happening from a window . and then he was describing it in a kind of . <u>arty</u> way whereas Wordsworth is much more <u>tangible</u> and . he's actually like . you get a sense that he <u>has</u> been out there and he's
> [★ ★ ★ ★
> T: [right . right . there's more of a sense of kind of . <u>rustic</u> <u>authenticity</u> . in Wordsworth isn't there . than that . sometimes very elaborate . uhm . <u>sensuousness</u> of Keats

Everything said in the above about Keats could equally well be said about the Della Cruscan movement as a whole; Della Cruscan poetry was characterized precisely by the 'arty' mannerism and 'elaborate sensuousness' that is here taken for Keats's singular contribution to the Romantic aesthetic. This style of reading can be exemplified in the work of Harold Bloom, perhaps the paragon reader of the canon as such. In the 72 pages of *The Visionary Company* (1971) that he devotes to Keats, the other poets to whom he most frequently refers or alludes to are Blake, Shelley and Wordsworth: three Romantic poets almost guaranteed to provide the greatest, the most miraculous contrasts with Keats and with one another.[7] This is no reproach: the pleasure of reading the canon perhaps results from taking it as a virtual text (a sort of ideal *Norton's Anthology*, one might say) in which the great poets of the past form adjacent (but startlingly distinct) chapters; this may even be the source of the strange and powerful experience that it is Attridge's (2004) purpose to describe. Reading the canon, we are like passengers in an aeroplane, soaring over a range of mountains all but submerged in cloud: seeing the peaks, but not the landscape, we remark upon their differences (and distant similarities) and marvel at their splendid isolation. But when we try to trace relationships between them – except where (Wordsworth/Coleridge, Shelley/Byron) the peaks are exceptionally close, connected by ridges that cut through the clouds – we might as well be sketching constellations, for we will often have no more to fall back upon than oracular insight. Thus, the speculative readings with which Bloom and others illustrate the dynastic narratives they project onto the canon: 'Stevens, possibly remembering Keats, even as Keats may be remembering Coleridge' (Bloom 1971: 434).

Of course, these narratives – in being accepted by successive generations of cultural producers – have a way of becoming subjectively true (at least with regard to relations between non-contemporaries), so that it is very easy to see how the idea that Wagner makes Schoenberg possible may have seemed as plausible to Schoenberg himself as it does to those of us who 'read' the canon-text of classical music in which Wagner and Schoenberg are both now embedded. But we should not forget that canons are always hostage to the present, so that the successions through which the poets and musicians (and screenwriters) of the past will have understood their traditions to have been handed down to them may well be different from those taught to undergraduates today. And so, if we truly want to understand the works of the canon, we must try to understand *both* the processes that made those works – scouring even the foothills and the valleys of the mountain ranges of which they have been made the peaks – *and* the processes that made them canonical – analysing the changing weather conditions that have spread such clouds across a lengthening past. Without the former set of processes, there would be no cultural change. Without the latter, there would be no 'creativity' – or rather, no island-peaks to which we might attribute it; no cloudy voids for its leaps across to explain.

Concluding Thoughts

This leaves the question of equivalent processes by which creativity might be ascribed to conversational utterances. These would have to be capable of establishing utterances as creative against a background of non-creative utterances, and they would have to be capable of preserving such utterances in cultural memory (however briefly). The existence of such processes might seem unlikely: as Carter observes, 'there is no *Palgrave's Golden Treasury* of Spoken Language' (2004: 55). But in fact there are several potential candidates. There is the conversational reenactment of witty utterances ('and then *she* said'). There is the institutional structuring of certain individuals (especially television and radio personalities) as people of exemplary wit. And there is the celebration in print of the most notable utterances of the most noted conversationalists (such as Samuel Johnson). All of these processes consecrate utterances, although with unequal degrees of influence and permanence.[8] They show not the extraordinary nature of ordinary language, but the ordinary exercise of power.

And this brings me to my final question, which is of what to do about 'creativity' – apart, of course, from analysing its production. Perhaps we could recognize it for the fiction that it is, and – openly acknowledging what we are doing – make a play to control it, calling 'creative' the works (and *oeuvres*) we want to see more widely appreciated (see Battersby 1994: 231–2 on the 'female genius'). But would it not be braver to talk about culture in ways that do not reduce to creators, creations and creativity – at the same time as analysing the cultural importance of the cult of the creator, the ideology of creation and the concept of 'creativity'? Battersby, Bourdieu and Roberts suggest alternative vocabularies; I point to them in hope.

NOTES

1. Cf. Rob Pope (2005: 19): '"creativity" only surfaced as an object of public concern in the mid-twentieth century, shortly after its appearance as a named subject of academic enquiry ... during the 1920s ... In this respect, "creativity" (narrowly conceived) is a product of the mid-twentieth century and of the modern West'. It is precisely with such 'narrowly conceived' creativity that this chapter is concerned; like Pope, I treat it as a development arising from older (though equally Western) concepts such as 'genius and talent, originality and invention' (ibid.); unlike Pope, I see little advantage in broadening the definition of creativity to encompass other concepts with different histories. See also note 2.

2. 'Creativity' is a Latin-derived English word referring to an important concept in Western culture; if certain non-Western languages have different words that are used in different ways, then both signifier and signified are different and it makes no sense to say that the cultures in which these languages are spoken conceive creativity differently. For example, where Lubart writes of 'the divergent conceptions that different cultures may have for the same term' (1999: 340), he would appear to misunderstand something: in the anthropological and theoretical works he surveys, the 'same term' (i.e. 'creativity') is interpretatively applied to different concepts from different cultures. In other words, the conceptions do not diverge; they are made to converge through the universalizing assumption that whatever concepts are employed in practices of painting, poetry, etc. must be variant conceptions of a real thing called 'creativity'. Thus, we cannot meaningfully say (with Lubart) that traditional painters in India have 'an Eastern view of creativity' (ibid.), unless our theory of concepts is Platonic; see first paragraph of this chapter. This is not to deny that it would be very interesting to study the adoption (or adaptation) of Western concepts such as (for example) creativity in non-Western cultures that have come to participate in (here) the global art market, nor that it would be equally interesting to study the adoption (or adaptation) of non-Western concepts such as (for example) 'umami' in Western cultures that have gained an enthusiasm for (here) Japanese cooking. But that is a different issue.

3. As of course do the populists, although in a different way: Carter (2004) considers it possible to *count* instances of creativity in everyday talk, although here the expert judgement is his own.

4. Attridge writes that 'works of art are distinctive in the demand they make for a performance ... in which the authored singularity, alterity, and inventiveness of the work as an exploitation of the multiple powers of language are experienced and affirmed in the present, in a creative, responsible reading' (2004: 136). Bourdieu, on the other hand, sees in the 'creator-to-creator relationship' only the demands of 'the social norms of reception' (1993a: 36); he argues, moreover, that 'the ideology of "re-creation" and "creative reading"' is merely a means by which to provide 'teachers – lectores assigned to commentary on the canonical texts – with a legitimate substitute for the ambition to act as auctores' (ibid.: 37).

5. This point could also be made with regard to the zombie formula. Brooker's reference to the 'George Romero zombies of yore' reflects the widespread opinion that the first zombie movie was *Night of the Living Dead* (1968), but (as Brian Hoyle has informed me) this film was preceded by numerous cinematic works such as *White Zombie* (1932) and *I Walked with a Zombie* (1943). These arguably represent a quite different formula – the voodoo movie – but the question of where to draw the line between the two will depend upon precisely what we require of the first instance of a new formula. *Plague of the Zombies* (1966),

for example, could be considered to challenge *Night of the Living Dead*'s priority. It owes more to the earlier formula than do the works most typical of the later, but so – as I have suggested above – does the Basilica of St Denis.

6. The 'agents or institutions' I have named are specific to cultural production in the Western world since the nineteenth century. In twelfth-century Europe, for example, galleries, publishers and critics did not exist, and holders of political and ecclesiastical authority – such as Abbott Suger – were the major players. See Allington (2008) for an attempt to theorize the relationships between the agents involved in literary production; Darnton (1982) is the classic study of such relationships, though in a highly specific historical context.

7. These three poets are each referred to on around 20 pages of Bloom's five chapters on Keats; Milton, the next most frequent, is referred to on ten, and the Della Cruscans, not at all. Wordsworth and Shelley represent competing Romantic movements; the poetry of Blake was in Keats's day almost totally unknown and without influence.

8. To them might be added the production of specific utterances as 'creative' by applied linguists. This process resembles the others, except in that the 'creator', being anonymous, can derive no benefit from it.

REFERENCES

Allington, D. (2008) 'How to do things with literature: blasphemous speech acts, satanic intentions, and the uncommunicativeness of verses'. *Poetics Today* 29(3): 473–523.

Attridge, D. 2004. *The Singularity of Literature*. London/New York: Routledge.

Battersby, C. (1994) *Gender and Genius: Towards a Feminist Aesthetics*. London: Woman's Press.

Bloom, H. (1971) *The Visionary Company: A Reading of English Romantic Poetry*, revised edn. Ithaca/London: Cornell University Press.

Bourdieu, P. (1993a) 'The field of cultural production, or: the economic world reversed', tr. Richard Nice, in Randal Johnson (ed.) *The Field of Cultural Production: Essays on Art and Literature*. Cambridge: Polity Press: 29–73.

Bourdieu, P. (1993b) 'The production of belief: contribution to an economy of symbolic goods', tr. Richard Nice, in Randal Johnson (ed.), *The Field of Cultural Production: Essays on Art and Literature*. Cambridge: Polity Press: 74–111.

Bourdieu, P. (1993c) 'The historical genesis of a pure aesthetic', tr. Charles Newman, in Randal Johnson (ed.), *The Field of Cultural Production: Essays on Art and Literature*. Cambridge: Polity Press: 254–66.

Brooker, C. (2008) 'Reality bites'. *Guardian Guide*, 18 October: 4.

Carter, R. (2004) *Language and Creativity: The Art of Common Talk*. London/New York: Routledge.

Darnton, R. (1982) 'What is the history of books?' *Daedalus* 111(3): 65–83.

Eysenck, H. (1995) *Genius: The Natural History of Creativity*. Cambridge/New York/Melbourne: Cambridge University Press.

Galton, F. (1869) *Hereditary Genius: An Inquiry into its Laws and Consequences*. London: Macmillan.

Galton, F. (1901) 'The possible improvement of the human breed under the existing conditions of law and sentiment'. *Man* 1(11): 161–4.

Hawking, S.W. (2003) *On the Shoulders of Giants: The Great Works of Physics and Astronomy*. Philadelphia/London: Running Press.

Jakobson, R. (1960) 'Closing statement: linguistics and poetics', in T.A. Seboek (ed.) *Style in Language*. Cambridge, MA: MIT Press: 350–77.

Kuhn, T.S. (1962) 'Historical structure of scientific discovery', *Science* 136(3518): 760–4.

Lubart, T.I. (1999) 'Creativity across cultures', in R.J. Sternberg (ed.) *Handbook of Creativity*. Cambridge: Cambridge University Press: 339–50.

Martindale, C. (1994) 'How can we measure a society's creativity?', in M.A. Boden (ed.) *Dimensions of Creativity*. Cambridge, MA/London: MIT Press: 159–98.

Martindale, C. (1999) 'Biological bases of creativity', in R.J. Sternberg (ed.) *Handbook of Creativity*. Cambridge: Cambridge University Press: 137–52.

McGann, J.J. (1993) *The New Oxford Book of Romantic Period Verse*. Oxford: Oxford University Press.

Pennycook, A. (2007) '"The rotation gets thick. The constraints get thin": creativity, recontextualisation, and difference'. *Applied Linguistics* 28(4): 597–608.

Pope, R. (2005) *Creativity: Theory, History, Practice*. London/New York: Routledge.

Proust, M. (1996 [1913]) 'Combray', in M. Proust, *Swann's Way*, trs C.K. Scott Moncrieff, Terence Kilmartin and D.J. Enright. London: Vintage: 1–224.

Roberts, T.J. (1990) *An Aesthetics of Junk Fiction*. Athens, GA/London: University of Georgia Press.

Schaffer, S. (1994) 'Making up discovery', in M.A. Boden (ed.) *Dimensions of Creativity*. Cambridge, MA/London: MIT Press: 13–51.

Sternberg, R.J. and Lubart, T.I. (1999) 'The concept of creativity: prospects and paradigms' in R.J. Sternberg (ed.) *Handbook of Creativity*. Cambridge: Cambridge University Press: 3–15.

Webster, G. (1999) 'Kurt Schwitters and Katherine Dreier'. *German Life and Letters* 52(4): 443–56.

24

In Defence of Genius

Guy Cook

The editors of this volume have all made persuasive contributions to the understanding of creativity, conceived both in general and in relation to language use in particular. Joan Swann, as both writer and editor, has surveyed, synthesized and advanced approaches in both applied and sociolinguistics and was the moving force behind the colloquium from which this book derives (Maybin and Swann 2006, 2007; Swann and Maybin 2007). Ron Carter has uncovered the ubiquity of creativity in everyday talk and spelt out the implications of his findings for linguistic and literary theory, both in his book *Language and Creativity: The Art of Common Talk*, and in other publications with his colleague Michael McCarthy. Rob Pope's book *Creativity: Theory, History, Practice* is an encyclopaedic survey and discussion of the history, uses and implications of the term. These are great achievements from which everyone interested in this elusive topic can benefit.

All three also share and promulgate a view, as do most of the other writers in this volume, that too much attention has been given in the recent past to what has been conceived of as extraordinary creativity, and in particular to so-called genius. Indeed they take this critique further, sometimes suggesting, with varying degrees of strength, that a distinction between extraordinary and ordinary creativity is unhelpful (because both are both), as is the associated concept of 'genius'. Recent work on everyday creativity, say Swann and Maybin, will 'disrupt ideas about creativity as an individual attribute' (2007: 495), while according to Carter (2004: 27) 'it would be a mistake to view creativity as a wholly individual act'. (The cautious word 'wholly' here avoids but also implies that creativity might however still validly be regarded as *partly* an individual act.)

My purpose in this chapter is to take issue with this party line. In this I do not question either the erudition or the importance of the work of the current editors, or the stimulus they have given to enquiry, but I do not accept the logic of their arguments, and consequently I do not accept their conclusions.

So it is not with the facts they present that I shall argue, but rather with the use of those facts as evidence for a particular view, and with the view itself. Consequently this chapter is concerned neither with reporting findings nor with surveying literature, but with arguing. It is intended to be a polemic – though not, I hope, a diatribe.

A good point of focus for my challenge is the opening chapters of Pope's *Creativity* (2005: 3–133), where his view of genius is expounded with particular plausibility and clarity. His statements are rather stronger than Swann's or Carter's – witness Carter's caution above – and therefore better for my purposes. Pope provides a mass of fascinating detail in support of his case, making these chapters informative reading, but I believe the fallacies of his argument are perhaps best exposed by stripping this scholarly casing away to reveal the bare propositions beneath. His case has a number of components, but the gist is summarized by the points below. Though he himself does not make the points as baldly as this, and the logic and the conclusion is in some cases implicit, I believe this is a fair summary, though much less entertaining in its starkness than the original:

1. Belief in genius posits a hierarchy of creativity, with some individuals occupying unassailable positions at its top. Therefore it is undemocratic. To this is attached a related minor claim 1(a) that belief in genius is expounded by right-wing writers. Pope's example is Roger Scruton (ibid.: 22–4). Therefore it is right wing.
2. Most of the individuals conventionally and popularly recognized as geniuses are men. Therefore the idea of genius is sexist ('phallologocentric' is Pope's term; ibid.: 23). They are also mostly white and from privileged social groups. Therefore the idea is also racist and classist. (The prioritization of gender among these parameters is Pope's – he devotes most space to it.)
3. The use of the term 'genius' in the modern sense of 'individuals who are supposedly outstanding in some way' (ibid.: 104) is comparatively recent, dating only from the late eighteenth century. Therefore it is historically contingent and socially constructed, and cannot refer to a general human phenomenon found across all periods and societies.
4. Creativity can be found in all human activity including the most mundane and everyday. Therefore there is no such thing as extraordinary creativity.
5. The term 'genius' is used loosely (an example of Pope's is 'that fence was a stroke of genius' (ibid.: 104)). Therefore it can't be taken seriously.
6. Genius is seen as an individual attribute. Yet many recognized geniuses produced their work in collaboration with others (Pope's example is Shakespeare). Therefore genius is not an individual attribute.

These are strong points. Yet none of them, however beguiling, stand up to scrutiny, and I shall attempt to demolish each in turn, arguing that while each premise above may be true, the conclusions drawn from them are non-sequiturs. Before I do so, however, it is necessary to say something about how I understand and use the notions I am defending.

As with any complex terms, there are, as Pope points out, many competing and sometimes incompatible attempts at definition, and some considerable variation across different historical periods. What I shall mean by 'extraordinary creativity' are creative artefacts, acts and ideas which are perceived as qualitatively different and superior to others; and by 'geniuses' I shall mean a small number of individuals who are perceived to consistently produce such extraordinary creativity in their fields (notably the arts, but also in scientific theorizing) in ways which are unattainable by the majority of others in those fields. I know that the problems with such definitions are legion, and that challenges and charges are now no doubt simmering or erupting in most readers' minds. This however is inevitable. I am not suggesting any kind of mechanical formula which will allocate individuals infallibly to one of two simple categories '+ genius' and '– genius', using the results of some kind of super IQ test. But this does not mean that the concept is invalid. Many important words denote concepts which are resistant to componential objective definitions and open to variable subjective interpretation. Similar problems pertain to the identification in individuals of 'goodness', 'kindness', 'beauty', 'intelligence', as do to the identification of 'genius'. Cultures and epochs will vary in whom they consider to be a genius. Even in one time and place, there is no absolute consensus about which individuals merit the accolade – though there is also often considerable agreement. There is difference of opinion as to how exclusively the term should be used. Some may think there are only half a dozen musical composers of genius, others that there are a hundred, and wherever the line is drawn there will be fuzzy borderline cases – as is usual with verbal categories (Rosch 1977). Yet none of these inevitable complications is a reason to abandon the term 'genius' as invalid. If we were limited only to the use of words which could be defined precisely, objectively and universally, we should not only have badly depleted vocabularies, but also very impoverished lives.

All this also means that when I give examples of geniuses in the course of my argument, they may not be universally accepted as such, even by those who agree with me about the validity of the concept. It does not matter in other words whether the reader agrees with me that, say, Jane Austen, Charlie Parker or Robert Burns were geniuses. I am not seeking agreement on a hit parade, but rather recognition that some human creative activity is perceived as extraordinary, and that some individuals who consistently produce such activity are perceived as extraordinary too.

Claims 1a, 5, 6: Right-wingedness, Loose use, Collaboration

Some of the claims made by Pope are substantial; others seem to form a kind of backdrop of circumstantial evidence, and as such can be countered fairly easily, in ways which Pope would probably accept.

The loose and/or hyperbolic or metaphorical use of a term (claim 5) does not preclude more precise and careful uses elsewhere. This is a general feature of language use. We may describe 100 degrees centigrade as 'boiling point' for water, but know that in fact there are variations dependent on altitude. We may say we have millions of empty wine bottles in the cellar, or that George W. Bush's head is full of crossed wires, without being so foolish as to believe these things literally. This is standard Gricean pragmatics (Grice 1975), and I do not imagine Pope would cling to his observation on the loose use of 'genius' as a major pillar of his case.

The same pertains to the notion (claim 1a) that an argument is right wing simply because it is expounded by a right-wing writer. This is what Aristotle called argument by *ethos*, the judgment of a claim on the basis of the character of the speaker, as opposed to argument by reason (Aristotle's *logos*). I disagree with Roger Scruton's politics, but that does not mean he is wrong about everything. He probably agrees with both me and Pope about the boiling point of water for example. So the fact that Roger Scruton supports the notion of genius is not an argument against it as such. Belief in genius is not a necessary, exclusive or defining element of being right wing.

As for collaboration (claim 6) it is hard to see why it precludes genius. Those widely regarded as geniuses seem indeed to be particularly responsive to the ideas of others, disposed to copying as a way of developing their own work (van Gogh of Millet, Mozart of Bach, etc.), and willing to incorporate what we should now call 'feedback from colleagues'. But there is nothing in this to disprove the idea that works of genius – including the plays of Shakespeare – are primarily (not necessarily 'wholly') the work of one person, even if part of that work involves that one person deciding what to accept or reject from others around. There is no reason why genius cannot involve collaboration and imitation among its attributes.

I turn now to the more substantial claims.

Claim 1: Undemocratic Elitism

A common thread in the case against genius is to link it with oppressive elitism of various kinds, particularly those promulgated in Western ideologies which thrived in the Romantic and post-Romantic eras when the notion of

genius was also particularly in evidence, contrasting it with the more enlight-
ened and progressive views of our own time when, in the demagogic words
of Swann and Maybin (2007: 495), 'the extension of "creativity" to everyday
contexts has been seen as a process of democratisation that challenges old
elites'. Yet there are important differences which this argument by association
needs to confront and counter. Hierarchies based upon categories of ethnicity, nation, class and gender are unjust, as they designate superiority for no
good reason. They are mutable, as they can be overturned. They also entail
oppression. Beliefs that men are superior to women, whites to blacks, upper
to lower classes, European to African nations, inevitably mean that those in
the favoured category have greater rights and are generally treated better than
those in the unfavoured category. In addition, any member of the favoured
category who accepts their own superiority, necessarily regards members of
the unfavoured category as inferior. In contrast, the notion that some human
beings are geniuses is not of this kind. Firstly, it is neither unjust nor oppressive, as it does not entail the deprivation or mistreatment of others. We do not
suffer in any way by acknowledging that the oratory of Martin Luther King
displayed a genius which we could never attain. Indeed many if not most of
those commonly designated as geniuses (including many Romantics) have
actively expressed opposition to the oppressive ideologies of their own time.
Secondly, those who are not geniuses generally regard our lives as enriched
rather than oppressed by those who are. Thirdly, while genius may benefit or even depend upon opportunities to develop in the form of education,
resources, patronage and encouragement, the reverse is not true: provision of
such advantages does not confer genius. Lastly, it is not the case – as in racist,
sexist and classist ideologies – that individuals of genius are necessarily proposed as superior overall, or should be afforded different rights, but only that
they excel in regard to their capacity in some particular field.

None of this entails a belief (though the charge will inevitably be levelled
against me) in any crass genetic determinism by which genius is seen as
entirely the result of nature and not at all of nurture. To say, as I do, that a
particular capacity for sustained extraordinary creativity is present in a small
number of individuals is not to offer any particular explanation as to why this
should be so. It remains an area for continuing enquiry – though one which
is in danger of being censored as reactionary and misguided if we follow the
editors of this volume.

Claim 2: Sexist, Racist and Classist

While there might be a case to be made that any elevation of individuals
partakes of patriarchal mores (Pope 2005: 78–84), the notion that 'genius'

is a sexist concept because the majority of those to whom the term has been applied are men (ibid.: 22–3, 99–106) is unconvincing. The feminist argument of Virginia Woolf on this issue in *A Room of One's Own* (1929), cited but never really countered by Pope (ibid.: 106), is simple but logical. As almost all known societies have suppressed opportunities for women and promoted them for men, it is not surprising that female potential genius has usually been lost, and that more male geniuses are known to us. There is nothing in this fact to disprove the assumption that potential to develop genius is equally distributed between the two sexes. The same injustice pertains in most areas of human activity, and far from being a sexist point itself, it is the main evidence of pervasive sexism. Woolf's argument is also strengthened by a parallel growth of the rights and education for women in most of the world with the numbers of women who are recognized as geniuses, notably in those areas of the arts which first opened up to women, such as poetry and the novel. The same argument pertains to the uneven representation of ethnic groups and social classes in the canon of genius. There was for example historically an absence of recognized African-American genius giving way initially to disproportionate representation in certain areas, such as jazz, before broadening – though still under-represented – into other areas.

Arguments linking genius to oppression are also highly selective, dwelling upon oppressed groups which are under-represented in the conventional canon, while conveniently overlooking others. The case Pope makes would not hold for homosexuals, an oppressed group which is well represented, or for the disproportionate number of writers of genius in the English literary canon who have come from Ireland or Britain's former colonies. Indeed it could be argued that in many cases genius is in part a response to oppression.

Even leaving this aside, there are many exceptions to the standard arguments that genius is accorded only to privileged white males. I have chosen my examples of genius so far deliberately: Jane Austen, a woman; Charlie Parker and Martin Luther King, African Americans; Robert Burns, a man born into rural poverty in an oppressed country.

Claim 3: A Recent Concept

Carter (2004: 25–7) and Pope (2005: 37–51) both recruit to their cause an account of the changing use and meaning of the words 'creativity' and 'genius' and other related words across the centuries. (Swann and Maybin 2007: 491 also allude to this etymological discussion.) They point out in particular how the Romantic notion of individual genius replaced a greater emphasis on the collaborative nature of art and how the Romantic notion of internal inspiration replaced the attribution of art to external – usually divine – inspiration.

Changes in meaning of both 'genius' and 'creativity' have been well documented (Williams 1983: 143, 230), and I do not contest them. Yet Carter's and Pope's use of these etymological facts as evidence for the notion of individual creative greatness as novel is another non sequitur. The changes they enlist refer less to the phenomenon itself than to how it has been named and explained, and it seems a strangely logocentric argument to suppose that a phenomenon does not exist because it is not named. 'Great' individuals, moreover, were recognized as such from at least classical times onwards. Indeed the authority of an Aristotle or a Vergil was if anything more fixed and unchallenged in pre-Romantic times than the status of modern geniuses is today. Such individuals may not have been named with the word 'genius', or, if they were, it may not have been with the modern meaning, but this does not entail that they were not recognized as extraordinary. There is a parallel here with arguments for 'the invention of childhood' (Cunningham 2006) and childhood innocence which find difficulty in accounting for counter-evidence from times prior to the supposed 'invention', such as Jesus's attribution of 'the kingdom of heaven' to 'little children' (Matthew 19:13–15) or Prospero's description of the infant Miranda as 'a cherubim ... that did preserve me' (*The Tempest*, Act I, scene 2). In a similar way, claims that 'genius' is a recent concept have to deal with counter-examples such as (to use Carter's and Pope's own example of Shakespeare) Ben Jonson's dedicatory poem to the First Folio, which not only attributes to Shakespeare qualities very much in line with the notion of individual genius which I am using here, but also places him in a pantheon of greats:

> ... I confess thy writings to be such
> As neither man nor Muse can praise too much.
>
>   ... Soul of the age!
> The applause! delight! the wonder of our stage!
> My Shakespeare, rise; I will not lodge thee by
> Chaucer or Spenser ...
>
> I should commit thee surely with thy peers,
>
> ... to honour thee I would not seek
> For names, but call forth thund'ring Aeschylus,
> Euripides, and Sophocles to us,
> Pacuvius, Accius, him of Cordova dead,
>
> ... Triumph, my Britain; thou hast one to show
> To whom all scenes of Europe homage owe.
> He was not of an age, but for all time!

Whatever Jonson's personal motives for praising his rival so effusively, and however much the competitive nationalism of the final lines may offend, there is little sense here of an age in which the notion of outstanding and extraordinary individual creativity – 'genius' in the modern sense of the term – was unknown.

Elitism and Language

I have argued above that there is a good deal of confused thinking in the yoking together of oppressive hierarchies and the notion of genius. This confusion has a particular history in linguistics which is especially pertinent here, as much of the work in this current volume, including contributions by the editors, is related to linguistic creativity.

Historically, the maintenance and creation of oppressive hierarchies has been expressed through attitudes, both popular and academic, to the language of the groups involved. Thus nineteenth-century linguists, working in the heyday of European nationalism and colonialism, believed that certain languages (and these always included inevitably their own) were, like the 'spirit' of the 'peoples' they expressed, superior to others, in logic or beauty or complexity (Sweet 1964 [1899]: 194; von Humboldt 1988 [1836]: 33). Meanwhile, within nations it was believed that certain varieties – always those of the powerful – were superior to the 'dialects' of lower classes and marginalized regions. In a similar way, the use of language by women was considered inferior to that of men: more garrulous, more emotional, more trivial. Work in both empirical and theoretical linguistics has disproved all of these complacent and convenient beliefs. Comparative descriptive linguistics shows the world's languages to have a common ancestry, as does humanity itself, and generally to be of equal formal complexity and functional power. If there is discrepancy, as some claim, it is the languages of the least powerful which are more complex, with complexity following isolation (Ellis and Larsen-Freeman 2006: 573). Sociolinguistics has shown dialects of languages to be equally complex, with the standard form generally reflecting the dialect of the dominant class and/or region. Studies of variation in language use by men and women have reached different conclusions, with some documenting regular differences (Lakoff 1975) and others showing a more complex picture (Cameron 2005), but none have found any difference which could be described in terms of superiority and inferiority.

In theoretical linguistics, the ideas of Noam Chomsky, though often criticized or even ridiculed in applied and functional linguistics, have also dealt a major blow to elitist conceptions of language, by stressing the universal and uniform nature of the language faculty as a species-specific attribute, rather than varying between groups or individuals. But care needs to be exercised in deploying Chomskyan theory in analysis of linguistic creativity. Chomsky has written of the creative power of languages to generate an infinity of novel sentences, and passages by him on this topic are frequently cited (Carter 2004: 77–8; Pope 2005: 55), or evoked (Swann and Maybin 2007: 491), even by those writing on linguistic creativity from a functional perspective. The universality of this creative power of language would seem at odds with the notion of genius, which stresses the uneven distribution of extraordinary creativity. It is important however to distinguish between the creativity *of* the system itself, which allows us all to be creative within the rules of our languages, and creativity *with* the system, when individuals depart from these rules, manipulating them to produce for example unorthodox word coinages and grammatical operations. Thus the almost certainly unique sentence

> There is a framed poem by May Sarton I cut out of *The Independent* in front of me on my desk.

is possible because of the creativity *of* the system, and has been generated by me within the rules of English, while the words Shakespeare gives to Cleopatra that

> I shall see some squeaking Cleopatra boy my greatness. (*Antony and Cleopatra*, Act V, scene 2)

is creativity *with* the system as its use of 'boy' as a verb is outside those rules (Widdowson 1975: 15). In Chomskyan terms, creativity *of* the system is an aspect of competence, creativity *with* the system is an aspect of performance – as is linguistic genius.

Claim 4: Ordinary and Extraordinary

Creativity *with* the system – an aspect of language play – has recently received extensive consideration in applied linguistics. Through their innovative work on the CANCODE corpus, Ron Carter and Mike McCarthy, by showing just how pervasive such creativity is in spoken English, have demonstrated that it is by no means a special or unusual aspect of language use (e.g. Carter and McCarthy 1995a, 1995b, 2006; Carter 1999). Collections edited by Swann and Maybin (Maybin and Swann 2006; Swann and Maybin 2007), as well as their own work on the topic (Maybin and Swann 2007), have also provided extensive examples of its use. Crystal (1998) has surveyed its use in such domains as puzzles, journalism, advertising and comedy, while in my own work I have documented and analysed it in a range of non-literary genres including rhymes, cartoons, riddles, songs and prayers (Cook 1996, 2000), advertising (2001a), language teaching materials (2001b), public relations (2007, 2008) and food labels (2004: 62–8, 82–9; Cook et al. 2009). There has also been extensive research into language play by language learners (e.g. Kramsch and Sullivan 1996; Cook 1997; Lantolf 1997; Sullivan 2000; Tarone and Broner 2000; Belz 2002; Broner and Tarone 2003; Bell 2005; Cekaite and Aronsson 2005; Kim and Kellogg 2007; Pomerantz and Bell 2007).

The issue at stake in this argument, however, is not whether such creativity *with* the system is prevalent in everyday language use – on this the writers cited seem to agree – but whether all instances are of equal value, and whether the fact that poetic language use such as patterning, coinage, form conversion, etc. are common in both literary and everyday discourse, somehow demotes instances which have previously been considered *extra*ordinary, putting the two on the same level. Is linguistic creativity in the Shakespeare line quoted above, and in the play and the *oeuvre* of which it is a part, of the same kind as that found in CANCODE when a speaker 'telling the story of a dangerous game he and his friends played as children, rolling down industrial spoil heaps inside old lorry tyres' says:

> And you'd just roll, like circusing right the way down and get right up to the top (Carter and McCarthy 1995a: 310)?

After all, the speaker here converts noun to verb in the same creative way as Shakespeare in the line from *Antony and Cleopatra* cited above. Carter agrees with me that it does not, observing that a one-off instance of such play is not the same as sustained and meaningful uses of play which

> operate on a much larger and more extended scale ... and ... contribute to the explication and representation of the human condition

concluding that

> to point out that creative language in such [literary] texts functions in ways similar to those in conversations does not explain why those texts have such importance in individual lives. (2004: 81)

These are perennial arguments going back at least to Jakobson's (1960) delineation of a poetic function and inattentive criticisms of it on the grounds that this function could be found outside literary texts (Werth 1976). (Jakobson never posited the poetic function as exclusive to poetry, and his own main example was the 1956 election slogan 'I like Ike'.)

Given that nobody now denies the presence of creativity with the system in both literary and non-literary texts (and perhaps nobody ever did!), it may seem that I am both aiming at a straw man and reviving a stale argument. Neither however is the case. Carter is real and his argument substantial, and, while related to the older argument, the points he is making (and therefore my opposition to them) are of a different nature. Summarizing the chapter in which the above quotation occurs, Carter comes up with the following bullet point, under the heading 'Towards the art of common talk':

> Creativity is both special and normal and is both ordinary and extraordinary. It is extraordinary in its ordinariness. Ordinary language, in so far as it exists, is the exception rather than the rule. It is problematic to make ordinariness a default condition.

Confusing but not confused, this apparently tautological declaration is itself an instance of language play and is self-reflective. Treated as ordinary reasoning it seems illogical, but this is because it redefines its own terms as it progresses, so that by its ending they no longer mean what they did at its beginning. Unpicked, it does not seem to abandon the terms 'ordinary/ extraordinary', 'special/normal', but to redefine them so that the attribute <creativity with the system> is now a characteristic of both, and it is language use without this characteristic (previously regarded as 'ordinary') which is now extra-ordinary or ab-normal, but in a different sense – giving us actually three categories where before there were two. This is a credible position, and the quantity of evidence Carter has presented is persuasive. But as with Pope's true premises and faulty sequiturs, we must beware of the conclusion which seems to be drawn. It does not follow from the presence of creativity with the system in everyday discourse that the distinction between ordinary and extraordinary creativity should be abandoned, but rather that the defining characteristics of the extraordinary are to be sought elsewhere. The ubiquity of creativity strongly suggests that the extraordinariness of the literary lies in some other aspect of creativity than mere play with the system. Rather than conflate what was previously considered to be the extraordinary and the ordinary, we should acknowledge that we have been looking in the wrong place, and that the fact of language play in everyday talk is not enough to turn it into art. The fact that Carter elsewhere talks of a cline of creativity from the extraordinary to the ordinary (2004: 66–7, 139–40) does not get him off the hook of this problem – for clines still have extremes, which can function in effect as binary opposites, and are used as such in the quotation above.

The possibility of pursuing difference between ordinary and extraordinary creativity does not however seem to be on the current agenda. In the forceful words of Maybin and Swann (2007: 514) 'it is pointless to try to judge wordplay according to its literary merit' and 'it makes little sense to compare conversational word play with a published poem in terms of their literary value'. To me, on the contrary, such 'pointless' comparisons remain one of the most interesting and as yet unsolved questions of linguistics: given their frequent formal similarities, what is it that distinguishes the banal from the sublime utterance? Why does a line of Yeats or Dylan cause such long-lasting reverberations in my mind, in ways which everyday banter does not.

The move away from interest in extraordinary creativity and genius not only seems unjustified, but also deprives us of a category. We need to ask what we gain and what we lose by abandoning these notions, tarring them with the brushes of elitism and sexism, relegating them to the status of a recent local historically contingent phenomenon, letting them melt away into the general hubbub of everyday language play. I have tried in this polemical paper to point out the loose argument and logical fallacies of the current orthodoxy, and in doing so to stay logical myself. But my motivation for the attack – as will readily be guessed, and as I have let slip at the end of the previous section – is more personal. Like many others, of both sexes, and all nations and classes, my life has been enriched by the creativity of those exceptional individuals to whom my attention has been directed by teachers, critics, publishers, colleagues and friends. Far from feeling that I have been socialized into conformity and obedience by this experience, it has on the contrary provided me with a counterbalance of beauty and sanity to everyday social existence. To lose this experience, and to deprive others of it, under the influence of illogical and falsely egalitarian arguments, would be a loss indeed.

By all means let us continue to study everyday creativity. But there are no *reasons* that I can find in the current debate to undermine the validity of the claim that there is also extraordinary creativity, unequally distributed among a very few individuals, to the great benefit of the rest of us.

REFERENCES

Bell, N.D. (2005) 'Exploring language play as an aid to SLL: a case study of humour in NS-NNS Interaction'. *Applied Linguistics* 26(2): 192–219.

Belz, J.A. (2002) 'Second language play as a representation of the multicompetent self in foreign language study'. *Journal of Language Identity, and Education* 1(1): 13–39.

Broner, M, and Tarone, E. (2003) 'Is it fun? Language play in a fifth-grade Spanish immersion classroom'. *The Modern Language Journal* 85(3): 363–79.

Cameron, D. (2005) 'Language, gender, and sexuality: current issues and new directions'. *Applied Linguistics* 26(4): 482–503.

Carter, R. (1999) 'Common language: corpus, creativity and cognition'. *Language and Literature* 8(3): 195–216.

Carter, R. (2004) *Language and Creativity: The Art of Common Talk*. London/New York: Routledge.

Carter, R. and McCarthy, M.J. (2004) 'Talking, creating: interactional language, creativity and context'. *Applied Linguistics* 25(1): 62–88.

Carter, R. and McCarthy, M.J. (1995a) 'Discourse and creativity: building the gap between language and literature', in G. Cook and B. Seidlhofer (eds) *Principle and Practice in Applied Linguistics*. Oxford: Oxford University Press.

Carter, R. and McCarthy, M.J. (1995b) 'Grammar and the spoken language'. *Applied Linguistics* 16(2): 141–58.

Carter, R. and McCarthy, M.J. (2006) *Cambridge Grammar of English*. Cambridge: Cambridge University Press.

Cekaite, A. and Aronsson, K. (2005) 'Language play, a collaborative resource in children's L2 learning'. *Applied Linguistics* 26(2): 169–92.

Cook, G. (1996) 'Language play in English', in J. Maybin and N. Mercer (eds) *Using English: From Conversation to Canon*. London: Routledge with the Open University.

Cook, G. (1997) 'Language play, language learning'. *English Language Teaching Journal* 51(3): 224–31.

Cook, G. (2000) *Language Play, Language Learning*. Oxford: Oxford University Press.

Cook, G. (2001a) *The Discourse of Advertising*, 2nd edn. London: Routledge.

Cook, G. (2001b) '"The philosopher pulled the lower jaw of the hen": ludicrous invented sentences in language teaching'. *Applied Linguistics* 22(3): 366–87.

Cook, G. (2004) *Genetically Modified Language*. London: Routledge.

Cook, G. (2007) '"This we have done." The different vagueness of poetry and PR', in J. Cutting (ed.) *Vague Language Explored*. Basingstoke: Palgrave Macmillan: 21–40.

Cook, G. (2008) 'Advertising and Public Relations', in V. Koller and R. Wodak (eds) *Handbook of Applied Linguistics, Volume 3: Language and Communication in the Public Sphere*. Berlin and New York: Mouton de Gruyter: 113–38.

Cook, G., Reed, M. and Twiner, A.J. (2009) '"But it's all true!" Commercialism and commitment in the discourse of organic food promotion'. *Text & Talk* 29(2): 151–73.

Crystal, D. (1998) *Language Play*. Harmondsworth: Penguin.

Cunningham, H. (2006) *The Invention of Childhood*. London: BBC books.

Ellis, N. and Larsen-Freeman, D. (2006) 'Language emergence: implications for applied linguistics'. Introduction to the Special Issue. *Applied Linguistics* 27(4): 558–90.

Grice, H.P. (1975) 'Logic and conversation', in P. Cole and J.L. Morgan (eds) *Syntax and Semantics, Volume 3: Speech Acts*. New York: Academic Press.

von Humboldt, W. (1988 [1836]) *On Language*. Cambridge: Cambridge University Press.

Jakobson, R. (1960) 'Closing statement: linguistics and poetics', in T.A. Sebeok (ed.) *Style in Language*. Cambridge, MA: MIT Press.

Kim, Y. and Kellogg, D. (2007) 'Rules out of roles: differences in play language and their developmental significance'. *Applied Linguistics* 28(1): 25–46.

Kramsch, C. and Sullivan, P. (1996) 'Appropriate pedagogy'. *English Language Teaching Journal* 50: 199–213.

Lakoff, R. (1975) *Language and Women's Place*. New York: Harper & Row.

Lantolf, J. (1997) 'The function of language play in the acquisition of L2 Spanish', in W.R. Glass and A.T. Pérez (eds) *Contemporary Perspectives on the Acquisition of Spanish, Volume 2: Production, Processing and Comprehension*. Somerville: Cascadilla Press.

Maybin, J. and Swann. J. (eds) (2006) *The Art of English: Everyday Creativity*. Milton Keynes: Palgrave Macmillan and The Open University.

Maybin, J. and Swann, J. (2007) 'Everyday creativity in language: textuality, contextuality, and critique'. *Applied Linguistics* 28(4): 497–518.

Pomerantz, A. and Bell, N.D. (2007) 'Learning to play, playing to learn: FL learners as multicompetent language users'. *Applied Linguistics* 28(4): 556–79.

Pope, R. (2005) *Creativity: Theory, History, Practices*. London: Routledge.

Rosch, E. (1977) 'Human categorization', in N. Warren (ed.) *Advances in Crosscultural Psychology*. New York: Academic Press.

Sullivan, P. (2000) 'Playfulness as mediation in communicative language teaching in a Vietnamese classroom', in J. Lantolf (ed.) *Sociocultural Theory and Second Language Learning*. Oxford: Oxford University Press.

Swann, J. and Maybin, J. (2007) 'Guest editors' introduction to the special issue: Language Creativity in Everyday Contexts'. *Applied Linguistics* 28(4): 491–7.

Sweet, H. (1964 [1899]) *The Practical Study of Languages: A Guide for Teachers and Learners*. Oxford: Oxford University Press.

Tarone, E. and Broner, M. (2000) 'Is it fun? Language play in a fifth grade Spanish immersion classroom'. *Modern Language Journal* 85.

Werth, P.W. (1976) 'Roman Jakobson's verbal analysis of poetry'. *Journal of Linguistics* 12: 21–73.

Widdowson, H.G. (1975) *Stylistics and the Teaching of Literature*. London: Longman.

Williams, R. (1983) *Keywords*. London: Collins Fontana.

Woolf, V. (1929) *A Room of One's Own*. London: Hogarth Press.

25

Creative Writing: Habitat Homo Sapiens

Graeme Harper

[A novelist and academic reflects on the nature of Creative Writing as 'action' and examines the implications for the national benchmarking statement he helped to draft.]

Habitats not Circles

Creative Writing begins in actions and ends, if indeed it ends, in actions. During, and in between, it produces artefacts, some public, many private, and it distributes those artefacts more or less, whether to a few or many readers, depending on the creative writer's thoughts on what is private or public and a culture's thoughts on what is culturally significant. As a set of actions, Creative Writing is poorly understood, yet some of its outputs, its public artefacts, are highly revered, most obviously as literature; and, in being highly revered, these artefacts have long encouraged us to turn back to consider the producers and consumers of Creative Writing. This again returns us to the human acts and actions which produce and consume Creative Writing; but these remain poorly understood, and so the circle completes, so it begins again. (An earlier, book-length treatment of these issues is my *On Creative Writing* (2010)).

I first considered whether creative and critical knowledge can be enhanced in such a circular fashion when I was undertaking a Masters in Historiography, taught enthusiastically at the University of New England in Armidale, New South Wales, in the middle of Australian wheat country. At the time, I was also writing my first novel, itself set in northern New South Wales in the early part of the twentieth century. The class did not deal with creative and critical knowledge, as such; rather, over a period of weeks it looked at what is known as the 'Hermeneutic Circle', an idea often attributed to the German philosopher Martin Heidegger, and referring to a more or less step-like relationship between human understanding, action and reflection, by which we engage with the world and, indeed, with the texts being produced within it.

What I was experiencing in simultaneously composing my novel while taking this class turned out not to be a Hermeneutic Circle because what I was considering was not a revolving pattern produced by the relationship between my perceived (and future) textual whole (my novel) and its textual parts. In fact, the notion of textual wholeness and textual parts, and the suggestion of primary textual existence, were themselves key components of my compositional problem!

Later in the same Masters course, when I was introduced more thoroughly to Martin Heidegger and to Hans-Georg Gadamer, who developed hermeneutics not least in what was an attractive-sounding area of 'practical wisdom', it seemed that elements of the discussion pointed to something about how existing texts might relate to the experience of creating and consuming texts – both of which I was very actively doing. But the pointing remained strangely inadequate, slightly off to the side, seemingly biased towards the text, leaving the acts and action as secondary. By 'acts' and 'actions' I am referring here to things that are actually *done* during Creative Writing (e.g. individual acts such as redrafting a sentence or a paragraph; or groups of acts, or what I call 'actions', such as collecting empirical evidence regarding some aspect of personal history or some social event, in order to draw upon during composition).

The collection of acts and actions I was envisaging was not an entirely open-ended system either, as perhaps some proponents of postmodernist theory favoured. My collection had systemic 'endness' to it; it was something that produced a definable result. Needless to say, there was still a great deal missing in all this thinking, and the revolving nature of act and action, creation and recreation, completion and beginning (potentially in that reverse order), seemed much less like a circle than like a habitat in which human beings dwelt and interacted, not in circular way, and not always linked, as if in a web; rather this habitat was generated and regenerated by acts and actions, artefacts and responses, not entirely randomly but certainly with some elements of fortuitousness. *Becoming*, in this sense, was more obviously a human activity than *being* and this becoming strongly favoured action as a mode of human engagement with the world, rather than passivity. Similarly, *becoming* involved the imagination; in fact, it could not exist without it because to intuit, which is essential to becoming, involves imaginative projections not restricted to acts of logic.

Other commentators, while offering some hope of reconciliation, similarly failed to capture what I was endeavouring to understand. For example, an excellent work by David A. Shon – *The Reflective Practitioner* (1983) – which said much on action and evolving plans of action in the realm of learning, suggested a 'spiral' founded in reflection, and seemed not quite to address the point that reflection was, in itself, static, often overly self-centred and, ultimately, uncommunicative. While Shon, in this work and in others, made reference to such things as 'reflection-in-action' and 'educating for artistry' and teaching itself becoming a form of 'reflection-in-action' the problem of the relationship between individual human acts and actions (in undertaking Creative Writing and as outlined above), the knowledge and understanding this involved (knowledge that might be acquired and further developed and, further still, disseminated via teaching) and the artefacts of Creative Writing that were almost exclusively touted in our cultures, was unresolved.

If only on reflection, I was sure, then the fluidity of this movement was unacknowledged. For creative writers, seeking to complete a work (at least to a point where they were comfortable letting it out into the public arena – the 'endness' to which I referred earlier), seeking to acquire knowledge about their actions and what results were likely to occur because of those actions, this was inadequate. It was inadequate for seeking to ground the desire to undertake Creative Writing in some sense of how Creative Writing was a holistic human activity, widely found throughout the world, undertaken in a great many forms, and often considerably valued by both creative writers and an even greater number of readers. In essence, the notion of action-and-reflection being a cycle of some step-by-step kind didn't work. And, if it didn't work for my personal learning and developing understanding as a creative writer, then there seemed little doubt that it was fairly inadequate for the constructing of teaching programmes in Creative Writing and, in addition, broadly for acting on the relationship between the creation and consumption of Creative Writing.

Creating, Learning, Understanding

What I was endeavouring to describe and, more importantly, *understand* was indeed the intersection of creativity, human language and what we have often been drawn to call 'literature' – but a specific instance of this intersection, or set of intersections, which created the habitat in which a creative writer (in this case, me) dwelt and confirmed that habitat as both a natural environment (that is, an ecological zone which might be experienced without concern that it was, as such, 'alien' to human life) and a person-made environment (that is, a zone of human choice and thus human construction, which was, metaphorically speaking, 'architecturally sound'). That is: that my choice and construction of a habitat was sound.

In teaching Creative Writing it feels both right in terms of the subject, and right in terms of the human exchanges that teaching involves, to provide students with the knowledge that will help them 'survive' – in this case, meaning 'bring them success in their chosen field' and 'improve their quality of life should they pursue this subject as a career'. Thus the key question emerges: what are the things we should be teaching Creative Writing students and how do they relate to our understanding of the interrelations between creativity, human language and literature? If there is an answer, it seems certain that an action–reflection circle does not provide it. Creative Writing learning does not involve a circular relationship. Such a circularity – whether action–reflection orientated or dialogic – is also not a good representation of how actual human life works more generally. It ignores the impact of memory, it leaves out the fortuitous and unpredictable, and it considerably downgrades evidence of complementary, entwined or parallel human activities (that is, those that appear not connected; those that appear to be peripheral to some central activity). If it were a good representation, we might travel around it but we would never advance.

Reflection or conversation, even 'in action', cannot make steps forward; it remains an idea based on a cycle of internalizing–applying–internalizing–applying. Thus it could be said that circularity, even if forming a wheel, can only roll forward if it relates to something beyond itself. Similarly, the relationship between creativity, human language and 'literature' cannot be understood by reference, first and foremost, to those artefacts of Creative Writing which we culturally have come most to revere. That is, if we begin by referencing 'literature' we do not understand the actions of creative writers; we understand, first and foremost, the actions of the market, the actions of publishers and booksellers, the actions of literary critics, the actions of cultural moments, the actions of public display, the actions of archivists and librarians in endeavouring to capture a notion of 'cultural value', the actions of educationalists as they endeavour to present education for the cultural and historical milieu. But we do not understand the actions of creative writers. And, with this in mind, it's essential for understanding Creative Writing that we approach the intersection of creativity, human language and 'literature' with a consideration not only of reflection but of *response*. Response, responsiveness, the act and actions and results of responding.

How this Impacts on Teaching and Research

As current Chair of the National Association of Writers in Education (NAWE) Higher Education Committee, the thoughts outlined above impacted on how I considered one of our recent (and, some have said, more significant)

Committee tasks. The Committee, which is elected from the membership of NAWE, consists of some ten members, all of whom are creative writers and have some connection with the teaching and learning of Creative Writing in Higher Education.

NAWE is the Subject Association for Creative Writing here in the United Kingdom. As the Subject Association, it seemed important that we were able to articulate what we felt were essentials for the teaching and research in the subject of Creative Writing in universities and colleges in the United Kingdom. With this in mind, we set forth to create what are usually referred to as Benchmark (or Hallmark) Statements and, after around four months of discussion, writing and rewriting we produced the Statements that are available in paper form or as a PDF document (www.creativewritingstatements.co.uk/). It would be inappropriate to speak formally for the Committee in this chapter, so I speak here personally in saying that the creation of the UK's first benchmark statements for the subject of Creative Writing naturally raised many issues. Among these were some relatively simple questions. For example, there is the question of 'differentiation' between entry-level and final-year undergraduate university modules or units in Creative Writing; the question of what sorts of things students might be assessed upon; the question of what Creative Writing, as a human activity, appears to offer humans; the question of what kinds of knowledge and understanding we were developing and disseminating.

So, perhaps not simple questions, after all! The key question, again speaking personally, often appeared to be: what are the things we should be teaching Creative Writing students in Higher Education and how do these things relate to our understanding of the interrelations between creativity, human language and the artefacts that this interrelation produces? Ultimately, this had to incorporate concepts of how the university *subject* of Creative Writing could be defined; and it had to include reference to what this subject fostered and encouraged, as ideals as well as practical skills, and in terms of learning, as well as of teaching. And it had to suggest what the study of Creative Writing brought about (that is, the results of undertaking a degree in which Creative Writing featured). Thus:

2.7   A Creative Writing degree develops:
- robust artistic practices;
- the capacity to be creative;
- an aesthetic sensibility;
- intellectual enquiry;
- the ability to apply the above to the production of the student's own textual material (either written or in other forms);
- skills in team working;
- an appreciation of diversity;

- the ability to conduct research in a variety of modes;
- the ability to reflect on one's own learning and development;
- the capacity to work independently, determining one's own future learning needs. (NAWE 2008: 5)

Later, in the section on Research, the same Benchmark Statement states:

3. Research Methodologies

3.1 Investigations in Creative Writing include creative practice, critical or theoretical reflection, and responses to advanced reading (in the broadest sense of the word 'reading').

3.2 Creative Writing is research in its own right. All Creative Writing involves research *in* Creative Writing whereby experience is transmuted into language (and some of that experience may concern language itself). (NAWE 2008: 13)

I'd add that the Committee's consideration, and writing, of the Benchmarks document brought it to consider (and its individual members to consider, personally) the habitat or habitats in which they dwelt, as creative writers. This was further developed in such sections as:

4.1 Creative Writing is in essence a developmental subject where the successful student is required to be an active participant in their own learning.

4.2 This developmental nature demands teaching which is informed and authoritative, but which also allows full scope for student participation and expression. (NAWE 2008: 7, 8)

Personally, I felt there was very little 'circular' discussion in the process of producing these benchmarks; though, certainly, there were long, and often difficult, explorations of the relationship between that which is being undertaken (the creation of works of Creative Writing) and that which exists (works of Creative Writing known by those in the Committee). Likewise, there was a strong sense of experiential knowledge – the knowledge of the Committee members themselves, relating in our university discipline at present to a great deal of knowledge that is ancient yet not widely analysed.

Creating 'Benchmark Statements' is a formal activity of contemporary academe; for better or worse, such documentation now forms part of university life. It was not always the case. As Charles Homer Haskins reminds us in his work on the rise of medieval universities:

the genesis of the mediaeval university was individuals with a common interest in a subject or in a teacher, who were attracted to a place, and who, over time, organized … Without buildings, a campus or much in the way of accouterments, the university – the community of teachers and students – was free to pack up and leave a locality if for some reason they felt mistreated or unhappy. (2004 [1923]: xi)

Evidence suggests that creative writers today are happy to be involved in academe – evidence, that is, provided by the vast numbers who choose to work in it, and work with it. Of course, throughout history creative writers have often had associations with the activities of higher learning, but the sheer numbers today, and the evolution of more formal institutional structures connected to higher learning, makes the current association historically distinctive. Evidence suggests also that today's students certainly appear to be happy to have Creative Writing available to them as a university subject – evidence, that is, provided by the considerable numbers of students studying the subject. These numbers continue to increase. As such, academe and Creative Writing in the twenty-first century go forward hand-in-hand, with many seeking to acquire knowledge about their Creative Writing actions and what the results are likely to be. They seek to ground their desire to undertake Creative Writing in some sense of how it is a holistic human activity, widely found throughout the world, undertaken in a great many forms – an activity that, at its core, is about human interaction. Being human-centred, Creative Writing asks us to consider how we, as individuals, pursue communication with each other and with our wider culture and society, as well as with the individuals, cultures and societies of the wider world. The fluidity of this communication, and its creative character, reminds us of the complex relationships that exist in human habitats and that initiate and inform the responses we choose to make to the world.

REFERENCES

Harper, G. (2010) *On Creative Writing*. Bristol: Multilingual Matters.
Haskins, C.H. (2004 [1923]) *The Rise of Universities*. Ithaca: Cornell University Press.
NAWE (National Association of Writers in Education). (2008) *Creative Writing Subject Benchmark Statement/Creative Writing Research Benchmark Statement*. York and London: NAWE.
Shon, D. (1983) *The Reflective Practitioner*. New York: Basic.

26

Three Reflections on Creativity and Writing

JON COOK

Any attempt to think about creative language is likely to encounter three objections at the outset. The first is that the very idea of 'creative language' is an arbitrary construct, not least because it could be argued that all language is creative and, if this is true, it follows that no significant distinction can be made between language that is and isn't creative. The second is the danger of identifying the creativity of language too narrowly with one linguistic feature, the existence, say, of metaphors or similes in literary and everyday language. The third is to argue that, even where the distinction between the creative and the uncreative uses of a medium might apply, it's very difficult to see how it could be applied to language in general.

An analogy might help to clarify what is at issue here. R. G. Collingwood's distinction between craft and art depends upon a distinction between a creative and uncreative use of a medium. Craft, according to Collingwood, is defined by a series of distinctions between a means and an end, between planning and execution, and a material on which it is exercised. Although art contains elements of craft, its priorities and its relation to a medium are very different:

> The theory of poetic technique implies that in the first place a poet has certain experiences which demand expression; then he conceives of the possibility of a poem in which they might be expressed; then this poem, as an unachieved end, demands for its realization, the exercise of certain powers or forms of skill, and these constitute the poet's technique. There is an element of truth in this...But the description of the unwritten poem as an end to which his technique is a means is false; it implies that before he has written his poem he knows, and could state, the specification of it in the kind of way in which a joiner knows the specification of a table he is about to make. This

is always true of a craftsman ... But it is wholly untrue of the artist in those cases where the work of art is not a work of craft; the poet extemporising his verses, the sculptor playing with his clay...In these cases...the artist has no idea what the experience is which demands expression until he has expressed it. (Collingwood 1938: 28)

The point here is not whether Collingwood's distinction is correct but the fact that it at least enables him to distinguish a domain where creative expression can take place by contrast with another kind of activity. Yet this kind of distinction just doesn't seem to apply to language in any way that intuitively makes sense. Or, if it does, our relation to language is much like that which he ascribes to poets, and, again, this leads us back to the idea that all language is in some sense creative.

These objections correspond to three obstacles in any discussion of creative language: the dangers of meaningless terms; thin description; and misleading analogy. One way of acknowledging, if not necessarily avoiding, these dangers is to identify specific instances of thought where a notion of creative language seems to arise, and then compare them to see if they bear any kind of resemblance to each other. This is the method of what follows. I've chosen three texts or loci of thought by three very different thinkers: Heinrich Von Kleist, Maurice Merleau-Ponty and Ludwig Wittgenstein. In each case I try to distinguish what they have to say about creative language, even though none use the phrase directly. In each case, and collectively, a question follows about whether the emerging account survives any or all of the three dangers outlined above.

Kleist

Heinrich Von Kleist published his short, conversational essay 'On the Gradual Production of Thoughts Whilst Speaking' in 1805. It begins with a familiar situation: someone sitting at a desk unable to work. There is a problem that needs be solved or an essay that needs to be written but no amount of sitting and thinking, no process of meditation or introspection, seems to help. Kleist's answer to this impasse is simple: find someone, almost anyone, to talk to. With any luck, the needed thoughts will emerge in the process of speaking.

Kleist is aware that his recommendation contradicts assumptions about intellectual rigour and system:

I see astonishment in your face. I hear you reply that when you were young you were advised only to speak of things you already understood. But in those days, doubtless, you spoke in the presumption of instructing others but my wish is that you speak in the sensible intention of instructing yourself. (Kleist 1997: 405)

Kleist's intention is to demonstrate the value of speaking about things you don't understand and, by speaking, come to understand them. Although he doesn't use the word, language is 'creative' because it brings thought into being in ways that often exceed the intentions of the speaker.

In elaborating this thought Kleist does not develop a theory of tropes so much as a comedy of contexts. His method – if he has one – is deliberately light-hearted and ironic. He imagines examples of what it might mean for thought to emerge in speech. His first is drawn from the French Revolution and consists in a reconstruction of Mirabeau's response to the King's messenger at the time of the first meetings of the Third Estate in 1789. But instead of writing about this as a turning point in history, a heroic moment in the development of liberty and human rights, Kleist imagines a hesitant and slightly terrified Mirabeau who doesn't actually have a clue about what he is going to say in response to the demands of the King's messenger. And so a resounding statement about the sources of political authority emerges in a comedy of hesitation and uncertainty. Mirabeau makes it up as he goes along and it's because he is improvising that he is able to say what he says:

> I think of the thunderbolt with which Mirabeau dismissed the Master of Ceremonies who, after the meeting of the 23rd June, the last under the *ancien régime*, when the King had ordered the estates to disperse, returned to the hall in which they were assembled and asked them had they heard the King's command. 'Yes' Mirabeau replied, 'we have heard the King's command.' – I am certain that beginning thus humanely he had not thought of the bayonets with which he would finish. 'Yes, my dear sir,' he repeated 'we have heard it.' – As we see, he is not yet exactly sure what he intends. 'But by what right ...' he continues, and suddenly a source of colossal ideas is opened up to him, do you give orders here? We are the representatives of the nation – That is what he needed! – 'The nation does not take orders. It gives them ...' (Ibid.: 406)

Kleist does not want us to view Mirabeau as a type of the Romantic genius with some special tap root into a source of creativity. But he does want to find a new ground for a Romantic value, spontaneity. It is one that depends upon a number of factors: a sense of emergency or threat, a setting of dialogue or debate, a heightened awareness that if something is not said in the moment an important opportunity will be lost. Mirabeau lives in his language in a way that surprises him. After some hesitation, the phrase arrives – 'by what right'– which will open out onto a thought he had not anticipated and an utterance he had not planned.

We might say that Kleist's account of 'creative' utterance shares something in common with Collingwood's contrast between the skills of the craftsman and the creativity of the artist. Like the artist, Mirabeau 'has no idea what experience demands expression until after he has expressed it'. But Kleist does not want to confine this kind of linguistic creativity to artists. It is a general potential in speech, one which Kleist wants to persuade us is largely impersonal.

He does this by way of another example, the exam room. Kleist reflects upon a contrast between two discussions, both of which attempt to respond to abstract questions about the political state and the nature of property. One occurs in the course of a conversation, the other in the context of a viva voce examination in which the two questions – 'What is the state?' 'What is property?' – are put to students by their examiners. In the absence of that conversation that had allowed thought to emerge, Kleist imagines his students unable to answer their examiner. The examiner will conclude that the students are ignorant. But Kleist's conclusion is different: 'For it is not *we* who know things but pre-eminently a certain *condition* of ours which knows' (ibid.: 408). Kleist does not develop this assertion, but instead returns to his attack on the conduct of public examinations. Here again we might assume that we are in familiar Romantic territory in the identification of the classroom as an oppressive place. In this setting language cannot discover thought because ritualized exchanges of question and answer do not allow for the kinds of spontaneous and improvised discourse that arise in conversation. Knowledge, in Kleist's view, is not a property of individual minds. It is held in language's distinctive temporality, at once an extended and diverse memory and a potential for new discoveries. Our words bear in them both the histories of their previous uses and the possibility that they might be applied ways that nobody planned or expected. What we know will always depend upon the relation that we bear to language and that relation is informed but not dictated by social and historical contexts. Mirabeau might, from one point of view, be saying the first thing that comes into his head. But his improvisations are timely and relevant. They bring an appropriate thought about rights to powerful expression, one that responds effectively to the occasion and transforms it. In this example language creates a thought that is timely in the way that it responds both to the present context and to its future possibilities. Although Kleist does not labour the point we can see how another dimension of linguistic creativity might reside in this sense of the timeliness of an utterance, the combination within it of accident and necessity.

Kleist's essay ends without an ending. A brief bracketed note tells us that it is 'to be continued'. It wasn't. The ploy may have been deliberate, part of Kleist's unmethodical method. We might find this a frustrating failure on Kleist's part to follow through and properly analyse his proposals about the emergence of thought in speech. The essay starts to explore ideas about creative language, but all it leaves us with is a set of intellectual vapour trails. Is the essay proposing a reform of education that might promote the conditions for the kinds of conversation that encourage the emergence of thought? And don't the two conditions that he sets out, one in which thought precedes language, the other in which thought emerges in language, need a fuller analysis and critique? Perhaps. But we might want to argue that really there's not a lot more to be said. Kleist's essay is a bit like a joke. You either get it or you don't. If you don't – if, for example, you say that there can be no thinking that precedes its expression – no amount of further argument will persuade you to think otherwise. If, on the other hand, you are persuaded, various quite radical things follow. Linguistic creativity is social through and through. It happens conversationally, but these conversations do not have to be either amicable or sympathetic. They are just as likely to happen in emergencies or in an encounter with an antagonist. But it does not follow that all antagonistic encounters will be creative. When authority is settled and dogmatic, as in Kleist's account of the examination room, thought will not emerge in speech. When authority is in doubt, as in Kleist's description of Mirabeau's speech, the possibility of linguistic improvisation arises.

Merleau-Ponty

Towards the end of his life, the French philosopher, Merleau-Ponty, was at work on a book whose title in translation is *The Prose of the World*. The book was left incomplete when he died in 1961 and wasn't published in France until 20 years after his death. The book's title, as Merleau-Ponty acknowledged, echoes Hegel's description of the Roman State as the 'prose of the world'. In his *Philosophy of History* Hegel contrasted two poetries, one from the East, the other from Greece, and then contrasted these further with an essentially prosaic ancient Roman state that lacked the freedom of ancient Greece and the passion for the infinite that characterized the East. But the echo is also a transformation. Merleau-Ponty's concerns are not with the history of political states but with the phenomenon of expression in language and how this phenomenon informs our experience of others and the world around us. The prose of the world for Merleau-Ponty contains possibilities for human self-realization. His book is, amongst other things, an argument in support of the creative power of the novel. Like Marx before him, he wants to stand Hegel on his head, but for different reasons.

The possibility that we might have a more or less creative relation to language is certainly one that Merleau-Ponty acknowledges. In the course of a discussion of the philosophy of language, he disagrees with the view that the purpose of such a philosophy is to establish clear and settled definitions of what words mean or to view language from the outset as something in need of reform. Nor does he adopt the view that there is a pure subjectivity that finds language an endlessly frustrating medium of expression. Language is not a disappointment, something that drags us down or away from an exalted state that might otherwise be ours:

> We must understand that language is not an impediment to consciousness and that there is no difference, for consciousness, between self-transcendence and self-expression. In its live and creative state, language is the gesture of renewal and recovery which unites me with myself and others. (Merleau-Ponty 1974: 17)

We are unlikely to know by reference to a set of rules or codes when language is in 'its live and creative state'. How then might it be manifest to us? One example that Merleau-Ponty explores might not at first sight seem an example of expressive language at all. Taking a cue from Sartre's discussion of the experience of reading in *What is Literature*, Merleau-Ponty sets out his understanding of what happens when a reading 'catches fire'. For him, such an experience depends upon the subtle mutation of a familiar language into something new:

> But the book would not interest me so much if it only told me about things I already know. It makes use of everything I have contributed in order to carry me beyond it. With the aid of signs agreed upon by the author and myself because we speak the same language, the book makes me believe that we had already shared a common stock of well-worn and readily available significations. The author has come to dwell in my world. Then, imperceptibly, he varies the ordinary meaning of the signs, and like a whirlwind they sweep me along toward the other meaning with which I am going to connect. (Ibid.: 11–12)

This passage resonates with many others in *The Prose of the World*. In its creative state language transports or moves us and this movement is always towards something: '*But therein lies the virtue of language*: it is language which propels us towards the thing it signifies' (ibid.: 10). This movement cannot happen without a place to start, and, in the case of reading, it is the agreement about meanings – language's common stock – that is the starting point for the writer and the reader.

Merleau-Ponty clarifies this process by using the example of reading Stendhal:

> Before I read Stendhal, I know what a rogue is. Thus I can understand what he means when he says that Rossi the revenue man is a rogue. But when Rossi

the rogue begins to live, it is no longer he who is a rogue: it is a rogue who is the revenue man Rossi. I have access to Stendhal's outlook through the common place words he uses. But, in his hands these words are given a new twist. The cross-references multiply. More and more arrows point in the direction of a thought I have never encountered before and perhaps would never have met without Stendhal. (Ibid.: 12)

At first reading this may seem to be saying something very familiar: creativity manifests itself in language by giving words a new twist. Mukarovsky, for example, in his influential essay, 'Standard language and Poetic Language', uses a similar distinction in his analysis of deviation.

But the differences between Mukarovsky and Merleau-Ponty are as telling as the similarities. Mukarovsky's preoccupations are with linguistic form. Deviations from the standard language manifest themselves through deviations of syntax, semantics and rhythm. As the context of his essay makes clear, the linguistic creativity he has in mind is exemplified by Gogol's use of vernacular speech in his stories. Language is always creating a standard version of itself, and, of course, what counts as the standard will vary over time. Creative language stands out against this background of normality.

Again, this looks like a similarity with Merleau-Ponty. In *The Prose of the World* he makes a distinction, vital for his whole argument, between 'sedimented language' (*le langage parlé*) and 'speech' (*le langage parlant*) (ibid.: 10). The distinction in the French original between the past and present participle is important. Language is all the time accumulating usage, protocols and conventions for utterance, and our experience of it is one of repetition. We use again and again the tried and trusted formulae, the professional jargons that give credibility to our utterances, the forms of speech that seem appropriate to the occasion. This Merleau-Ponty describes as 'language after the fact, or language as an institution'. 'Speech' or '*le langage parlant*' assumes all this and then seeks to depart from it. But these departures are not necessarily manifest in linguistic form, although they may be enabled by literary form. This is part of the point of Merleau-Ponty's invocation of Stendhal. He does not use a new or vernacular word for 'rogue', but, nonetheless, our understanding of what the word can mean is transformed. The agency of this transformation is subtle and complex. When Merleau-Ponty refers to 'cross-references' multiplying, I think he means that in the form of the novel there is an opportunity for ordinary words to interact in ways that alter their sense. They establish patterns and possibilities for recollection which suspends the usual oblivion of speech. We have an experience of language seeking out new significations. But there is something more than this – something like an erotic encounter. We accept a voice into our linguistic world, and, in doing that, the thoughts carried by that voice intertwine themselves with ours.

In a way that echoes, although not as far as I know deliberately, Kleist's trust in the powers of linguistic possession. Merleau-Ponty's version of reading is not bothered with the ways that literary works 'construct' their readers with all the accompanying anxieties about who is included in the construction and who isn't, as though the most important thing about reading a novel is a decision about whether it's a party you've been invited to or not. Reading – perhaps reading creatively – has the form of an encounter and one that has its moments of struggle and conflict:

> The relations between the reader and the book are like those loves in which one partner initially dominates because he was more proud or more temperamental, and the situation changes and the other, more wise and more silent, rules. The expressive moment occurs where the relationship reverses itself, where the book takes possession of the reader. (Ibid.: 12–13)

Merleau-Ponty's account of language assumes that speaking and listening, writing and reading, are not strictly demarcated. One kind of linguistic act flows into the other, and creativity is not attributed exclusively to any one of them. In this example, the expressive act – one that we might conventionally think of as to do with moments of speech or writing – occurs when a reader is taken over by the language of another. If this possession by another's language is a form of domination, it is also the harbinger of another moment of creation: the moment when the author – the imaginary self created by the writer – also becomes the reader's creation: 'I create Stendhal: I am Stendhal while reading him' (ibid.: 12). It is, of course, a kind of dialogue, but it does not require and even may be inhibited by a reader who comes to a text armed with an array of analytic techniques or ideological requirements. Part of the value of Merleau-Ponty's account is that it guides us towards the importance of our pre-critical relation to language if we are to let it work creatively in us.

Wittgenstein

Kleist suggests language can have the power to create thought. Merleau-Ponty argues that being possessed by the language of others can create new linguistic meanings in the texture of our own utterances. Each attempts to describe those moments when language appears to turn towards new possibilities of sense. In this final section I want briefly to explore another perspective: that the creative potential of language depends upon our experience of its being on display.

This idea has its most immediate philosophical origin in the work of Wittgenstein. One maxim in reading his work, especially his later work, is that the meaning of language resides in its use. Words are like tools. They help us to do things and it's exactly because of this that they are meaningful. I ask someone to pass the salt and they do. A parliament debates a law and it then passes into legislation. A vicar pronounces two people man and wife and they become so. All these things can and do go wrong and, when they do, we can feel that meaning drains away from language. But that just reinforces the point. As one recent commentator on Wittgenstein, James Guetti, has put it, 'a use of language for him [Wittgenstein] is not a mere saying of words; it is an application of words to do something, an application that is both purposive and consequential' (Guetti 1993: 3).

But this, as Guetti, acknowledges, is only one aspect of Wittgenstein's approach to language. The 'mere saying of words' interested him greatly, and especially the endless confusions that can arise when 'mere saying' gets confused with meaningful application, as in this famous little anecdote about the philosopher and the tree:

> I am sitting with a philosopher in the garden; he says again and again 'I know that that's a tree', pointing to a tree that is near us. Someone else arrives and hears this, and I tell him: 'This fellow isn't insane. We are only doing philosophy.' (Wittgenstein 1960: 61e)

The philosopher thinks that he is meaningfully applying words when all he is doing is 'saying' them. We might go on to draw two erroneous conclusions from this anecdote. One is to assume that it is a satire on philosophy and not a tender defence of it (it may be both). The other is that the purpose of Wittgenstein's philosophy is to regulate language so we only use it in meaningful ways. He was just as interested in what happens when language is in a condition of 'mere saying'.

A lot of 'mere saying' goes on in just talking and it's not always something that speakers intend. We often play with language by echoing an utterance, parodying it, or taking it out of its context of intended use. It is these occasions that form the basis for Guetti's ideas about language being on display. His argument is, in some ways, close to Jakobson's analysis of the poetic function discussed elsewhere in this volume. When language is on display we develop a heightened awareness of the linguistic medium itself. Language in use, on the other hand, does not draw attention to itself in this way. Another idea of Wittgenstein's is relevant here. Its source is in the *Tractatus* and his remarks about the logical form of propositions. It is there that he makes the famously gnomic remark that 'What expresses *itself* in language we cannot express by means of language' (Wittgenstein 1961: 51). Even, that is, when language is in use, there is something about language that is being shown in its grammatical and syntactic forms. Another way of putting this takes us back to the question of what is being expressed in any utterance. One way of answering the question is to say that what is being expressed is language itself not just in a particular use but in all its potential for other and further uses. Telling is always accompanied by showing.

Our awareness of this potential in language is especially heightened in certain conditions, and, for Guetti, the major instance of this is in works of literature. It is here that language is especially on display, and this has as much to do with what we hear in a poem or a story as what we imagine we see. The auditory imagination is as important as the visual, and the polemical edge to Guetti's argument is that much literature teaching, in its preoccupation with theme, character and structure, has forgotten this fact.

We might ask what this might look or sound like in practice. How do we experience language on display in a work of literature? Wallace Stevens's poem, '13 Ways of Looking at a Blackbird', is an interesting case because at first reading, and following the prompting of the poem's title, it may appear to have little to do with the sound of language. The poem's first stanza or section sets the tone of what is to follow:

> Among twenty snowy mountains
> The only moving thing
> Was the eye of a blackbird

In its entirety the poem appears to be what its title indicates. It records or reports or proposes 13 ways of looking at a blackbird. Each section of the poem contains one of these 13 ways, often in haiku-like three or four or five line stanzas. In each section there is a deceptive simplicity of utterance, as though nothing in the poem required further elaboration.

The poem's sounds play a distinctive role. Each of its 13 sections sounds like a saying or a proverb. It is as though the poem might be taken from a sampler, or a school book, or the verbal text to a set of illustrations, each one showing a blackbird. The grammar of each section takes the form of an assertion. But these assertions take on a particular quality because of the way they sound idiomatic, something that is reinforced by the poem's second section:

> I was of three minds
> Like a tree
> In which there are three blackbirds

Whatever this section means – and it may not be very much – its first line echoes an idiom: 'being in two minds' as a way of describing indecision. But this sound, an echoic sound, is caught up in a subtle, and possibly comic, tension, with the fact that each of its sections sounds decisive. Its imaginary speaker knows what he is saying and has some wisdom to impart, not just about blackbirds, but also about the world and its weather, and about poetry and its sounds.

A fuller reading of the poem would go on to show how these sounds are playing with the equivocal character of its assertiveness. The 13 ways of looking turn out to be about the problems of looking, or, to put it in a language that connects Stevens's poem to one of modern art's experiments, it explores the relation between what can be presented and what always eludes presentation:

> When the blackbird flew out of sight
> It marked the edge
> Of one of many circles

It would though be a mistake, I think, to say that what Stevens is attempting to do is create a new set of proverbs in his poem. What is happening instead is that the form and the sound of the proverb are being displayed in the poem, and this is just one of the ways we might want to say about Stevens's poem, and many others, that they are putting language on display. It's here that an important dimension of linguistic creativity resides. (For a fuller discussion of issues raised in this section see Cook and Read 2010).

Conclusion

What has been attempted here is three brief sketches of how we might think about the different dimensions of linguistic creativity. One attends to the element of spontaneity and improvisation as aspects of language's own curious powers of inventiveness. The second attends to the issues of intersubjectivity in the experience of creative language, and reminds us that our sense of linguistic creativity should not be confined by a restricted notion of expression or an exclusive attention to tropes. The third reminds us that creative language may not make sense in the way everyday language use does. Instead it displays language's inventive powers in ways that can be occluded by too great an insistence on the fact that, faced with a literary text, for example, the most important thing to do is find a meaning hidden in it.

REFERENCES

Collingwood, R.G. (1938) *The Principles of Art*. Oxford: Clarendon Press.
Cook, J. and Read, R. (2010) 'Wittgenstein and literary criticism', in G. Hagberg and W. Joost (eds), *The Blackwell Companion to the Philosophy of Literature*. Oxford: Blackwell-Wiley: 467–90.

Guetti, J. (1993) *Wittgenstein and the Grammar of Literary Experience*. Athens, GA and London: University of Georgia Press.

Merleau-Ponty, M. (1974) *The Prose of the World*, ed. C. Lefort, tr. J. O'Neill. London: Heinemann.

Mukarovsky, J. (1964 [1932]) 'Standard language and poetic language', in Garvin, P. (ed.), *Prague School Reader in Esthetics, Literary Structure and Style*. Washington, DC: Georgetown University Press.

Stevens, W. (1955) *Collected Poems*. London: Faber and Faber.

Von Kleist, H. (1997) *Selected Writings*, ed. and tr. D. Constantine. London: J. M. Dent.

Wittgenstein, L. (1960) *On Certainty*, eds G.E.M. Anscombe and G.H. von Wright, trs Denis Paul and G.E.M. Anscombe. Oxford: Basil Blackwell.

Wittgenstein, L. (1961) *Tractatus logico-philosophicus*, trs D.F. Pears and B.F. McGuiness. London: Routledge and Kegan Paul.

27

Creativity Looks at Language

Ruth Finnegan

Are language and literature indeed sites for creativity? The answer must surely be yes, amply displayed in this volume. That answer is filled out and at the same time problematized by the probing discussions of just what 'creativity' is or isn't. Controversies emerge around its definition, incidence, functioning, foundation, boundaries, even existence. Creativity is undoubtedly a topic of interest and debate, rightly treated with seriousness in this volume.

Here however I want to turn the spotlight onto the other two terms in our volume's triad – onto 'language' and 'literature'. What light does this scrutiny of creativity throw on language and, by extension, on literature? Or, better, how have the contributors here approached language and literature as arenas for creativity and what if any are the implications?

Let me open with some preliminary background points. I do not have space to engage directly with the interesting controversies that have emerged over the continuity – or is it contrast? or interaction? – between 'ordinary' and 'literary' language or, in Lynne Cameron's terminology, between 'prosaic' and 'poetic' (it seems to me that all the chapters here have insights to bring). But the fact that this question was in the editors' plan from the outset is significant. It doubtless underlay the volume's notable breadth, a wonderfully roomy sphere for the consideration of diverse approaches to creativity. It has meant too that it has not seemed out of the way to see 'literature', at least in some contexts, as not confined to the great works of the conventional high-art canon, but also treatable in the untrammelled sense that extends beyond the traditionally primary referent of *written* text into genres that are additionally – sometimes principally – performed or oral (another controversy I cannot pursue here, but see Finnegan 1992, 2005; Foley 2002). Further, it is not just in fixed 'works' that the contributors have sought creativity. It is also in performances and renderings, and in how readers and audiences engage with them. The analyses here are not just of products but of processes, not just of texts but of how readers creatively experience them, not only 'the page' but, as Patience Agbabi has it, 'the stage'.

By now this broadening beyond the once-conventional limitation to static verbal text is doubtless a relatively uncontroversial element in the current state of the art. It also arguably follows on smoothly from the notion of 'creativity' with its connotations of action, of activity. It is nonetheless worthy of note as the context for the commentaries here. A text-based focus on written works has after all had a long run in scholarship, not least literary scholarship, the more so for its link with dominant Western ideologies by which literacy and alphabetic writing have been privileged among the high achievements and destiny of Western civilization. Despite the well-known challenges, that grand story retains a hold on our imaginations. We grow up with the idea that *the* reality of linguistic – and literary – expression is captured quintessentially in writable text, bolstered as this is by the continuingly pre-eminent position of writing in educational curricula and bureaucracies of power. It is a still-potent historical legacy even as the gate-keepers are to an extent changing with a wider range of communication modes and media calling attention to themselves.

It is noteworthy then that in their quest to uncover creativity, many contributors here have moved out from that text-based perspective to include performance, practice and experience. As well as direct treatments of performance they consider people's active processing of texts and reflect on how people creatively interpret and engage with literary works. This is well demonstrated, if in their differing ways, in the analyses by Peter Stockwell, Fiona Sampson, Joan Swann, Jane Spiro and, not least, Rob Pope's scrutiny of creativity in transformed texts, parodies and, memorably, the Ten Commandments (on such textual transformation see also Finnegan 2011). It is not the only perspective of course. As Lynne Cameron for one insists, there is still a place for viewing the 'finished work' – a poem, a painting – as different from performance, something that, in Cameron's words, ' "leaves" the artist and begins a life of its own out in the world'. Given the current zest for performance and practice, this point is still worth stressing (with debates which again cannot be followed here). But in general the balance in the volume could be said to be towards the processual, the emergent, the experiential, rather than the fixed text.

This brings me to the nub of my interest here. For it is perhaps the enhanced sensitivity to the performed, experiential and actively manipulated dimensions of creativity in language and literature that leads to what I find the most striking feature of the volume – the importance attached to elements other than the purely verbal. This is in fact remarkable in a volume setting itself up to be about language and literature. And it comes not just in the part entitled 'Creativity across Modes, Media and Technologies', where we might indeed expect it, but in one way or another across the volume.

The explorations of creativity in language and literature frequently allude, for example, to the importance of audition. The 'oral–aural' process of writing and the shared 'auditory thrill' of performance are prominent themes in Patience Agbabi's reflections in 'Give Me (Deep Intake of Breath) Inspiration', while Richard Danson Brown aptly draws attention to the aural elements and tones of the voice. In Louis MacNeice's 'Can't we ever, my love ...', the meaning is in part brought out aurally by ruptures in the formal pattern. And even though focusing primarily on verbal text and the connotative interiors of words, Rukmini Bhaya Nair's piece cannot avoid reference to the 'combinations of sound and sense' that make up a poem.

It is also sound-as-music. Explicit references to music constantly enter in, remarkably so, in fact, given how music so often tends to be submerged in the schooled paradigms of language and literature. Music is explicitly part of Michelene Wandor's poetry readings, and in her work as writer she aims to combine words and music in new and different ways. Music comes profusely into the analyses of the films – recall 'Arranged Marriage' and 'Heavy Water'. In similar vein, though from a different angle, Patience Agbabi's 'wordshops' challenge 'the literary hierarchy that says the condensed stuff replete with classical literary allusion is superior to the musical stuff replete with popular cultural allusion'.

That there can be an acoustic side even to language-as-written also comes through, if less explicitly. Certain sonic elements like rhythm, rhyme or metre are directly signalled in print format, others created through the reader's ear where, above all for poetry or dialogue, the auditory resonances can be created and re-created in the reading. As well, written texts have of course often been realized through being performed aloud, something of the present not just the past. 'Audio books' and multimedia forms blur the boundaries between sounded and visible text, poetry readings flourish, and for many religious adherents the full experience of sacred writing is a sonic one. The one-line model of language and literature by which the reception of written text is a matter merely for the eye and mind is belied both by the implications of some of the accounts here and, more directly, in the comparative literature on reading (e.g. Boyarin 1993; Cavallo and Chartier 1999; Coleman 1996).

The contributors here also advert to the visual features of language and literature. These come most prominently in the analyses of live verbal performance that recur throughout the volume, interacting with the established literature of performance studies (e.g. Bauman 2004; Bauman and Briggs 1990; Sawyer 1997; Schechner 2002). The examples here remind us of the potentials for creativity in gesture, in facial expression, body language, visible movement, personal charisma and also, if less explicitly, in costume, accoutrements, colour and lighting. Visual elements are also featured alongside words in staged works, live or recorded, as in the two films described here and the synchronous computer-mediated interchanges so vividly conveyed in Angela Goddard's chapter.

In written text too there is a significant visual dimension. It comes not just in the displayed words but in their formatting and presentation, something often forgotten but not overlooked here. Richard Danson Brown depicts written poetry as 'a sophisticated use of language which relies on visual as well as aural cues', while in her 'Mature Poet Steals', Patience Agbabi focuses attention on the visual layout of her sonneted prose versions of 'My light is spent', where the format is essential for her creative redressing of words. The *look* of typography – its layout, type, orthography – are all part of the whole. In alphabetic representations as they now stand, where would we be without the visual signalling of prose, poetry, quotation, emphasis or dialogue, intrinsic to the written literary art? So too with the materials and surfaces for graphic depictions, the illustrations and images that work creatively with them, the revealing styles of handwritten texts, the textures and colours through which written materials communicate, the icons, animations and scrolling through which writing lives on the computer screen.

The modes in which creativity is detected by the writers here are complex and multiple indeed. Several accounts take us across a wide range, all of which can have their relevance. Mario Petrucci exemplifies the creative plurality of his Chernobyl film based in 'poetic and filmic imagery commingled with music and other dubbed audio' and its 'visual and textual interpenetration'. The combination of visual and text-based imagery, he remarks, exploits

> a new set of co-sensory pungencies. As a poet used to page and voice, this co-existence … of visual and aural forms felt like adding a third dimension to the familiar board version of chess.

For her *Arranged Marriage* film G. D. Jayalakshmi repeatedly emphasizes the critical importance of mixed modes working together: of speech, of music and of complex visual moves in a creative interplay of shot sizes and transitions, panning and cutting. The opening scene and the specific music chosen for the start of the film set up the mood, as the film-maker uses 'all the tools available – language, gestures, non-verbal communication, camera angles, the pace of editing and finally music'. In a different context but equally strikingly Agbabi reflects on the multisensory ambience essential to rap when she describes her mentor as 'totally immersed in hip hop culture. He wore the clothes, he walked the walk, he talked the talk. Rap was the soundtrack to his life …'.

The near-inextricable intertwining of modes in or around linguistic communication is well demonstrated in Angela Goddard's remarkable account of users' creative marshalling and manipulating of both long-established and more recently available communication technologies in CMC (computer mediated communication). She reveals the resourceful deploying of graphics, webcam images, sound, icons and animations, such as those for 'lots of laughing' or the 'wink', where a large pink heart splits into little ones fluttering down to acoustic pulsations matching their visual throbbing. She shows how participants can simultaneously speak and listen via acoustic devices, write in a text box and interact via a webcam, emoticons and animations, as well as sharing sites and creating joint plans or documents. Here writing is not visual fixity but dynamically materialized, and sound intermingles with moving graphics and images set in dynamic exchanges within real time as text scrollingly appears and disappears. Synchronous computer mediated communication of this kind takes us beyond the standard speech/writing contrasts to a model that is essentially and simultaneously multimodal. Goddard pertinently emphasizes that the participants are not only handling multiple systems alongside each other but systems that are interwoven. Research which focuses on one communicative element cannot therefore capture the way the communication works..

If all this now seems fairly obvious, it might be useful to reiterate how easy it is to overlook the multidimensionalities critical to much of our communication but only explicitly noticed when we make the effort to search them out. If Patience Agbabi had chosen to give us only the verbal text of her poem 'Word' we might still have been impressed and rested content with that, not appreciating its partialness. The same goes for Angela Goddard's CMC examples, which could indeed have appeared as merely a printout without an explication of the multimedia dynamics. That indeed has been a common approach in the past, whether in the prioritizing of fixed text while overlooking readers' creative input, or in the widely practised transcripts of multimodal live performance which have so often hidden much that in actuality made them creative. Even now it is common to analyse the art of songs by focusing on their verbal texts – but as Simon Frith expressed it some years ago:

> A song is always a performance and song words are always spoken out, heard in someone's accent. Songs are more like plays than poems; song words ... [bear] meaning not just semantically, but also as structures of sound. ... It is not just what they sing, but the way they sing it, that determines what singers mean to us. (Frith 1988: 120–1)

Schooled as we are to look at the unilinear writeable words, we systematically overlook these multiple dimensions. We know in practice they are there and are skilled in working with them. But they often enough remain below the level of explicit awareness. The technology of writing has for long been *the* high-status and academically validated mode for capturing reality – but this also too often lulls us into forgetting that it captures only certain elements, blotting out the rest. The pages of this book, like thousands of others, present their verbal descriptions with wonderful efficiency and directness but only faintly convey the musical, pictorial and moving-image dimensions that, as several contributors insist, also form part of the creativity they aim to uncover. The multiple dimensions illustrated in this volume may in one way be obvious – but still emphatically need flagging up.

Indeed both their potential significance and at the same time their missibility come across when we consider not only the chapters that directly explicate them but also those which bypass or allude to them only briefly. In Janet Maybin's perceptive account of penfriend correspondence, for example, she makes clear that the creativity also arose from, and perhaps in part lay in, the pictures and photos enclosed with the letters. But it might also have been found in their layout, texture and perhaps handwriting, and it would have been great to have had illustrations and reproductions from the manuscripts to explore this possibility, not just the transcribed extracts. Similarly Elena Semino writes fascinatingly about verbal attempts to describe pain, revealing rich metaphorical creativities. It would have been equally fascinating to know of the gestures and body language that in the spoken cases went along with these endeavours – or perhaps, indeed, creatively elaborated, pictured or even in some cases qualified them. Kate Pahl's analysis of linguistic and visual interrelations in children's accounts of their multimodal box projects brings insight into certain dimensions of creativity; but she also goes out of her way to remind us that a full account would also need to include three dimensional, tactile and gestural dimensions. Despite the richness of the accounts here, it is accepted that much is missing too – omissions that the volume itself has so successfully now drawn to our attention.

What can be left out emerges even more strongly in Lynne Cameron's transcripts from reconciliation talks arising from an IRA killing. The words, interjections, dialogic interactions and hesitations are meticulously reproduced. They are impressive and moving indeed, illustrating the speakers' creative lexical choices in their metaphor shifting and symbolisms. But what if we had also had access to the tones and resonances of the voices and silences, to their cadences and to the non-verbal bodily expression which might have formed equally emotion-drenched and meaningful – and creative – elements in the interchanges? As for the films: without the chance to actually experience their aural and visual qualities, readers of this volume can gain only a limited appreciation of the creative pluralities and sequences involved.

So it is still worthy of remark that, even amidst the omissions and the constraints of our print technology, so many of the contributors seem to take it for granted, without apology, that approaching language and literature under the 'creativity' rubric justifies exploring a multiplicity of modes. Their search leads them not just to words or verbal texts in the narrow sense, but to a host of multisensory channels and resonances.

The result is that it is not just 'creativity' that has now become problematic but also 'language' and, by the same signal, 'literature'. If the contributors include gestures, music, typographical format, non-verbal indicators, film shots, animations or computer smileys, then have they exceeded their brief? Or, alternatively, do we need to rethink our views of the margins of language and of literature?

There is indeed a good case for the second position. Take for instance the boundaries between language and music. They may seem immutable, a fact of nature. But it has in fact been argued for some time that the language/music distinction is better represented as a continuum rather than a dichotomy (List 1963; also more recently Banti and Giannatasio 2004; Clayton 2007; Feld et al. 2004; Finnegan 2008). It is true that in some cultural contexts the division is taken as self-evident. In the European high-art song tradition of 'text-setting', for example, words and music are indeed in a sense separated. But the classifications of different cultures vary. Not all have a differentiated concept of 'music', and even when they do this can be defined and split up in diverse ways. The classical Greek *mousiké* encompassed what we would now differentiate as music, poetry and dance, while the mediaeval *musica* meant spoken as well as sung performance, with little idea of words and music as separate media. So today, can one really separate out the musical from the linguistic in vocal art: Edith Sitwell's voice in 'Façade', say, a resonant rendering of a Milton sonnet, a Beatles' song, a contemporary rap performance? It is no surprise that intonation, song, voice, music all come into the discussions of creativity here, and some performances could be equally described as 'sung poetry' or as 'vocal music'. People can deploy an infinite wealth of sonic resources across a spectrum covering speaking, intoning, recitative, chanting, plain song, cantillating, tuneful lamenting, melodic singing, and much else where it is really not possible to apply some global opposition between language and music. They merge into each other, and any borders are fuzzy and shifting.

The boundaries between linguistic and somatic expression can prove equally elusive. Many examples are given in these chapters. In communication more generally, it is accepted that people make regular use of gesture, facial expression, eye glances, bodily orientation, demeanour, gait and movement (for examples see Finnegan 2002). In a guide to improving your French the first main section opens with 'French body language': gestures, eye contact, stance (Schorr 2004: 19ff.) – and rightly so, for to speak a language fluently must surely include mastering its gesturing. Modern communication technologies have expanded our capacity to capture – and thus notice – the significance of movement and gesture, endowing them with a solidity veiled in script-based tools. In song and poetic performance, movement is part of the creative act, sometimes in the fully crafted form best described as dance. I think for example of the classic Fijian *meke* – integrated words *and* music *and* dance – where all are necessary for the genre's realization, or similarly, closer to home, of Michael Jackson's danced-sung-poetry where the styled movements are part of the creative artistry. Seen through the lens of creativity, a clear-cut line between the linguistic and the bodily becomes near-impossible to trace. Indeed studies of the intimate ways in which gestures are systematically coordinated with speech have already raised the question of whether the boundaries of language should be widened to include gesture (Kendon 2004; McNeill 2000; Streeck and Knapp 1992). And if gesture, why not other bodily enactments?

Written language merges into other spatial representations too, both fixed and fleeting: in script, graphics, images and icons. This comes in several examples here, as also in comparative accounts. A growing number of cross-cultural studies of literacy have challenged the Western high-culture ideology of 'the written word' as something essentially abstract, mental and context-free, instead bringing out its multimodality and materiality (Bauman and Briggs 2003; Finnegan 2002: esp. 229ff.; Kress 2003). In the Japanese tradition of literary texts as art objects, a poem is recognized not only as performance but as physical object, realized through its calligraphy, illustrations and the materiality of its choice of paper (Gerstle 2005), while in earlier Western calligraphies as in the pictorially rich non-alphabetic systems of Meso-America or Asia, writing can lie as much in scintillating visual display as in words (well illustrated in Tonfoni's aptly titled *Writing as a Visual Art*, 1994). So too in the long tradition of illustrations, graphic craft and picture books, as well as in current computer generated extravaganzas where not only (malleable) script but colour, shape, icon and moving image are part of the display. The margin between (written) language on the one side and picture, graphic and moving image on the other is scarcely hard and fast, and in several accounts here it is usefully eroded.

Under the spotlight of this exploration of creativity, language spills over the banks once so confidently set around it. Far from being confined to one clearly demarcated channel, it is realized through a spectrum of overlapping modes and media creatively deployed in human usages, temporal moments, spatial incarnations and more, brought together in multiple manifestations. Multimodality may be more to the fore in some genres than in others. But the accounts here demonstrate the unwisdom of screening it out in advance by implicitly invoking a model of language where such dimensions are discounted. This volume illustrates the rewards of slackening the bonds and allowing the imagination to range beyond the strict limits which in the past have so often been set around 'language' and, in consequence, around 'literature'.

All this brings a serious challenge to a restrictive model of language. Given the difficulty – indeed the ethnocentric short-sightedness – of setting fixed boundaries there is indeed much to be said for widening our view of 'language' (and literature). This is where this volume has by now unavoidably led us. For the dominant emphasis has been not on 'language *and ...*' but on the merging of arts that make no sense if we try to split them apart.

There might also be grounds for an alternative position, however: one where we retain a relatively narrow delimitation of language precisely to make clear the need to uncover those other modes with which it so intimately works. Taking the linguistic as a focus can be a jumping-off ground for arguing all the more forcibly that it is not in the verbal alone that creativity can be found, but in the interplay of language with other modes and dimensions. This still needs saying loud and clear, for the powerful tradition of hard-copy written text inevitably steers us towards a unidimensional take on verbal art. This volume itself bears witness to the technological constraints of print. The music and artful moving shots of film which some of us remember from their initial live presentation, the dramatic modulations of performing voice, the interaction of power-point visuals with spoken commentary, the scrolling words – all have now disappeared behind the superficial simplicity of static text-on-page. We have to struggle to remind ourselves that that is not the whole of what is there, that when we try to uncover the creativity it is needful to look further, unpicking the interwoven elements so as to bring out the multidimensional creativity.

There might be a balance to be kept here. In some cases, as in certain of the examples here, separating out the strands can be to misread the web as a whole. On the other hand disentangling them can sometimes be illuminating, both for analysis and to bring up the threads into clearer view. Differing elements, furthermore, do not necessarily always sit happily together, indeed in some cases can compete, qualify, even fight. Mario Petrucci interestingly comments on the energetic debate during the making of his film over 'the ways in which visual (filmed) imagery and text-based imagery could combine forces (or, if handled poorly, compete)'. We know in practice that body language and spoken words do not always convey the same thing – one may modify even contradict the other, and the verbal does not necessarily have automatic domination. So too with the way that a smiley or other emoticon can soften or humorize the words of an email, or metacommentaries be effective precisely by utilizing simultaneous but differently functioning modes. Given that these intermixtures so often tend to be below the level of consciousness there is indeed an argument for drawing explicit attention to them, sometimes perhaps best achieved by seeing them as separate and additional features over and above the linguistic.

Whichever position we end with here, the boundaries of language and of literature emerge as intriguing and pressing questions for our attention. If for no other reason, the issues and topics treated so illuminatingly in this volume make this necessary. 'Creativity' has here been the key to unlock some of the gates to let us into less fenced pastures, pushing controversially at the edges that, whether explicitly or implicitly, are so often put around language and literature. The debate needs to proceed on where we now locate the fields for language and literature, be they bordered, emergent or unconfined.

In their vision for the volume the editors rightly prefigured the (debatable) continuities between 'everyday' and 'literary' language, issues well followed out in its chapters. To this we must surely now add the equally fascinating and debatable continuities between language and the broader galaxy of arts that might – if inadequately – be roughly indicated by such notions as (among others) music, gesture, dance, image, graphics, movement, material, sound or touch. Perhaps it is only when we turn the lens onto all of these that the overflowing and intermingled splendours of language and literature as arenas for creativity can shine out with their true brilliance.

REFERENCES

Banti, G. and Giannatasio, F. (2004) 'Poetry', in Duranti, A. (ed.), op. cit.

Bauman, R. (2004) *A World of Others' Words: Cross-cultural Perspectives on Intertextuality.* Oxford: Blackwell.

Bauman, R. and Briggs, C.L. (1990) 'Poetics and performance as critical perspectives on language and social life'. *Annual Review of Anthropology* 19: 59–88.

Bauman, R. and Briggs, C.L. (2003) *Voices of Modernity: Language Ideologies and the Politics of Inequality.* Cambridge: Cambridge University Press.

Boyarin, J. (ed.) (1993) *The Ethnography of Reading.* Berkeley: University of California Press.

Cavallo, G. and Chartier, R. (eds) (1999) *A History of Reading in the West.* Cambridge: Polity.

Clayton, M. (ed.) (2007) *Music, Words and Voice: A Reader.* Manchester: Manchester University Press.

Coleman, J. (1996) *Public Reading and the Reading Public in Late Medieval England and France.* Cambridge: Cambridge University Press.

Duranti, A. (ed.) (2004) *A Companion to Linguistic Anthropology.* Oxford: Blackwell.

Feld, S., Fox, A.A., Porcello, T. and Samuels, D. (2004) 'Vocal anthropology: from the music of language to the language of song', in Duranti, A., op. cit.

Finnegan, R. (1992) *Oral Traditions and the Verbal Arts.* London: Routledge.

Finnegan, R. (2002) *Communicating: The Multiple Modes of Human Interconnection.* London: Routledge.

Finnegan, R. (2005) 'The how of literature', in Gerstle, A., Jones, S. and Thomas, R. (eds) *Performance Literature.* Special issue, *Oral Tradition* 20(2): 164–87.

Finnegan, R. (2008) 'O que vem primeiro: o texto, a música ou a performance?' ['Which comes first: the words, the music or the performance?'], in de Matos, Cláudia Neiva, Travassos, Elizabeth and de Medeiros, Fernanda Teixeira (eds) *Palabra Cantada: Ensaios sobre Poesia, Musica e Voz*. Rio de Janeiro: 7Letras.

Finnegan, R. (2011) *Why Do We Quote? The Culture and History of Quotation*. Cambridge: OpenBook Publishers.

Foley, J.M. (2002) *How to Read an Oral Poem*. Urbana: University of Illinois Press.

Frith, S. (1988) 'Why do songs have words?', in Frith, S. (ed.) *Music for Pleasure*. Cambridge: Polity.

Gerstle, C.A. (2005) 'The culture of play: Kabuki and the production of texts'. *Oral Tradition* 20: 188–216.

Kendon, A. (2004) *Gesture: Visible Action as Utterance*. Cambridge: Cambridge University Press.

Kress, G. (2003) *Literacy in the New Media Age*. London: Routledge.

List, G. (1963) 'The boundaries of speech and song'. *Ethnomusicology* 7(1): 1–16.

McNeill, D. (ed.) (2000) *Language and Gesture*. Cambridge: Cambridge University Press.

Sawyer, R.K. (ed.) (1997) *Creativity in Performance*. Greenwich: Ablex.

Schechner, R. (2002) *Performance Studies: An Introduction*. London: Routledge.

Schorr, N. (2004) *Tune up your French*. New York: McGraw Hill.

Streeck, J. and Knapp, M.L. (1992) 'The interaction of visual and verbal features in human communication', in Poyatos, F. (ed.) *Advances in Nonverbal Communication*. Amsterdam: Benjamins.

Tonfoni, G. (1994) *Writing as a Visual Art*. Exeter: Intellect.

Tracey, K. (ed.) (1999) 'Language and social interaction at the century's turn'. Special issue, *Research on Language and Social Interaction* 32(1/2).

28

Epilogue – Creativity: Postscripts and Prospects

RONALD CARTER

The current position of work in the field of creativity studies is a vibrant one. As this volume attests, much work is continuing apace in both theory and practice; colleges and universities worldwide are seeing new courses in creative writing develop in response to growing demand from students while the subject has also enjoyed a reawakening in the field of linguistics. Schools of English worldwide are employing creative writers as faculty members in greater numbers than ever before; research continues to be undertaken widely from experimental psychology to business and management studies, with research methods similarly developing in range and scope to embrace everything from laboratory experiments (involving brain scans) to detailed ethnographic studies in which individuals are captured producing creative talk in a variety of different social contexts or in which individuals talk about different aspects of their experience of reading creative works.

In this connection it is worth noting too how the word 'creativity' has begun to acquire further connotations and functions in much contemporary discourse – both in the UK and increasingly worldwide – in an ever expanding range of official publications, including educational policy documents. The word has been used repeatedly by politicians in budget statements and debates and is commonly employed in discussions of the economy. Indeed, the word 'creativity' or 'creative' collocates quite freely not just in phrases such as 'creative writing; creative pleasure and enjoyment' or 'creative classrooms' but also, more functionally (and sometimes pejoratively), in 'creativity in business, creative industries, enterprise and creativity, creative accounting' and 'creative problem solving'.

Such a rebirth should not, however, suggest that the field of creativity studies in English language and literature studies is marked by either a uniformity of approach or a commonality of purpose. Inevitably, there are differences in emphasis and orientation, differences in theory and, crucially, differences in what is actually delineated and defined as creative. Attempts to summarize inevitably lead to oversimplification and do not adequately capture continuities; but sometimes even crude summaries help to point to directions and pathways for future development. Accordingly, I would suggest that there are three main landmarks that need to be recognized which, for the sake of convenience and with no little imagination, I have called Creativity 1, 2 and 3.

Creativity 1: A More Literary Focus

Creativity 1 takes place largely within the domain of literary studies and involves explorations of what are taken to be examples of creative literary art. Under this heading 'creativity' is seen principally as an act of individual self-expression with the creative impulse and process resulting in the articulation of a distinctively shaped personal vision. Creativity 1 is confined largely to writing and defined largely both by means of formal aesthetic criteria and by evaluative criteria that seek to establish the originality of a work of verbal art. The concern is to establish and to demonstrate the ways in which things are made new, as a result of norms being broken or as a result of challenges to established ways of seeing. The norms here are in the first instance textual and linguistic forms, but a departure from established forms which can also sometimes accompany a challenge to established practice which is more divergent from cultural and ideological norms as well as from the norms of literary forms and techniques. These challenges can involve working within an existing tradition to inflect established themes differently; or it can involve an altogether more radical expression of difference resulting in a marked departure from literary traditions and histories.

The concern with norms and regularities in ways of seeing is also vital to a full *contextualization* of the creative work within the practices associated with Creativity 1. The place of historical *context* is commonly seen as instrumental to a full interpretive reading of a text which is in turn resistant to seeing a text outside the conditions in which it was produced. A work cannot simply be original in itself; it can only be seen as original and inventive with reference to a background norm or horizon of expectations, and one aim of literary research is to reconstruct actively that context.

In addition to this originality and inventiveness, what Derek Attridge (2004) refers to as the 'singularity' of creative work is also a major defining criterion. Attridge suggests that verbal art requires inventiveness to be singular (in the way that the enduring poetry is singular). The key word here is 'enduring' as it underlines that the greatest art is a permanent and enduring challenge, not simply to present culture but to all culture, so that in this sense a literary text's signification is both embedded within the context and culture of its time and yet comparatively free of (without transcending) the controlling and shaping forces of history. This view risks reinforcing a view of enduring texts as autonomous and self-referring that doesn't entirely do service to the ways in which such texts by definition also raise profound ethical questions with which responsible readers can engage politically and socially, in the process relating the texts to their own lives and to the lives of others in their surrounding cultures.

With the exception of now very few societies that support (or control) literary creativity for purposes of social and political enrichment, such a definition of Creativity 1 is the most culturally powerful definition of creativity and is enshrined in numerous high prestige cultural events and products that celebrate the individual artist. Examples would be literary prizes such as the Booker prize, the award of Nobel prizes for literature, the authors studied in most university degree courses in literature, designations by publishers of works as 'modern classics' and so on. The emphasis is on the individual creativity of the artists and on the creative capacity of the critic or cultural commentator to isolate the distinctiveness and originality of the work in question and to argue for what is more and what is less creative.

There is a tendency to resist too great a degree of overt analysis of the processes of Creativity 1 on the grounds that too much dissection can be inhibiting to and for the artist and may, on the other hand, be deemed both too reductive and too reifying against the background of the more holistic hermeneutic aims of the literary critic and the literary critical community. Resistance may also be on the grounds that, for the artist, language alone can be inadequate for the purposes of discussing creative processes. This can be seen as romanticizing the creative process as something too numinous or mystical to describe; or it can be a realistic assessment of the inadequacy of critical metalanguage in particular and language in general. On the other hand, it is worth noting that the growth of pedagogic programmes in creative writing has resulted in the development of valuable analytical guidance on the teaching of creative writing and in numerous publications offering explicit classroom-oriented support across a wide variety of social and institutional contexts.

The aim of the literary critic with respect to Creativity 1 is also broadly holistic in another sense. It is important to show that creative effects are cumulative and organic over a complete work with resonances that interact across stanzas or chapters or dramatic scenes and are not simply the result of a single instance or local effect. For example, the existence of a metaphor or metaphor set within a single paragraph may result in some striking local effects and may indeed underline, as adherents of a Creativity 2 model frequently emphasize, the continuum between everyday language and literary language (that is, metaphors are not simply a literary figure of speech); but the creative power of the metaphor is only ever fully realized if it has resonances across the whole work and can be seen to reinforce meanings in more than one place in an interrelated and mutually reinforcing and mutually deepening texture of meaning creation. If common everyday language exists in a text it will, adherents of Creativity 1 argue, be literary only if it can be creatively embedded and reconfigured, given order and shape and pattern in the service of literary meanings. It is this kind of effect to which the sensitive literary critic will remain vigilant; it is this kind of effect that characterizes creativity that is likely to be more universal and enduring from creativity that is likely to be more ephemeral.

Creativity 2: A More Linguistic Focus

As discussed above, in culturally powerful contemporary conceptions of creativity such as Creativity 1, the phenomenon has been isolated and promoted (at least within Western cultures) as a product of an inspired individual (the term 'genius' is, as we have seen, not uncommonly used). Most contemporary uses of the word carry to some degree a post-Romantic or at least posteighteenth-century heritage into discussion in which the often lone artist is celebrated and the often lone literary critic accepts the task of elucidation and exegesis. (Of course, 'lone' here may be mythical for in reality creative work is more collaborative and team-based than the culture sometimes allows.) Analysts of Creativity 2 challenge such assumptions by exploring the extent to which creativity can be common and can be analysed in a wide range of contexts of communication. Creativity is not therefore simply the exclusive preserve of the individual genius or the pathological outsider. Neither is creativity simply an act of mind; it is also a contextual act, more likely to occur in some types of interaction and certain modes of communication than in others. It is not simply or exclusively a 'literary' act. Such linguistic creativity is both a common property and can be properly spoken of in terms of creativities. The introduction to this volume and the discussions of 'genius' in Part 4 discuss further the histories and contested meanings of words surrounding the lexicon of creativity.

Definitions of creativity under a heading of Creativity 2 underline that ordinary, demotic, common language is artful and has continuities with and exists along clines with forms that are valued by societies as art. Creativity is also closely related to language play and to games that may and often do involve humour for both light and serious as well as for both interpersonal and transactional purposes. (It is no semantic accident that the words 'creation' and 'recreation' are etymologically linked.) As a result of the strong current emphasis on self-expression and distinctive personal visions based on difference, the recursive, cyclical and echoic nature of creative language common in everyday conversation, often for playful purposes or for purposes of entertainment, prompts some rethinking of more established ways of theorizing creativity.

Ordinary everyday creative language operates in two contrasting directions, as Cook (2000) persuasively reminds us. It is a force for conformity and solidarity, creating and reinforcing intimate interpersonal relations, and delineating the boundaries between group insiders and outsiders. It is also a resource for ideological resistance and sometimes for rebellion, allowing the individual to break free, internally and/or through action, from social, cultural and institutional constraints. Creativity in everyday language exchanges can, for example, involve acts of hostility and aggression, jokes can cause pain as well as laughter, creative chants at football matches can be hostile and racist as well as a source for humour; children's playground games (where repetitive words, song and group movement prevail) can exclude as well as include. Such textures of everyday experience are not generally seen as the province of the more literary focus of Creativity 1, and adherents of Creativity 2 would argue that much is being missed as a result. Many of those embracing Creativity 1 would feel that much of this everyday discourse is ephemeral, relativistically valued and of limited – and certainly not lasting – cultural significance.

The phenomenon of Creativity 2 is most salient in interactional language encounters. It is often produced and coproduced in domains in which new forms of social encounter, such as those that occur in online communities require and create the formation of different interactive practices as well as new linguistic forms and identities. Creativity 2 thus entails plurality. Those investigating Creativity 2 argue that in many instances it is important to attend to values as well as to value, accepting relativism as a positive not a negative outcome. There are other values than aesthetic values. Aesthetic values are important but should not be primary: there are, for example, social, political, affective, communal and entertainment values too. The basic position here is one that is not wholly comfortable with the idea that there should be a coherent essentialist or universal specification of art. It is also a position that entails a consideration and specification of *values* rather than *value* and of *creativities* rather than *creativity*.

Creativity 2 thus underlines that creativity is not a wholly written phenomenon and is not the exclusive preserve of an individual creator. Creative texts can be coproduced, that is, they can be the result of creative interactions between individuals or within groups. Creativity 2 phenomena can be subject to aesthetic criteria (it is naive not to recognize the influence of Creativity 1 definitions and practices) and to the intricacies of judgement and evaluation naturalized within approaches that embrace Creativity 1; but definitions under the heading of Creativity 2 are undertaken by means of what might be termed a more broadly 'sociological aesthetics'.

The more 'sociological' or socio-cultural position embraced within Creativity 2 entails something altogether more plural, suggesting that a more collective, temporally variable and contextualized aesthetics should be embraced rather than the singular, individualist and universalist aesthetics conventionally associated with much post-Romantic culture. The process was foreshadowed by the early work of Czech structuralists such as Jan Mukarovsky who in their turn were reacting to the largely decontextualized and self-referring focus of the early Russian formalists who have had such an influence on Western modernist aesthetics. To paraphrase Mukarovsky: cultural and aesthetic variationism and the boundaries between the various realms of culture are permeable, shifting and variable from community to community. Aesthetics is for Mukarovsky domain and culture specific: 'the attitude which the individual takes toward reality and to the reality depicted by the artistic object…is determined by the social relationships in which the individual is involved' (Mukarovksky 1970 [1936]: 16).

As we have seen in numerous chapters in this volume, such a position will necessarily raise issues to do with high and low cultures, as well as clines and continua between the literary and non-literary, canonical and non-canonical, literary creativity and 'everyday' creativity. We should note though that the assumptions regarding creativity associated with the culturally assigned pre-eminence of Creativity 1 mean that definitions of Creativity 2 take place within the lens of Creativity 1 but also serve to problematize the processes by which definitions are made and assumptions constructed in both Creativity 1 and Creativity 2.

Methods for Analysing Creativity 1 and 2

Perhaps predictably, methods for analysing and discussing creativity may also be demarcated under the same broad headings. Work valued as Creativity 1 is normally assigned a value through a careful process of personal hermeneutic exploration, with evidence drawn from textual extracts, comparisons with other works by the same writer or by other writers (within a broad historical lens and with close attention to the importance of historical context), with attention devoted to the extent to which the text under discussion accords with non-transient values, universal validity and enduring significance (Attridge's 'singularity' above). The ascription of value is made and registered through the sensibility of the individual literary critic and the accumulated experience that informs the sensibility and judgement of that individual. Although context is viewed as significant for interpretation, and although biographical evidence, alongside socio-historical, economic and political details, is frequently drawn on, just as there are concerns that too much text-intrinsic analysis can be reductive, so are there concerns that such information can also be reductive and should therefore be treated cautiously when interpretations of texts are made. The reader, it should be underlined, is therefore more often than not an individual, professional reader; there is limited interest in ordinary readers or in the products of reading groups. The preferred perspective entails a singular voice.

Analysis of Creativity 2 involves in parts a not dissimilar process to explorations of Creativity 1 but with (normally) greater attention to the linguistic particulars of the texts. Indeed, the narrower linguistic focus often results in text-intrinsic features of language being highlighted but isolated from broader contexts of significance. There is less concern for historical context and correspondingly greater concern for social context and for the social relationships which result in the co-construction of the creative text. Analysis draws on established linguistic-stylistic methods with attention given, as appropriate, to different levels of language organization from sound systems to syntactic and discoursal patterning, extending into cognitive poetic consideration of the role of cognition in the interpretation of tropes such as metaphors.

Creativity 3: Moving beyond Either/or

There are several problems with having in the above pages divided definitions and practices associated with literary and linguistic creativity into two main types: Creativity 1 and Creativity 2. It serves to oversimplify the different positions, and in formulating the categories the tendency is to exclude and make oppositional when those occupying particular territories would say that there are more subtle similarities than there are crude differences. In this final section therefore the aim is to look to the future, to explore connections, to seek ways of reconciling different positions and to try to get beyond an *either/or* position towards one in which *both/and* or *this-as-well-as-that* may be delineated under a heading we might call 'Creativity 3'. The trends and tendencies in this view of creativity are at more formative stages of development but are united by possibilities for fusion and some new directions for the study, theory and practice of creativity. Needless to say, what are highlighted here as key areas for development are no more or less than my own views.

Creativity 3 involves more prospective, contextualized and emergent definitions of creativity and a focus on creativity as a dynamic process as well as on creativity as a completed product. It is a more discourse-based view of creativity. Much of the work examined under the headings of Creativity 1 and 2 focuses on discourse as 'text'. This volume has illustrated how in recent years the view of discourse has expanded beyond traditional notions of 'text' to include multimodal and multimedia semiotics and to consider more thoroughly the role of discourse in the creation and reception of different texts. This means that there is increased interest in how people, not exclusively professional linguists or literary critics, receive, interpret and use discourse in modes other than written and spoken language, including images, video, film, sonic patterns and music, and in how these different modes interact with verbal communication and with more traditional and established notions of the literary.

There is also a developing awareness of the crucial role played by new media technologies such as various mobile devices, social networking sites and of the creative interaction and relationship between these technologies and the discourse-based creativities produced by these technologies. With first, second or foreign language users of English, examples abound of creative code-mixing and crossing between linguistic codes, scripts and language forms in situations when feelings or emotions are intensified or when physical conditions are strained. Email, text messaging and internet chat systems such as skype and IRC also generate conditions of communication in which 'speakers' commonly appropriate a 'between' language which is not simply standard English but which enables users to give creative expression to their feelings of friendship, intimacy and involvement with each other's feelings and attitudes, and accordingly new modes of speaking/writing are invented, creatively developed and facilitated by the technology.

In this connection there is also a tendency in discussions of creativity to assume that it is a monolingual phenomenon. Increasingly, routine perceptions in dominant first language English-speaking contexts that the world is monolingual are catching up with a world of multilingualism and linguistic diversity where monolingual speakers of English find themselves in a minority. As illustrated in this volume, bi- and multilingual creativity is significant, with a major world language such as English becoming the site for new creativities, involving owners of the language whose first language is not English, whose culture exhibits different inflections and who, in a range of discourses extending from everyday interaction to hip hop to more canonical creative writing, push back the creative resources of the language. The kinds of theories and practices explored in this concern with creative communication 'beyond text' lead to shifts in the way in which verbal and non-verbal creativity is conceptualized and addressed analytically, in its more traditional literary modes, in its more everyday manifestations and in cross- and intercultural contexts.

A discourse-based view of creativity is also emerging to embrace a view of writing as *rewriting*. This kind of analysis is built on similar assumptions to those of close reading but it is augmented by a methodology of *active reading* (Knights and Thurgar-Dawson 2006). 'Transformative' analysis is built on a pedagogic assumption that close reading has tendencies towards a more passive reception of the text and that putting the reader into a more active role by forcing the text into a different linguistic or generic design will lead to more active engagement with its specific textuality. Transformative text analysis therefore assumes that response and engagement are more likely to take place if features of language and textual organization are drawn to a reader's attention as a result of the text having been deliberately manipu-lated in some way. The process here is one in which the reader compares the original text with one which has been rewritten, transformed or re-regis-tered. Rewriting involves making use of a different range of linguistic choices, building as it does always on the fundamental notion of translation and its classroom value to close reading of texts along a critical–creative–reading–writing continuum.

Transformative writing extends a discourse-based, variational view of crea-tivity, along the lines argued by Mukarovsky (above), underlining apprecia-tion of the distinctive characteristics of different modes and genres of writ-ing, including both the 'literary' and the 'non-literary', and fostering at the same time the important connections between the critical and the creative illustrated throughout this volume. Among the most striking of developments have been those that focus on 'textual transformations' using comparative text analysis by means of processes of rewriting from different angles and positions, 'translating' the text from one medium to another along an axis of spoken to written, verbal to visual, textual to dramatic.

Also significant is the *social ethnography of reading*. This approach has gained considerable impetus in recent times and offers further potential for Creativity 3 studies which moves beyond either/or differences and accepts more inclusive both/and possibilities. Such studies show how creative lan-guage is received as well as produced in and out of different contexts, of how different values come in and out of play in different contexts of reading, revealing individuals in the process of recognizing themes, aesthetic form and meanings that can be *both* of universal *and* of local contingent relevance. It involves studies of readers reading literary texts, adding the valuable dimen-sion of a sustained focus on the reception of creative texts as well as on their production and, in several respects, paralleling the interest of many linguis-tic researchers in the creative language produced by 'ordinary' speakers and writers. Here readers are indeed plural and are not necessarily trained profes-sionally in the institutional practices of reading. The different perspectives brought to bear on texts, shared within the reading group and then recorded and analysed ethnographically, reveal a different process, but one no less illu-minating, of what is involved in creative reception. The studies in this domain undertaken so far, including those reported in this volume, also argue that we need to develop a variable rather than a unitary, a collective rather than an individualist, a pre-Romantic rather than a post-Romantic, aesthetics of creativity with attention to both 'pre-text' and 'post-text' as well as to 'text'. The data recorded from group reading sessions provide a valuable empirical dimension to our understanding of literary response, our engagement with the meanings texts have for different people and how they come to produce those meanings, what linguistic, textual or thematic triggers generate them, how they share them, modify them and develop them both as individuals and as part of a group process of further reading and discussion. It is an approach that involves close attention to the formulation of response through language, it often involves readers responding to core canonical and enduring texts in a specific literary tradition or canon and offers rich possibilities for bringing together the concerns of Creativity 1 and Creativity 2 under a reconfigured Creativity 3.

Finally, an approach to creativity that is not covered in detail in this volume is corpus-based approaches. Increasingly, corpus-based approaches to discourse are developing so that electronically accessible multimillion word computer-stored records of the patterns and forms of a language at a particular time can be captured and then used to benchmark the uses of language drawn from corpora of the works of individual writers (and increasingly speakers). The growing assembly of historically attuned corpora means too that investigations of texts and discourses can take place at different points in literary and textual history. The speed and the level of sophistication with which corpus annotation is evolving today means that more layers of social and cultural information are being added (see Vo and Carter 2010 for a full review). This will arguably bridge more gaps in corpus linguistic creativity studies in the near future, enabling richer, more variational and contextualized paradigms for the study and practice of creativity as discourse, supporting practices embraced within the domains of Creativity 1, 2 and, in particular, Creativity 3.

Conclusion

The contributors to this volume cover many of the issues highlighted in this epilogue and the volume as a whole points collectively and cumulatively to a position, where, in spite of the title selected for the book, we may in future be better served not by the 'positions' enshrined in Creativity 1, 2 and 3 but by a fuller enumeration which goes beyond 'creativity' (to Creativity 4, 5, 6 ...) towards a fuller and more inclusive use of a plural 'creativities'. The challenge is to find ways of moving beyond 'language' and 'literature' while at the same time continuing to address the theoretical, analytical and pedagogic concerns of all committed to creative practice. There are, of course, inevitably issues of institutional and cultural power that stand in the way; but it is hoped that this volume may have helped in the process of taking some first steps.

REFERENCES

Attridge, D. (2004) *The Singularity of Literature*. London: Routledge.
Cook, G. (2000) *Language Play, Language Learning*. Oxford: Oxford University Press.
Knights, B. and Thurgar-Dawson, C. (2006) *Active Reading*. London: Continuum.
Mukarovsky, J. (1970 [1936]) *Aesthetic Function, Norm and Value as Social Fact*, tr. E. Suino Mark. Ann Arbor, MI: University of Michigan Press.
Vo, Thuc Ahn and Carter, R. (2010) 'What a corpus can tell us about creativity', in O'Keeffe, A. and McCarthy M. (eds) *Routledge Handbook of Corpus Linguistics*. London and New York: Routledge: 181–99.

Index